D1521635

TIME OF ANARCHY

TIME OF ANARCHY

Indigenous Power and the Crisis of

Colonialism in Early America

MATTHEW KRUER

HARVARD UNIVERSITY PRESS

Cambridge, Massachusetts

London, England

2021

Publication of this book has been supported through the generous provisions of the
Maurice and Lula Bradley Smith Memorial Fund.

First printing

Library of Congress Cataloging-in-Publication Data
Names: Kruer, Matthew, 1981– author.
Title: Time of anarchy : indigenous power and the crisis of colonialism in early America /
Matthew Kruer.
Description: Cambridge, Massachusetts : Harvard University Press, 2021. | Includes index.
Identifiers: LCCN 2021018621 | ISBN 9780674976177 (cloth)
Subjects: LCSH: Susquehanna Indians—Government relations—History—17th century. |
Susquehanna Indians—Politics and government—17th century. | Indians of North
America—East (U.S.)—Government relations—To 1789. | Indians of North America—East
(U.S.)—Politics and government—17th century. | Anarchism—East
(U.S.)—History—17th century. | Emotions—Political aspects. | United States—History—
Colonial period, ca. 1600-1775. | Great Britain—Colonies—America—Race relations.
Classification: LCC E99.S9 K78 2021 | DDC 974.8/004975—dc23
LC record available at https://lccn.loc.gov/2021018621

To Katie

For Warre, consisteth not in Battell onely, or the act of fighting; but in a tract of time, wherein the Will to contend by Battell is sufficiently known: and therefore, the notion of *Time* is to be considered in the nature of Warre.

—THOMAS HOBBES, *Leviathan* (1651)

We have wars of our own.

—JOY HARJO, *In Mad Love and War* (1990)

· CONTENTS ·

· NOTE ON NAMES AND DATES ·

THIS BOOK IS ABOUT the power of Indigenous peoples in North America and the limits of European colonialism. One of the weapons in the colonizers' arsenal was language, which included the power of naming to define and order the conceptual universe of everyone in early America. In writing this book, I have tried to communicate clearly without doing violence to Indigenous peoples by inaccurately describing them with the words of their colonizers.

I use the terms *Native* and *Indigenous* interchangeably to describe the original peoples of North America. Both are capitalized to reflect Indigenous peoples' belonging to sovereign nations, just as English and French are capitalized. I sometimes use *Native American* and *Indian,* the latter primarily when describing settler points of view. I reserve these terms for occasions when multiple groups are under discussion or it is impossible to determine their national affiliation. When some degree of accuracy is possible, I use terms that describe broadly similar cultural groups, such as *Algonquian* or *Siouan.* Whenever referring to specific peoples, I use the proper name for that group using the spelling preferred by modern tribal nations, such as *Pamunkey.* In some cases, this practice prefers terms less familiar to non-Native audiences, such as *Haudenosaunee* ("People of the Longhouse") rather than *Iroquois.*

I use the terms *colonist* and *settler* interchangeably, both of which describe a person of European descent participating in the colonization of North America. *African* and *black* (in lowercase) refer to people of African descent. I rarely use the uppercase *Black,* which conveys a shared sense of culture and historically rooted identity, because in seventeenth-century North America this form of blackness had not yet taken shape. For the same reason, I generally avoid the use of the word *white* for people of European descent, who likewise had not yet come to think of themselves in such terms. Indeed, this book tells part of the story in which these color-coded racial identities, along with categories like *Indian,* began to take on meanings familiar to twenty-first-century readers.

The Indigenous people at the center of this book, whom I describe throughout as *Susquehannock,* appear in documentary sources under many names. Most Iroquoian speakers called them *Andastoerrhonon* or *Andastes*; among the Haudenosaunee they were known as *Andastogues* or *Andastogueronnons.* French sources usually rely on one of these appellations. Speakers of Munsee and Unami, including the Munsees and Lenapes of the Delaware Valley, called them *Minquas,* which Dutch, Swedish, Finnish, and German colonists adopted. Algonquian speakers in the Chesapeake called them *Sasquahanoughs* or *Susquehannocks,* and English colonists followed suit. The inevitable distortions produced by settlers recording Indigenous phonemes as echoed through European ears, combined with the creative orthographies beloved by early modern writers, have created an enormous catalog of variations on these terms. The Susquehannock autonym was never recorded, but linguistic comparisons with other Iroquoian languages suggest that it was something very close to *Gandastogues* or *Conestogas.* However, because the name they called themselves is not entirely certain, and because they are best known in English-language scholarship as Susquehannocks, I have (though with some reluctance) chosen to use the term *Susquehannock.*

I cite the most accessible versions of sources whenever possible, and I have kept the original spelling in those sources. However, for readability I have made alterations for a few early modern orthographic quirks. The interchangeable *i* and *j* and *u* and *v* have been standardized. The majuscule *ff* has been replaced with *F* and the thorn (*y*) with *th.* Abbreviations have been expanded and symbols translated, for example *and* instead of *&.* I sometimes alter capitalization and punctuation for the sake of clarity. In rare cases I change the spelling when the meaning might otherwise be obscured. Many of the standard printed sources for early American history contain transcribing errors that mangle Indigenous names even more than settlers did when they first wrote them down. I have corrected such errors after comparison with the original manuscripts but have not otherwise modernized their spelling.

Seventeenth-century English peoples used the Julian, or "Old Style," calendar, which ran behind the modern Gregorian calendar by ten days and began new years on March 25. I have adjusted dates so that years begin on January 1 but have left the months and days unchanged.

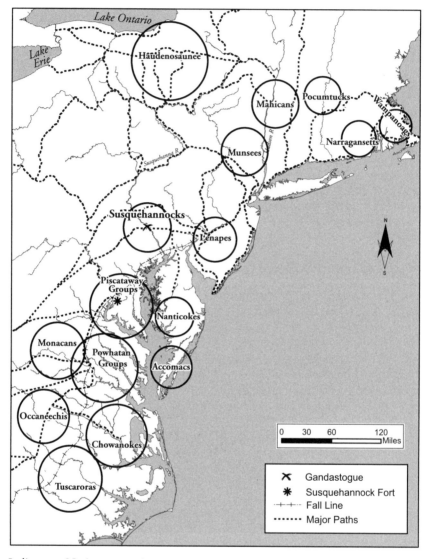

Indigenous Nations, ca. 1675

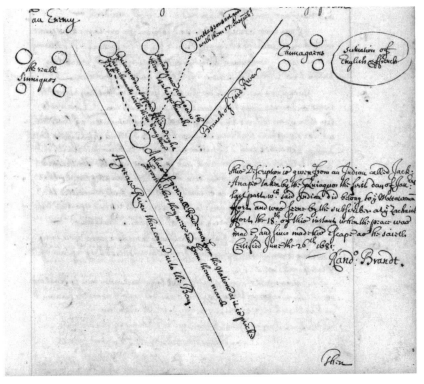

When seventeenth-century Indigenous peoples drew maps, they often focused on relationships among peoples rather than topographical precision. This map of Iroquoia, made by a Chesapeake Algonquian who had been adopted into the Haudenosaunee (Five Nations Iroquois), depicts each nation as one or more circles with straight lines showing the paths and rivers that connected them. Proceedings of the Governor and Council (1678–1683). Collections of the Maryland State Archives.

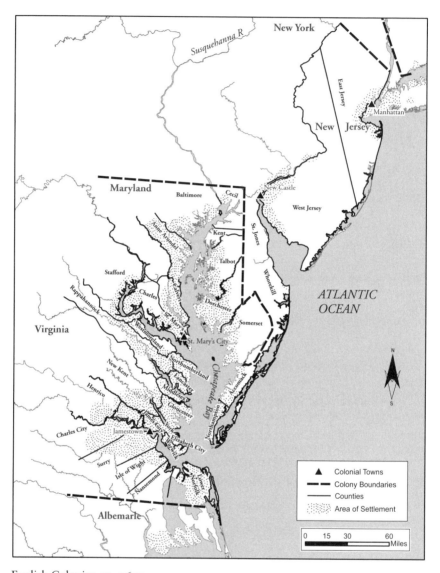

English Colonies, ca. 1675

Seventeenth-century English settlements in North America were limited to the Atlantic seaboard, penetrating into the interior only a few miles along major rivers. This map of the Chesapeake region, drawn by a Dutch colonist who became a naturalized resident of Maryland, reveals these limits in its depiction of individual plantations along the water. Augustine Herrman, *Virginia and Maryland as it is Planted and Inhabited this present year 1670* (London, 1673). Courtesy of the John Carter Brown Library at Brown University.

PROLOGUE

ONCE, THE SUSQUEHANNOCKS had been a mighty nation. From humble origins in the late sixteenth century as newly arrived migrants to the Susquehanna Valley, by the 1650s they were more formidable than any competing power, Indigenous or European. Commanding the crossroads of the region's fur trade, they played Dutch, Swedish, and English allies against each other to their own advantage. They grew numerous, wealthy, and strong. But their fortunes rapidly declined. Waves of epidemic disease and years of grinding war with the Haudenosaunee (Five Nations Iroquois) left them weak and divided. By 1675, when English allies suddenly turned against it, the Susquehannock nation was a shadow of its former self. Forced to abandon their homes and scatter, by the 1680s only a few hundred Susquehannocks remained as captives of the Haudenosaunee and refugees among Lenapes in the Delaware Valley. They survived through migration and adaptation, retaining a surprising degree of power as their nation transformed. But that is not what settlers saw. According to a pronouncement by Charles Calvert, the Baron Baltimore and Lord Proprietor of Maryland, "the Susquehannoks and theire Country were Conquered by the Marylanders . . . and the Susquehanohs are now noe Nation." To English eyes, the people who had been giants of the mid-Atlantic had withered and their nation was dead.[1]

Calvert was disastrously wrong, as he should have been able to see by the pivotal role that Susquehannocks played in the 1682 treason trial of Jacob Young. Born Jacob Claesen, a young man of undistinguished background in the Dutch United Provinces, Jacob had immigrated to New Netherland in the 1640s and spent the next decade in Susquehannock country as a fur trader for the Westindische Compagnie (West India Company, or WIC).

In the 1660s, he jumped the sinking ship of Dutch America, changed his name to Jacob Young, and became a naturalized Englishman in Maryland. His mastery of the Susquehannock language and personal relationships with their sachems (chiefs) made him a natural messenger, negotiator, and diplomat. He became the nexus of an alliance between the Susquehannock nation and the province of Maryland. By the 1680s, Jacob was a tobacco planter, slaveholder, and tavern keeper, a successful businessman among the colonial elite. He owed much of this success to his talent for communication and a knack for gaining peoples' trust. His nickname, "Jacob My Friend," was repeated so often by so many people that it became a kind of alias. There was only one Jacob who was everybody's friend.[2]

To Susquehannocks, Jacob was more than a friend: he was a member of the nation, part of the circle of kin that defined their political community. According to his former employer, New Netherland director Petrus Stuyvesant, during the years Jacob lived among the Susquehannocks he married a Susquehannock woman and had children with her. This kinship bond would have been central to his standing in the community and no doubt accounts for the influence that made him an effective diplomat. In the eyes of Jacob's Susquehannock kin, he was one of them. According to the rulers of Maryland, that was precisely the problem. Their list of allegations began with the charge that Jacob "did Contract Marriage and take to Wife an Indian Woman of the Susquehannah Nation, by whom the said Jacob had Several Children, one or more of which is now amongst the Indians." This union was a primal act of disloyalty. His kinship with the Susquehannocks made him "alienate his Affection from the . . . Lord Proprietary and his Government," and become "more nearly Concerned for those Indians even against his Majesties Subjects the good Christian People of this Province." Jacob, in other words, was not an Englishman at all. His marriage to an Indigenous woman and love for his Indigenous children showed that in his heart he was really a Susquehannock.[3]

The indictment inverted Jacob's life story, turning his tireless dedication to the Susquehannock-Maryland alliance into a series of devious betrayals. According to the charges, when conflict broke out in 1675 he took their side without hesitation. He gave the province's enemies aid and comfort, sending them guns, food, and blankets. He abused his position as interpreter to twist messages for Susquehannock gain, spreading lies and disinformation. He sabotaged peace talks that could have saved the lives of loyal Marylanders. He ordered Susquehannock goon squads to murder his rivals, growing rich by fencing goods plundered from English homes. The indictment went so far as to claim that Jacob "travell[ed] to Several parties of the said Susquehannahs . . . then Scattered into Several parts of this Province and Virginia, and to rally them together," then personally led them "in Arms" against Maryland as a Susquehannock war captain.[4]

As news of the trial coursed through Maryland, Susquehannocks remembered Jacob, their friend. A week after Jacob was brought to the bar, Susquehannocks living in the Delaware Valley sent a message to the Maryland assembly: "whatever could be Alledged against Jacob Young touching any thing concerning the Indian Affairs was all false." They insisted that Jacob was a true friend to Maryland and had always used his influence to urge peace, even when emotions were running hot and angry voices demanded action. But he was not there to counsel restraint now, and if his trial ended in conviction then Susquehannock warriors would avenge him with a slaughter like nothing the English had ever seen. They warned the assembly, "in case the Life of the said Jacob Young be taken away . . . they would have 500 lives more for him out of Maryland." The burgesses backed down without a moment's hesitation. They canceled the proceedings, concluding, "it is Absolutly unsafe for the Province to bring the said Jacob to Tryall."[5]

This was not the end of Jacob's trial—indeed it was only the beginning—but it is worth pausing for a moment to consider the strangeness of the whole affair. Lord Baltimore brought Jacob to an emergency trial for intimate connections to a supposedly vanquished nation that his province no longer recognized. Then the trial was interrupted by a handful of refugees who threatened to bring a colony of twenty thousand people to its knees. Rather than dismiss the threat, Maryland legislators fell over themselves in their rush to capitulate. Jacob was the crucial broker to a broken people; both his influence and the Susquehannocks' power to menace should have been a thing of the past. Yet in 1682, the Susquehannocks cast as long a shadow over the mid-Atlantic as they ever had. The trial of Jacob My Friend offers two puzzles. Why would the Maryland burgesses quiver with fear over a Susquehannock ultimatum? And how could a small and scattered Indigenous remnant exert such magnetic power over an entire colony?

Susquehannock intervention in Jacob's trial took place amid a decade of upheaval, when chaos engulfed English colonies and Native nations from the Great Lakes to the Deep South. It started in 1675 along the Potomac River, where skirmishes between Susquehannocks and Virginia colonists escalated into full-scale war. Disagreement among colonists over the proper response—cautious defense or aggressive offense—became a political crisis in 1676, snowballing into a rebellion known after its ostensible leader, Nathaniel Bacon. The tide of insurrection spilled across colonial borders. Discontented Maryland colonists rallied under the banner of a Protestant crusade to overthrow the Catholic Lord Baltimore. A secessionist movement swept through New Jersey and ethnic riots threatened to engulf Manhattan and Albany in New York. Rival factions in Albemarle, the northernmost province of the proprietary Carolina colony, lurched toward a full-blown revolution called Culpeper's Rebellion after one of its ringleaders. Even when colonists were not in open revolt, or when their uprisings were violently suppressed, the spirit of rebellion seemed to hover over the colonies, only barely contained.[6]

These outbursts of civil disorder were entangled with conflicts among Indigenous nations, which invariably included bloodshed between Natives and settlers. Algonquians in Virginia, although allies of the colonial government, were targeted not only by Susquehannock raiders but also by colonists unable or unwilling to distinguish between friendly and hostile Indians. Similarly, Susquehannock and Haudenosaunee raids on Algonquians in Maryland sparked retaliatory murders between colonists and their Native allies. Political struggles in Albemarle unfolded in the midst of a war between colonists and neighboring Indigenous peoples. Instability in the Delaware and Hudson Valleys took place in the shadow of King Philip's War in New England. Colonial rebellion, Anglo-Indian war, and battles among Native nations did not just coincide in time: they shaped each other, connecting dozens of peoples and colonies in a spasm of conflict that washed over eastern North America. Colonial orders broke down, Indigenous nations broke apart, and violence surged unrestrained by any power.[7]

Historians are familiar with most of these conflicts—indeed, some are among the most studied events in early American history—yet they are nearly always examined in isolation. This book focuses on the one factor that tied them all together: the Susquehannocks. After clashes with settler militias in 1675, the Susquehannock people splintered into at least six groups and scattered in every direction. Small bands traveled to places as far flung as the Delaware Valley, the eastern Great Lakes, the upper Ohio Valley, the southern piedmont, and Albemarle Sound. Forced into flight by colonial violence, these bands adopted widely differing strategies in response to their predicament. Many sought to keep their heads down and evade colonial eyes. Others joined Indigenous neighbors for protection. Some worked to forge a new peace, and some confronted their enemies, whether those enemies were English or Indigenous. Each of these initiatives had consequences. Although the Susquehannock nation was small, its actions caused repercussions far out of proportion to its numbers. In most cases it tipped volatile colonial societies, already riven by internal social and economic discord, into political strife. Susquehannock influence was often

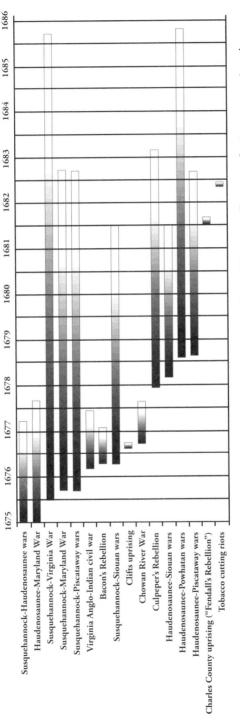

Constituent conflicts of the Time of Anarchy. While often seen as separate conflicts, this image illustrates the interconnections between Indigenous wars, Anglo-Indian violence, and civil strife in the colonies between 1675 and 1685.

indirect, but it had enormous geographical breadth and transformative intensity.[8]

This book tells, for the first time, the history of Susquehannock migrations and their ramifications in the English colonies between 1675 and 1685. Historians have perceived only parts of this event at a time without grasping the larger whole. It was not a single struggle but a time of many entangled struggles. Taking my cue from a pithy pair of contemporary descriptions, I call this event the Time of Anarchy.

The first description comes from George Alsop, an indentured servant in Maryland who strained to understand the deliberative process of Susquehannock council politics. "Their Government is wrapt up in so various and intricate a Laborynth," Alsop wrote, that he "cannot see into the rule or sway of these Indians, to distinguish what name of Government to call them by." He settled on "Anarchy" as the most accurate term. It was a colorful way to draw attention to the Susquehannocks' supposed savagery, evoking a Hobbesian state of nature without any real authority or stable political order. The second description comes from Virginia governor Thomas Lord Culpeper, writing in the aftermath of Bacon's Rebellion, who described the turmoil as "our Time of Anarchy." This turn of phrase stripped the defeated rebels of legitimacy by bringing to mind the chaotic violence of civil war, social upheaval, and moral disorder. In two different contexts, Alsop and Culpeper captured something important about the essence of the troubled decade between 1675 and 1685. It was a time of anarchy for Natives and settlers alike: a period defined by intense political conflict within societies as well as contention between polities. Before it was over, central authority had collapsed in several English colonies and the political shape of many Indigenous nations had transformed.[9]

There is no need, however, to remain hostage to the pejorative sense of anarchy inherited from seventeenth-century philosophy. Alsop was onto something, even if his ethnocentrism led him to misunderstand what he saw. The Susquehannocks' "laborynth" was a form of politics with consensus building as its foundation, which bound the community together through collective deliberation rather than coercive authority. From the nineteenth century to the twenty-first, the example of Indigenous politics has led theorists to reject the Hobbesian view of existence as a pitiless war of all against all, inspired foundational works of social science questioning the state—with its institutionalized forms of inequality and violence—as the pinnacle of political evolution, and galvanized activists to practice radical forms of self-governance. Indigenous scholars such as J. Kēhaulani Kauanui, Audra Simpson, and Leanne Betasamosake Simpson, among others, have refused to accept the hegemony of the nation-state and championed alternative modes of political society predicated on kinship and reciprocity. Susquehannock "anarchy," far from the failure to achieve order that Alsop depicted, points toward forms of order radically different from anything that English colonists—or most modern Americans—could imagine.[10]

Rather than assuming that power is a force exerted from the top down by chiefs or kings, we should instead imagine power flowing upward from the bottom. The primary agents of political movement, in this view, are families and households, the most basic units in which individuals translate their desires into collective action. Flipping our perspective in this way, which one scholar has termed "anarchist history," is a fruitful way to approach not only nonstate societies in Native North America, but also the settler societies established by European states. Nations and empires, which we tend to treat as solid objects, are better conceived as contingent entities that emerge from smaller collectivities joining together. Political power, this model suggests, is never as concentrated at the top as those at the top might like it to be, and actors who seem marginal can marshal surprisingly powerful forces. I also use "Time of Anarchy" in this sense: not to denote chaos, but rather to focus attention on the origins of order. The distinct ways that English colonists and Indigenous peoples understood the sources and operation of political power were central to the conflicts among them. Those differential understandings shaped both the ways that they broke apart and their struggles to put themselves back together.[11]

Because this story has never been told in its entirety, the chapters that follow narrate the origins, progress, and conclusion of the Time of Anarchy. It begins with an account of the deeply intertwined history of Susquehannocks and English settlers from their first meetings in the early seventeenth century. Most of the narrative, however, focuses on the years 1675–1685, between the Susquehannocks' scattering in the face of colonial aggression and the decision of the last Susquehannock holdouts to cease warring against the English colonies. These events do not unfold in a neat or linear manner, and the multiple groups of people in separate geographical spaces can at times threaten to talk over each other in a chorus of clashing voices. To bring some coherence to this polyphonic simultaneity, each chapter employs a different mode of analysis. Successive chapters explore emotional cultures, rumors, migrations, conspiracy theory, peacemaking, captivity, and racial thinking as phenomena that drove different phases of the Time of Anarchy. These distinct bodies of interdisciplinary literature offer new opportunities to understand the ways that the histories of Susquehannocks and colonists were braided together.

Although Indigenous histories and settler histories took shape in dialogue, *Time of Anarchy* argues that Susquehannock voices, so to speak, determined the topics of conversation. Accordingly, this book is centered on them. The sources for their history, like Susquehannocks themselves, are scattered across a huge geographical space. They appear in the archives of half a dozen English colonies, ranging from trial depositions in Carolina, military dispatches in Virginia, legislative proceedings in Maryland, lawsuits in Delaware, land deeds in Pennsylvania, treaty councils in New York, and even trader accounts in Connecticut. Moreover, their nation occupied the crossroads of contending European empires, so traces appear in the records of four imperial zones on both sides of the Atlantic, including missionary relations in New France, corporate reports in New Netherland, executive correspondence in New Sweden, and shipping news in London. Finally, material evidence offers insights into aspects of Susquehannock life that elude European documents, and the archaeological literature is extraordinarily rich.

Yet these appearances are usually fragmentary, brief, and frustratingly vague. For most of the seventeenth century, Susquehannocks engaged with Europeans on their own terms. As a result, most Europeans encountered Susquehannocks—almost always men—traveling for trade, diplomacy, and war, and had little opportunity to observe their culture and society at home. Virtually nothing is known of their spiritual beliefs or the stories they told about their origins and history. Colonists often did not bother to record names or describe personalities, referring to faceless individuals as "sachems" or "great men" and referring to their nation as a vague collective. I have been able to locate references to only forty-three named Susquehannocks before the eighteenth century. Of this already small cast, thirty-eight appear only once, twenty-seven sign a document but offer no further details about their lives, nine appear only offstage in secondhand references, and none are women. Even the material record has enormous gaps. There is no way to know how many Susquehannock sites were drowned by modern hydroelectric dams that flooded the Susquehanna River Valley or paved over by the steel towns that those dams powered. One painful indication of the scale of loss: a nineteenth-century traveler, passing through what once was the heart of Susquehannock country, noted that canal builders had dismantled a Native burial mound, "out of which were taken hundreds of Cartloads of human bones and used as filling-in materials for one of the bastions or shoulders of the Dam." These problems are compounded by the destruction of the Susquehannock polity in an eighteenth-century massacre perpetrated by white colonists, leaving no organized descendant community, and thus no elders or knowledge-keepers who could speak to this history themselves.[12]

Faced with such limitations, I make no claim to have recovered Susquehannock perspectives. Even if I could, I have no right to speak for them, which would be a form of ventriloquism that can do just as much violence to Indigenous people as histories that erase them altogether. Whenever possible, I account for the reasoning behind Susquehannock actions. Occasionally, I offer conjectures based on circumstantial evidence or speculations beyond the limits of available sources, explaining why I think my conclusions are plausible but allowing for differences of interpretation. However, much remains unknown and perhaps unknowable. Just as there were many individual Susquehannocks whose names I cannot know, I have undoubtedly left out factors influencing the choices they made.[13]

Instead, this book tells a story that crosses colonial borders and the artificial boundaries created by manuscript collectors, a story that places the Susquehannock people at the center of the action. It pieces together the fragments of documents and material evidence into a coherent mosaic, interpreting them through the lens of ethnohistory and the methods developed by scholars of Native American and Indigenous Studies. This means using sources produced by Natives whenever possible and reading them with an eye toward Indigenous epistemologies. It also requires using colonial documents without privileging colonial perspectives. Reading between the lines, it is possible to pick up on subtle clues about society and culture embedded in seemingly superficial interactions; reading against the grain highlights the moments when hapless European observers such as George Alsop point toward important insights despite their own obliviousness. To use a cinematic metaphor, my approach is to make the Susquehannocks the stars of the film. The camera is fixed on them, following as they move, watching events unfold as a consequence of their actions. Because the Susquehannock nation scattered into many groups during the Time of Anarchy, this requires multiple camera crews operating simultaneously, with frequent changes of scene. Each set has its own cast of European actors whose more famous dramas were entangled with Indigenous peoples, all of which appear differently from this new angle. With Susquehannocks in the spotlight, events that previously seemed to be fragmented parts of colonial histories resolve into an Indigenous whole.[14]

A holistic view from Susquehannock country offers a fresh look at one of the best-known debates in early American history: the development of racial slavery. Historians have interpreted Bacon's Rebellion as an eruption of class conflict that led to the consolidation of black slavery as the core of Southern economy and society. As this argument goes, wealthy planters, anxious about rebellious solidarities between exploited English servants and enslaved Africans, cultivated ties with poor white men based on a shared sense of racial superiority. Planters, in other words, defused class conflict by embracing racial slavery. This Black story, so familiar to historians of early America, is intertwined with a Native story that is less well known; both are necessary to understand how English colonies became slave societies. Although evidence about peoples of African descent is comparatively scarce during this decade—it is outweighed by sources related to Indigenous peoples by orders of magnitude—I have sought to highlight those sources whenever possible to explore the relationship between Black and Native histories. As scholars of slavery have shown, every plantation was a forced-labor camp where white colonists developed a system of racial mastery. *Time of Anarchy* suggests that in the turbulent 1670s and 1680s every plantation was also a war zone in which settlers often felt mastered by Indigenous power. The distinctive forms of racial thinking that emerged during warfare with Native nations shaped the ways that slavery and race evolved in the late seventeenth century.[15]

Framing the Time of Anarchy around the Susquehannocks solves one of the puzzles of Jacob's trial by illuminating their surprising sources of power. Scholars have grown increasingly attentive to the ways that Native peoples could not only defend their sovereignty and independence in the face of European colonialism, but also turn ostensibly colonized territories into zones of Indigenous ascendancy. For obvious reasons, these histories typically focus on large, populous, militarily powerful nations, and by 1675 the Susquehannocks were none of those things. *Time of Anarchy* suggests that even small Indigenous nations could and did shape the course of American history. As with many other Native peoples, Susquehannock power was not built on conquest and rule, but alliance—a relationship that involved ritual acts of reciprocity, mutually advantageous exchange, and kinship ties built through intermarriage, adoption, and ceremony. The networks they wove through a century of alliance building possessed tremendous flexibility and resilience, and remained intact through the years of their precipitous decline. When Susquehannocks scattered, they remained enmeshed in the social fabrics of many nations across a vast geographical space. Even when they were seemingly weak and divided, their actions could unleash titanic forces—forces that might make the burgesses of Maryland tremble and save their friend Jacob.[16]

Although Susquehannocks were central to the Time of Anarchy, they are only half the story. Cracking the second puzzle of Jacob's trial requires a turn toward the other half: the English colonies. Marylanders did not tremble only because they recognized Susquehannock military capabilities, but also because they understood that Susquehannock power placed pressure on fault lines in their society. In contrast to the supple networks of Indigenous polities, English power structures were far more brittle. The English imperial state was organized, at least in theory, as a chain linking the sovereign to his subjects in a hierarchy of command and obedience. In practice, the realities of politics on the periphery created a variety of ad hoc arrangements based in part on local negotiations between rulers and ruled. In moments of crisis, especially times of war, humble subjects could make extraordinary demands on their governments to protect them from hostile forces, such as Susquehannock raiders. To some colonists, however, tributary Natives—who recognized the king as their sovereign and possessed rights as subjects of the crown—were an intolerable threat. This perception placed governments in the untenable position of having to protect one group of subjects from the other. Officials who ignored demands for action discovered, as protest slid into riot and rebellion, the fragility of their control. Lord Baltimore might bow to a Susquehannock ultimatum because he feared that war could, in an instant, lead his own people to rise up against him.[17]

The Susquehannocks' story is important not only in its own right but also because their actions reshaped eastern North America. In the process of breaking apart and struggling to come together again, Susquehannocks changed the balance of power among Native nations. Susquehannock enemies, such as Algonquians and Siouans in the South, suffered devastating losses that left them more vulnerable to colonial incursions, leading to land loss and mass enslavement. Susquehannock alliance building infused the Haudenosaunee with new energy, channeling both war and diplomacy in new directions. Colonists under assault by Susquehannock enemies displaced their fears onto Native friends and came to see them in newly racialized terms, lumping different Indigenous peoples together into a single—and inherently antagonistic—category. Imperial officials seized on the chaos as an opportunity to impose greater control over the fractious colonies. Some colonists resented these schemes, while others embraced them as the only means of coping with Native adversaries whose power seemed as irresistible as it was elusive. Out of these rancorous battles emerged an imperial framework for the governance of Indigenous subjects and an intercultural framework that came to be known as the Covenant Chain, both of which shaped Anglo-Indian relations well into the eighteenth century.

Susquehannocks did not set out to accomplish any of this in 1675. Many of these developments were the indirect result of their actions, ripple effects of warfighting and peacemaking, sometimes based on nothing more than rumors of their passing and settlers' fevered imaginations. In asserting the primacy of their power to reshape eastern North America, we do not have to imagine them as masterminds or juggernauts. We can see them instead as the proverbial butterfly in the mathematics of chaos theory, whose fluttering wings start a chain reaction that determines the course of a tornado on the other side of the world. In a time of anarchy, small decisions could have enormous consequences.

· 1 ·

THE STRUGGLE FOR ORDER
IN GANDASTOGUE AND
ENGLISH AMERICA

SUSQUEHANNOCKS FIRST ENCOUNTERED Europeans in 1608. News, carried by Algonquian allies, had reached their connadago (town) that foreigners carrying rare and valuable goods had arrived in the Chesapeake. After holding a council and consulting with the elder women that led each extended family, a delegation of five sachems and sixty warriors traveled south to meet them. A storm arose. The fierce winds made the bay's waters choppy and dangerous. Rather than risk a crossing in lightweight birchbark canoes, the sachems beckoned the strangers toward the shore and stepped aboard their hulking ship. The sachems did not bring warriors to guard them; this was their country and they were not afraid. As they sat down for a council, the English captain began with a religious ceremony, chanting and reciting his people's mythic history. The sachems reciprocated with a ceremony of their own, performing a sacred dance and singing a song to mark the occasion. They presented the English with strings of wampum, beads chiseled from cream white whelk and rippling purple quahog shells, a tangible expression of their desire for peace. Wrapping the captain in a beautifully painted bearskin mantle, showing him the luxurious furs that their people could trade, they proposed a lasting alliance. While wind and rain raged outside, in a cabin redolent with tobacco smoke and tanned leather and human bodies in motion, the sachems concluded with a moving speech that the captain interpreted as "an oration of their loves."[1]

Decades later, expressions of peace and love gave way to betrayal and grief in the midst of a war that neither people had expected. After decades of alliance, Virginia colonists turned on the Susquehannock nation. Militia expelled Susquehannocks from their town and murdered five sachems negotiating under a flag of truce. Susquehannocks retaliated by killing several dozen colonists along the frontier. One Susquehannock captain—as so often, colonial authors did not bother to identify him by name—asked the Virginia governor, "what was it that moved him to take up Arms, against . . . his professed friend"? He declared "as well his owne as subjects greife to finde the Verginians, of Friends, without any cause given, to becom his foes." It was this grief that cast the Susquehannocks into a state their Indigenous relatives described as "a turbulent bloody mind," moving them to take revenge for the Virginians' treachery and seek restitution for their slain kindred. They fought a war that brought "violent and deadly fears" into the life of every colonist.[2]

Emotions traced a long arc in the entangled histories of Susquehannocks and English colonists in the seventeenth century, from promising first contact to bloody breakdown. But these expressions of feeling were more complex than they seem. Modern readers might assume that the meanings of these visceral elements of human experience are intuitive. If we make such assumptions, however, we misinterpret the historically and culturally specific associations that words like "love" and "grief" represented. In every culture, feelings emerge from the intersection of physical sensation and linguistic expression, taking shape in the space between shimmering storms of synaptic fire and the echo chamber of social communication. To process emotions we translate experience into words, and the words we use influence our experience. This circuit has no beginning and no end. However primal feelings may seem, however personal to our subjective experience of the world, they are fundamentally shaped by our social context. The encounter between Susquehannocks and English, therefore, was conditioned by distinctive cultures of emotion.[3]

Feelings were profoundly political, and politics was inseparable from emotion. In the emotional arc that connected Susquehannocks and settlers in the seventeenth century, love and grief shaped collective actions that led peoples to peace, or war. These particular emotions were fundamental to the ways they understood the proper organization of the body politic, the healthy functioning of society, and the correct methods of dealing with outsiders. Emotions formed the ligaments of political order. Both peoples struggled to create and maintain order amid the upheavals introduced by European colonization, seizing opportunities and minimizing dangers in order to create powerful nations. They were, in every sense, emotional struggles. The emotional basis of society and politics shaped how Susquehannock and English societies evolved over the course of the seventeenth century. It braided their struggles together, even when order broke down and their nations fell apart.[4]

The Susquehannock sachems who traveled south in 1608 represented a rising nation. The core of their homeland was the lower Susquehanna Valley, a country they called Gandastogue. It was a relatively recent creation, coalescing from people of diverse ethnic and linguistic backgrounds in the fifteenth and sixteenth centuries. Those who fissioned off from Owasco peoples, ancestors of the Haudenosaunee (Five Nations Iroquois) and neighboring Iroquoian groups, were the seed. "Proto-Susquehannocks" (as archaeologists, unable to know what they called themselves, designate these people) and related "Peri-Susquehannocks" lived throughout the upper Susquehanna Valley in autonomous bands as small as a single family. The environmental pressures of the Little Ice Age, a global cooling that shortened growing seasons and reduced crop yields, caused conflict with neighbors over scarcer resources. The increasingly distinctive Susquehannocks moved south and west and concentrated in larger, defensible settlements. In a decades-long chain of migrations, previously separate peoples gradually merged into the nation of Gandastogue. Susquehannock society arose from the mechanisms that held this motley body politic together, above all the processes of transforming strangers into kin rooted in their emotional worlds.[5]

The paramount social value of the Susquehannocks was peace, which signified not only the absence of conflict but also emotional calm and mutual goodwill. Peace was essential to their newly formed country. Gandastogue's political structures were egalitarian, built around complementarity and reciprocity rather than the hierarchical institutions of Eurasian states. Men and women exercised authority over different spheres of life. The town and surrounding fields were women's spaces. Female elders, or matrons, governed the extended families that shared a longhouse, which housed up to forty people related by a common matrilineage and whose interdependence was symbolized by the common pot in the house's heart. Men governed relations with outsiders. Younger men were war chiefs, whose thirst for reputation inspired them to great exploits in service to their kin and community, while elders became civil chiefs, whose wisdom helped maintain stability and harmony. These leaders exercised power through persuasion and consensus rather than command and coercion. Collective action arose from deliberation in search of harmonious agreement. "Some six of them get into a corner, and sit in Juncto," one colonist described their process of governance, "and if thought fit, their business is made popular, and immediately put into action; if not, they make a full stop to it, and are silently reserved." Cultivating an environment of peaceful emotional balance was essential to this work of consensus politics.[6]

Grief was the most dangerous threat to peace. Susquehannocks experienced the death of loved ones as a trauma that caused fury, despair, and self-destructive madness. Without healing, that trauma would consume the deranged individual and could damage or destroy the entire community. Condolence rituals were designed to restore peace, but sometimes ceremony was not enough. Matrons of the bereaved family could channel destructive feelings toward outsiders by calling a "mourning war," asking men to raid enemies for captives who would restore wholeness to the community in one of two ways. Matrons could promote healing by adopting the captive to fill the social absence left by death. When Susquehannocks "make warres, and incursions upon the neighboring Indians," observed one colonist, it was "partly for to get their Women," who would contribute to the nation's strength through labor and childbearing. In other cases, mourners might expiate their rage on the captive's body in a communal ritual of torture, dismemberment, and consumption. An English trader reported that "prisoners in warre" were brought back to the connadago until "their great feast, at which times they bring them forth, and binde them to trees, makeing a hott fire about them at first, and still bigger by degrees, until they be dead; in the meanewhile they use to cut out peeces of their flesh, and boile it and eat it before them from whom they cut it." The integration of captives into the community, either through adoption or ingestion, was the dark side of Susquehannock emotional culture. Cultivating peace could be bloody work.[7]

Mourning wars contributed to Gandastogue's expansion and transformation. During their sixteenth-century migrations they absorbed the original inhabitants of the lower Susquehanna Valley, known to archaeologists as "Shenks Ferry people." Excavations of palisaded villages and skeletons with the scars of combat testify to the violence that caused the disappearance of the Shenks Ferry as an independent group. The "Keyser people" of the upper Potomac Valley met a similar fate. As Susquehannocks built towns atop the ruins of enemy villages, absorbed captives exerted a quiet but profound influence on their captors. Shenks Ferry and Keyser women continued to craft ceramics in the styles of their natal cultures for decades after their peoples were absorbed but also experimented with new aesthetics that blended their traditions with those of Susquehannock kinswomen. Judging by Gandastogue's graveyards, Susquehannocks did not demand the captives' assimilation and even celebrated their cultural distinctiveness. Cemeteries include many graves with multiple bodies, usually in positions that suggest kinship ties and emotional relationships. For example, the

Ibaugh cemetery, near what is currently Lancaster, Pennsylvania, contains a grave with two adults facing each other and a child nestled between them. Some multiple burials reflected more than one set of mortuary rituals. Another grave contains one body arranged with the knees drawn up to the chest, reflecting Susquehannock customs, the other in a Shenks Ferry manner of extended, or laying down position, with pottery of both peoples' manufacture. The practice of honoring multiple cultural traditions through mourning suggests that a distinctively "Susquehannock" national identity was cultivated through connection to and engagement with peoples of diverse origins.[8]

Although war was a powerful force driving Gandastogue's expansion, peaceful forms of alliance building were equally important. From their core in the Susquehanna Valley, Susquehannock traders traveled along paths and portages that made Gandastogue into a major transportation nexus linking the Great Lakes to the Atlantic coast. They traded with the Senecas, one of the nations of the Haudenosaunee, for Lake Superior copper, a material whose brilliance suggested associations with the sun, and catlinite, a red mineral easily worked into ceremonial objects such as tobacco pipes. Copper was especially prized by coastal Algonquians, who exchanged it for wampum, beads crafted from marine shells and lined on strings or woven into belts. Wampum was central to diplomatic rituals. It imbued words with sincerity because the collective labor that crafted it symbolized community support for the speech, transforming ephemeral breath into durable memory. It healed grief in condolence rituals, wiping away the blood and tears of past discord and clearing the way for peace. Copper and wampum were not inert repositories of value, but objects of spiritual power. Their exchange was never a market transaction for profit but part of ceremonies that affirmed connection in a circle of reciprocity and mutual obligation, creating and reinforcing the bonds of alliance. Susquehannocks did not trade with strangers. Rather, trade was the means by which strangers became friends and friends became kin.[9]

The rituals of mourning that bound Susquehannocks to each other also connected them to these foreign friends. Long after they completed their southward migrations, Susquehannocks made pilgrimages to an ancient burial ground near what is currently Nichols, New York, which had originally been used by Owasco peoples. They practiced a ceremony in which they unearthed an ancestor buried decades earlier, rearranged the skeleton to cradle a recently deceased Susquehannock, and reburied the two in a loving embrace. Archaeologists believe the ceremony memorialized a historic kinship with the Haudenosaunee, building bridges between peoples who had grown into separate nations. They practiced similar burials with

Wendats (Hurons), who interred the dismembered skeletons of many dead in one ossuary, mingling the bodies, arts, and spirits of different peoples. One Dutch traveler, describing a ritual known as the Feast of the Dead in which "their friends come from other nations," explained that the burial was the occasion to "contract new alliances of friendship with their neighbors; saying, that as the bones of their ancestors and friends are together . . . so may their bones be together in the same place, and that as long as their lives shall last, they ought to be united in friendship and concord, as were their ancestors and friends." Through such rituals of grief and healing, Susquehannocks and their neighbors created sacred links of friendship, kinship, and alliance.[10]

Gandastogue was not a nation of static borders, territorial, ethnic, or cultural. It was more like a network of connections, densely woven in the Susquehanna Valley core, sparser the farther it traveled, which knit together many nations. The nodes of this network were people, bound by a shared emotional culture that prized peace, who maintained harmony through shared mourning and the violent deflection of dangerous feelings. These emotions shaped the process of nation building that made Gandastogue a mid-Atlantic power by the turn of the seventeenth century. This is what those five Susquehannock sachems meant to communicate when they met with the English captain in the midst of a storm in 1608. They hung wampum around his neck, their desire for peace made manifest; rich northern furs and tobacco pipes of exotic stone, an invitation to join their far-reaching network of exchange and reciprocity; bows and arrows "sutable to their greatnesse and conditions," to promise that allies would defend each other from their enemies. Presenting him with these gifts, professing their "loves" and "stroking their ceremonious handes about his necke," was the Susquehannocks' way of asking the English to take a first step into the sacred circle of kin that bound the diverse peoples of Gandastogue into a nation.[11]

The English captain in 1608—his name was John Smith, and he is a rather famous representative of the Jamestown colony in Virginia—had a different perspective on what Susquehannocks were after. Smith had no understanding of Susquehannock culture; he had been in North America for only a year and had interacted only with coastal Algonquians who were as culturally different from Susquehannocks as the English were from Ottoman Turks. Nevertheless, he lavished praise on what seemed a magnificent but pliable people. "Such great and well proportioned men, are seldome seene, for they seemed like Giants," he wrote. His admiration for the principal sachem, "the goodliest man that ever we beheld," like a hero out of European antiquity decked in the furs of ferocious beasts, was emblazoned on Smith's iconic map of Virginia. Despite Susquehannock confidence and

John Smith's map of Virginia included two illustrations of Indigenous peoples: Powhatan holding court (left), and a wild, giant-like Susquehannock sachem (right). One of the earliest Native Americans depicted by English authors, this often-reproduced sachem has erroneously become synonymous with Virginia Indians. John Smith, *Map of Virginia* (London, 1624). Courtesy of the John Carter Brown Library at Brown University.

power, however, they had "an honest and simple disposition," marveling at English superiority and "adorning the discoverers as Gods." Viewing the Susquehannock ceremony through an ethnocentric lens, what Smith saw was not a proposal for alliance but an offer of submission. "Stroking their ceremonious handes" was a gesture of adulation. Their promises of "aids, victuals, or what they had to bee his" was a pledge to pay tribute. They wanted "his creation to be their governour," he believed, and for the colonists at Jamestown to "defend and revenge them of the Massawom-ecks," an Iroquoian people to the north who were the Susquehannocks' "mortall enimies." In Smith's view, the "oration of their loves" expressed desire for a political compact: subjection in exchange for protection. It was natural for him to make this assumption. That compact was the core of the English understanding of a properly ordered body politic: a hierar-chical relationship between sovereign and subject, expressed through an emotional language of love.[12]

The English saw the universe as a series of nested hierarchies resembling each other across scale, each centered on a patriarch. A father sat at the head of every household, responsible for its governance and expected to care for his dependents—wife, children, and servants—in exchange for their obedience. In the household's heavenly reflection, God offered salvation to his human children, and in turn they recognized God's sovereignty and obeyed his divine will. In between these poles sat the king, father of his nation, with all the subjects of the realm his symbolic children. The patriarch's authority derived from a sacred fountainhead. "The Lord hath set superiours in the places of eminencie, wherein they beare the image of God," wrote the minister William Gouge in a manual on household governance. King James I, an enthusiast of the divine right of kings, took the analogy to heart. "The King towardes his people is rightly compared to a father of children," he wrote, describing a king as "a little God to sitte on his Throne, and rule over other men." Arguments for the monarch's absolute power were fiercely contested in the seventeenth century, but even vehement critics shared its underlying assumptions about the household and its patriarch. The republican theorist James Harrington conceded, "paternal power is in the right of nature; and this is no other than the derivation of power from Fathers of Families, as the natural Root of a Common-wealth." Less a coherent ideology than a set of deeply rooted beliefs about the origins of social order, patriarchalism was shared by nearly everyone in England and English America.[13]

Love between the patriarch and his dependents was the glue that held family and society together. The first duty of "all godly servants" to their masters, wrote puritan ministers John Dod and Robert Cleaver, was "to love them, and to be affectioned towards them, as a dutifull childe is to his father," and "to be reverent and lowly to them." Love was essential not just to familiar order but also to social stability, explained Thomas Hobbes, because "obedience, is sometimes called by the names of Charity, and Love, because they imply a Will to Obey." The obligation to love was a reciprocal one, however, as even the most extreme advocates of absolutism acknowledged. "As the father over one family," wrote Sir Robert Filmer, "so the king, as father over many families, extends his care to preserve, feed, clothe, instruct and defend the whole commonwealth . . . so that all the duties of a king are summed up in an universal fatherly care of his people." The word "love" thus mingled emotional affection, paternalistic care, and reverence of a subordinate for a superior. As James I put it, "as their naturall father and kindly maister," a good king must provide for his subjects and consider "his greatest suretie in having their hearts." Accordingly, matters of state were routinely expressed in the language of love. In the Virginia Company of London's charter, King James I called the stock-holders "our loving and well-disposed subjects" who "have been humble suitors unto us," and promised that his foremost goal was to "secure the safety of our loving subjects." Inextricable from loyalty to God, king, and family, love was the bedrock of political order.[14]

The corollary to the equation of affection with obedience was punishment for disobedience. According to Gouge, the sinful condition of humanity mandated "an awfull respect of the divine Majestie" and mortal terror for the state of one's soul. Existential trembling was the surest foundation for moral order, and by extension order in the temporal realm. Cleaver and Dod defined reverence for parents as cheerful obedience combined with "a bashfull awfullnesse, and standing in feare of them." While God held souls in his hands, however, princes and parents had to rely on corporeal forms of violence to chastise the disobedient—"correction," as it was generally called. Violence, wielded properly, not only punished wrongdoing but also encouraged right action in the future through fear of the consequences. Terror of patriarchal violence was therefore desirable so long as it fostered an environment of love. Gouge distilled the ideal relationship between patriarch and dependents as the symbiosis of these emotions: "Their distinct duties are noted in two words, Love, Feare." In the English imagination, terror was indivisible from the love that united in harmony God, king, and humanity.[15]

English colonists brought this emotional culture to North America. Jamestown's planners imagined an ordered commonwealth with laboring freemen and servants governed by gentlemen endowed with the natural right to rule. When it turned out be a pestilential deathtrap populated by "loose, leawd, licentious, riotous, and disordered men," the gentlemen did not hesitate to rule through brutal discipline. The *Lawes Divine, Morall and Martiall* (1610) prescribed draconian punishments for even petty offenses. Capital crimes included lying, blasphemy, and killing a chicken. Governor Sir Thomas Dale carried out sentence with maximal cruelty as an example to others. Men guilty of "beinge Idell" were hanged, shot, or broken on the rack, and "all theis extreme and crewell tortures he used and inflicted upon them to terrefy the reste." Thus was discipline maintained by the "trusty and well beloved" governors and captains to whom the king entrusted "the good Order and Government . . . to be made by our loving subjects" in Virginia.[16]

English relations with Indigenous peoples were structured by the paradoxical fusion of love and fear. The booster literature for colonization was filled with enthusiastic schemes to Christianize, civilize, and Anglicize Native Americans, turning them into proper subjects of the king. Thomas

Harriot concluded his ethnography of Chesapeake Algonquians with his "good hope they may be brought through discreet dealing and governement to the imbracing of the trueth, and consequently to honour, obey, feare and love us." Virginia's charter espoused the goal of conversion "unto the true worshipp of God and Christian religion," and ministers such as Robert Johnson exhorted colonists to evangelize "by faire and loving meanes, suiting to our English natures." William Crashaw optimistically predicted, "when they are converted and love their owne soules, then they will love us also." Loving colonization aimed to inspire Indigenous reverence for English authority, a project synonymous with instilling a healthy sense of fear. Indian children should be "brought up in the feare of God and Christian religion," Company shareholders asserted, preparing them for the imperial hierarchy of obedience. If these lessons failed to take hold, there were other methods. When Governor Dale suspected that Native traders bringing food to Jamestown "did rather come as Spyes then any good affectyon they did beare unto us," he had them "apprehended and executed for a Terrour to the Reste, to cawse them to desiste from their Subtell practyses." Dale thought that violence would hasten the Indians' acceptance of English authority and ultimately their embrace of subjection to the crown.[17]

Chesapeake Algonquians had different ideas about political order and the proper means of incorporating outsiders. Most Indigenous peoples near Jamestown were part of the Powhatan paramount chiefdom, a polity composed of many chiefdoms that paid tribute to a single mamanatowick (paramount chief). As a political structure, the paramountcy combined hierarchy and autonomy. Werowances (chiefs) of each nation generally governed their internal affairs without interference. Unlike consensus-seeking Susquehannock matrons and sachems, however, the mamanatowick known as Powhatan wielded coercive authority. Werowances paid tribute in goods, providing Powhatan with the material means of rewarding followers, making war, and crafting alliances. He used these tools to transform outsiders into Powhatans through the threat of conquest and the promise of prosperity, enlarging his domain from six chiefdoms in the 1560s to more than thirty by 1608. With the confidence appropriate to an ambitious ruler of an expanding people, he used the same tools to incorporate English newcomers. Powhatan elevated John Smith to werowance of Jamestown, promising to provide for the newest members of Tsenacomoco (Powhatan country) in exchange for tribute in weapons and metalwork. Powhatan, Smith wrote, "promised to give me Corne, Venison, or what I wanted to feede us, Hatchets and Copper wee should make him, and none should disturbe us." Being English, Smith could conceptualize this power relationship only through the lens of affection. In his telling, Powhatan told his new subordinate, "I never use any Werowance so kindely as your selfe," and Smith reciprocated by professing "our true love."[18]

Whether English and Powhatans understood each other's politics, they grasped each other's designs for dominance. Instead of paying tribute, colonists extorted food at gunpoint and killed any who refused. Powhatan asserted his authority by chastising his unruly tributaries. Colonists justified the resort to arms in patriarchal terms as correction of the wayward Powhatans. "It is as much," wrote William Strachey of the merciless fighting during the First Anglo-Powhatan War (1609–1614), "as if a father should be said to offer violence to his child, when he beats him, to bringe him to goodnes." The diplomatic marriage of Powhatan's daughter Matoaka (Pocahontas) to John Rolfe offered an opportunity for peace. Yet the burgesses of the first assembly in 1619 complained, "we never Perceaved that the natives of the Countrey did voluntarily yeeld themselves subjects to our gracyous Sovraigne." Their good behavior "proceeded from feare and not love," but fear alone was not enough. Rolfe's introduction of tobacco generated a scramble for land that left little room for compromise. In 1622, Opechancanough, Powhatan's successor, orchestrated the massacre of over three hundred settlers. The nine hundred survivors huddled behind Jamestown's flimsy palisade, terrified of Powhatan power. "Wee live in feare of the Enimy everie hower," wrote one servant to his parents in England. Others noted the militia's impotence in the face of warriors "who like violent lightening are gone as soon as perceived." The aspiring planter William Capps was outraged by this breach of the patriarchal compact. "Our worthier men" did nothing to defend the colony, he wrote, cynically imagining the gentlemen allowing men like himself to "first be Crusht alitle" until desperation forced them to fight for survival. "I would God had their soules," he cursed his leaders, and if peace returned, "I will forsweare ever bending my mind for publique good, and betake me to my owne profit." The feeling of being betrayed led Capps to lose faith in his country and absolve himself of a subject's duties.[19]

Despite Capps's frustrations, the English waged the Second Anglo-Powhatan War (1622–1632) with unflinching savagery. Company orders instructed, "roote out [the Powhatans] from being any longer a people, so cursed a nation, ungratefull to all benefittes, and uncapable of all goodnesse." If extirpation was impractical, then expel them "so farr from you, as you may not only be out of danger, but out of feare of them." English militia slaughtered Powhatan noncombatants, burned towns, and destroyed food stores in regular raids. Their conduct demonstrates that fragile English dreams of coexistence could easily shift toward genocide. However, they did not target Natives as a racial or ethnic group, but rather the Powhatans as a polity and the core Pamunkey nation in particular. Virginia's leadership eagerly sought Indigenous allies, and several nations agreed to become tributaries of the English. In 1614, the Chickahominies, who had long struggled to fend off Powhatan expansion and saw the English as a natural ally, swore they would "become not onely our trustie friends, but even King James his subjects and tributaries." They signaled an Indigenous understanding of tributary autonomy when they stated that "their desire was to injoy their owne lawes and liberties." The English crafted their treaty as a protection compact, stipulating that Chickahominies "should for ever bee called Englishmen, and bee true subjects to King James and his Deputies," and in exchange "we would defend them from the furie of Powhatan, or any enemie whatsoever." As colonial forces gained ground, they recruited an increasing number of Chesapeake nations who became English tributaries.[20]

These ad hoc tributary relationships were formalized after the Third Anglo-Powhatan War (1644–1646). Opechancanough launched a desperate bid to push back the English, killing as many as five hundred colonists. But the balance of power had shifted too decisively in Virginia's favor for Powhatan warriors to consolidate their initial success. The recently installed governor, Sir William Berkeley, established an effective strategy for defeating Indigenous foes. A line of fortifications guarded the frontier, each serving as a base for rangers who targeted Powhatan towns and crops, while Indian allies served as scouts and spies. Their value to colonial security was "an undisputable truth," asserted the burgesses as they sent William Claiborne to enlist Rappahannocks and Eastern Shore nations "for the further discovery of the enemie." The Powhatan paramountcy disintegrated under the onslaught. In 1646, militia captured and unceremoniously murdered Opechancanough. His successor, Necotowance, signed a treaty that surrendered Powhatan independence and made its nations tributaries of Virginia. "Necotowance do[es] acknowledge to hold his kingdome from the King's Majestie of England," the treaty read, and in exchange the Virginian government would "undertake to protect him . . . against any rebells or other enemies whatsoever." It is unlikely Necotowance bore much affection for his conquerors, but after years of war his people had learned to fear the English and agreed to exchange obedience for protection as subjects of the "little God" across the sea.[21]

The Anglo-Powhatan wars brought Virginians and Susquehannocks in contact again two decades after their first meeting in the middle of a storm. The Susquehannocks' flexible political structures and the cultural value they placed on incorporating outsiders allowed Gandastogue to grow in power and influence at the same time that colonists searched for Native allies. In 1627, they encountered William Claiborne, who was looking for new trade routes to finance "a continued and settled course of warre" against the Powhatans "to their utter exterpation." No documents record their meeting, but it established a mutually advantageous alliance. In 1629, Gandastogue's sachems allowed Claiborne to build a trading post on an island called Monoponson, which Claiborne renamed Kent. In 1638, they expanded the grant to include Palmers Island, at the mouth of the Susquehanna River. This was the origin of what the sachem in 1676 called their "ancient league of amety." It gave the Virginian Claiborne a "Plantation in the Sasquesahonoughs Country" and the Susquehannocks a gateway to the wider Atlantic world.[22]

They were promiscuous in their desire to fold foreigners, both Indigenous and European, into a web of alliance. Although Susquehannock expansion into the Delaware Valley initially led to mourning wars against Lenapes in the 1620s, by the 1630s they had made peace and consolidated their friendship through intermarriage. Together, the people of Gandastogue and Lenapehoking (Lenape country) traded with merchants of the Dutch Westindische Compagnie (WIC) based in an outpost called Fort Nassau. They also, "with the common consent of the nations," welcomed a motley mix of Swedes, Finns, Dutch, and Germans representing the Swedish Söderkompaniet, or South Company. New Sweden (Nya Sverige) built its main trading post on the west shore of Minquas Kil—a Unami-Dutch mashup best translated as "Susquehannock Creek"—on land "close to the Minquas country," with another outpost "directly on the trail of the Minquas." Excavations of Susquehannock hunting camps show a surge in animals butchered for fur rather than meat. Those furs were what made the Delaware Valley valuable to Europeans. One WIC employee stated that without "trade with the Minquas . . . this river would be of very little importance." Anyone walking through the Dutch outpost New Amstel (later English New Castle) could not fail to notice that its handful of streets were named Beaver, Otter, Mink, and Minquas. For Susquehannocks, Delaware thus became another space populated with allies bound by exchange and mutual friendship.[23]

Gandastogue's networks to the west grew as well. Building on what Jesuit missionaries described as "close alliances with the Hurons," some Susquehannocks relocated to Wendake (Wendat country) in the 1630s. Nearly two decades later Jesuits reported, "there are still found in the Huron country people from their districts." It is likely that some of these migrants married and created multiethnic families. Characteristically for a people who embraced cultural blending, some Susquehannocks converted to Catholicism and took French names. Estienne Arenhouta, for example, kept his new faith after returning to Gandastogue in the 1640s. The nation absorbed most Indigenous groups in the Upper Susquehanna Valley, who apparently retained both political autonomy and connections to their natal identities. The Skanendowa, for example, were described by Dutch mapmakers as an independent polity in 1616, but by the 1650s they signed treaties with Europeans alongside sachems of the "true Minqueser," the core Susquehannock community. While the Skanendowa's incorporation may have been peaceful, in other cases it was not. By the end of the 1630s, the Susquehannocks and their allies had defeated their "mortall enimies," the Massawomecks, and "destroyed that very great Nation." Archaeologists have noted a corresponding influx of Massawomeck-style ceramics (called Monongahela) into Susquehannock communities and an increase of Massawomeck burials in Susquehannock graveyards, suggesting that some of this "destroyed" nation was incorporated. This diverse and extensive network of political connections led one European to describe Gandastogue as "the Minquas council and their united federation."[24]

Despite their ecumenical embrace of outsiders, the Susquehannocks did refuse one important alliance. In 1638, what seemed to the Susquehannocks like an aggressive group of interlopers muscled their way into the Chesapeake. They spoke English and brandished a paper from their king naming them owners of the lands that sachems had granted to William Claiborne. Their militia declared Claiborne a pirate and conquered his trading posts on Kent Island and Palmers Island. Their leaders imperiously demanded that Susquehannocks direct their furs toward the new colony of Maryland and transfer their alliance to its proprietor, Cecil Calvert, the Baron Baltimore. The sachems declined. To trade was to cultivate peace between friends, express political solidarity, and gradually transform friends into kin. Of course they were interested in beneficial exchange and the power that trade afforded, but they traded only with trusted allies, not with people who made themselves enemies by waging war at the watery gates of Gandastogue. One Chesapeake merchant explained the Susquehannock rebuff in a language the English could understand: "the Indians exceedingly seemed to love the said Clayborne."[25]

Lord Baltimore understood the power of love in politics. In a 1649 address to Maryland colonists, he professed "our sincere affection to them," and hoped they would "unite themselves in their affection and fidellity to us." Affective bonds would hold their new society together. In Maryland they would realize that "wee are all members of one Body Politique," he reasoned, "in their Unanimous, and cheerfull obedience to the Civill

Government." Unity was the corollary of the divine commandment "to love one another," which would allow them to achieve "temporall felicity in this World" and the "accomplishment of Eternal happiness." Love and obedience were the essence of the patriarchal compact, constituting a political order on earth that mirrored divine perfection. Unfortunately for Baltimore, however, the creation of his colony represented division rather than unity and upheaval rather than order. In contrast to Gandastogue's experience, in which the incorporation of foreign peoples was a source of strength, the expansion of English America brought a tangle of incompatible allegiances that promoted factionalism, crisis, and civil war.[26]

Rejected by Susquehannocks, Maryland's ruling Calvert family reached toward other Indigenous nations and found partners in the Piscataway paramount chiefdom. Algonquian peoples culturally similar to the Powhatans, Piscataways had suffered from mourning war raids during Gandastogue's expansion and saw Maryland as a natural ally. Kittamaquund, the Piscataway tayac (paramount chief, usually translated by English writers as "emperor"), welcomed settlement by the English at the mouth of the Potomac River and invited them to build a Jesuit mission. Over one hundred Piscataways converted to Catholicism in the first few years, including Kittamaquund. His daughter was christened Mary, given an English education, and married to the colonist Giles Brent. Father Andrew White delighted in the Piscataways' apparent love for Christ and their gentle embrace into Maryland's political order, but acknowledged its basis in a protection compact. He explained, "they had warres with the Sasquasahannockes," who "waste and spoile them and their country," and therefore the Piscataways "like us better . . . assuring themselves of greater safety, by liveing by us." In 1641, the tayac ceded the right to choose his successor to Lord Baltimore, beginning the process of transforming his chiefdom into a tributary of Maryland that was formalized in 1666.[27]

Unfortunately, Maryland's acquisition of tributary nations added fuel to ongoing conflicts between Indigenous powers and sparked colonial rivalries over the Indians they saw as "theirs." The Calverts procured a royal order prohibiting Virginian trade within Maryland's boundaries, which Virginia's governor Sir John Harvey enforced despite William Claiborne's vehement objections. Harvey complained that Claiborne and his allies in the Governor's Council were consumed by "malice," a dangerous inversion of love that made them "more likelye to effect Mutinye, then good lawes and Orders." Indeed, Claiborne orchestrated a coup against Harvey and funneled public resources toward a private war on Maryland. Baltimore believed Claiborne "did practise and conspire with the Sasquisahanoughes . . . against the inhabitants of this colony." But Susquehannocks did not need his prodding; they were already enemies of the Piscataways and resisted Maryland's attempts to engross the fur trade. Their raids destroyed the Jesuit mission in 1642 and threatened the fledgling colony's capital at St. Mary's City. Caught in the middle of this Indigenous rivalry and beholden to Piscataway allies, Governor Leonard Calvert declared Susquehannocks "enemies of this Province" but failed to find money to pay for a military expedition or men willing to fight. His best effort mustered only thirteen volunteers and twenty conscripts, which probably did not cause much worry among Gandastogue's thousand seasoned fighters. Contemptuous of Maryland's toothless militia, Claiborne diverted men from the Third Anglo-Powhatan War to retake Kent Island and overthrow the Calvert regime. English alliances with Natives drew colonies into Indigenous wars and pitted colonists against each other in a chaotic tangle of conflicts.[28]

Because Lord Baltimore was Irish and Catholic, Maryland also became embroiled in the transatlantic religious and political upheaval of the English Civil Wars. After England's violent experience of the Reformation, most English people considered their nation Protestant to the core. Catholics represented the essence of everything that was un-English, a perfect antithesis against which English identity could be defined. The Stuart king Charles I was insufficiently hostile to Catholicism—or was, in the eyes of puritans, sympathetic to it—causing radical ministers to fulminate against his "papist" contaminations of the Church of England. Charles, like his father, claimed a divine right to unfettered monarchical power, which his opponents denounced as a fusion of Catholicism and tyranny often expressed as "arbitrary rule." Civil war erupted between Charles I and his Parliament in 1642, spreading throughout the British Isles and across the Atlantic. In 1646, Captain Richard Ingle, bearing a Parliamentary letter of marque to prey on royalist ships, invaded Maryland on the pretext that Lord Baltimore was plotting to wield "tyrannicall power against the Protestants . . . and to endeavor their Extirpation." With prodding from William Claiborne, Protestants joined the cause. As the province descended into sporadic civil wars lasting into the 1650s, the Calverts denounced the "Subtile Matchiavilians" who wielded sophistries about republican liberty to "alienate their affections" from their patriarchal lord.[29]

Battles between Protestants and Catholics in England were bitter, but in North America they were complicated by the presence of Indigenous peoples. In 1652, violence between Kent Island settlers and Eastern Shore Algonquians sowed terror on the frontier. "Some are Soe dreaded and affrighted they have left their plantations," complained colonists, petitioning the government to fulfill its patriarchal duty to act for "the preservation of our Lives with our wives and Children." In the midst of challenges to the government's legitimacy, it was imperative for the Calvert regime to protect its people to retain their loyalty. Yet when religious strife returned, the Calverts were hard pressed to fight rebels and Indians at the same time. In 1655, government forces impressed men and confiscated weapons from suspected rebels in the frontier county of Anne Arundel, but these security measures left colonists vulnerable to attack. In a polemical pamphlet, Leonard Strong capitalized on well-worn English nightmares of Catholic conspiracy with dangerous foreigners, such as French Jesuits, and added an American flourish. He claimed that disarming colonists was not callous indifference but a malign plot. "The Indians," he wrote, "were set on by the Popish faction," who incited Native peoples to massacre defenseless Protestants. In subsequent decades, this image of Indian-Catholic collusion, and its mobilization to justify armed resistance, became a central feature of political disorder in the Chesapeake.[30]

During the Civil Wars, Virginians also forged arguments that resurfaced in the 1670s. Parliament's execution of Charles I in 1649 and proclamation of a kingless Commonwealth threw patriarchal politics into a spin. Governor Berkeley announced his colony's allegiance to the king-in-exile Charles II and declared that a nation without a monarch was nothing but anarchy. Parliament's laws, he charged, were a vehicle "for the accomplishment of their lawless and tyrannous intentions." The 1651 assembly declared, "the Lawes of England . . . tell us, that no power on earth can absolve or manumit us from our obedience to our Prince." Any body that compelled an alternate allegiance asserted an absurdity and possessed no legitimacy. Berkeley marshaled familiar arguments about a government's obligation to protect its people, stating, "the afflicted English Nation now groanes" under such "heavy burthens" that "wifes pray for barrenness and their husbands deafnes to exclude the cryes of their succourles, starving children." Rebellion was justified in self-defense of these suffering families. He reasoned, "we may resist violence with force, and in a lawfull defence of our selves, destroy any that shall endeavour to take away our lives." The argument that defiance of the state was actually a proper veneration of the sovereign allowed Berkeley to unite the colony behind him. A generation later, it served disaffected colonists challenging his regime just as well.[31]

Although England's troubles destabilized the emotional languages of loyalty and obligation, in one case the rhetoric of political affection played a familiar role. In 1652, a Commonwealth fleet forced the Chesapeake colonies to capitulate and took control of their governments. Commonwealth commissioners, among them William Claiborne, brokered a formal end to hostilities between Maryland and Gandastogue. Six sachems led by Sawahegeh, representing "the Indian Nation of Sasquesahanogh," signed

"Articles of Peace and freindshipp" with "the English Nation in the Province of Maryland." The terms of the treaty affirmed that the two nations "promise and agree to walke together and Carry one towards another in all things as freinds and to assist one another accordingly," a bond that would remain "for Ever, to the End of the World." Friendship between equals was at the heart of the agreement. Unlike the Algonquian nations conquered or converted by Virginia and Maryland, Gandastogue did not offer subjection. Rather, Maryland joined the Susquehannock network of allies. After 1652, the two peoples would act "as in Reason should be done betweene those that are freinds," and in the process changed the political landscape of the mid-Atlantic.[32]

Gandastogue reached its height in the 1650s as seeds of alliance blossomed and bore fruit. Susquehannock relations with Munsees and Lenapes in the Delaware Valley illustrate the depth of their blending. Adopted captives from mourning wars and relations gained through intermarriage produced a new generation of leaders who claimed multiple ancestries. Minqua-Sachemack, one of the Hackensack proprietors of Manacknong (Staten Island), announced his hybrid identity every time he introduced himself: his name literally translates as "Susquehannock chief." He was one of several multiethnic leaders mentioned in European records, and doubtless many more lived and died without leaving a documentary trace. Settlers were often confused about the identities of these figures, struggling to pin down their political affiliation to ensure the legitimacy of land sales and diplomatic agreements. From Indigenous points of view, however, it was possible to belong to more than one community. People like Minqua-Sachemack were both Susquehannock and Hackensack, and they possessed rights—including land rights—inherited from all the lineages that produced them. As the Lenape sachems Mattehorn, Sinquees, and Pemenacka stated in 1651, "they were great Chiefs and Proprietors of the lands, both by ownership and by descent and appointment of Minquaas and River Indians," and they could grant rights to those lands on behalf of "ourselves, our heirs and co-heirs." These multiethnic leaders represented an extension of Susquehannock space that overlapped with and interpenetrated the spaces of their neighbors.[33]

Susquehannocks surrounded themselves with a mantle of European allies through strategic land grants. Four Susquehannock sachems—Jonnay, Tonnahoorn, Pimadaase, and Cannowa Rocquaes—witnessed the 1651 grant by Mattehorn and other mixed-ancestry leaders, which conveyed the territory between Bombay Hook and "the bounds and limits of the Minquaes country" to New Netherland (Nieu Nederlandt). It established the legality of the trading post at New Amstel despite Swedish protests. In 1652, they offered Maryland land north of the Patuxent River on the western shore and the Choptank River on the eastern shore, covering nearly half of Chesapeake Bay. They insisted that Kent Island and Palmers Island belonged to Claiborne, but allowed Marylanders to "build a Howse or Fort for trade." This grant ensured that Maryland would prosper, Virginians could trade, and Susquehannocks would enjoy three English entrepots on their doorstep. Finally, in 1655, sachems conveyed the corridor between the Delaware River and the upper Chesapeake to New Sweden. They asked Governor Johan Risingh to "establish blacksmiths and shotmakers on the land, who should make their guns and other things for good pay," and hoped to buy "cloth, guns and all other goods." The territory would serve Gandastogue as munitions factory and trading post.[34]

Susquehannocks made these grants from a position of strength. In the case of New Sweden, Gandastogue was clearly the superior party in what colonists understood as a protection compact. Risingh described a signing ceremony in which the spokesman Svanahändär "took me by the hand and led me forward on the floor and said: 'As I now lead you by the hand, so will we lead your people into the country, and maintain you there and defend you against Indians and Christian enemies.'" Like their Indigenous neighbors, Susquehannocks understood territorial rights in relational terms: rather than alienating the soil in a market transaction, they exchanged gifts for the right to perform specific actions, such as hunting, farming, or trade. What Europeans understood as "sales" did not, in Susquehannock eyes, relinquish their sovereignty, and they did not hesitate to "sell" the same territory to different buyers when it served their interests. Susquehannocks granted land to invite Europeans closer to Gandastogue, creating new nodes in their networks among four colonies representing three different European empires. No other seventeenth-century Indigenous power enjoyed so many European connections at one time.[35]

European allies allowed Gandastogue to survive waves of Haudenosaunee mourning wars that crashed over the Great Lakes. In 1649, Five Nations warriors attacked Wendake in raids of unprecedented size and intensity. They destroyed most Wendat towns, killed thousands and carried away thousands more in fetters, and forced survivors to flee. Haudenosaunee campaigns targeted other nations friendly to Gandastogue one by one: Petuns in 1650, Neutrals in 1651, and Eries by 1656. Although Gandastogue could not field nearly as many fighters as the Wendats or Eries, between 1651 and 1655 it repeatedly repulsed attackers with the help of English, Swedish, and Dutch firearms. Susquehannocks not only weathered the Haudenosaunee storm, but also offered refuge to allied peoples. A Jesuit

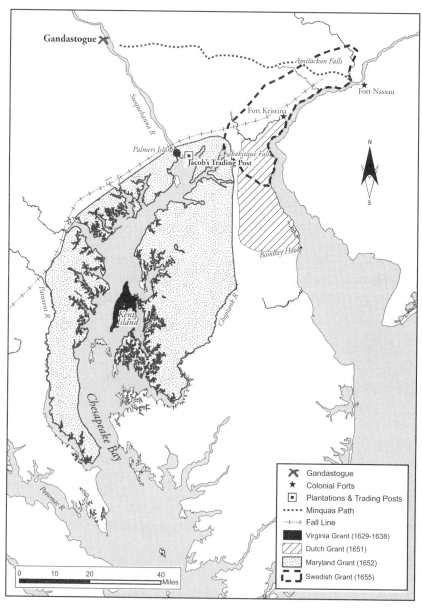

Susquehannock Land Grants, 1629–1655

observer reported that Wendats searching for safety "take their route toward the people of Andastoe [Gandastogue]." Although Jesuits portrayed this migration as a desperate flight into the dark, some refugees may have been Susquehannock immigrants who moved to Wendake in the 1630s, or their children, now returning home. Others no doubt had kinfolk or spiritual brethren, such as the Catholic Estienne Arenhouta, waiting for them on the other side. In either case, the violence of the Haudenosaunee wars led streams of people to join the Susquehannock nation.[36]

Violence and dislocation offered opportunities for Susquehannocks to expand their influence. In 1656, hundreds of Eries migrated south toward Rickahock, an outpost above the falls of the James River that they had established for trade with Susquehannocks. Within a few years they continued into the Savannah River Valley, where they became known as the Westos. The Erie-Susquehannock alliance endured through this migration, opening new paths to power. In 1662, the Virginia assembly noted, "the Susquehannock . . . in considerable numbers frequently come to the heads of our rivers; whereby plain paths will soone be made." Susquehannock paths would allow them to "gett the whole trade from our neighbouring and tributary Indians." Gandastogue also grew by accepting refugees from Dutch-Indian wars in the Hudson Valley. According to a 1660 report, "seven canoes full of Indians with wives and children" from the Minisinks "came down and proceeded to the Minquas country." A steady flow of people from the Esopus, Raritans, Navesinks, Hackensacks, and Mahicans followed. Susquehannocks further expanded their influence by acting as mediators. The "chief sachem from the Minquas country" told WIC officers he wanted to broker a peace between their Indigenous allies and Director-General Petrus Stuyvesant, dangling the carrot that "when they see that there is everywhere peace between the Dutch and the Indians, then they will come with all their beavers to Stuyvesant's land." Putting this economic clout to good use, the sachem Onderischoghque presided over the conference that ended the conflict. In the 1660s, Susquehannock influence grew to such an extent that one historian characterizes Gandastogue as a "regional great power."[37]

By the early 1670s, Susquehannock space reached its most extraordinary expanse. Its geographic reach and social diversity can be glimpsed in the journals of the German explorer John Lederer, who sought to blaze trails beyond Virginia's southern frontier. His only successful expedition relied exclusively on a Susquehannock guide named Jackzetavon. Though operating hundreds of miles from his homeland in the Susquehanna Valley, Jackzetavon had the social connections to secure safe passage and hospitality from at least ten Indigenous nations as far south as Ushery (Catawba) country in what is currently South Carolina. In fact, when southeastern Natives traveled, they followed protocols based on their extensive familiarity with Susquehannocks and their goods. If an Indigenous nation "hold any correspondence with the Sasquesahanaughs," Lederer wrote, "you must give notice of your approach by a Gun; which amongst other Indians is to be avoided, because being ignorant of their use, it would affright and dispose them to some treacherous practice against you." Susquehannock friends, such as the Monacans who celebrated Jackzetavon's arrival "with Volleys of Shot," Occaneechis living on an island in the Roanoke River, and the Westos, who wielded iron hatchets and were "addicted to Arms," were all nodes in Gandastogue's network of trade and alliance.[38]

Mutual enmity was no less powerful than mutual exchange. There is suggestive evidence that Susquehannock-Haudenosaunee hostility may have added northeastern nodes to Gandastogue's network. In 1671, the trader John Pynchon observed a delegation of Pocumtucks from the Connecticut Valley "going a great journey . . . all along the sea coast and so on toward Virginia" in search of allies against the Five Nations. Having recently suffered a devastating defeat at Mohawk hands, they intended "to make a league with the Nowgehowenock Indians (as they call them)," a nation "beyond Delaware" who were needed for "their ability to carry on their wars and encourage them and receive encouragement from them." Nowgehowenock was most likely the name that New England Algonquians used for Susquehannock, the only Native nation between Delaware and Virginia renowned for its martial prowess and access to European firepower. There are no records indicating whether the Pocumtuck embassy was successful. If it had been, Gandastogue's tendrils would have stretched all the way into Massachusetts.[39]

Susquehannock influence reached west as well. Although the Haudenosaunee wars forced Susquehannocks to abandon their towns in the upper Potomac Valley, hunters probably continued to use these settlements as temporary camps, and as late as 1670 fighters used the streams and paths of the Ohio to range deep into Haudenosaunee territory. A French map noted that Lake Erie and the western end of Lake Ontario "are infested with Gantastogeronons," and French explorers observed Senecas camouflaging their longhouses to evade Susquehannock attack. They noted, "the Antastogué [Susquehannocks] . . . are continually roving about in the outskirts of their country," so far west that "we ran a great risk along the Ohio River of encountering the Antastoez." The sources are too scanty to say whether Susquehannocks moved through this war zone alone or if they established relationships with nearby Indigenous groups such as the Shawnees. It is suggestive, however, that archaeologists have uncovered evidence of trade links between "Proto-Susquehannocks" and the Shawnees' progenitors, the Fort Ancient culture, reaching back to the sixteenth century. Moreover, by the 1690s Susquehannock and Shawnee communities had become so deeply interwoven that they traveled, fought, and lived together. It is plausible that they formed their alliance earlier than it was observed by Europeans, facing the Haudenosaunee threat together.[40]

Gandastogue's expansion was dramatic. During a time when war, disease, and dislocation claimed half the Haudenosaunee and 80 percent of Powhatans, the Susquehannock population doubled from roughly 2,500 in 1608 to more than 5,000 at their zenith in the 1650s. Archaeological excavations attest to the wealth that flowed into Gandastogue, ranging from

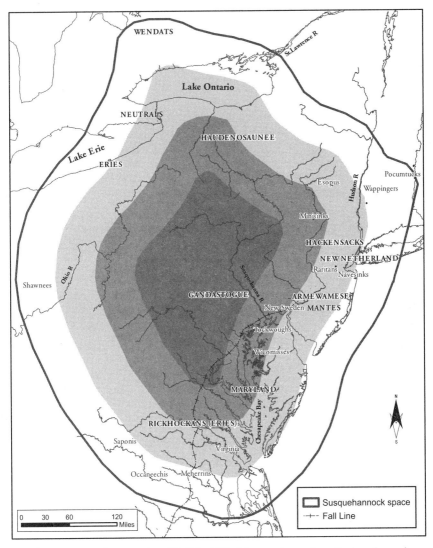

The Susquehannocks' Social and Political World, ca. 1650–1675. Rather than a bordered territory with an ethnically homogenous population, Gandastogue is better imagined as a network of affiliated peoples from many nations.

utilitarian items such as brass kettles and iron fishhooks to glass beads whose luminous beauty inspired Susquehannock craftswomen to sew them into patterned belts like wampum. Flintlock muskets, lead shot, and steel hatchets became the standard weapons of a Susquehannock warrior, which made them fearsome opponents and desirable allies. Their access to material forms of power from several European markets, combined with a culture that drew strength from the mixing of heterogeneous people, allowed them to weave a web of affiliations embracing a multitude of nations over a vast geographical space. From a core in the Susquehanna Valley, Gandastogue's network radiated outward, overflowing the boundary lines that European cartographers inscribed on their maps. When crisis struck in 1675, this was the canvas on which the Time of Anarchy unfolded.[41]

England's years of war and revolution abated in 1660, when Parliament restored the monarchy and invited the Stuart heir to take the throne. Southern colonies embraced the Restoration of Charles II in the effusive terms a sovereign might expect from his subjects. The Virginia assembly, technically complicit in rebellion for capitulating to the Commonwealth, professed "all due obedience and reverence," and sent Sir William Berkeley to beg the king for a pardon and "reacceptance of them into his sacred Majesties favour and protection." Thankfully, Charles II cultivated a spirit of reconciliation. One of his first acts wiped the slate clean by pardoning all of his subjects for crimes committed during the time of troubles. The only exceptions were the men who signed his father's execution order, the so-called Regicides. These men were publicly drawn and quartered, a choreographed spectacle of terror in which the victims were hanged, castrated, disemboweled, and forced to watch their entrails set on fire before they were beheaded and dismembered. Such was the restoration of the patriarchal compact between the king and his people. Colonists professed that they were "his majesties loveinge subjects," but they meant what they said when they called him "our dread soverain."[42]

The Restoration promoted a surge of interest in overseas empire. Charles II maintained the Stuart ardor for absolutist rule, and his inner circle saw colonies as a source of revenue outside Parliament's control over spending. Colonies were therefore critical to sovereign power, argued the royalist Sir John Knight, and Virginia in particular was "of as great importance to his Majesty as the Spanish Indies are to Spaine." Within months of his coronation, Charles II chartered the Royal African Company and gave it a monopoly over the shipment of enslaved Africans to American plantations. At this point, slavery was less important to Virginia's economy than indentured servitude. As late as 1680 there were only about three thousand people of African descent in a total population of forty thousand, one-sixth the number of English servants and one-third the number of tributary Natives. The form of racialized chattel slavery that came to characterize the eighteenth- and nineteenth-century plantation South, moreover, had not yet taken shape. Not all African-descended peoples were enslaved; some were legally indentured servants and a few were free. Nevertheless, black slavery was present almost as soon as Virginians planted tobacco on seized Indigenous lands—by 1619, if not earlier—and the wealthiest planters displayed an early preference for perpetually exploitable slaves over servants who could be squeezed for only a few years. The Stuarts encouraged this trend by expanding England's participation in the Atlantic slave trade, profiting from slaving itself as well as customs duties on the aromatic gold that black lives were sacrificed to grow. Considering that critics of the Stuarts denounced absolute monarchy for stripping their liberties and reducing Englishman to slavery, it is perversely fitting that Charles II built an empire on the backs of enslaved Africans.[43]

Pursuing an imperial vision in which colonial profits fueled monarchical consolidation at home, the Stuarts treated North America like a blank slate upon which they could project a neofeudal fantasy. In 1663, Charles II chartered Carolina as a proprietary grant to his eight closest supporters. The Lords Proprietors, as they were called, created a framework for government that mandated an elaborate hierarchy of titled nobility, English serfs, and black slaves. The following year, Charles II named "our Dearest Brother" James, Duke of York, the proprietor of a vast domain including all of New Netherland, branding the Dutch as interlopers in their own colony. In 1664, a fleet under the command of Richard Nicolls forced Manhattan's surrender. New Netherland transformed into New York, an imperial province that was also the personal possession of the Duke of York.[44]

The conquest of New Netherland displayed the scope of Stuart ambitions, but it also demonstrated the fragility of the patriarchal compact on which imperial order depended. The equation of obedience for protection was most commonly invoked by sovereigns, but the unprotected could do the same math to absolve themselves of the duty to obey. Thomas Hobbes considered this one of the limitations of sovereign power. "The end of Obedience is Protection," and therefore "the Obligation of Subjects to the Soveraign, is understood to last as long, and no longer, than the power lasteth, by which he is able to protect them." Although many political theorists would have disagreed, colonists of all nations subscribed to the same

rough logic. So when the invading English fleet approached Long Island in
1664, Dutch colonists warned Director-General Stuyvesant that if he could
not protect them, they "shall be obliged, to our hearts' grief, to seek, by
submission to another government, better protection." When Stuyvesant
failed, Dutch colonists joined the English and became New Yorkers. The
belief that a government that failed to protect its people could command
no allegiance and deserved no loyalty weakened colonial regimes when
they most needed staunch support. A decade later, this structural flaw in
the patriarchal compact accelerated political fracturing during the Time of
Anarchy.[45]

New York served as a laboratory for Stuart experiments in colonial rule,
especially in Native affairs. The king instructed Richard Nicolls, his "trusty
and well beloved" agent, to address Algonquian complaints against New
England colonists, with authority to circumvent local magistrates and make
new treaties. He justified this broad and intrusive mandate as a "manifes-
tation of Our Fatherly affection towards all Our Subjects," English and
Indian alike. Beneath the rhetoric this was realpolitik: direct relationships
between Native nations and the crown would undermine the authority of
New England officials, many of whom were unrepentant Commonwealthmen
who hated the new king, and undermine their claims to territory within
the Duke of York's charter. Even if the primary goal was to humble recu-
sant colonists, however, the recognition of Indians as subjects elevated the
importance of Indigenous peoples by tying the defense of their rights to the
expansion of imperial power. As governor of New York, Nicolls oversaw
the passage of a legal code known as the Duke's Laws, which guaranteed
Native access to courts and promised that even in suits against colonists
they would receive justice "in as full and Ample manner . . . as if the Case
had been betwixt Christian and Christian." Indigenous peoples within
New York would be subjects of the crown with rights and protections
under the law. Over the next two decades, the recognition of Native subjecthood made for a powerful cudgel that royal authorities could wield
against truculent colonists in the name of the king's fatherly love for his Indian children.[46]

Imperial goals mandated that New York preserve amicable relations between settlers, tributary Indians, and independent Native nations. While
the Chesapeake grew tobacco on expropriated Native land, New York's
economic lifeblood was furs, and the fur trade required willing Indian partners; "otherwise His Majestyes expences" in funding the conquest, Nicolls
observed, "will not turne to any account." In 1664, Nicolls's agents concluded a treaty with Mohawks and Senecas that established a relationship

between sovereign nations. The Haudenosaunee indicated they were merely transferring the alliance they had with the Dutch so that things continued "as formerly." Unlike the Dutch, however, the English stipulated, "all such as have submitted themselves under the protection of his Majesty are included in these Articles." The alliance would depend on the Five Nations' willingness to include tributary Indians in the deal. Nicolls, understanding that interactions among these three constituencies offered many opportunities for small incidents to become diplomatic crises, established regulations in the Duke's Laws. Trading required a license, so only a select group of merchants would be trusted with the protocols of exchange. Guns and liquor, staples of the fur trade economy but volatile commodities even in the best of times, required additional licensing. Land, the most volatile commodity of all, required the governor's permission to purchase, creating a centralized system for the orderly transfer of Indigenous territory to English hands. Aside from these regulations at the point of intercultural contact, New York Indians were, like tributaries in Virginia and Maryland, left to govern their own affairs.[47]

New York's tributary system reflected the Stuarts' cultivation of pluralism. Scarred by puritan extremism during the Commonwealth and personally attracted to Catholicism, they judged religious toleration important to political stability. Puritans found this cause abhorrent and some Anglicans continued to persecute dissenters, but new proprietary colonies were free to etch toleration into their foundations. Carolina's Fundamental Constitutions allowed "any religion," including "Jews, Heathens, and other dissenters," to worship without interference. East and West New Jersey, two proprietorships carved out of New Netherland, guaranteed liberty of conscience and became havens for Quakers and Presbyterians. In New York's Delaware Valley, conquered Dutch, Swedes, Finns, and Germans were allowed to observe their own religious traditions and governed their own "national" communities with minimal English supervision. By accident if not design, the accommodations meant to govern heterogeneous European populations resembled those for tributary Indian nations. In New York, in contrast to Virginia and Maryland, the composite legalities created to incorporate Indigenous peoples were not anomalous but part of a larger pattern of pluralism built into the DNA of Restoration imperialism.[48]

It would be too generous to call New York's bricolage of Indian treaties and legal accommodations a "system." Nonetheless, Nicolls and his subordinates cobbled together a structure of rule in which Natives not only held a meaningful place as subjects of the Crown but also served an important role in royal designs for colonial development. For the first decade after the Restoration, these arrangements were limited to the new proprietaries, where royal agents faced less opposition from entrenched elites than in colonies such as Virginia or Maryland. However, it set a crucial precedent for the coming time when established orders tottered and fell, opening opportunities for aggressive intervention and the expansion of the Stuarts' improvised multicultural empire.

Susquehannocks slipped into precipitous decline in the early 1660s as all five Haudenosaunee nations intensified their wars with Gandastogue. Susquehannocks survived repeated assaults by forces as large as eight hundred men, thanks in part to their extensive network of allies. In 1661, invaders found the Susquehannock connadago defended by European-engineered bastions bristling with Dutch muskets and Swedish cannons. Auxiliary forces included hundreds of Lenapes and "Black Minquas [Eries]," as well as fifty militia the Maryland government dispatched after sachems "assured us of their affections and friendship" and conveyed that "they expected the like from us." Susquehannock counterattacks were fierce. Warriors penetrated deep into Cayuga territory and stalked Seneca transportation routes, forcing Haudenosaunee traders to move in caravans to avoid ambush. In 1666 and 1669, they inflicted major defeats on Onondagas, who according to one Jesuit "have been much humbled of late by the Gandastogué." Despite these victories, fighting consumed the nation. Combat losses were heavy and epidemic disease struck in 1661 and 1663 in the aftermath of sieges. In 1647, there were more than five thousand Susquehannocks. By their own report, that number had been cut in half by 1663. In 1671, Jesuits estimated only one thousand. By 1675, less than four hundred Susquehannocks remained. A Quaker who visited Gandastogue during these days witnessed despair, writing, "its douted by som that in a litle space they will be soe destroyed that they will not bee a people." In little more than a single generation, 90 percent of the nation was lost.[49]

It is difficult to imagine how people raised in an emotional culture equating grief with destructive insanity would have experienced loss on this scale, but transformations in society and politics offer a glimpse into the impact of those experiences. Judging from their changing practice of war, the controlled rituals of mourning war mutated into chaotic violence and murderous rage. As manpower diminished, Susquehannock warriors became younger. By 1670, entire war parties were composed of boys as young as fifteen, who raided Cayuga country without the leadership of experienced war captains. Instead of avoiding casualties and maximizing captives, these "Andastogué boys," as a Jesuit called them, killed as many of their enemies as possible through bold assaults that cost many lives. Ar-

Signatures of Susquehannock ambassadors Wastahanda-Harignera and Goswein-gwerackqua, both described as Gandastogue's war captains. "Articles of Peace and friendshipp," 29 June 1666. Collection of the Maryland State Archives.

chaeological excavations demonstrate a spike in violent death among adolescent males, and the presence of prestige goods associated with martial power—European flintlocks, for example—indicates that youths took on the leadership roles traditionally held by older men. As Alsop crudely phrased it, "he that is the most cruelly Valorous, is accounted the most Noble," so that in struggles for political influence "he that fights best carries it here." Before the 1660s, Susquehannock leaders were either war captains or peace chiefs, but Wastahanda-Harignera—the only sachem whose leadership remained constant during these years of decline—was both "Cheife Generall Councellor" and one of their "warre Captaines." According to neighboring Lenapes, this fusion of opposing roles signaled a deranged slide away from the ideal of peace that held society together.[50]

Death and militarization transformed Susquehannock mourning war. Instead of achieving glory by taking captives, young warriors sought to terrorize their enemies. A Marylander had earlier observed, "what Prisoners fall into their hands by the destiny of War, they treat them very civilly while they remain with them abroad." Instead of taking prisoners back to the community for judgment by the matrons, warriors began to execute captives while still in the field. In 1672, Susquehannock men killed two Oneida women within sight of their town so their kinfolk could watch and listen as they died. When warriors did bring captives back, the community stretched out their tortures, keeping enemies alive for days before allowing them to die. Haudenosaunee retaliated with equally prolonged executions, but understood that Susquehannocks intended these actions to strike fear into their hearts. It worked. In 1668, an Oneida elder opposing Jesuit evangelizing framed his arguments in relation to Susquehannock violence: "in Heaven," he claimed, "all those who should go there would fall into the hands of the Andastoguez" and be "treated as Captives." Instead of eternal bliss, he warned, Oneida converts seeking the Catholic paradise would find Susquehannocks waiting to cut off their fingers, mutilate their faces, and scatter their blood across the sky. Despite the Susquehannock slippage toward defeat, they terrified the Haudenosaunee more than ever before.[51]

Susquehannocks punched above their weight in part because of their wide-ranging networks of support. One might reasonably assume that their ability to mobilize European allies grew smaller as New Netherland swallowed New Sweden and New Netherland became New York, which committed to a Haudenosaunee alliance. But the nodes of their networks were people, and many of the people who traded with Susquehannocks under one imperial regime continued to do so after they exchanged allegiances. The most important of these figures was Jacob My Friend. Beginning as a WIC employee at Fort Nassau, he joined the Susquehannock circle of kinship by marrying a woman of Gandastogue and carried those relationships with him when he moved to Maryland. His trading "howse," located just a few miles from Palmers Island, hosted negotiations with Susquehannock sachems and served as the provincial entrepot for shipments of guns and ammunition to Gandastogue. He was a member of an intercolonial frontier elite, with an estate of 1,280 acres along St. Georges Creek in New York's jurisdiction in addition to his Maryland trading post, making him one of the wealthiest men in the Delaware Valley. Jacob risked his life and reputation on the Susquehannocks' behalf. In 1664, he accompanied Wastahanda-Harignera on a diplomatic mission to Iroquoia, and advocated for Maryland's leaders to consider the Susquehannocks "a Bullwarke and Security of the Northerne parts of this Province." Through tumultuous years of imperial conquest and Indigenous warfare, Jacob remained a steadfast friend of the Susquehannocks and served as the nexus for their alliance with Maryland.[52]

Counterintuitively, Gandastogue's networks flourished even as its population withered. The unprecedented scale of Haudenosaunee wars brought thousands of foreigners into Iroquoia. By 1660, one Jesuit claimed, "the Five Nations . . . are, for the most part, only aggregations of different tribes whom they have conquered." Others estimated that adoptees made up two-thirds of some nations. Susquehannocks were among these captives. Although many would have been ritually executed, flayed by knives and burned by fires, others were adopted. After Haudenosaunee invasions of "the country of the Andastes and the Chaoüanons [Shawnees]," noted a French traveler, "they considerably augmented their own forces, by the great numbers of children or other prisoners whose lives they spared." In 1668, a missionary estimated that "Andastogué prisoners of war," a common French term for adopted captives, composed as much as one-third of the Cayuga villages Onontaré and Thiohero. In the early 1670s, "people from Andastogué" lived among the "free iroquois" at the mission community of La Prairie de la Madeleine (later Kahnawake), "dwellers there as prisoners of war." By the early 1680s, Susquehannocks could be found in several other multiethnic missions, including Lorette and Sillery (Québec). As captives in Iroquoia, Susquehannocks survived and made new lives.[53]

According to traditional Haudenosaunee practice, these captives would have been purged of their previous identities and "requickened" as new members of a Haudenosaunee family. But these were not traditional times. Many requickened foreigners retained connections to their natal identities in Iroquoia's melting pot. At least one community of Wendat captives reconstituted their entire town in Iroquoia, and Jesuits observed several multiethnic communities without any native-born Haudenosaunee. "My heart is all Huron," declared one Wendat living among the Onondagas, "I have not changed my soul, despite my change of country." Fragmentary evidence suggests that Susquehannocks not only held on to their hearts, but also infused Iroquoia with their culture. By 1675, most ceramics in Seneca towns were in the style of Susquehannocks and other peoples of the Ohio Valley, produced either by captive women or Senecas influenced by them. This process echoed the captive Shenks Ferry, Keyser, and Massawomeck women who brought their culture into Gandastogue in the early seventeenth century. Susquehannocks were among many peoples who experienced something short of complete assimilation despite their forced relocation. As one man who had been born Wendat told a group of Haudenosaunee, "the country of the Hurons is no longer where it was,—you have transported it into your own." In a manner not entirely metaphorical, the apparent decline of the Susquehannock population was a transportation of "countries"—nations made from webs of kin—into Iroquoia. Even as independent Gandastogue fell into eclipse, a new kind of Gandastogue grew year by year in the shadow of the Iroquois Longhouse.[54]

While Gandastogue proved surprisingly supple in the face of disaster, the English colonies demonstrated remarkable fragility even as they expanded. By 1670, the population of Virginia had grown to thirty thousand, Maryland eleven thousand, New York and the Delaware Valley six thousand,

and Carolina four thousand. King Charles II hoped that sovereign love would bind them together, assuring colonists of "our extraordinary and fatherly care towards those our subjects" and of his determination "to unite them all in a joynt dependance and firme loyalty to our selfe." Much to his disappointment, chronic instability and spasmodic violence plagued the colonies. In 1660, Maryland governor Josias Fendall fused anti-Catholicism and antiroyalism into a rebellion against the Calverts. Dutch resistance to English occupation manifested in 1665 as riots in New York City, holdouts in Albany promoting armed resistance, and skirmishes between militia and the garrison at Kingston. In 1669, a Scandinavian who took the nom de guerre Königsmark convinced one-third of the Delaware population to rebel with grandiose promises that a Swedish fleet had set sail to reconquer New Sweden. When a Dutch fleet actually did sail in 1673 to force Manhattan's surrender and resurrect New Netherland, not only did Dutch colonists gleefully switch their allegiance but so did English colonists in New Jersey. In Virginia, where a planter elite squeezed laborers for every drop of profit, insurrections erupted in 1661, 1663, 1671, and 1674. Exploited servants justified their actions as protests against their reduction to "slavery" by tyrannical masters. For officials, however, the cause was obvious: "the feare of God in their harts not haveing," the disaffected intended to "extinguish the hearty love and the true, and due obedience which a true, and faithfull subject of the King should beare."[55]

Modern historians have offered more compelling explanations for this endemic disorder, which varied from colony to colony and ranged from ethnic tensions and religious antagonisms to a depressed tobacco economy and factionalism among elites. However, few scholars have appreciated the extent to which the ambiguous status of tributary Indians placed pressure on these fault lines and pushed them to the breaking point. Each colony offered its Native subjects a range of rights and protections. New York had the Duke's Laws. Virginia's 1662 legal code codified Indigenous rights to land, property, and personal safety, with provisions to evict English squatters, control ranging cattle, and prohibit Native enslavement. Maryland's 1666 treaty with its twelve tributary nations established reservation lands and proscribed forced removal; subsequent laws passed in 1669 limited encroaching settlement. While these provisions fell short of English birthright liberties, they were nonetheless the antithesis of extirpative warfare in earlier decades. At least on paper, the tributary relationship established Indian subjects as rightsbearers under the principle that "they shall have equall justice with our owne nation."[56]

This legal framework enabled tributary nations to weather the storms of colonialism. Despite second-class status, many Indigenous leaders considered it the best means of securing their survival. Native men earned wages as fishermen and farmhands, fur trappers, animal hunters, whalers, and wilderness guides. Women found employment as domestic servants or crafted baskets, pottery, and tobacco pipes for sale in the marketplace. Some Indigenous elites were attracted to the possibilities offered by engagement with English people and culture. Cockacoeske, who in 1656 became the Pamunkey weroansqua (female chief), took the English planter John West as a lover and bore a son also named John West, who became "a great warr Captaine among the Indians." In the 1660s, she developed a warm relationship with deputy governor Francis Moryson, to whom she affectionately referred to as "good Netop," the Algonquian word for friend. Cockacoeske was by no means a typical figure, but she exemplifies the Indigenous determination to thrive within the limits of colonization.[57]

The tributary system should not be romanticized, however; settler colonialism was inherently violent and Natives suffered under English rule. Werowances continually complained of aggressive squatters and destructive livestock, which broke the promises written in treaties. As the Portobacco weroansqua stated, fears that they "will soon come to destruction" forced one community after another to move away from intruding colonists. Dislocation damaged harvests and reduced Indigenous health, causing a decrease in fertility, an increase in susceptibility to disease, and a calamitous loss of population. Local English officials often abused their positions to swindle Indians of their land or trap them in forms of debt peonage scarcely distinguishable from slavery. Finally, allegiance to an English sovereign subjected Natives to the political culture of love and fear. When New Castle magistrates executed a Lenape for murder in 1671, Governor Francis Lovelace congratulated them for causing the convicted man to "suffer in the most Exemplary way" and hanging his decaying body for public display. He mused, "I doubt not but the Novelty of it may produce good Effects, to restrayne the Exorbitancyes of any Indyans from the like Attempts." Tributary Indians could usually count on access to courts, but the courts often failed to deliver justice and exposed them to a judicial culture that maintained order by inflicting terror.[58]

Tributary structures, despite some benefits, ensured that both Natives and settlers became entangled in larger patterns of violence. Virginian planters, legally barred from enslaving Indians themselves but allowed to buy slaves from distant countries, sold guns to Native partners to do the dirty work of enslavement. In the early 1660s, Thomas Stegge and his wife, Sarah Stegge (who later remarried as Sarah Grendon), partnered with the Westos at Rickahock to funnel enslaved Indians to Virginia plantations. Governor Berkeley and his circle of favored oligarchs, called the Green Spring faction after Berkeley's plantation, used the assembly to crack down on this "private sinister comerce," ostensibly because irresponsible gun running could "bring a warre upon the country." They then turned around and established a legal monopoly on trade with Native peoples and made the same guns-for-slaves deal with the Occaneechis, a chiefdom of Siouan-speakers whose towns were located at the strategic crossroads of the southeastern road system. They targeted nations beyond Virginia's frontier, which spared Native tributaries from slave raids. Some tributaries actually prospered, such as the Appamattucks who did most of the labor on the paths between Virginia and Occaneechi Island. Yet this participation fueled dangerous competition. Traders such as Grendon and her nephew William Byrd bitterly resented the tributary Indians who served the Green Spring monopoly and covertly pursued opportunities that drew new Native nations into the maw. This tangle of Anglo-Indian partnerships and rivalries contributed to colonial factionalism and promoted bad blood between settlers and tributaries.[59]

Pledges of mutual defense, whether part of the patriarchal compact undergirding the tributary relationship or treaties of alliance between equals, also encouraged a lethal entanglement of enmities. Maryland's alliance with Gandastogue caused the Five Nations to view Maryland as an enemy. Raids by "Senecas"—a catchall term Marylanders used in ignorance of Iroquoia's distinct nations—claimed at least thirty English lives between 1661 and 1666. Tributary Algonquians were sucked into the fray, noted Philip Calvert in 1660, "for being freinds to us and the Susquehannoughs." This was particularly galling to Piscataways because Susquehannock warriors had raided their communities for decades before the English crafted an alliance without consulting them. Colonists complained as well, not only that Susquehannocks had brought violence to their doorsteps but also for the financial burden that war imposed on struggling planters. Burgesses protested "the Greate Expense they must be at to defend the Province against the Incursions of the Sanecoe [Seneca] Indians" and demanded that Lord Baltimore reduce taxes to compensate. But the province was beholden to protect its imperiled tributaries and assist Gandastogue. In 1664, the assembly grudgingly granted Governor Calvert "full power to Lay a tax . . . toward the aydinge and assistinge the sasquahanna Indians." This expansion of executive power over spending rankled many colonists, who thereafter twisted together economic distress from poor tobacco prices, dissatisfaction with Baltimore's "arbitrary" rule, and the blowback from Indigenous alliances. This noxious cocktail of resentments only grew worse as Haudenosaunee raiders continued to haunt the frontiers and Susquehannocks became less capable of fighting them.[60]

The confusing lines of allegiance that bound governments, tributaries, and foreign nations made for a volatile combination with colonists impatient with Indian rights and weary of Indian violence. Settlers could be bewildered by the variety of Indigenous peoples around them, dressing in different styles and speaking different languages, each with their own cultural norms and protocols of civil behavior. They did not always have the ability—or inclination—to tell the difference between friend and foe. Maryland's 1666 treaty bluntly stated something that colonists often expressed: "the English cannot easily distinguish one Indian from another." Virginia burgesses complained how difficult it was to enforce the law when colonists suffered from this handicap and shunted the responsibility onto tributaries. The 1662 law code mandated that tributaries give intelligence if foreign Indians approached, "to the end that the nations may be distinguished" and authorities could know who was responsible for subsequent violence. But it was easy for Natives to lie, and when they told the truth it was easy for settlers to distrust them. In 1661, Maryland colonists accused a party who identified themselves as "all Sasquehannoughs" of being Haudenosaunee in disguise, resulting in a gunfight between supposed allies. Sachems later claimed that the men responsible for attacks on colonists were "a Company of Vagabond Rogues that delighted in mischeife and run from nation to nation." Rather than parse the meaning of such a statement, which gestured toward the multiplicity and mobility of Native identities, colonists settlers found it easier to fear allies as well as enemies.[61]

Colonists' mistrust made it difficult for governments to honor obligations to Native subjects. Indeed, settler frustrations with their rulers became intertwined with their animosity toward Indian rights. Virginian oligarchs used the legal protections for Indigenous lands to limit the expansion of tobacco-growing areas to preserve their wealth and power. Young freemen, eager for land after fulfilling their contracts as indentured servants, found their dreams of becoming patriarchs of their own small households dashed. The lawyer William Sherwood explained, "rather then to be Tennants"—servants in all but name—"too many . . . seate upon the remote barren Land, whereby contentions arrise betweene them and the Indians." Enforcement of legal provisions to evict squatters and burn their houses did not diminish demand for Native land, but it did link popular impatience with Indigenous rights to resentment of the elite men who monopolized the levers of power. The fusion of these resentments had incendiary potential. Lord Baltimore denounced colonists who demonstrated their lack of "loyall affection and fidellity to us" by disregarding protections for tributary land. Those who had "acquired great Proportions of land . . . from the Indians and have possessed them without our Consent" hoped to foster "Great division and Faction among the People" and ultimately "adventure the ruine of all the People there, by Civill warrs." In settler struggles over political rights, religious allegiance, economic opportunity, and social power, Natives unwillingly occupied the field on which those battles were fought, with the stability of the colonial order hanging in the balance.[62]

In the first three-quarters of the seventeenth century, the Susquehannock nation experienced a meteoric rise and a catastrophic fall. Their emotional culture of mourning offered potent mechanisms for building links with outsiders through war and peace. They assembled an extensive network of kinfolk and allies across much of eastern North America, stretching from the Delaware to the Ohio, from the Great Lakes to the southern piedmont. By 1675, however, they were not a great power but a small and embattled remnant. What residual might they marshaled came from terrorizing enemies through brutal and costly displays of violence. Yet their decline was not as apocalyptic as bare population figures suggest. Nodes of alliance persisted in the form of personal connections with people who might shift from Wendat to Mohawk, or Dutch to English, and remain committed to their Susquehannock friends. These connections gave Gandastogue flexibility and strength even as the nation seemed to fall apart. After 1675, Susquehannocks mobilized this hidden reservoir to astonishing effect. They experienced unfathomable loss, but they also retained sources of influence so subtle as to be nearly invisible. This paradox of vulnerability and power was one of the central factors driving the Time of Anarchy.

The countervailing brittleness of England's colonies came not only from tensions the settlers imported from England but also from the piecemeal, ambiguous, and contentious incorporation of Native peoples into an unstable empire. The project of creating settler colonies required the appropriation of Indigenous land, which rendered Indigenous nations an intolerable impediment. Yet the faded remnants of early designs for assimilating Indians, manifesting in an improvised accretion of legal protections, created a class of Indian tributaries. Native subjects were expected to love and fear the dread sovereign; they received rights and protections under the law. But to colonists seeking their fortune, Indians remained a barrier. For some settlers, tributaries were not just an obstacle to their ambitions but a threat to their safety, a danger to their families, a source of fear. Governments, obligated by the patriarchal compact to defend their subjects from harm, found themselves in the difficult position of protecting one group of subjects from another.

Colonial leaders understood the predicament. In 1662, Virginia burgesses acknowledged that "the mutuall discontents, complaints, jealousies and

Feares of English and Indians proceed cheifly from the violent intrusions of diverse English made into their lands." Indians retaliated in self-defense, "tending infinitely to the disturbance of the peace of his majesty's country." It disturbed the peace because of the power of fear in English political culture. Addressing colonists in the frontier county of Charles City, deputy governor Francis Moryson pointed out that war was unjust, unnecessary, and expensive, yet popular fears placed pressure on the government. Fear led men to accuse their leaders of "neglect[ing] the defence of this Countrey," thereby betraying the patriarchal duty "committed by his Majestie to [their] charge and care." Failure to assuage these fears through action could lead to a political crisis. "These Panick feares stop not with the particular trouble," he concluded, "but for the most part breake out into murmurings and repinings against their Governours and the Government for not following their rash humours and immediately involveing the Countrey in a destructive warr." The peculiar ability of even groundless terror to tear asunder the fragile bonds of political community, leading to disobedience, insurrection, and war, was the second force that shaped the Time of Anarchy.[63]

· 2 ·

RUMORS OF WARS

THE SUSQUEHANNOCKS FLED IN WINTER, and rumors followed in their wake. In late 1674 or early 1675, the western Haudenosaunee nations forced their enemies to abandon their homeland. Susquehannocks went south and camped above the reaches of the Patuxent River on Maryland's northwestern frontier. Wastahanda-Harignera, the sachem who had been his nation's one steady leader through decades of loss, met with the Maryland Council at Mattapany, the estate of Governor Charles Calvert. He spoke, the secretary noted, through "their Interpreter"—probably Jacob My Friend standing beside his kin in this moment of crisis. Wastahanda-Harignera asked "if the English would lett him and the Susquehannahs live at the falls of Patowmack." But the sudden arrival of the entire nation at the province's borders alarmed colonists, who could not be sure why they were there. Their migration coincided with several "murthers and Outrages" in nearby Baltimore County. No doubt Wastahanda-Harignera assured the council that the perpetrators were Haudenosaunee, but word spread that the killings were actually committed by "the Susquehanna Indians and other their Confederates." In February 1675, burgesses at the assembly speculated that perhaps "the Susquehannahs and Senecas have private Correspondence together Notwithstanding the Seeming Warr between them." If Gandastogue had forged a separate peace with Iroquoia, then the supposed refugees camped on the Patuxent were the vanguard for a Haudenosaunee invasion. Therefore the burgesses "hath reason to Suspect . . . the Designs of the Susquehannahs."[1]

In the absence of reliable intelligence, the Maryland government enacted contradictory policies. Several "Great Men of the Susquehannahs" attended the assembly, asking "what part of the Province Should be Allotted for them to live upon," in fulfillment of Maryland's treaty obligation for mutual protection. The council directed them to build a new settlement above the falls of the Potomac, a generous distance from English and tributary Algonquian settlements. Wastahanda-Harignera did not want to settle above the fall line, a no-man's-land traversed by Iroquoian raiders coming south, but "after Some tedious Debate" he signaled that his people "would Condescend to remove as farr as the head of Potowmack." After the sachems' departure, however, the assembly prepared for other eventualities. They authorized Governor Calvert to "make Peace with the Cynego [Seneca] Indians" if possible, to renew the war against the Haudenosaunee "if his Excellency and Councill shall thinke expedient," and—if it turned out that Gandastogue had betrayed them—to launch a preemptive strike against their erstwhile allies. They claimed these measures were warranted by "certaine credible Informations" that Susquehannocks were untrustworthy, which meant "a Warr is likely to ensue." But they offered no informant, no evidence, no grounds at all save their suspicions and whispers based on fear.[2]

Colonial suspicions extended to tributary Algonquians. The burgesses worried that Susquehannock migrants, "should they be evily inclined," might "Corrupt Our Indians and Mould them So to their own future Designs." Despite earlier conflicts, fighting on the same side against the Haudenosaunee had built mutual trust between the Susquehannock and Algonquian nations. In 1670, the Piscataway tayac, Nicotaughsen, paid the compliment of visiting Gandastogue for diplomatic talks. Such visits seem to have paved the way for the Susquehannocks to move into an abandoned town on Piscataway Creek, just a few miles from Moyaone, the Piscataways' current town. The migrants apparently had Nicotaughsen's blessing. As one colonist described it, Susquehannocks "sought Protection under the Pascataway Indians," disobeying the governor's orders to settle above the falls and instead coming to a separate agreement with Algonquians. Wastahanda-Harignera may have thought this the only prudent course of action, as the English did not seem to have their best interests at heart. Surely he could not help but notice that Marylanders radiated distrust, demanding "they shall go where the Governor pleaseth to appoint them or . . . they shall be forced by Warr." Nevertheless, private communications between Wastahanda-Harignera and Nicotaughsen fed into the assembly's fears of "corruption" among Indigenous peoples they would rather keep separated. Like neighbors everywhere, Natives in close proximity inevitably got to talking, and colonists were unsure of what plans they might hatch when English ears could not hear.[3]

Confusion often reigned during the Time of Anarchy, and rumors flourished in the gap between supposition and certainty. Not all rumors are false, and even false rumors usually contain a seed of truth, but their defining attribute is the lack of conclusive evidence that would prove one way or the other. They swirl around uncertainties, circulated by people searching for reliable information, forming a continuous stream of conversation that flows just beneath the level of public debate. Rumors thus operate as a forum for the discussion of current events, where theories are iteratively formulated, elaborated, and tested for their ability to explain whatever is going on. These ephemeral conversations have a precarious relationship to the truth. They are inherently untrustworthy. Yet rumors have a peculiar power because they are almost impossible for anyone to control. When the rumors fixate on uncertain dangers and impending violence, spreading news means spreading fear. In the early stages of the Time of Anarchy, rumors were the fuel that brought Indian and English societies into spectacular collision.[4]

In a time of war, good information can be essential to survival and the most crucial information concerns the enemy. Where are they? What are their plans? What will our leaders do to protect us?—these are the sorts of questions that define everyday life on a military front, and in early America every frontier was a potential combat zone. Producing the answers was a social process. In fields and taverns, during church services and ceremonial dances, during militia drills and hunting expeditions, huddled behind walls and in remote holdfasts, early American peoples talked. They talked in groups and they tended to talk about other groups, such as the enemies on the other side of the front. They also talked, in hushed tones or angry denunciations, about those on this side, insufficiently zealous in their hatred of the enemy. When the identity of the enemy was itself uncertain—when Susquehannocks and colonists had to ask themselves whether they could trust their own allies—those conversations were fertile breeding grounds for suspicion, and suspicion could lead in a flash to violence.[5]

Such a flashpoint came a few months after Susquehannocks built new longhouses, raised a palisade, and planted corn for the autumn harvest. In July 1675, a group of Doegs, one of Maryland's tributary nations, took some hogs from Thomas Mathew, a Northumberland County planter with estates in Stafford County, Virginia, who owed them money but refused to pay. The Doegs considered this fair recompense; Mathew saw it as brazen theft. His servants and overseer chased them across the Potomac, retrieving the hogs in a skirmish that left several Doegs dead. Doeg raiders returned and killed the overseer and an enslaved Native working on Mathew's plantation. Thirty Stafford County militia, with orders from Governor Sir William Berkeley and permission from the Maryland government, pursued them across the Potomac under cover of night. Near dawn they surrounded two Indian encampments, assuming both were Doeg. Captain George Brent confronted the Doeg headman, progressing swiftly from accusations to gunfire. Hearing shots, Captain George Mason ordered his men to fire on the other camp while the people still slept. Mathew later recounted that a Susquehannock man ducked through the hail of bullets to reach for Mason and "Shook him (friendly) by one Arm Saying *Susquehanougs Netoughs i. e.* Susquehanaugh friends." The Susquehannock shouted in pidgin Algonquian; in his own language he might have said something more like "Gandastogue generoo." He probably did not speak any English, and perhaps in a surge of adrenaline reached for whatever phrase he thought the English might understand. In the dark he might not have known the assailants were English and assumed it was Doegs who had opened fire. It may be telling, in either case, that he should be so willing to trust English friendship or that trust of Algonquian neighbors should be so fragile. Mason, who spoke enough Algonquian to understand his mistake, "ran amongst his Men, Crying out 'For the Lords sake Shoot no more, these are our friends the Susquehanoughs.'"[6]

Between eight and fourteen Susquehannocks died before Mason's men ceased fire. It may seem like a small number, but the slain amounted to around 10 percent of the entire adult male population of Gandastogue. It must have been a painful loss to an already ravaged people, all the more shocking because it was wrought by allies after a sojourn in search of safety. Neither Virginia nor Maryland officials bothered to offer condolences, a callous disregard for the emotional protocols of Susquehannock diplomacy tantamount to a breach of their alliance. The response in the Susquehannock connadago can only be imagined, but in the short term restraint prevailed over retaliation. For more than a month after the shootout, neither Doeg nor Susquehannock took up arms. Eventually, though, simmering rage boiled over. In late August, mixed parties of Susquehannocks and Doegs killed two Virginians in Stafford County. They followed these attacks on people with attacks on property, slashing crops and slaughtering cattle. The council noted, "the Doegs and the Sucahanno Indians as confederates . . . make Dayly incursions" across the frontier, "appearing Armed in considerable numbers to the terrifying the inhabitants of those parts and to the apparant indainger of the whole County." These small raids spread panic across northern Virginia.[7]

News traveled fast, especially bad news, and nothing traveled faster than fear. Two weeks later, the brash young aristocrat Nathaniel Bacon wrote to Berkeley, his cousin-in-law, that neighbors in Henrico County were constantly talking about "these late rumores of Indians." Bacon was a newcomer to Virginia, having arrived in 1674, and he confessed that it was difficult for him to tell the difference between truth and falsehood. The torrent of "continued reports and alarumes," however, had convinced him that no Indian could be trusted, Susquehannock or otherwise. He was not alone in this opinion. Berkeley acknowledged, "the Country was all Armed by a feare and Jelousie that all the Indians were conspired against us," including tributary nations within the colony's borders. Such rumors inspired Bacon to arrest a group of Appamattuck traders on dubious charges of theft. His overreaction, executed without a shred of legal authority, threw Berkeley into a paroxysm of outrage. Castigating Bacon's "rash heady accction," Berkeley spelled out the danger. If spreading rumors created panic, and panic led settlers to take the law into their own hands, they would alienate friendly Indians, destroy the tributary system that Berkeley had constructed over the last three decades, and bring about the very result they feared: "a Generall Combination of all the Indians against us."[8]

Berkeley appreciated the power of rumor. It was difficult to monitor and easily turned subversive. Publications, such as the polemical pamphlets that fueled religious controversy and political upheaval during the English Civil Wars, required expensive machinery and might be suppressed by authorities. It was far more difficult to police dangerous talk. Early modern societies, even literate ones, were oral cultures. Printed papers and manuscripts were often read aloud in social spaces like town squares and taverns, serving as raw material for tellings and retellings that spread from mouth to mouth. But there was a difference, in the English imagination, between news and rumor. News was not always rock-solid truth, of course, and intelligence reports required corroboration. Rumors, on the other hand, were disruptive to social order and good government. They comprised misinformation spread with malign intent. Colonial authorities therefore tried to control rumors through the force of law. Shortly after the execution of Charles I in 1649, the Virginia assembly criminalized "false reports and malicious rumors . . . tending to change of government, or to the lessening of the power and authority of the Governor or government," mandating that "the authors of such reports and rumours" and "the reporters and divulgers thereof . . . shall be adjudged equally guilty." Such statutes were common everywhere in English America, invariably conflating rumors with "false News" that caused "Disturbance of the publique peace."[9]

The most dangerous kind of rumors concerned Native Americans. Francis Moryson, acting as governor in 1662 while Berkeley visited England, provided an astute analysis of the problem. He noted that the "annuall feares of the Indians . . . distract[ing] the Inhabitants of this Country" were caused "more from their own Jealousies than any reall dangers." Jealousy—meaning a tangle of suspicion, fear, and wrath—was, upon investigation, invariably caused by insubstantial wisps of hearsay, nothing but a "light and frivolous report." Nevertheless, the rumors frightened colonists, who demanded their government protect them by going to war—even when the suspected Indians were tributary Algonquians entitled to legal protection. Moryson acknowledged that failure to respond to colonists' demands would be dangerous, arousing "vaine feares" that he would "neglect the defence of this Countrey" and thus betray his patriarchal duty. Decisive action was necessary to "assure all men against the feares of any greate destruction" and prevent "murmurings and repinings against their Governours and the Government." When people *murmur*—a literary trope describing the irrational, deliberately unintelligible, and politically subversive speech of the lower classes—those in power best pay attention, for sedition was not far behind. It did not matter that the peoples' fears were groundless; the government would have no choice unless it wanted to risk insurrection. Rumor spun into fear, and fury would force their hand.[10]

As rumors of Susquehannock violence and tributary complicity spread through the colony, Berkeley was determined to act before fear became a force he could not control. On August 31, he mobilized 750 men from the northern county militias and commissioned Westmoreland County commanders John Washington and Isaac Allerton to conduct a "full And thorough inquisittion . . . of the true causes of the severall Murthers and spoyles." The outcome of the investigation was never really in doubt. Susquehannocks and Doegs would either give "sattisfaction"—surrender the killers for trial and give financial restitution for destroyed property—or face "such Executions . . . as shall be found necessary and Just." He emphasized the importance of constant communication, instructing Washington and Allerton to "give speedy notice to the Honorable Governor of theire severall proceedings" so he could give further orders. To contain the violence, it was imperative for Berkeley to retain executive control.[11]

Just a few days after Berkeley dispatched his orders, Natives of unknown identity killed several colonists in Anne Arundel County on Maryland's northwestern frontier. Calvert and the Maryland Council, having just received news of Susquehannock and Doeg raids in Virginia, leapt to the conclusion that the same culprits were responsible. They decided a sharp response was necessary to forestall a larger "insurrection of the Indians." On September 3, the council raised 250 militia from the southern counties and additional fighters from Algonquian tributaries, with Councilor Thomas Truman in command. After receiving an invitation from Washington and Allerton to confront the Susquehannocks, the Maryland militia planned to rendezvous with the Virginians and forcibly relocate them to the Potomac falls.[12]

Miscommunication and uncertainty hovered over the negotiations between Susquehannocks and settlers. Truman, arriving at the connadago a day before the Virginians, demanded to speak to Wastahanda-Harignera. From atop the palisades, Susquehannock spokesmen responded that Wastahanda-Harignera could not speak because he had died earlier that summer. English documents make no further comment, but the silence probably covers a ripple of sadness and shock. For Iroquoians, the names of dead kinfolk were reminders of the emotional pain of social rupture. To speak the name of the dead was a powerful affront—especially if, as seems likely, Wastahanda-Harignera had been one of the casualties of English gunfire over the matter of a few stolen pigs. Despite Truman's unintentional insult, a small group of "some other great men" emerged from the connadago to talk, followed by a larger group of thirty or forty once they felt it was safe. Spokesmen denied any role in the attacks on Anne Arundel colonists, insisting "it was the Senecaes." They lent sincerity to their words with objects of power, brandishing a copy of the Gandastogue-Maryland treaty and a medal bound with black and yellow ribbon, a gift from Lord Baltimore that they kept as a "Token of amity and friendship" that bound the two peoples in brotherhood for as long as "Sun and Moone Should last."[13]

The sachems' invocation of friendship could not prevent the rumor-fueled bloodshed that ensued. Truman demanded that Susquehannocks provide men to assist in hunting for the alleged Haudenosaunee culprits. He took their reticence as proof of their complicity. Sensing the mood, most Susquehannocks quietly filtered back behind the safety of their walls, leaving only five or six sachems to continue negotiations. The arrival of the Virginia militia escalated tensions. Washington and Allerton accused the Susquehannocks not only of the killings in Stafford and Anne Arundel, but also a third attack perpetrated just days earlier. They cited dubious reports of Susquehannocks dressed in English clothes stripped off the bodies of their victims, ferrying canoes full of plundered beef and pork back to the connadago. Scouts brought word that the rumors were true, claiming that bodies of Susquehannock warriors killed by the doomed defenders were left unburied. According to Maryland captain John Allen, "the Sight of the Christians Murdered" incited fury among the militia and caused a "generall Impetuosity of the Whole feild." While Washington, Allerton, and Truman bickered over what to do, tempers flared and the mood turned murderous. Militia from both colonies, unconvinced by the sachems' dodge that "the mischieffs were done by the Senecas and not by them," became less and less patient with their leaders' inaction. The commanders conferred privately, hoping they could find a way to "prevent a mutiny of the Whole Army." Someone—it is unclear, from conflicting testimonies eager to shunt the blame, exactly who—bound the Susquehannock sachems, carried them away, and smashed in their skulls.[14]

Horrified Susquehannocks manned their palisades while militia settled into a siege. They were at a serious disadvantage: even counting elders, women, and children, the entire nation was outnumbered three to one by the attackers surrounding them. Their numbers continued to dwindle as hunger and disease took their toll. Archaeologists have uncovered forty-two burials at this site, including seven children, a staggering number considering the Susquehannocks had inhabited the connadago less than a year. On the field, however, "bold and formidable" Susquehannocks, hardened veterans of war with the Haudenosaunee, quickly gained the upper hand against the poorly trained and undisciplined militia. One colonist observed that heavily armed warriors "made so many salleys, and the besiegers kep such negligent gards" that they created "remarkeable mischeife." They raided the cavalry's horse corral to bolster their food supply and killed over fifty militia over the course of the month-long siege. At the end of October, the remaining Susquehannocks gambled on a daring breakout. They packed everything they could carry, destroyed whatever they were forced to leave behind to deprive their enemies of plunder, and readied for a rough journey. In the moonlit dark they slipped out of the connadago, silencing colonial sentries before they could raise an alarm. As frustrated militia set fire to their abandoned longhouses, Susquehannocks withdrew above the fall line, beyond easy pursuit.[15]

The rumors that led to a near mutiny, the summary execution of ambassadors under a flag of truce, and the bloody debacle that followed: this was the first wave of political devolution that propelled the Time of Anarchy. The militia's murderous actions were apparently popular; mariners carrying news across the Atlantic depicted the siege as a heroic victory in which every last Susquehannock was put to the sword. That popularity was precisely the problem. English authorities in Virginia and Maryland recognized the dangerous precedent, whether it was the result of rogue commanders or uncontrollable young men. Berkeley's views were not recorded, but it is likely he would have agreed with John Cotton, a resident of Queen Creek, who stated that the killings were "Diametrecall to the Law of Arms." Given the sentiments expressed to Nathaniel Bacon earlier that summer, Berkeley probably believed this butchery would undermine colonial authority rather than encouraging Indians to submit to it, accomplishing little but escalating hostilities. The Maryland Council recognized that men on the margins taking matters into their own hands would encourage civil disorder. They

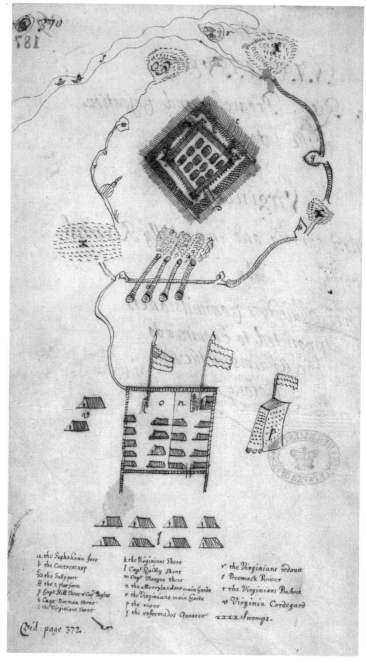

English siege of the Susquehannock connadago. Frontispiece from John Berry and Francis Moryson, "A True Narrative of the Rise, Progresse, and Cessation of the Late Rebellion in Virginia." The National Archives of the United Kingdom.

warned, "by this meanes and through Such proceedings as these, noe Co-missions, Instructions, powers and directions for the future will ever be Ob-served." The inevitable result: "all Authority will become Rediculous and Contemptible."[16]

These auguries were ominous enough, but subsequent events were worse than anything that Berkeley or Baltimore could have predicted. Royal in-vestigators later identified the siege as a turning point. Their 500-page man-uscript report was ostensibly dedicated to the causes of the civil disorder among settlers that came to be known as Bacon's Rebellion. The report contained only one illustration, a sketch that graced the frontispiece, but it had nothing to do with Bacon or rebellion. It depicted the siege of the con-nadago, advertising this incident as the cause of everything that followed. The English assault on the Susquehannocks, intended to bludgeon a weak and vulnerable people into submission, was instead the trigger that set the Time of Anarchy in motion.

In the months after they escaped the siege, Susquehannocks were quiet. Co-lonial records do not include even rumors of their whereabouts. It was as if an expectant hush fell over the Chesapeake. Then, on January 25, 1676, they went to war. The timing suggests a deep cultural significance to their decision. Indigenous war parties typically mobilized in the summer. These attacks, however, occurred just a few days after the Midwinter Ceremony, an annual celebration of purification and thanksgiving that prominently featured the interpretation of dreams. Iroquoians ascribed a special power to dreams, which expressed the soul's deepest desires and mandated col-lective action to fulfill those desires. There is no way to know what kinds of dreams Susquehannocks dreamed during their winter of exile. The war captain Monges, at least, remained full of sorrow over colonists' betrayal twenty years later, and said he "had still tears in his Eyes when he thought of it." Although evidence among Susquehannocks is sparse, Jesuits noted that nightmares of violence and despair had become increasingly common among the Haudenosaunee during the years of war with Gandastogue, often fueling longings for vengeance. A Quaker missionary visiting Susque-hannock descendants in 1706 observed that matrons, one of whom he described as "an ancient grave Woman," were central to political decision making based on dream interpretation. If the same was true in earlier de-cades, it is reasonable to conclude that midwinter dreams led Susquehan-nock matrons to call for a mourning war.[17]

While motivation for Susquehannock attacks fell within traditional cultural patterns, the forms of violence reflected newer practices emphasizing terror. War parties raided English settlements in the upper Rappahannock

Valley, killing several dozen colonists. Raiders took almost no captives except for a few they immediately tortured to death. Thomas Wilford, a veteran Indian trader, claimed to have witnessed "an English man (that was then prisoner) taken and tied to a tree his nayels pulled off and Used in very barberous maner then taken and Rosted in hot Embers." According to other accounts, Susquehannocks "devised a hundred ways to torter and torment those poore soules," including "sticking feathers in their flesh," while "some they ripp open, and make run their gutts round trees." War breeds sensational stories of enemy atrocities, but there is reason to give some credence to these reports. Susquehannocks were deliberate in their choreography of violence. They staged grisly executions near isolated farmsteads so that settlers huddled behind barricades and nervously gripping their muskets had to listen to the screams of the dying. Traumatized witnesses reported that this experience was so horrible it "makes our harts Ready to bleed to heare." Petitioners described "sad Spectacles of Blood and Ruin ly every wher at our Doores," while "our Freinds and Neighbours that Survive [are] the living monuments of Callamity and greife." Raiders amplified the survivors' fear by mutilating corpses, leaving their "brutish Markes upon there fenceless bodies, that might testifye it could be none but they who had commited the fact." Susquehannocks spoke in the symbolic language of burned flesh and scattered blood, leaving echoes of suffering calculated to inflict fear among the survivors.[18]

The raids unleashed a wave of terror. Although the number of casualties was relatively small—thirty-six, according to the most reliable reports—colonists in the epicenter of violence in Rappahannock County fled en masse. Six of every seven plantations were abandoned, leaving raiders to set deserted farmsteads aflame. Frightened refugees carried stories of what they called "the fury of the enimy" to every corner of Virginia. Older colonists could not help but recall haunting fears of annihilation during the earlier Anglo-Powhatan Wars. Nathaniel Bacon wrote, "how this His Majesties Colony of Virginia was formerly Overrun and almost Depopulated by the Barbarous Indians is not yet worn out of the Knowledge and sad Remembrance of some surviving Inhabitants." These elders feared "being again overrun and ruined by these Heathens." For those too young to remember, the unprecedented sense of vulnerability was no less excruciating. Thomas Mathew later recalled "these frightfull times," when "the most Exposed small families withdrew into our houses of better Numbers, which we fortified with Pallisadoes and redoubts, Neighbours in Bodies Joined their Labours from each Plantation to others Alternately, taking their Arms into the Fields, and Setting Centinels." Native warriors struck suddenly and without warning; terror spread dark wings at the slightest hint of impending violence. "No man Stirred out of Door unarmed," he wrote, "Indians were (ever and anon) espied, Three, 4, 5, or 6 in a Party Lurking throughout the Whole Land." Everywhere outside the fortified plantations was a potential war zone.[19]

A letter from Elizabeth Bacon, wife of Nathaniel, poignantly captures colonists' feelings of bleak horror and harrowing fear. "I pray God keep the worst Enemy I have from ever being in such a sad condition as I have been in," she wrote to her sister in London. The Bacons were a wealthy family and, judging by a 1677 inventory, enjoyed luxuries uncommon in seventeenth-century Virginia: a brick house, fine linens and silks, stuffed chairs, a library full of books. But Bacon, with an infant daughter and pregnant with her second child, lived at Curles Neck, a plantation near the fall line that was vulnerable to sudden attack. Nathaniel, called to Jamestown as a member of the Governor's Council, was not there to protect them. Perhaps that is why she kept a small arsenal next to her fine feather bed, including a "baskitt with 8 hand granados, Iron shells Loaden and fitted." Bacon told her sister that the frontier was taut with fear. "If you had been here," she wrote, "it would have grieved your heart to hear the pitiful complaints of the people." Many of her neighbors had fled, and now "nobody durst come" to Curles Neck, leaving her isolated, lonely, and practically defenseless. Indians, Bacon concluded ominously, "are come verry nigh our Plantation."[20]

The patriarchal ideal shaped colonists' experiences of these attacks. One author claimed that Susquehannocks assaulted not only English bodies but also English manhood, calling Virginians "Cowwards and childeren to fight with." Even without such taunts, the trembling of women like Elizabeth Bacon meant that Virginian men had failed to protect their dependents, the most basic patriarchal obligation. A group of petitioners from Charles City County, writing in early 1677, recalled the "violent and deadly fears of danger wee apprehended from the Indian, many of the people haveing . . . drawne togeather inwards to secure their wives and children, whose daylye cryes made our lives uncomfortable." Living under siege in their own homes, which transformed a space of care and love into one of violence and fear, accentuated the emotional pain of their failure.[21]

If individual men had failed to protect their wives and children, by implication the government had failed to protect its subjects. Helplessness in the face of Indigenous power was emasculating, but the image of domestic distress also possessed immense political potency. The Charles City petitioners believed it "our duty incumbent on us . . . to take up armes, many of us for the just defence of ourselves, wives and children," an imperative mandated "by the laws of God and nature" that superseded the laws of men. Invoking the emotional suffering of families was not just a compelling way for colonists to frame requests for help, but also a coded challenge to the legitimacy of a government that had failed them.[22]

Colonists—"we of the Frontiers," as Bacon called them, a reminder that these families were on the front lines—called on the government to fulfill the patriarchal obligation of the rulers to protect the ruled. Mary Byrd, a neighbor and friend of Elizabeth Bacon, wrote, "posts came in daily to the Governor," flooding Berkeley's desk with reports that Susquehannocks "dayly make Incursions upon us." Colonists must have cheered when Berkeley mobilized militia under deputy governor Sir Henry Chicheley, assuming they would pursue and destroy the Susquehannock raiders. Berkeley had more cautious measures in mind. Chicheley's mission was to "march out and disarme the Neighboring Indians," probably with the goal of reassuring panicked colonists and pressuring Algonquians to comply with government directives. To everyone's surprise, Berkeley abruptly canceled the mission, disbanded the militia, and called for an assembly the following month to formulate a war strategy. In the meantime, colonists were ordered to cluster together and fortify their homes, bunkering down in conditions of tension and tedium that inevitably fueled rumors.[23]

Berkeley probably changed tack because an opportunity presented itself to bring a swift end to the war. He had wanted to regain command since events had spun out of his control the previous year, hoping "to finde out the cause of this their breach of peace" with the Susquehannocks, "soe if possible he might have produced all to a right understanding, and that thereby a faire and friendly accomodation." According to John Cotton, following the February raids a Susquehannock sachem requested parlay. "What was it that moved him to take up Arms, against him, his professed friend," the unnamed sachem asked Berkeley. He declared "as well his owne as subjects greife to finde the Verginians, of Friends, without any cause given, to becom his foes." This grief, he explained, motivated their attacks in restitution for the "grate men murthered" in front of the connadago. Having vented their anger on English bodies, his men were ready "to renew and confirm the ancient league of amety" between Gandastogue and Virginia—provided that Berkeley provide a "valluable satisfaction for the damage." Unfortunately, allowing Susquehannocks to escape punishment after spilling English blood would compromise Berkeley's credibility, and he considered the prospect of compensation downright offensive. "These proposealls," wrote Cotton, were "derogetory and point blanke, both to honour and intress." Despite the sachem's warning that his people "were resalved to fite it out to the last man," the Virginia Council refused the peace offer and apparently rejected any future negotiations.[24]

Without the prospect of a negotiated peace, Berkeley relied on the slow machinery of government to stem the tide of panic. The assembly met in early March, declared war on the Susquehannocks and their Indigenous allies, and organized the colony's defenses. It ordered the construction of six new forts, garrisons totaling 500 men, and an additional 125 cavalry providing a defensive screen spanning from the Potomac to the Blackwater. Because "wee are to warr with an enemy whose retirements are not easily discovered to us," these forces were intended only to secure the frontier and protect settlements. The main offensive force would consist of Algonquian fighters, who "shall goe in search of all murderers, and all other Indians enemies to the English," with financial rewards for every prisoner and severed Susquehannock head. The war provisions forbade militia commanders from aggressive action without first dispatching a detailed report to the governor and receiving authorization for an assault. Berkeley, recognizing that Algonquian allies were crucial, insisted that executive control was the only way to prevent local militias from getting swept along by fear and anger, antagonizing friendly Indians and driving them into the arms of Susquehannocks. The March assembly's plans placed the colony on a firm defensive footing, with a strategy that relied on cooperation and trust between settlers and tributary Natives.[25]

At least that was how it looked from the state house in Jamestown. Viewed from the frontier, the assembly's war provisions were absurd. Susquehannock stealth and mobility rendered static fortifications useless, and the rangers could not hope to cover such a vast frontier. As Bacon explained a few months later, "the Enemy never approach[ed] nigh any of the said Forts," but simply skirted around them, slipped past the patrols, "firing, plundering and killing where they found no competent Resistance." Berkeley's prohibition on offensive operations seemed even more preposterous. County militias could not respond to attacks until they had dispatched messengers to Berkeley at Green Spring and waited for the messengers to return, a round trip of two hundred miles for the most remote settlements. It did not take much military expertise to grasp that this procedure allowed Susquehannock war parties—who traveled quickly, struck without warning, and disappeared down paths unknown to settlers—to kill with impunity. Cotton expressed the colonists' despair, writing that their condition was "every whit as bad, if not worse since, as before the forts were made," because they had no permitted means of defense except "prayers, and miss spent teares and intreties." Colonists expecting a decisive response were baffled. Thomas Mathew recalled, "The Misteryes of these Delays were Wondred at and which I ne're heard any coud Penetrate into." While Berkeley had hoped to reassure colonists with vigorous action, instead he invited talk about the causes for his indolence in the face of crisis. Into the gap, wrote Mathew, "Popular Surmizes and Murmurings" fluttered and took flight.[26]

The bits of news and conjecture that circulated as rumors among colonists were, often enough, interpretations of Native communications. Although they did not write using ink and paper, Indigenous peoples had their own methods of transforming breath and sound into durable configurations of history and memory. In eastern North America, wampum was the most widely used form of what scholars call alternative literacies. Like early modern Europeans, though, Native peoples had powerfully oral cultures. Information traveled by word of mouth, speeding along river bottoms and upland paths, borne by travelers exchanging news over a friendly pipe, spread in the formal setting of international councils, forming a vast circuit of talk. Some of that talk was ordinary news and could be accepted as fact. Some of it, inevitably, was less certain, flickering along a spectrum ranging from speculation and misinformation to outright lies. Settlers, who produced all the surviving documents by translating Indian rumors into English writing, seldom understood the context of such transmissions and filled in the gaps with their own fears and fantasies. To the modern reader, Indigenous communications appear in this attenuated form, like a whisper we strain to hear through the wind whose beginning and end are lost.[27]

Around the same time that scuffles over stolen pigs escalated into open war in the Chesapeake, another Anglo-Indian conflict broke out in New England. In 1675 the magistrates of Plymouth, seeking to extend their authority over neighboring Indigenous nations, intervened in a suspected murder of a Wampanoag man by several other Wampanoags. When these men were tried and executed by an English court in June, Wampanoags violently resisted this assault on their sovereignty. King Philip's War, as it was called after the Wampanoag sachem Metacom (Philip), became one of the bloodiest wars in American history. Algonquian combatants inflicted crippling losses on English forces and razed colonial settlements. In late December New England settlers, driven by suspicion and desperation, massacred several hundred Narragansett noncombatants in the Great Swamp. Many neutral and formerly allied Natives chose to side with their endangered kin. By the time Susquehannocks struck Virginia's frontier in early 1676, most Algonquian nations east of the Hudson River had aligned against the English. Rumors of dark designs suggested that the coalition might stretch even farther.[28]

As New England's news swept across English America, some colonists thought the simultaneous outbreaks of violence were connected. The

Virginia assembly noted, "the defection their and here, though at least three hundred miles distance from the other happened neer the same time." This coincidence led them to believe that Susquehannocks "have been and still are endeavoring" to create "a generall Combination of all from New-England hither." Berkeley reversed the direction of causation but came to a similar conclusion. Having nursed a grudge against puritans since the English Civil Wars, Berkeley blamed New Englanders for Virginia's woes. He wrote, "when the New England Indians resolved to attaque the New-England men they sent Emmissaries as farr as our parts to seduce our Indians to doe the like." New York governor Edmund Andros, who was better informed than most, expressed similarly grandiose concerns. Algonquians in New England had already "engaged all others their neighbors," he noted, and were presently "endeavouring by all meanes of command and proffitt to engage the Maques [Mohawks], and sent to all other parts as farre as Canada." Even "all our Indyans as farre as Delaware thought only to wait opportunityes." These rumors found their way across the Atlantic. Ship captains in England passed along what was "confidently reported a long time": Natives "are so bold they come at Noontime into theire plantations and kill the English and that they are fitted with all manor of Artilory from France." Credible information was scant, and no colonist could claim to really know what these Indigenous groups were saying to each other. But they had to face the possibility that New England Algonquians, Susquehannocks, Munsees, Lenapes, Haudenosaunee, and even New France and its Native allies, were arraying themselves against the English colonies.[29]

These specters haunted colonists as they barricaded themselves in lonely farmsteads, edgy, bored, and awash in terrifying rumors. Susquehannocks seemed to surface in the midst of the March assembly's deliberations. The burgesses noted, "to our griefe we find by certain intelligence . . . that a very considerable bodie of them are come downe upon James River, within fifty or sixty miles of the plantations, where they lye hovering over us." According to some rumors, Susquehannock warriors did not merely hover, they flitted through colonial defenses like shadows in the wind. As word spread, the number of reported casualties ballooned. Reliable reports said two but soon it was two hundred, then five hundred or more. In their writings, many colonists evoked an undifferentiated smear of carnage, such as Cotton's description of "dayly commited abundance of ungarded and unrevenged murthers." Examined in the cold light, the evidence suggests a less bloody spring than these narratives suggest, with Susquehannock warriors mounting only sporadic attacks that caused as few as two or three casualties. There is a strong possibility that most sightings of Susquehannock warriors, and most reports of the devastation they wrought, were fantasies or fabrications. Of course, that was the whole point of using terror as a tactic: to make the enemy's imagination work against them. The reality was less important than the rumor.[30]

The climate of fear encouraged settler suspicions of tributary Algonquians. While colonists near the James River braced for an onslaught, colonists in Rappahannock County discovered a murdered English man just a mile away from a Nanzatico town. Colonists insisted that Nanzaticos, not Susquehannocks, were the killers and called loudly for the government to punish them. Within a few days the Nanzaticos abandoned their town and sought refuge in inaccessible marshes. Soon afterward, colonists in neighboring Lancaster County claimed that Wicocomocos were responsible for a second spate of killings. As news of these killings spread, the conversation of rumors centered on the question of whether these were isolated incidents or declarations of war. Writing from Rappahannock Valley, one colonist confessed that he was bewildered by the profusion of circulating stories. He wrote, "there are soe many various Reports that a man Knowes not how to thinke." Some of the possibilities were alarming, such as the rumor that Algonquian hostility was the result of Susquehannock coalition building. Cotton reported a common belief that Susquehannocks were courting tributary nations, hoping to "draw in others (formerly in subjection to the Verginians) to there aides" and attack "in seperate and united parties."[31]

It is plausible that Susquehannocks would have made diplomatic overtures to Virginia Algonquians, but if they did there is no evidence that Algonquians accepted. Virginia's tributary nations did not have any history of friendship with Gandastogue. They had little to gain by joining a dwindling band of desperadoes and stood to lose everything if they sided against colonists in another major war. The leaders of most tributary nations supported the English. Cockacoeske, the weroansqua (female chief) of the Pamunkey nation, "offered their assistance against all enimies." According to the lawyer William Sherwood, Pamunkeys served as "spyes to finde out the Susquehanoes." Other tributaries followed, each with its own reasons for rendering assistance. For some, the war may have offered economic opportunity. George Mason reported that Indians in Stafford County took up their guns in pursuit of bounties offered by the assembly. Others may have sought to consolidate their personal power. The ambitious Appamattuck Perecuta, for example, was a longtime associate of Abraham Wood in the southeastern trade and an avowed anglophile; in 1671 he had stated his desire that "he would be an English man." Perecuta appeared before the assembly to signal his martial support, and in turn the burgesses confirmed him as the Appamattuck "King." Whatever the motives, it was a fateful decision for each nation. By siding with settlers, Algonquians made themselves enemies of Susquehannocks.[32]

While Indigenous peoples were often the subject of rumors circulating among colonists, they could also be the rumor's origin. Tributary Algonquians were crucial to colonial intelligence gathering, as suggested by the phrases peppering English records: "we find by certain intelligence" or "I am informed," invariably constructions that concealed the source. Berkeley tipped his hand when he marveled, "it is almost incredible what intelligence distant Indians hold one with the other." He understood their incredible intelligence because he depended on it. Natives knew the interior road system, they spoke the languages, and they possessed the social connections needed to gather information from sources beyond the limits of colonial observation. Their importance granted them power to shape the flow of information, and sometimes Indigenous leaders tried to manipulate rumor to their advantage. Werowances looking to reassure skittish settlers might even attempt to demonstrate their loyalty by fabricating information about the enemy. Appamattucks, whose main town was located south of the James River falls, were almost certainly the origin of intelligence about the approaching Susquehannocks. Despite colonists' professed terror, however, their fears turned out to be groundless, the rumored Susquehannock warriors just shadows and smoke. We can only speculate about the reasons why Perecuta and other Appamattucks might spread this rumor, but it may have been an attempt to allay colonial suspicions, redirecting the fears of men like Nathaniel Bacon away from them and onto their proper targets.[33]

Native attempts to control the flow of information could easily backfire. Virginia's tributaries had not been politically united since the 1646 treaty dismembered the Powhatan paramountcy. Their interests did not always align and in the face of colonial suspicion they did not necessarily stand together. Some tributary nations, confronted with accusations of secret dealings or collusion with the enemy, appear to have shifted blame onto other Algonquians. One group of colonists complained that Native informants engaged in "promiscuous impeaching of one the other," blaming other tributary nations for whatever "evills and mischeifes" they were accused of by the settlers. Colonial rumors about the culpability of Nanzaticos and Wicocomocos may even have originated with neighboring Algonquians seeking to protect themselves. Given the tightrope that tributaries had to walk between Susquehannock raiders and English neighbors whose friendship was increasingly dubious, their attempts to use rumors to their own advantage had the unfortunate effect of feeding settler fears about Indians in general.[34]

Even Indigenous attempts to prepare defenses and build solidarity may have fed colonial fears by playing into expectations established by rumors of secret communications. Pamunkey warriors readying their arms and ammunition to hunt down Susquehannocks could easily appear, to wary colonists, like Indians preparing to massacre their English neighbors. Colonists may have misinterpreted innocent actions. Tributary leaders surely talked to each other, passing messages and arranging councils. It was standard practice to give gifts at such meetings, especially wampum, to recall histories of friendship or smooth over past rivalries. Glimpses of wampum exchange may have been the source of the rumor that Indians were "offering Vast Summes of their wealth" to "hyre other nations of Indians," which misinterpreted diplomatic protocols as the market transactions of warlords and mercenaries. The passage of envoys from one tributary nation to another, the treaty councils and ceremonial dances that made up Native politics, could easily appear to nervous English eyes as scarcely concealed preparations for war.[35]

By spring 1676, colonial attempts to understand the circulation of rumors among Natives, complicated by the pervasive atmosphere of confusion and mistrust, completed the circuit from speculation to certainty. At the conclusion of the assembly in late March, the burgesses noted, "all Indians as well our neer Neighbours as those more remote" were "giveing us dayly suspitions." Berkeley insisted on retaining tributary nations as allies, if only to prevent them from rushing into the arms of the enemy. Other colonists thought this was wishful thinking with potentially lethal consequences. Bacon wrote to Berkeley, "this story of siding with or protecting any Indians is wholly a thing in the Clouds." No matter what shows of loyalty Pamunkeys or Appamattucks gave, colonists such as Bacon believed there was no such thing as Indian allies, only Indian conspirators. By the end of April, what once had seemed to be sporadic bursts of violence, their origins and meaning debated in rounds of rumor, resolved into a chilling pattern. Giles Bland, an aristocratic newcomer critical of Berkeley and his government, summarized the general opinion of his countrymen. "The Indians seem to have all conspired," he wrote, "as the others have done near New-England."[36]

Although rumors are inherently mercurial, they do not always spread hurly-burly. Colonists often spread rumors in genuine attempts to understand and explain ongoing events, but others deployed them to direct the public conversation. People outside the corridors of power, without public office or excluded from the realm of elite politics, could empower themselves by uncovering truths that the authorities would rather suppress. Their rumors were insurgent communications, a language that expressed subversive political aspirations and mobilized action. In the hands of such figures, rumor slipped into something more than dubious news about current events. The rumor *was* the event, feeding discontent and sparking rebellion.[37]

During the Time of Anarchy, women's voices were especially effective at using rumor to galvanize popular opinion. Despite patriarchal limitations on female participation in politics, Virginia women could operate as public figures by adopting the mantle of "good wives," with the moral authority to enforce communal standards of propriety. They could not sit as magistrates but they could damage or destroy reputations through gossip about scandalous secrets. Gossip made it possible to subvert patriarchal authority and indirectly express political dissent. Moreover, many women were well positioned to serve as vectors for rumor. Widows, who could own property in their own name and had standing under the law without the mediating figures of husbands or fathers, were often tavern keepers, presiding over a major space for socializing and news sharing. In a time of war, the rhetoric that male colonists used to decry Indian violence—endangered families, suffering women and children, the disrupted domestic sphere—opened the door for women to speak on their own behalf. Rumor was a source of power that allowed Virginia women to become speaking political subjects, criticizing unpopular policies and encouraging a movement toward open defiance.[38]

Sarah Grendon, a veteran Indian trader and personal enemy of William Berkeley, sabotaged the assembly's defensive strategy by spreading rumors about oligarchical corruption. The assembly levied a tax of 60 lbs. of tobacco per poll (titheable person) to pay for the new forts and their garrisons. This war tax was quadruple the operating cost of the government in 1674, and it was added onto an already onerous poll tax of 50 lbs. of tobacco for other expenses. For small planters and freeholders already struggling to stay afloat amid depressed tobacco prices, the tax increased the risk of losing their land and slipping into tenancy on properties owned by the wealthy planters. Adding insult to injury, the proceeds of the tax went into the pockets of the oligarchs contracted to build the forts, who profited doubly by having their land protected from attack at public expense. Rumors spread that the assembly's strategy was a corrupt bargain to fleece the people in the midst of crisis, which Berkeley blamed on Grendon. "Mrs. Grindon," he complained, "told hundreds" that those too poor to pay the tax would have their property confiscated so the big planters could line their pockets. The hundreds told hundreds more. As a result, Berkeley's policies were "throughout the country universally disliked . . . as being a matter from which was expected great charge and little or noe security to the Inhabitants." It became commonplace to denounce the forts as "a great Grievance, Juggle and cheat," the whole war strategy "meerly a designe of the Grandees to engrosse all their Tobacco into their owne hands."[39]

Scattered pockets of colonists on the frontier, styling themselves Volunteers, organized to act on these rumors. They drafted a petition, "the humble Appeale of the Voluntiers," criticizing the government's strategy. They charged that the forts "only defend that ground on which they stand," allowing Susquehannocks "in constant motions" to "privily and silently attacque the weakest and most unguarded places." And the cost was crippling. "By whom can soe vast a Tax bee paid," they asked, pointing out that frontier defense had "drawn soe many men from their Occupations" and exacerbated economic distress. The petitioners offered a solution with a lofty promise of relief from death and taxes. Arguing that offensive action was imperative, the Volunteers offered to "fight for their own Lives and Liberties with their own Armes," funding military operations to spare the people any further expense. All Berkeley had to do was issue a commission investing them with the authority to wage war on their own account.[40]

Berkeley was outraged by the "humble Appeale," sensing that the Volunteers threatened his tenuous control of the Susquehannock-Virginia War. "Some seditious sperits," he wrote, "spred amongst the People the intollerablenesse of this most necessary charge of the warr." According to some rumors, Berkeley was so furious that he declared any breach of his command not to attack Indians would be considered open insurrection, and "by proclamation under great pennalty prohibited the like petitioning for the future." This charge was hearsay; it was first recorded after the end of the rebellion by colonists from Charles City County—including Sarah Grendon's husband, Thomas—who claimed only "wee did heare" about Berkeley's interdiction. Had the rumor been true, though, it would have been a startling violation of the right to petition for redress of grievances, which the English cherished as a fundamental bulwark of liberty. In all likelihood Berkeley simply ignored the "humble Appeale," but the rumor spread anyway. Colonists already confused by military policy and angry about onerous taxes started to wonder if Berkeley intended to govern behind a cloak of secrecy, out of sight and impervious to the influence of the people.[41]

Grendon and other rumorers played on suspicion of Berkeley's motives, twisting anti-government sentiment and anti-Indian sentiment together. The March assembly's war provisions outlawed trade with Natives on pain of death, ostensibly to prevent unscrupulous arms dealers from compromising colonial security. However, the law allowed licensed agents, appointed by the county courts, to continue selling munitions to encourage the loyalty of tributary Indians and equip them for combat against the heavily armed Susquehannocks. To a cynical eye, it was a brazen attempt by Berkeley and the Green Spring men to appropriate the trade under the cover of public crisis. Sarah Grendon professed that Berkeley "was a greater frend to the Indians then to the English," protecting his profits rather than his people. She was hardly a disinterested commentator—Grendon and her nephew William Byrd were among the merchants locked out by the assembly's ban—but her stories quickly gained traction. According to the royal commissioners, "this made the people jealous that the Governour for the Lucre of the Beaver and otter trade . . . privately gave comission to some of his Friendes to truck with them, and that those persons furnished the Indians with Powder, Shott, etc." Grendon's rumors, which "presently spread through the whole country," conflated fears of Indians with denunciations of the regime. The government had failed its duty to protect English subjects, then compounded that failure by diverting resources to Natives, breaking the reciprocal obligation between the ruler and the ruled that held the patriarchal state together.[42]

Rumors that Berkeley's government was sympathetic to Indians terrorizing the frontier began to fracture the structures of authority in Virginia. Colonists progressed from merely discussing matters to taking them into their own hands. Men in the frontier counties of Charles City, Henrico, and New Kent gathered in camps that were part public caucus and part military base. Women with newfound access to politicized speech were no doubt instrumental in convincing fathers, husbands, and brothers to join the movement, encouraging their men to live up to the ideal of the patriarchal defender and belittling the manliness of the hesitant. These men "beat up drums for Volunteers to goe out against the Indians and soe continued Sundry dayes drawing into armes." Despite Berkeley's best attempts to contain the effects of Anglo-Indian violence, his actions—and rumors about those actions—only accelerated the devolution of political power to actors beyond his control. They awaited only a leader to direct their energies, a mouthpiece to harmonize their chorus of voices into an incendiary unity.[43]

Rumors of Indigenous violence had primed Nathaniel Bacon to take action; personal tragedy pushed him over the edge. Bacon agreed with the Volunteers' antipathy toward Indians but conceded that forming an uncommissioned militia would be illegal. As a cousin of Berkeley's wife, Frances Culpeper Berkeley, Bacon initially refused to defy the governor out of respect for their kinship. Nevertheless, rumors of daily Indian attacks and a rising English body count so frustrated Bacon that "hee in som elated and passionate expressions sware, Commission or no Commission, the next man or woman that he heard of that should be kild by the Indians, he would goe out against them." Soon afterward, Native warriors assaulted one of Bacon's plantations and killed the overseer, "one of his owne Familey" and a man, recalled confidant Thomas Mathew, "whom He much Loved." Bacon met with his friends William Byrd, Henry Isham, and James Crews, all leaders in the growing Volunteer movement. They uncorked their rum, "growing to a height of Drinking and makinge the Sadness of the times there Discourse, and the fear they all lived in, because of the Susquaha-nocks." Crews, who believed the Volunteers needed a leader of wealth and distinction to give them legitimacy, convinced Bacon to visit a camp of three hundred men across the river at Jordan's Point. They brought rum to share. The crowd, lubricated with fear, anger, and alcohol, did not even allow Bacon to greet them before they named him their captain with ferocious cheers. According to Elizabeth Bacon, Nathaniel was "very much concerned for the losse of his Overseer, and for the losse of so many men and women and children's lives every day," so "hee was willing to doe them all the good he could." His failure to protect the dependents in his own family, and fear for the families of fellow Virginians, led him to take up arms without legal authority.[44]

The Volunteers gave the government one last chance to avoid insurrection by repeating their request for a military commission. Their petition to Berkeley was a revealing distillation of the link between Anglo-Indian violence and colonial rebellion. The Volunteers spoke on behalf of "the poore distressed subjects in the upper parts of James River," using emotional language designed to evoke pathos and dehumanize their enemies. They complained that "the Indians hath allready most barberously and Inhumanly taken and Murdered severall of our bretheren and put them to most cruell torture," leaving everyone "in dayly dandger of Loosing our lives by the Heathen" and "afraid of goeing about our demesticall affaires." By highlighting their struggle to fulfill the patriarchal obligation to protect their families, they implicitly drew attention to Berkeley's failure to live up to his obligation and thus questioned the legitimacy of his regime. Then they offered a solution: "grant us a Committion . . . to take armes in defence of our lives and estates." Berkeley could recover his authority by investing the Volunteers with the power to act. In the same breath, however, they also requested "to make choice of Commitioned Officers to lead this party now redy." The allusion to an already mobilized army was a threat that the Volunteers intended to take the offensive against Indians whether Berkeley granted them legal authority or not. By presenting this veiled ultimatum, the petitioners assumed the mantle of loyal subjects even as they prepared for extralegal action.[45]

Popular antipathy toward Natives went hand in hand with the breakdown of central authority. The rustling of rumor led Volunteers to attack friendly Algonquians instead of enemy Susquehannocks. As the Charles City men marched toward New Kent County to link up with other groups of armed volunteers, they grabbed a Pamunkey man and his son. Although both were known to be close friends of their English neighbors, wrote Virginia secretary Philip Ludwell, the Volunteers lynched them "with much Horror and cruelty." They then used rumors to terrorize Algonquians in the York Valley. Thomas Wilford, the Volunteers' interpreter, fed the Pamunkey weroansqua Cockacoeske "very false storyes" that Berkeley was convinced of their hostility and intended to destroy them. This lie, recounted William Sherwood, "soe terrified and threatned the pamunkey Indians that they fled for security." Wilford spread the same stories among the Chickahominies, "and with Continuall threatning never left till they had Driven" them "away from their Townes." Upon receiving this news, Berkeley ordered the Volunteers to disperse and summoned Bacon to Green Spring to explain himself. When Bacon demurred, Berkeley mobilized a party of 250 supporters and marched toward New Kent. He intended to bolster public confidence by conducting a circuit of frontier defenses, "to settle the hearts of the people, and to call Mr Bacon to accompt."[46]

In early May 1676, Susquehannocks surfaced again in an urgent flight of rumors, and it caused relations between Volunteers and the government to break. "We have fresh intelligence," wrote Bacon from his camp, "that the Susquehannocks are joyned with the Ockaneechesh [Occaneechis] and killed the King of the Tuskarores [Tuscaroras] and disobliged almost all the Indians in those parts." The news caused such a panic that New Kent County militia commander George Lydall ordered his neighbors, and even his wife, to stand vigil all night with loaded muskets. Gunshots rang out as sleepless men and women raised alarms, glimpsing shadows in the moonlight and catching noises in the dark. Algonquians who had not already fled left their towns quickly and quietly to avoid colonists' hair-trigger tempers. They took their arms and ammunition with them, forming multinational camps in remote swamps. To Volunteers, the concentration of armed Algonquians suggested that "the feare of Generall Combination" was "not without reason." Bacon responded to Berkeley's furious orders to stand down by claiming that it would be impossible to disband the Volunteers without leaving the whole frontier vulnerable to imminent Indian invasion. Instead, they set out to intercept the Susquehannocks and determine the truth behind the rumors.[47]

Mistrust from the ceaseless flight of rumors guided the confused proceedings of the Volunteers' mission to Occaneechi Island. As it turned out, the news of a Susquehannock alliance with the Occaneechis that had caused panic in New Kent and spurred the Volunteers southward had originated

from the Occaneechis themselves. According to Philip Ludwell, Susquehannock emissaries "tempted them, with great offers of wealth if they
would . . . help to destroy the English, and severel threats if they refused."
But the Occaneechis, like tributary Algonquians, had little incentive to accept. As one of Virginia's principal trading partners, their interests were
aligned with the English. Their chief, Posseclay, refused Susquehannock
overtures and "sent in Runers to Give notion to the English, of what was
done." He offered solid intelligence about Susquehannock movements, including the location of two new settlements along the Meherrin River, not
far from Occaneechi Island. In Jamestown, the members of the Governor's
Council had no doubt of "the Occaneechees freindship to us." But out on
the frontiers, where the Volunteers marched, the winds of rumor inverted
Occaneechi intentions, turning a show of solidarity with colonists into evidence of Indigenous conspiracy.[48]

It is difficult to know what happened when the Volunteers reached Occaneechi Island because extant accounts contradict each other on almost
every detail. According to an anonymous Volunteer, friendship and cooperation gradually eroded through mutual suspicion and misunderstanding,
ending in a massacre of Occaneechis at English hands. Nathaniel Bacon,
who penned the only other eyewitness account, depicted a march to war
against the Occaneechis, known enemies from the moment he set out, culminating in a glorious slaughter. William Berkeley and his supporter William
Sherwood both told stories of Bacon's perfidious betrayal of Occaneechi
allies out of greed and stupidity, leading to a humiliating defeat at Occaneechi hands. Narrative differences did not always align with factional loyalties. The account of Philip Ludwell, one of Berkley's inner circle, was
similar to the anonymous Volunteer's story and unlike Berkeley's as much
as it was unlike Bacon's. The Indigenous perspective was different from all
of the English versions. Abraham Wood recorded intelligence gleaned from
Native informants, relating a minor encounter in which Volunteers stumbled into the middle of a Susquehannock-Occaneechi conflict but quickly
retreated. Like the eyewitnesses to murder in Akira Kurosawa's *Rashomon*,
each narrator told a coherent story, but the stories cannot be reconciled.[49]

Most accounts agree that an initially friendly meeting between Volunteers and Occaneechis slowly degenerated into havoc. Bacon and his men—
somewhere between fifty and three hundred, depending on the source—
arrived at Occaneechi Island after a long march. Almost a hundred miles
beyond Virginia's frontier, they were physically exhausted and short on supplies. Posseclay offered shelter, hospitality, and military assistance, sending
a war party to attack the Susquehannocks. Posseclay wanted to honor his

alliance with the English, and also to free several captive Monacans and other Siouans allied to the Occaneechis who had been taken captive by Susquehannocks. Occaneechi warriors destroyed the nearest connadago, killed most of its inhabitants, freed the Monacans, and offered a handful of captive Susquehannocks to Bacon as a gift.[50]

Bacon's detractors claimed he picked a fight with Posseclay over the spoils of war, making increasingly belligerent demands until the Siouans had no choice but to fire on the Volunteers in self-defense. There is probably some element of truth to this story: the Volunteers had promised their cause would not cause taxpayers a penny, so financing their campaign required plunder. Even pro-Volunteer accounts portray an estrangement of the Occaneechis from the English as tensions over hospitality compounded cultural misunderstandings and bred rumors of ill intent. Posseclay apparently invited the Volunteers to remain as his guests after the destruction of the Susquehannock town, but the English remained longer than he expected. The days passed, and Volunteers watched Siouan warriors—Occaneechis as well as men from several allied nations—gather on the north side of the river. Perceptive men began to realize they were trapped on the island and dependent on Occaneechis for food and transportation. Posseclay became less forthcoming with provisions, perhaps hoping the Volunteers would take the hint and be on their way. Rumors spread among the Volunteers that Posseclay's "Delusive procrastinations" were the result of "private Messages from the Governour," who had convinced the Occaneechis to show their friendship—not to the English in general, but specifically to Berkeley—by slaughtering the men he had branded rebels. Meanwhile, rumors spread among the Siouans that the English were demanding the liberated Monacans as slaves and that Posseclay might cave to their demands. In the mounting concern and confusion, someone went too far: an Englishman wading across the river begging for food, in one telling, or a Monacan determined to fight rather than be sold as a slave, in another. Guns were fired and chaos erupted.[51]

Occaneechis and other Siouans died in their confrontation with the Volunteers, between fifty and 150, depending on the account, possibly including chief Posseclay. Several more were captured and enslaved. Englishmen died as well, probably between ten and fifteen but possibly dozens more. Historians have tended to accept the higher numbers of Occaneechi casualties and the lower numbers of English ones, depicting the encounter as an English massacre of Occaneechis. Berkeley, however, claimed the opposite: that well-armed Siouans mowed down the disorganized rabble, trapping and slaughtering every Volunteer who could not find a horse to cross the

shallows and escape the island. Wood's story, the closest we have to an Indigenous account, describes an inconclusive engagement that claimed only
a handful of lives on either side, without any lasting impact.[52]

Just as contemporaries advanced various explanations for Bacon's hostility toward the Occaneechis, so have scholars in the centuries since. Recent
historians, giving credence to accounts emphasizing Bacon's destructive
impact, have portrayed his actions as determination to break into the
Native slave trade. Berkeley and the Green Spring men, through veteran
trader Abraham Wood and his Appamattuck agents, held a monopoly on
this trade in partnership with the Occaneechi chiefs. Therefore, this argument goes, Bacon and other prominent Volunteers—including William
Byrd—used the groundswell of popular support to destroy that monopoly
at both ends, shattering the Occaneechis and opening opportunities for aggressive entrepreneurs. However, it is unlikely that Bacon or Byrd had
such plans. In 1675 Bacon had accepted a proposition from Berkeley to
"joyne with Mr. Bird for the farming of . . . the Indian trade," effectively
becoming one of the Green Spring men growing rich from the slave trade.
There would have been no percentage in breaking the monopoly in which
they were partners. Moreover, the Volunteer assault was not as destructive
as Bacon claimed. Rather than becoming refugees forced to disperse into
the Appalachians, the Occaneechis survived the Volunteer assault and remained in control of their island, as well as the southeastern transportation network, for years afterward. We must therefore lend at least equal
weight to the accounts that depict the campaign as a debacle for the Volunteers as those that claim a catastrophe for the Occaneechis. Much like
the unenviable magistrates of Rashōmon, scholars sifting through incompatible accounts cannot afford to trust some but not others.[53]

Whatever happened, the encounter on Occaneechi Island in May 1676
was a pivotal moment in the Time of Anarchy. Posseclay's decision to assault the Susquehannocks on the Meherrin River began an Indigenous war
that spread across the piedmont. Siouan warriors destroyed one town,
massacring a band of about one hundred men, women, and children. As
Ludwell noted, however, the larger second town was unscathed. Posseclay,
in a conversation with Bacon before relations descended into bloody
mayhem, reminded him that this second band remained a threat. "The
susquehanos," he said, were "a stout nation, and never forget an Injurie."
Posseclay was right: the Susquehannocks did not forget. One of the principal effects of the Volunteer incursion into the piedmont, as the anonymous trooper observed, was to leave "all Nations of Indians . . . ingaged
in a civill Warre amongst themselves."[54]

For the English, Occaneechi Island marked the beginning of a new phase in their political disintegration. What actually happened at Occaneechi Island was lost in the deluge of stories that came out of it, each purporting to capture the truth of the encounter. The Volunteers marched back to Virginia, spreading tales of Indian treachery, of conspiracies between Indians and oligarchs, and of the brave stand of the Volunteers on behalf of the poor suffering English families on the frontier. The stories spawned rumors and, as rumors tend to do, multiplied in the telling. The rumors created a web of interpretive possibilities, networking settlers across space as they struggled to interpret the spreading chaos around them. The urgent chatter amplified colonists' fears of their enemies and fed suspicions of their neighbors, each new round dividing them further from Native allies. The rumors ramified across the colonies and Indigenous nations, and became the seeds of much larger narratives about the true nature of the chaos spreading through eastern North America.

THE SUSQUEHANNOCK
SCATTERING

WHEN IT CAME TO THE ENCOUNTER on Occaneechi Island, Nathaniel Bacon and Sir William Berkeley did not agree on much. Bacon argued that Indians "are now if not all a vast number of them confederated, and have for some time been in open wars with us." The Volunteers did what was necessary. He trumpeted that the battle on Occaneechi Island was "a greater victory from sharper conflict than ever yett has been known in these parts of the world." In contrast, Berkeley painted the Volunteers as villains who butchered loyal Indian allies. He declared, "this very action wherein he so much boastes was fully foolishly and . . . Treacherously carried to the dishonor of the English nation." Despite their disagreements, both sides implied that the Susquehannock-Virginia War was essentially over. Bacon crowed that the brave Volunteers "destroyed. . . . 2 of their most valiant nations," the Susquehannocks and their Occaneechi confederates. Berkeley boasted that he had secured the frontiers, claiming that there had not been a single casualty since executing his military strategy. After the Susquehannocks' winter raids, he wrote, they fled toward the mountains where "they live only on Acornes." He concluded confidently, "we have now such a strength on the frontiers of al our Plantations that we cannot feare them if they were ten times more in Number then they are." The governor and the rebel agreed on this much at least: the Susquehannocks were finished.[1]

They were both wrong. Whether due to bad intelligence or self-serving swagger, English writers exaggerated the severity of the Susquehannock plight. The land over the Appalachian mountains was not the desolate wilderness that Berkeley depicted but a familiar node in Gandastogue's spatial network. Susquehannock farmers and traders had settled the Upper Potomac Valley by the late sixteenth century. Although they abandoned those settlements during the Haudenosaunee wars, generations of hunters and warriors continued to range deep into the Ohio Valley, probably using the same sites as temporary camps. These would have been obvious choices for shelter in a time of need. Even Berkeley's spiteful comment that Susquehannock migrants were reduced to eating acorns was misleading. Spring was always a lean time for Native peoples, coming after the end of the winter hunting season but before the first runs of fish or ripening of early crops. To fill the gap women cultivated nut trees, particularly hickory and walnut. In other words, what the English saw as a wasteland was an Indigenous garden, and Berkeley was merely describing a traditional Susquehannock diet. The group of Susquehannocks who went west after their expulsion from the Potomac were not desperate refugees. They were returning to a place their people had once called home.[2]

As Susquehannocks scattered, Gandastogue was not destroyed but transformed. Some had decided to stalk the Virginia borderlands to strike back at the settlers who had betrayed them. However, these warriors' actions were not the result of decisions made by the leaders of a united nation, which had always been, in essence, the contingent creation of many families and their individual longhouses. Power devolved from the level of the nation to smaller collectives: a band of related households, a single extended family, or just a small cadre of young men. The Virginia group was only a splinter, acting independently. Other bands chose other paths. One went west, back to the Ohio country. Two went south, toward the Roanoke River. At least three additional bands went their own ways, moving north and east. As they scattered, these groups of Susquehannocks carried different political agendas with them, seeking refuge, reconciliation, or revenge.[3]

The actions of migrating Susquehannocks had seismic effects on their neighbors, both Natives and settlers. The ramifications of those actions restored stability in some regions but in others they created new zones of violence. Colonists, often poorly informed and motivated as much by apprehension and hearsay as reliable intelligence, struggled to understand the turmoil that Susquehannock movements unleashed. Officials sought to restore order through assemblies and treaty councils, but in each case they failed, leaving the colonies further embroiled in factionalism and strife. The fault line in these battles was a disagreement about the future of Indigenous peoples in the colonial order—not only the elusive Susquehannocks but also the tributary Algonquians that increasingly became the focus of settler fear and rage. Those who defied the government did not act on behalf of their whole colony, much less the empire, both of which had always been constituted by many families and individual households. As structures of central authority crumbled, smaller collectives—volunteer militias, neighborhood associations, or even single families—flexed their political muscles. This devolution of power across English America rippled

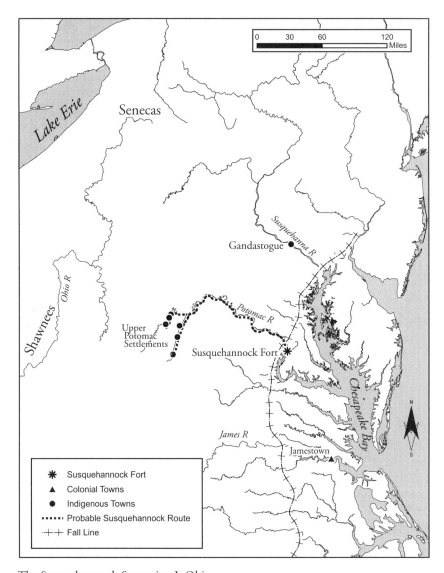

The Susquehannock Scattering I: Ohio

outward from Indigenous nations, with Susquehannocks at the center. Everywhere they went, tremors followed in their footsteps.[4]

Susquehannocks may not have been as desperate as Berkeley imagined, but they had endured a wrenching series of tragedies. They fled their homeland with Haudenosaunee raiders at their backs. Algonquian allies and colonial friends offered protection and then betrayed them. Militia killed a dozen of their men in a senseless accident then murdered five more with deliberate brutality. They abandoned another home in a second violent expulsion within one year. It must have taken heroic efforts for leaders to hold their people together and prevent them from succumbing to sorrow. But Washahanda-Harignera was dead, along with their five principal sachems, robbing them of their most respected, experienced, and effective leaders. One colonist explained the impact of their loss using the metaphor of a card game, suggesting that Susquehannocks "lost som of their prime court cards, without a faire dealeing." Yet some powers remained: the matrons would have continued to lead their households, and they would be responsible for choosing new male leaders. These men were probably younger, less experienced, and without established supporters. It is likely that some of them, like headmen during the years of conflict with Iroquoia, were war captains with different priorities than civil chiefs.[5]

There are no records detailing the political controversies that ensued as Susquehannocks decided what to do next, but given what we know about consensus-based politics we can imagine what it might have looked like. There must have been deliberative councils featuring appeals for one course of action or another, with heroic contests of oratory among untested leaders. Perhaps there were also tense disagreements or even angry arguments, some favoring flight to uncertain safety, others the strenuous work of diplomacy to stop the fighting, and a few insisting on battle even if it cost them everything. Women and men would have listened knowing that the fate of their people hung by a thread. With the stakes so high and contradictory positions on the table, emotions could easily run hot, a distressing breakdown of the peaceful minds and hearts essential to consensus politics. This much is certain: no one position prevailed. Rather than defer to the most respected voices—voices that had been silenced by recent tragedies—Susquehannocks agreed to disagree, so that multiple leaders could follow different courses of action without coming into conflict with the others. Power diffused among many bands, each one likely just a collection of households bound by allegiance to kin from affiliated lineages. Gandastogue broke up and its people scattered in every direction.[6]

The Susquehannock history of connections with peoples across eastern North America shaped their choices of destination. Although the sources offer only fugitive glimpses of most of these groups in 1676, making it difficult to decipher their intentions, it would have been logical for each to pursue a course of action based on their social networks. Thus two bands went south. The Susquehannock traveler Jackzetavon had demonstrated, as John Lederer's guide in 1670, that he had friendly links with a dozen different Indigenous nations of the Southeast, including enough goodwill with the Occaneechis to secure hospitality. Not all Susquehannocks would have traveled so widely throughout the region, but Jackzetavon did. He or someone like him was likely the reason why two bands of Susquehannocks decided to make a two-hundred-mile trek from Piscataway Creek to the Meherrin River, on the border of Occaneechi country. Perhaps Jackzetavon himself was the envoy who "tempted" Posseclay with an offer to join to-gether and "destroy the English," hoping to build on his existing connec-tions to forge a stronger alliance between their peoples. It was a risky gamble but, because Occaneechi Island was already a node in Gandastogue's net-work, not an unreasonable one.[7]

Unfortunately for these Susquehannocks, led by the new "prime court cards" who rose to leadership, the gamble ended in disaster. Initially, "the fled Susquehanoes came" to the Occaneechis "for succor, and were for some time reelieved." Posseclay permitted them to rebuild two abandoned towns on the Meherrin River which had once belonged to the Saponi nation, trib-utaries of the Occaneechis. But the relationship soured when Posseclay refused to attack the English. According to Philip Ludwell, passing on in-formation gleaned from Posseclay's messengers, Susquehannocks resorted to "severe menaces," and William Sherwood claimed they even "endeav-oured to beat the Ockinagees off their own Island." Occaneechi warriors infiltrated one connadago and massacred its inhabitants, carried the sa-chem's scalp back "in triumph," and all captives "they cruelly tortured and killed runing fyer brands up their bodys." Of the Susquehannocks who went south, one band was annihilated.[8]

But the second town, "a very considerable party of men, besides woemen and Children," survived. Their movements are all but invisible in the con-temporary records, but according to local tradition among North Caro-lina colonists they continued east along the Meherrin River. They came to Cowinchahawkon, the main town of the Meherrins, a small nation of about two hundred people. Susquehannocks and Meherrins forged an alliance. It was a natural combination. Both peoples were Iroquoian speakers and they already had friendly relations, as demonstrated by Jackzetavon's smooth journey through Meherrin country in 1670. Moreover, they shared a common enemy. Meherrins had been the targets of Occaneechi warriors hunting for slaves to sell in Virginia's voracious labor market. Meherrins and Susquehannocks immediately faced war parties from the damaged but still dangerous Occaneechis, who attacked Cowinchahawkon soon after the Susquehannock relocation and forced both peoples to abandon it. Together, they moved farther southeast, toward coastal Algonquian communities whose people had also suffered from Occaneechi slave raids. Arriving in the town of Katoking, Meherrins and Susquehannocks received a Chowanoke offer of protection, with permission to settle in the northern reaches of

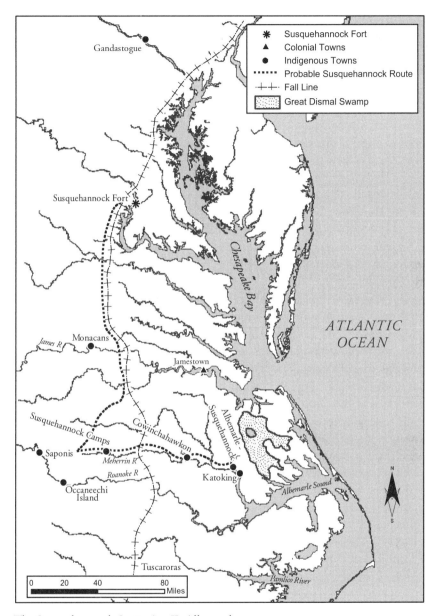

The Susquehannock Scattering II: Albemarle

Chowanoke country. Over time "they began to take the name of Maherrin Indians," the two communities amalgamating along Albemarle Sound.[9]

We will call this group the Albemarle-Susquehannocks to distinguish them from the other scattered Susquehannocks. (I will continue referring to different bands of Susquehannocks by hyphenated names based on their geographical location throughout this book.) Their motives and actions, like those of many of the other groups, can be seen only in shadowed glimpses. The documentary record for the northern part of Carolina is sparse even by seventeenth-century standards and the recollections of later North Carolina colonists require caution because they were far from disinterested observers. The reason for their recitation of Indigenous migration was to dispossess Meherrin Indians on the dubious charge that they were Susquehannock imposters with no rightful title to the land. Meherrins, for their part, insisted they had "lived there for many years" but quietly declined to respond to allegations about Susquehannock descendants among them.[10]

Susquehannock blending with Meherrins and Chowanokes explains an otherwise puzzling fact: the sudden outbreak of war between Natives and settlers in Albemarle Sound during 1676. There was little reason for conflict in Albemarle. Chowanokes had been enthusiastic allies and trade partners with colonists since the days of the Roanoke colony. Chowanoke land was far enough away from colonial settlements that territorial encroachment and roving livestock, so often causes of friction between colonists and Natives, were not an issue. A fragment of evidence from 1707 suggests that the outbreak of war in 1676 was the result of the Susquehannocks' arrival. The North Carolina Council wrote that the Chowanoke nation had been peaceful neighbors until, "by incitements of the Rebelious Indians of Virginia who fled to them they committed hostility upon the Inhabitants of this Government." Albemarle-Susquehannocks were the only Indigenous peoples who moved from Virginia to Carolina in 1676, so they were almost certainly the "Rebelious Indians" whose arrival spawned violence and political crisis. The Time of Anarchy's geographical scope expanded with the scattering of Susquehannocks into Carolina.[11]

Other Susquehannock families remained closer to their homeland. English observers in New Castle noted a scout in January 1676, a "Suschannyock Indian" who "came upon the River." By May, several groups of Susquehannocks had followed and according to Indigenous informants "intend here to abide." They initially dispersed throughout the upper and lower Delaware Valley but eventually established a new community along the Schuylkill River. It was a sensible destination. Over the course of the seventeenth century, Gandastogue has expanded its network of political, economic, and social ties throughout the Delaware Valley. If not quite home to most Susquehannocks, it was at least a familiar place filled with friends and kinfolk.[12]

Calling on connections with Lenapes and Munsees, these Delaware-Susquehannocks sought sanctuary rather than confrontation. They could count on the multiethnic descendants of marriage alliances, headmen such as Minqua-Sachemack and Achipoor Minquaes who proudly claimed Susquehannock heritage and would have made natural advocates for endangered kinfolk. Their relationship had endured through Gandastogue's tribulations, as one sachem testified in 1670 when he affirmed that Susquehannocks and Lenapes "were brothers of one another." The principal Lenape spokesman, Renowewan, not only reciprocated with the ritual gift of a wampum belt but also referred to "the Mincquas . . . whom we had also with us," suggesting that some Susquehannocks already lived in Lenapehoking before the scattering. Gandastogue's people included a significant number of Minisinks and Esopus who had sought refuge during wars with Europeans in the 1650s. In the scattering, Delaware-Susquehannocks rejoined these friends and kinfolk throughout the Delaware Valley, building on familiar ties with Armewamese and Mantes in the lower valley as well as Hackensacks, Navesinks, and Minisinks above the falls.[13]

Delaware Valley colonists, listening to the flurry of reports from colonies north and south descending into carnage, observed these movements nervously. A series of violent incidents left Natives and settlers on edge: the 1673 murder of John Roades and Thomas Tilley by unknown Natives in Delaware Bay; the suspicious death of a Lenape man after leaving a New Jersey tavern in 1674; the murder of Peeques, a Navesink man, by James Sandelands in a rum-soaked argument and reprisal killings committed by Peeques's grieving brother in early 1675. These were the sort of small incidents that, handled incompetently, had tumbled into war in New England and the Chesapeake. Thankfully, the Delaware Valley benefited from strong leaders on both sides who successfully defused the tensions. Renowewan, who was an "old Acquaintance [of] Peter Rambo and Peter Cock" as well as other members of the Swedish and Dutch communities, promoted reconciliation and expressed "readinesse to continue in good friendship." Edmund Andros, the governor of New York, satisfied Lenapes by offering presents to cover the dead and reassured colonists by bringing a retinue of professional soldiers to keep the peace. Despite this record of conflict resolution, escalating wars in surrounding regions encouraged Natives and settlers to distrust each other. In November 1675, New Castle commander Edmund Cantwell reported that the loyalties of Lenapes were "wavering."

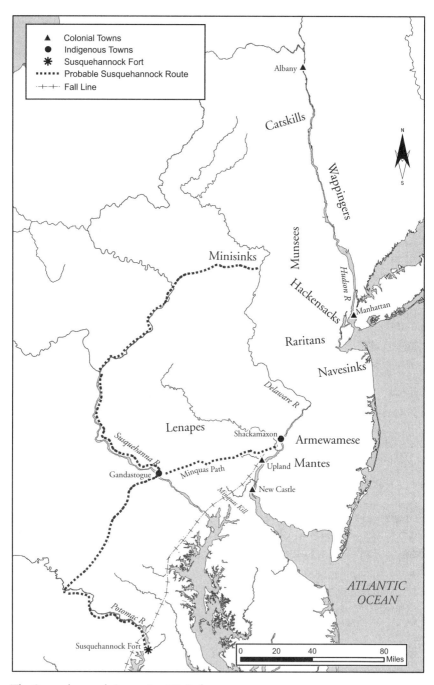

The Susquehannock Scattering III: Delaware

Andros trusted Renowewan, "who shall not loose for his Constancy," but he could not discount the rumors suggesting "all our Indyans as farre as Delaware" are "thought only to wait opportunityes" and quietly sent arms and ammunition to New Castle.[14]

Edmund Andros understood the importance of alliances with Indigenous peoples. Military experience in the Caribbean had taught him that diplomacy, not force, was the best way to protect colonists, preserve stability, and pursue the Stuart vision of imperial centralization. Upon his arrival as the new governor-general in November 1674, returning English rule to the region after the brief resurrection of New Netherland, he immediately reestablished the tributary status of Native nations in New York. Over the course of 1675 he crafted a chain of alliances—if not securing subjection then at least affirming mutual friendship—with Lenapes, Munsees, and Algonquians from Delaware Bay to the central Hudson Valley. Given that the Haudenosaunee were the dominant military power in the Northeast, no doubt Andros would have reached out to them next had the Mohawks not beaten him to it. In April 1675, Mohawk sachems asked the magistrates of Albany, whom they knew and trusted, to forward a set of "proposicions and desires, of a continued Friendship" to Andros. Andros considered Haudenosaunee allies a crucial counterweight to the outbreak of King Philip's War and Susquehannock wars and embraced the opportunity. He traveled to Albany in autumn 1675, "engaging Maques [Mohawks] and Sinnekes, not anywayes to injure any Christians to the Eastward, and particularly . . . South-ward." He also encouraged Five Nations warriors to leave the tributary nations of New York alone and instead pursue mourning wars against enemies of the English. As defeated Algonquians streamed westward seeking to escape from the violence of King Philip's War, Andros drew them into New York's orbit. He offered groups such as the Mahicans of the central Hudson Valley and the Wiechquaesgecks of southern Connecticut protection, guaranteeing their safety from New England militia and Haudenosaunee raids. In exchange for recognizing New York's authority they were promised "equall Justice, according to Law" and allotted land in a new community called Schaghticoke.[15]

This chain of Anglo-Indian alliances benefited all parties. Embattled Algonquians received shelter from the war in New England. The Haudenosaunee secured the blessing of the English to extend the branches of the Tree of Peace to cover new nations. New York gained a web of Indian allies whose allegiance not only protected the province's borders but also provided leverage against the ambitions of rival colonies. As the governor of a proprietary colony, Andros was a personal agent of the Duke of York and one of his principal tasks was to establish the Duke's territorial claims. Schaghticoke was strategically placed to stake New York's claim to an area contested by Massachusetts and New France. Andros hoped to do the same for the Delaware Valley, putting to rest the Calverts' insistence that it fell within Maryland's boundaries. This required that Susquehannocks sign on to the alliance chain, placing Gandastogue's territory under New York's jurisdiction. If Andros could gain Susquehannock allegiance, he could use his relationship with the Haudenosaunee to place New York at the center of English diplomacy with Native peoples, turning the Duke's province into the core of a burgeoning American empire.[16]

Despite Andros's determination to make diplomatic contact, Delaware-Susquehannocks were wary and avoided colonial agents. When Andros first caught the Susquehannocks' scent in February 1676, he chastised his subordinates for allowing them to slip away. "I am Surprized," he wrote to Edmund Cantwell in New Castle, "you did not make means, to speake to, or gett the Suschannyock Indian . . . to be brought [to] me." Cantwell, hoping to avoid accidentally causing an incident, ordered colonists to keep their distance from the new arrivals but followed Andros's injunction to initiate talks. Lenapes, unsure of English intentions toward their kinfolk, shielded Delaware-Susquehannocks from these entreaties. Rumors had been spreading—probably by Dutch and Scandinavian colonists, many of whom had longstanding relationships with Lenapes and Susquehannocks but little love for their English conquerors—that Cantwell intended to lure Susquehannocks into a trap, capturing their sachems and shipping them to Manhattan in chains. In May, Cantwell traveled to the falls of the Delaware and apparently convinced two Delaware-Susquehannocks, Conachoweedo and Sneedo, to give Andros a hearing. English documents described them as "sachems" of "some Susquehanna Indyans from Delaware and the head of the bay and those parts," indicating that they spoke for some but not all of the scattered Susquehannocks. This was the first time either man appears in any documentary source, suggesting they were new sachems who came to prominence after the deaths of Gandastogue's leadership.[17]

The council, which took place on June 2–3 at Fort James on Manhattan, demonstrated that even weakened and scattered Susquehannocks had the power to frustrate colonial designs. Andros adeptly followed the protocols of Indigenous diplomacy, welcoming them, offering condolences for their grief, and stating "hee is sorry from his heart at their Troubles." He positioned himself as peacemaker, volunteering to broker an agreement with the Mohawks as well as Virginia and Maryland, and proposing that Susquehannocks should join New York's chain of alliances. Andros promised, "if they are afraid and not well where they are, if they will come into this government, they shall bee welcome and protected from their Ennemys." He gifted Conachoweedo and Sneedo with matchcoats—mantles of woven cloth, a staple of the fur trade economy—and offered hospitality, urging them "to goe eate and drinke and thinke upon what they have to say, and come again tomorrow." Andros's offer of protection was the same one that he had made to several other Native nations and he had every expectation that the weakened Susquehannocks would leap at the chance.[18]

They did not. Conachoweedo and Sneedo ate, drank, and rested, met with Andros again on June 3, and gave their answer: a polite but firm no. Conachoweedo, the senior spokesman, said, "they have no mind to goe up to Albany but to returne to the South [Delaware] River, to their folkes." Declining the offer of mediation, Conachoweedo preferred to rely on his own resources among Lenape and Munsee kinfolk. Andros, surprised, tried to regroup by offering another option. Instead of coming to live in New York they could join the Mohawks, who "have promised . . . they may goe and live with them." Conachoweedo again declined and evasively replied, "they are but two so can give no other answer then that they will goe to the rest of their people and tell them what the Governor saith, and will return with an answer." As new leaders representing splinters of the nation, they did not have the power to make such a decision without community consensus.[19]

Conachoweedo and Sneedo also rebuffed Andros because they did not want or need New York's interference. During spring 1676, Delaware-Susquehannocks focused their energies on diplomacy among Indigenous nations, seeking to end their wars with the Haudenosaunee. By the time they met with Andros these initiatives had been underway for some time. Mohawks, who had never pursued war against Gandastogue with the same tenacity as the western Haudenosaunee, had extended several peace offerings in 1675. In April, the Mohawks revealed that they had "preserved 17 Minquas Indyans alive," and released these captives as a show of goodwill. In late June, an embassy of Wappingers had passed through Manhattan on their way to visit Susquehannocks in their new home on the Potomac. Their spokesman, Mawhoscan, informed the English that his mission was to mediate a peace between the Mohawk nation and the "Susquehannas Indyans" to end their sixteen years of war. They carried gifts from the Mohawks with them: twenty-four belts of wampum along with another band woven into a circle, an enormous offering that signaled the Mohawks' sincerity. With such warm overtures from Mohawks and assistance from

Munsees and Lenapes, Delaware-Susquehannocks had reason to hope for the future.[20]

Negotiations between Susquehannocks and Haudenosaunee were still tentative, however, and serious obstacles remained in the way of a permanent settlement. In contrast to the Mohawk leadership, the western Haudenosaunee nations—Seneca, Cayuga, Onondaga, and Oneida—refused to consider peace. Seneca spokesmen told Andros that they were "wholly adverse" to peace with Susquehannocks, instead "desiring their Extirpacion." They wanted not just to defeat Gandastogue but to destroy it as they had destroyed Wendake, the Neutral Confederacy, the Erie Confederacy, and so many others. Mourning wars had already resulted in Susquehannock captives adopted by the dozens and hundreds, constituting a wholesale transfer of population from Gandastogue to Iroquoia. The western Haudenosaunee simply wanted to finish the process through a victor's peace, incorporating the last Susquehannocks into the Longhouse.[21]

The growing numbers of adopted Susquehannocks in Iroquoia was also a motive for the Mohawks, whose goal was not very different from that of the other four League nations. Andros, after listening to the Mohawk position at Albany, wrote, "the Susquehannas being reputed by the Maques of their Off-Spring . . . they might bee brought to some Peace, or Concorporate againe." They wished to honor their familiar connections with Susquehannocks by joining together into one people, as they had been in the days of Owasco ancestors before their nations went separate ways. Healing the bitterness from years of war through gifts of wampum and offers of voluntary relocation was surely tempting in comparison to the Senecas' promise of violence, but the result would be the same: the dissolution of Gandastogue as an independent polity and absorption of its people into the League. Given the number of Susquehannocks already incorporated into Iroquoia during the midcentury mourning wars, this may have been a far more appealing prospect to Conachoweedo and Sneedo than becoming tributaries dependent on the good graces of New York's imperious English.[22]

The Delaware-Susquehannocks were no doubt struggling to walk this tightrope and debating among themselves how to deal with the Haudenosaunee now that military resistance was no longer a viable option. Nevertheless, they had more room for maneuver than Andros imagined. Wappinger mediators were laying the groundwork for peace with the Mohawk nation. It is likely that other allies made similar overtures toward the western Haudenosaunee nations, which were probably the source of recurring rumors in the Chesapeake that "they have made peace with their Old Enemy the Senecas." This dance of Indigenous diplomacy may be responsible for a lull in fighting between Susquehannocks and Haudeno-

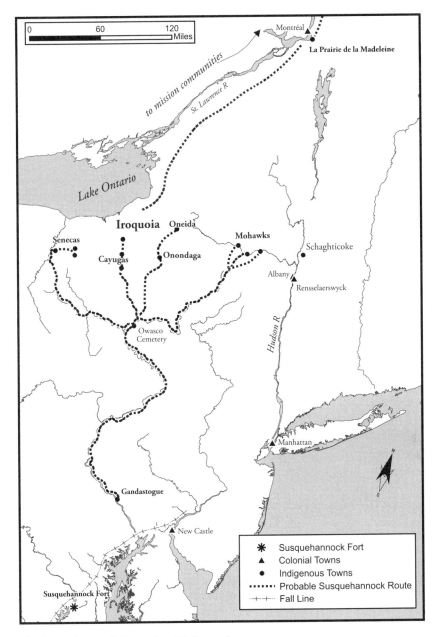

The Susquehannock Scattering IV: Iroquoia

saunee between 1675 and 1676. Andros took the credit for brokering this détente, but Conachoweedo's and Sneedo's words at the June conference suggest that it was the result of diplomacy conducted among Native nations, with little or no influence from New York. Indigenous negotiations, only barely visible in the colonial records, explain why Conachoweedo and Sneedo proved so cagey in their conference with Andros.[23]

To soften their rejection—no need to burn bridges with new neighbors, after all—the sachems promised to return to Manhattan, this time bearing proper gifts. They had been unable to bring wampum to signal their community's commitment to peace and create the bonds of friendship. Serial migrations from the Susquehanna to the Potomac and then to the Delaware, each time in flight from merciless enemies, had left them with precious little to give. Conachoweedo was clearly distressed by their poverty and resulting breach of protocol. Next time, he vowed, "they would bring some present with them to appeare like themselves"—to become again the proud and wealthy Susquehannocks of old.[24]

Andros pounced on this apparent vulnerability, telling them, "its no matter . . . they shall bee welcome whither they bring any thing or not." By absolving the sachems from the obligation to bring gifts, Andros indicated that in New York the people of Gandastogue would not be equals in a circle of reciprocity but dependents on colonial powers. Perhaps he believed they had little choice but to accept. Yet his last proposal was oddly plaintive: "They should say whether they will come into the Government or no, if they will not t'is well, if they will hee will make provision for them, and they shall bee protected and welcome: so that when they returne—They should make answer whether they will come or no in briefe." As though grasping at straws, Andros pressed them for some answer, any answer.[25]

Conachoweedo and Sneedo did not reply. They were probably offended by Andros's crass rejection of promised gifts. Even if they could forgive this faux pas, they surely understood the implications: that accepting New York's protection spelled the death of an independent Gandastogue. According to the English secretary recording the council, Conachoweedo and Sneedo "departed well satisfyed." Yet they never answered Andros's question about their intentions and they never returned to Manhattan. Despite Andros's careful efforts, he could not bend Susquehannocks into the shape he needed them to take as the linchpin in his alliance chain. Thanks to the shelter offered by Lenape and Munsee kinfolk, as well as talks with the Haudenosaunee, they had confidence in their ability to shape their own futures.[26]

Some Susquehannocks decided to return to Gandastogue during the spring of 1676. Turning their backs on the troubles that came from their southward migration, they moved to the Susquehanna Valley and built a "new Fort" just one mile south of the one they had abandoned the previous year. Perhaps they were encouraged by the ongoing diplomatic talks that held the possibility of peace with the Five Nations. Perhaps, in the midst of hardship and dislocation, they could not resist the lure of home. Whatever their motivations, they intended to stay. Susquehannock men cut timber and sunk fresh palisades into a hilltop near the riverbank. Women prepared new fields for a crop of maize. Writing later in 1676, Maryland Councilors noted that Susquehannocks had lived in the connadago "for so many months that they have now Corne fitt to roast." Yet colonists heard barely a whisper from them throughout spring and early summer. Gandastogue-Susquehannocks seemed keen to avoid the English altogether as they settled back into their embattled homeland.[27]

Their designs toward Maryland Algonquians were a different matter. The Mattawoman headman, Maquata, seeing the winds of fortune turn against Gandastogue, made an ostentatious show of loyalty to the English. The Maryland Council noted that Maquata "came first in to Major Truman Voluntaryly and offered all his men to Serve us against the Susquehanoughs." Several nations of the Western Shore—Piscataway, Pamunky, Choptico, and Nanjemoy—followed his example, sending warriors "in pursuite of the Enemy." Tributary leaders prevailed upon the government to pay a bounty of four matchcoats for each Susquehannock prisoner. Judging by the payout, Algonquian warriors were zealous in the hunt. By May 1676 they had delivered more than thirty Susquehannock captives. Records are scanty about the fate of these captives, but at least some were sold into slavery as laborers on English plantations. In 1681 the Charles County planter Henry Hawkins complained about "an Indian man of his Susquehannoh." The warriors received their matchcoats and ammunition for further raids "by way of gratification for the Services done . . . in the late Warre against the Susquehannough Indians." Susquehannock enslavement financed Maryland's war effort while Mattawomans, Piscataways, and other Algonquians profited.[28]

The capture and enslavement of Susquehannocks both hearkened back to earlier decades of English settlement and presaged the future of Anglo-Indian warfare. As in Virginia, slavery came early to Maryland and enslaved Africans were important to its economy as both plantation laborers and Indian traders. In fact, the first recorded interpreter to the Susquehannocks was an unnamed "Negroe, which lived among them for to learne the language." However much colonists might have preferred enslaved Africans to other forms of labor, there were not enough black men and women to fulfill English demand. By 1670 there were about seven hundred Marylanders of African descent and over ten thousand English settlers,

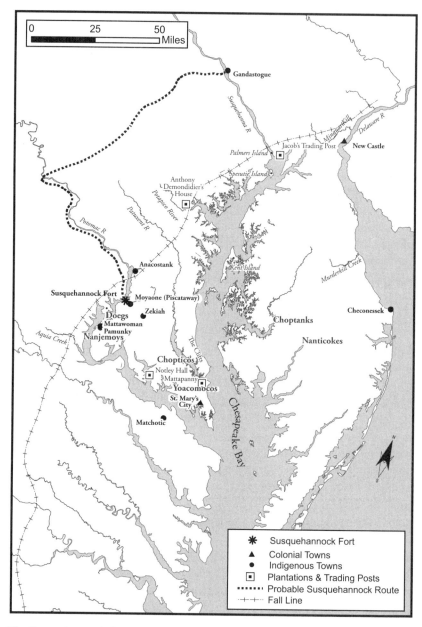

The following labels appear on the map:

0 25 50 Miles

Gandastogue

Susquehanna R.

Minguankill

Delaware R.

Jacob's Trading Post

New Castle

Palmers Island

Spesutie Island

Anthony Demondidier's House

Patapsco River

Patuxent R.

Potomac R.

Kent Island

Murderkill Creek

Anacostank

Susquehannock Fort

Moyaone (Piscataway)

Zekiah

Doegs

Mattawoman

Pamunky

Nanjemoys

Choptanks

Checonessek

Nanticokes

Aquia Creek

The Cliffs

Chopticos

Notley Hall

Mattapanny

Yoacomocos

St. Mary's City

Chesapeake Bay

Matchotic

Legend:

✴ Susquehannock Fort
▲ Colonial Towns
● Indigenous Towns
☐ Plantations & Trading Posts
•••••• Probable Susquehannock Route
-+-+- Fall Line

The Susquehannock Scattering V: Gandastogue

comprising only 6 percent of the population. Instead, early settlers made unfree laborers through small-scale Indian slaving. The government had cracked down on this practice in 1649, at least for Algonquian tributaries, but soon thereafter introduced an innovation: enslavement through plunder. In 1652 and again in 1667, the cash-strapped government financed expeditions against Native nations on the Eastern Shore by promising soldiers that "every and all such Indian or Indians So taken and made lawfull prisonner" were theirs to "convert and improve to his and their Owne use and benefitt." Data on these enslaved Natives is scarce, but they were sufficiently numerous to be included in a 1664 law that defined "all Negroes and *other slaves*"—that is, Indigenous peoples—as slaves for life, further mandating that the children of enslaved people would inherit the condition of their father. In 1676 Susquehannocks became victims of this cruel circuit between warfare and capital accumulation, unwillingly financing further violence against their people as human plunder. The system worked so well that it became a common feature of Anglo-Indian war in the late seventeenth century.[29]

Gandastogue-Susquehannocks' response to this assault was animated by the same emotional calculus that drove others to attack Virginia settlers. In this case, however, the targets were Algonquians responsible for killing and capturing their kindred. Maquata spelled out the logic behind Susquehannock retribution to the Maryland Council, explaining "the Susquehanoughs . . . are now his Enemyes Only because he hath espoused [Maryland's] quarrell against them." The fighting occurred largely beyond the limits of colonial observation, but it seems that after early Algonquian successes, Susquehannock warriors gained the upper hand by mid-1676. Maquata was forced to move to a more defensible location and "infort himselfe for the security of himselfe and people against the Susquehanoughs." In May, Maquata claimed that the Mattawomans were "in great danger of being destroyed by the common Enemy, and therefore feared his Owne life." Susquehannocks may have been scattered but they were far from weak, and the Western Shore became a battleground between Indigenous combatants.[30]

The violence engulfing Native communities was a colonial crisis waiting to happen. Although colonists initially went unscathed by Susquehannock assault, they could not help but feel vulnerable. Men and women on the northern frontier had been concentrated in fortified plantations over the winter, creating the combination of terror and tedium in which rumors flourished. Small incidents piled up: livestock killings by Indians of uncertain identity, stories of "mischeife intended" by disaffected friends, children taken captive near the ominously named Murderkill Creek. Maryland officials needed to ensure that colonists felt protected before fear led to another version of the Volunteer movement rumbling across the province's southern border. However, they also needed Algonquians to believe that the government would protect their communities from English vigilantism as they bore the brunt of the Susquehannock offensive. The government was committed to two potentially antagonistic populations: Algonquians nervous about their vulnerability to violence committed by rogue colonists and colonists nervous about their vulnerability to violence committed by rogue Indians.[31]

The Maryland government had been incapacitated by the absence of Governor Charles Calvert, who had become the new Lord Baltimore upon the death of his father in November 1675 and traveled to England to settle his affairs, but called an assembly for May 15 to address the brewing crisis. Baltimore and his inner circle had no choice but to navigate the double bind between their two groups of subjects. The proprietary party, made up of the Calvert family and their largely Catholic supporters, was adamant that Maryland must stand by friendly Algonquians. Like Berkeley, they considered tributary Indians a bulwark of provincial security. Unfortunately, this position encouraged an alliance of convenience between colonists with longstanding grievances against the Calverts and colonists more immediately concerned with Indigenous violence. Antiproprietary resentment mixed together planter frustration with the stagnating tobacco economy, Protestant opposition to Catholic rule, and popular resistance to the exceptional powers wielded by the government of a proprietary colony. Denunciations of corruption, tyranny, and arbitrary rule—battle cries that had created more than one crisis for the Lords Baltimore already—became highly charged when those allegedly corrupt interests seemed to weigh in on the side of Native nations. Debates over policies about war with Susquehannocks or the place of tributary Algonquians in the colonial order were not, in this light, simply practical matters of security. They were battles for the soul of the province.[32]

The trial of Thomas Truman demonstrated how this struggle corroded formal authority and encouraged the devolution of power. After the assembly convened, the first act of the Upper House—another name for the Governor's Council, a body dominated by the proprietary party—was to impeach Truman for the "barbarous and inhumane Murder of five Susquehannough Indians." They charged that the summary execution of sachems at the beginning of the 1675 siege violated orders issued by the Lord Proprietor in Truman's commission and therefore amounted to treason. Truman did not contest his guilt but did justify his failure, claiming that militia from

Virginia and Maryland had committed these killings without orders after the discovery of several murdered colonists nearby. The representatives in the Lower House—the legislative body packed with Protestants and Calvert opponents—were apparently convinced by these extenuating circumstances. They agreed that Truman could not be held responsible for the behavior of a crowd enraged by the spilling of innocent blood. Instead of capital punishment, the typical sentence for treason, they slapped Truman with a fine.[33]

The Upper House was incensed by the implied endorsement of vigilante violence. They warned that the government's complicity in murder would arouse the distrust of tributary Indians, "with whome the publick Faith hath been broke," causing them to lose confidence in "any Treaties We Shall have with them Which in this Dangerous Juncture of affaires the Country will Stand in need of and on which we must in some measure depend." Hanging Truman would signal that friendly Indians could expect the protection of the law and encourage their loyalty. Moreover, making an example of Truman would maintain order among colonists. Even the Lower House admitted that a crime like treason must be punished harshly to encourage "terror of others to bewarr of Such Offences against your Lordship for the future." If terrible criminals did not receive terrible punishments then no one would fear the sovereign power of the Lord Proprietor. Colonists, even government officers, would hold themselves free from any bond of obedience, ignoring commissions and instructions as they pleased. "Soe all Authority will become Rediculous and Contemptible," the Upper House predicted, "and Soe Render the Government Odious To all people." The Lower House refused to budge, allowing Truman to escape justice. The Upper House issued a grim prophecy. "Whether by [Truman's] action the Province Will not be Prejudiced and many English murdered," they warned, "his Lordship and this house Leaves to the further Consideration of the Lower house." Vigilantism, left unchecked, would bring war and anarchy.[34]

The Lower House sought to subvert the Calverts' alliances with tributary nations, giving popular fears of Indians a veneer of public approval. One bill proposed a ban on the sale of guns and ammunition to all Natives, including tributaries. This measure would not increase security—there were already laws on the books that prohibited unlicensed arms dealing—but it would force the government to break its treaties, which included promises to distribute weapons for self-defense and military service on the colony's behalf. Rather than protecting colonists, the Upper House argued, the law would force friendly Algonquians "to Joyne with the Indians that are our declared Enemies." In all likelihood this was the very outcome that some burgesses wanted: a bright line designating tributary Indians enemies of the province.[35]

Despite the Upper House's determination to show solidarity with Native allies, they were not without reservations. On the one hand, they made strenuous efforts to uphold legal protections and encourage military service. Governor Calvert used his executive powers to kill the proposed arms embargo and send large shipments of powder and shot to "the friend Indians." Bounties were raised to five matchcoats for live Susquehannocks and three for every scalp (the higher bounty revealing a clear preference for captives who could be made into slaves). The council heard petitions from several Algonquians complaining of mistreatment, ordered restitution for property illegally confiscated by settlers, and called English criminals to account in the courts. On the other hand, they also questioned the dependability of Indigenous allies, using the chaos in Virginia as a cautionary tale. "We See the Woefull Condition our Neighboures are in," they stated, "by Neglecting to make Certaine their owne Security by theire owne forces and depending Wholly upon the Indians." They demanded that each tributary nation deliver hostages for their good behavior as mandated by treaty. The councilors even pandered to popular anti-Indian sentiment by arguing that colonial rangers would not only repel Susquehannock incursions but also keep tributary Indians in line. They explained, "noe neighbour Indian will attempt any thing to the prejudice of the people here untill they shall have removed theire Wives and Children out of the danger of our forces." The proprietary party courted Algonquian subjects to secure their loyalty, but their ostensibly pro-Indian policies did not shy away from the threat of destruction for disloyalty.[36]

Tributary leaders attended the assembly and watched tensely from the galleries. They could not participate in the debates but they used their experience with English political culture to influence the proceedings. None were savvier than the Mattawoman werowance Maquata. When he claimed that Susquehannocks were his enemies only because of his people's loyalty to Maryland, he was being disingenuous. Like all Potomac Algonquians, the Mattawomans had a history of war with Gandastogue before mutual enmity with Iroquoia turned them into allies. By implying otherwise, however, he placed Mattawoman military service in the framework of patriarchal obligation: they obeyed the sovereign to whom they owed allegiance and therefore the Lord Proprietor owed them protection. In a meeting with Lord Baltimore, Maquata emphasized that his warriors provided English colonists with a shield against Susquehannock attack. He expressed solidarity with them as fellow subjects, stating, "the security of the English" was just as important as "his owne security." His appeal was remarkably successful. Baltimore ordered a garrison of twenty men to guard the Mattawoman town, which allocated half of the province's English troops to the protection of Indigenous tributaries. In recognition of Maquata's loyal service the council gave him a gift: a medal bound in yellow and black ribbon, stamped with the image of Lord Baltimore and the province of Maryland. It was very like the one that Susquehannock envoys had presented to Truman as a reminder of their friendship just before they were clubbed to death by an enraged mob. Maquata was no doubt pleased that his clever performance of English subjecthood was rewarded with a garrison of protectors, but he was probably wise enough not to trust too much in the medal's power.[37]

Demonstrating loyalty to the English, Maquata and other tributary leaders discovered, meant walking a razor's edge. Mattawomans fulfilled their end of the bargain not only by repelling Susquehannock raiders but also guarding the border against spillover violence from Virginia. In early June, Mattawomans captured a Virginian Pamunkey escorted by Piscataway, Choptico, and Yoacomoco werowances. They were on their way to Moyaone, the Piscataway town. According to Maquata, who assisted with the interrogations, the "Pamunckye Indian prisoner" was "a person violently suspected to have had his hand in blood on that side potomack River." The Pamunkey, he believed, was a spy on behalf of a coalition of Susquehannocks and Virginia Algonquians who came to scout Maryland's defenses. This clandestine embassy offered Maquata an opportunity to reinforce his depiction of Mattawomans standing shoulder to shoulder with settlers against a common enemy. The Pamunkey revealed that Virginia Indians from the town of Matchotic, seeking to escape Susquehannock raiders and Volunteer vigilantes, planned to cross the border into Maryland. Maquata insisted the refugees would include "spyes . . . for Some evill intent." He told the council, "there will be many Indians . . . in his Quarters ere long," and added, "whether enemyes or Freinds he knowes not but feares the worst."[38]

Maquata's attempt to score points by siding with settlers against other Natives was no more successful than similar gambits by Cockacoeske and Posseclay. The council concluded that the Maryland Algonquians were innocent but issued a stern reminder that "it was agreed betweene his said Lordshipp and the said King and the other Kings that neither he nor any Other should entertaine any Indians that should at any time come from Virginia." Colonists on either side of the Potomac were not likely reassured by the unsettling implication of Maquata's suspicions: factions among Maryland's tributary nations were in contact with known enemies of the

English. To allay such worries, the council instructed the captured werow-ances to escort the Pamunkey prisoner to Virginia, "tell them the newes," and then return to Maryland "to live with their Freinds." Perhaps they hoped to reassure Virginia colonists that the hostile Indigenous coalition did not extent to Maryland, prompting the Volunteers to think twice be-fore bringing their riot into the Lord Proprietor's domain. Maryland colo-nists, however, must have puzzled over the proprietary party's motives in using suspected conspirators as emissaries of fidelity. For antiproprietary forces—the sort of men who advocated breaking Maryland's treaties, dis-arming the province's Indigenous defenders, and absolving Indian-killers of their crimes—the entire affair would only have fueled popular distrust. The Calverts' use of turncoat tributaries to do the colony's business looked, at best, naïve and stupid. At worst, it looked like popish lords colluding with Indians at the expense of good Protestant Englishmen.[39]

Although the May assembly's major goal was to organize the colony's defenses to defeat Susquehannock raiders, it only created more disarray. Compared to Virginia's mobilization of military resources, Maryland's preparations were minimal. Twenty rangers were supposed to guard the entire frontier. The "Act Proveiding for the Security and Defence of this Province" authorized commissioned captains of the county militias to raise forces on an ad hoc basis "upon any Warre with the Indians, which may hereafter chance to break out, (which God forbid)." Lacking direct attacks on colonial communities, it was left to Mattawomans, Piscataways, and the other Algonquian tributaries to take the fight to Gandastogue. Yet the "Security and Defence" mentioned in the act's title was not limited to Na-tives. Militia officers with the power to mobilize men in the event of Susque-hannock invasion had the same power for another eventuality: "for the opposeing and suppressing of . . . any domestick Insurrection, or Rebellion within this Province." Even though the Gandastogue-Susquehannocks are little more than ghosts flitting through the surviving documents, their war against Algonquians nonetheless exerted such political force that Maryland drifted inexorably toward crisis.[40]

We have already met the Susquehannocks who decided to remain in Virginia, meeting colonial aggression with mourning war. It was probably just a small band of warriors rather than the families that migrated to other destinations. Jacob My Friend described them as "severall troops," war par-ties that settlers understood as the "incendaries of the mischeifs" in Virginia. For some of these men, the raids in early 1676 apparently sated their desire for revenge. By summer 1676, English observers noted Susquehannocks leaving Virginia to "returne to their old habitations" in Gandastogue. At least a few, however—perhaps as few as eight—decided to stay to repay the Virginians' treachery. They camped in the bluffs above the James River, where in earlier decades Susquehannock moccasins had trodden "plain paths" to their Erie allies' town Rickahock. The sources are inconsistent on the activities of these Virginia-Susquehannocks during the spring of 1676. The rumors flew thick and fast, but reliable reports were rare birds. It is possible that the raiders simply laid low and let the flutters of panic over their winter raids brew into a storm.[41]

The repercussions of their decision to attack Virginia colonists were indirect, but one of the ripple effects was a profound shift in English attitudes toward Native peoples. Modern readers conditioned by the virulent racism of later centuries might assume that colonists felt a blanket antipathy toward Indigenous peoples and that hatred motivated their vigilante attacks. To be sure, the English considered themselves and their civilization superior to the supposed savagery of Indians, and settlers frequently exploited their power over tributaries to defraud them of land, exploit their labor, and undermine their sovereignty. But even if their relationship was fraught, it *was* a relationship: settlers and Natives lived in close proximity, part of the same multicultural society. Algonquian men and women worked on plantations alongside English servants and enslaved Africans, as both wage earners and indentured servants. Indigenous artisans crafted baskets, blankets, canoes, and tobacco pipes, shaping the everyday material experience of most colonists. Natives were regular visitors to English settlements and mainstays of social spaces such as taverns; English men visited Native towns for companionship and sex. The development of ethnic hatred was not neither preordained nor automatic. It was the result of violent ideological work that men like Nathaniel Bacon performed in the midst of war with Susquehannocks. Indian-hating, in other words, was not a cause of the Time of Anarchy. It was its consequence.[42]

By May 1676, pervasive rumors that Susquehannocks had recruited Algonquians encouraged colonists to interpret acts allegedly perpetrated by tributaries as part of the Susquehannock-Virginia War. In mid-May, Native raiders assaulted an isolated plantation house in Rappahannock County and slaughtered its defenders to the last man. Militia captain Thomas Goodrich, in pursuit, thought "tis the susquehannos that has done us this mischife." His fellow officers William Travers and Thomas Hawkins, however, assumed that Goodrich "has not bin Rightley informed" because obviously the killers were tributary Portobaccos. This story, if accurate, was probably the outcome of bad blood between settlers and Algonquians. By the end of 1675, in the tense pause after the Susquehannock breakout, colonists in Northumberland County robbed and beat a Wicocomoco

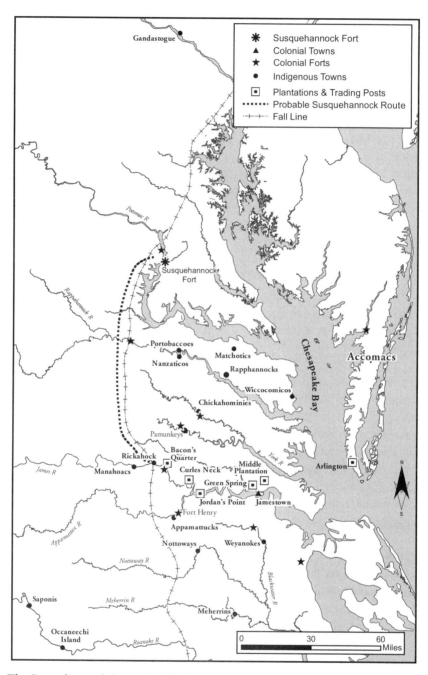

The Susquehannock Scattering VI: Virginia

employed as a deer hunter. Similar but unreported incidents were undoubtedly on the rise as panic over Susquehannock raids spread, leading Nanzaticos to relocate in January 1676. Moreover, the May raid occurred just one week after 110 dragoons rode through Rappahannock towns on their way to build a new fort for frontier defense. Coinciding with the Volunteers' treachery against allied Occaneechis—news which would have spread from mouth to mouth among Natives just as it did among settlers—Algonquians deserted their towns and joined the growing Indigenous camps in the Tidewater swamps. Whether they left after assaulting their English neighbors or because they feared English attack, many colonists interpreted their move as evidence of collusion with Susquehannock enemies.[43]

Algonquian tributaries were caught between the hammer of vigilante violence and the anvil of government policy. The Pamunkey weroansqua, Cockacoeske, delivered on her promise to provide intelligence to colonists. While Berkeley conducted a tour of frontier defenses, camping near the falls of the James, she "sent the Governour word . . . that there was a great force of Indians neare him and therfor advisd him to be gon in time, least they should destroy him." Despite this show of loyalty, the Volunteers lumped Pamunkeys in with Susquehannocks as "barbarous Enemies" and terrorized their communities. Although Berkeley had issued orders for tributary Indians to remain in their towns, Cockacoeske chose survival over obedience and led her people to the Great Dragon Swamp to escape Volunteer marauders. With few good options, Pamunkeys not only faced hostility from Susquehannock raiders and rogue militia but also risked alienating Berkeley's government.[44]

Cockacoeske, like Maquata in Maryland, was a shrewd student of English political culture and played the role of patriarchal dependent to her peoples' advantage. The Pamunkeys' hidden refuge was discovered by militia captain William Claiborne Jr., son of the William Claiborne who had forged an alliance with Gandastogue half a century earlier. Cockacoeske dodged an order to return to the Pamunkey town and told Claiborne "she would most willingly returne and be under the Governors protection" but Berkeley's militia "could not protect" Pamunkeys "from Mr Bacons violence." Cockacoeske's justification for her defiance was strikingly similar to the Volunteers' justification for theirs: Berkeley's patriarchal failure to provide protection subverted his authority and invited ostensibly illegal action for self-preservation. Philip Ludwell explained, "if the Governor could not Rule Mr. Bacon and his crue, they [Pamunkeys] could not Imagine how he could protect them." Cockacoeske shamed Berkeley, who could not deny the justice of her argument, into allowing Pamunkeys to remain in the Great Dragon Swamp. She reduced him to a grumbling resolution to find a suitable punishment for them after the Volunteer movement was crushed.[45]

Just as English authorities faced a crisis stemming from colonists acting without sanction, Algonquian authorities struggled to prevent divisions among their people. Tributary Natives surely felt their share of fear as they were dragged into a war against Susquehannocks that they did not start, as well as anger as settlers began pointing guns at every Indian in sight. Civil leaders like Cockacoeske, pondering the ruinous cost of war against the English, used their power to urge restraint and advocated that Natives abide by the 1646 treaty for their own survival. Some Algonquians, however, would not abide the Volunteers' indiscriminate violence and the government's failure to honor the treaty's promises of protection. After moving to the Great Dragon Swamp, Cockacoeske summoned a trusted interpreter to carry a message to Berkeley. She was absent when the interpreter arrived and dissident Pamunkey leaders made their play. According to an anonymous report, "the great men tooke him and bound him naked to a tree there whipped him . . . derideing him In a very scurrilous manner." The torture might have gone further if Cockacoeske had not arrived and ordered the interpreter set loose. Sources provide few hints about the extent of this power struggle between Cockacoeske and rival werowances, but it appears that structures of authority—and the forces preventing an escalation of ethnic violence—were nearly as strained in Native communities as among settlers.[46]

By the middle of May 1676 the movement toward civil war between Virginia colonists and the Native people of Virginia had gathered its own momentum. It required no further Susquehannock intervention to careen toward disaster. Volunteer suspicions about Algonquians inspired preemptive violence. English fears and fantasies became self-fulfilling prophecies, causing at least some Natives to respond in kind. Philip Ludwell lamented, "by this meanes we have not now, that we know of, hardly 100 Friend Indians on all our Borders Round, and at least 1500 enemies more then wee needed to have." Berkeley fumed that the Volunteers were the cause of, rather than the solution to, Indian violence. "These poore men that have beene killed will have their bloods laid to Bacons charge as well as to the barbarous Enemies," he wrote. Nevertheless, he had to admit the growing evidence of Algonquian hostility. "I believe all the Indians our neighbours are engaged with the Susquahannocks," he wrote to militia commanders in Rappahannock. "Therefore I beseech you doe your best to destroy all of what Nations soever they are."[47]

The widening Anglo-Algonquian war was at the center of the confrontation between Volunteers and the government. Berkeley accepted his patriarchal duty to protect English subjects but insisted that the authority to wage war belonged to him alone. On May 10 the governor branded the Volunteers rebels for taking up arms without a legal commission. "Mr. Bacon's proceedings are," the council proclaimed, "rash, illegal, unwarrantable, and most rebellious, and consequently destructive to all Government and Lawes." In a "Declaration and Remonstrance" issued on May 29, Berkeley reminded the people of Virginia, his "loving frends," of the subject's duties to fear and revere. He admitted that "if any Ennimies should envade" it was the responsibility of government officers to "rayse what forces they could to protect his majesties subjects." However, taking up the sword without authority, even with honorable intentions, was treason. "I can shew," he stated, "an hundred examples where brave and greate men have been put to death for gaining victories against the command of their superiors." The Volunteers did not contest the point but maintained that Berkeley's failure compelled them to act out of their own patriarchal duty. Bacon made an emotional appeal to his kinsman, begging the governor "to believe mee in my heart" when he swore his "abhorrence of Mutiny and rebellion, our Loyallty to our King and obedience to your Honor." Nevertheless, "if noe body were present and I had noe orders," he wrote, "I would still goe in the defense of the Country against All Indians in general"—not just Susquehannocks but all Indians because "they were all enemies." This basic disagreement about the proper response to Anglo-Indian violence was the issue driving colonists toward civil war.[48]

Berkeley hoped to prevent an irreparable rift by calling a new assembly "for the better security of the Country from our Barbarous Enemies the Indians and better settling and quieting our domestick disorders and discontents." He put a brave face on it, announcing that he was responding to the people's "soe earnest desires," but his control was slipping. Royal investigators later noted that calling the election was a gamble to head off the threat of "force from Bacon or his Confederates." Unfortunately the election demonstrated how polarized colonists had become over the issue of Anglo-Indian violence. Even as copies of Berkeley's declaration circulated, the voters of Henrico County chose Nathaniel Bacon and James Crews—Volunteer leaders in open rebellion—as their burgesses. Scandalized by this popular endorsement of the Volunteers, Berkeley's supporters claimed the men had won their seats by fraud, bursting into the county courthouse "with about 40 armed men" and forcing voters to cast their ballots under the gun. But whether they came into office as Indian-fighting heroes or brutal strongmen was irrelevant. Rebels were going to join the governor in the state house to decide the fate of Native peoples in Virginia.[49]

Indian affairs was the incendiary issue that dominated the June assembly. All other matters were overshadowed by the Volunteers' demand for a commission to wage war against Indians and Berkeley's refusal to delegate Indian policy to what he considered an unruly mob. Bacon made a public plea that popular complaints about inequality should be buried so that colonists could unite against Indians. "Discontents," he wrote, were "best diverted . . . and safest leveled at the Center of them, these barbarous Aggressors." The grievances against Berkeley's government that most concerned the Volunteers and their supporters were "those that tended to protect and cherish the Enemy and hinder our opposing them." Six or seven hundred armed colonists, double the number that had first taken up arms in April, camped around Jamestown to pressure the burgesses into granting the commission. "Our taking up Arms so disorderly and our such earnest pressing of our Right Honorable Governor to Comissionate and put us in some better Posture of Defense against these bloody Heathens," said Bacon, "was purely intended . . . to preserve our very Being." The burgesses knew the Volunteers could not be suppressed by force. According to Philip Ludwell, even if there were enough soldiers in Jamestown to match them— which there were not—the loyalties of government militia could not be trusted because "not a part of the Country" was "free From the taint of this poyson." The longer Berkeley delayed, the more seriously the encamped Volunteers, with "rage heightened beyond Imagination," considered storming the capital. Granting the Volunteers the commission they demanded was, Ludwell wrote, an "unavoydable necessitie . . . to prevent the whole Country falling in a moment to ashes." Berkeley concluded that it was the only way to stave off insurrection.[50]

The burgesses, who included many men sympathetic to the Volunteer cause, found a compromise that bestowed the Volunteers with legitimacy but also shackled it with restraints. The assembly offered what was in essence a letter of marque for a privateer army. It authorized "divers gentlemen and Soldiers as Reformades, Volunteers or Privateers" to mobilize "for the Service of the Country against the Common Enimy." Much as Maryland's militia had done in previous wars, Volunteers were permitted to finance their campaign through plunder and enslavement. This was a significant victory for Bacon and men of like mind, who resented the rights and protections afforded to Indigenous peoples. However, the assembly's order prohibited "the falling upon or injureing in any sort any Indians, who are and continue in friendship with us." Susquehannocks were fair game, but tributaries remained off limits. Despite the harder line that Berkeley was taking with recalcitrant Algonquians, he clung to the hope that he could resolve the crisis without power devolving to forces beyond his control. For the moment, he was successful. According to the royal investigators, "the people were soe well pacified . . . that every man with great Gladness returned to his own home" before the commission was even finalized. The Volunteers were mollified by their transformation from unsanctioned pirates into agents of the government and returned home to protect their families from Indigenous raiders.[51]

Yet the assembly was nearly derailed because of Berkeley's resistance to this compromise. Once the Volunteers dispersed and Bacon went home to attend to his pregnant wife, Berkeley refused to sign the promised commission. When Bacon arrived in Henrico, "impatient people run to him to aske how affaires stood, exclaiminge more and more against the Indians, and desired to know if he had gott a Commission." The frontier people grew furious at Berkeley's foot-dragging and stated their intent to obtain the commission by any means necessary. According to the royal commissioners, "they began to sett upp their throats in one common Kry of oaths and curses, and cryd out aloud that they would either have a Commission for Bacon that they might serve under his conduct, or else they would pull down the Town." Between five and six hundred Volunteers from Henrico and New Kent shouldered their muskets and marched—not against Indians this time but against the government that insisted on protecting those Indians. On June 23 the Volunteers seized control of the capital and surrounded the State House with the governor, council, and burgesses locked inside. Bacon and his men threatened to burn down the State House if Berkeley did not deliver a signed commission. Berkeley later claimed that the councilors told him "unlesse I would yeald to inevitible necessity they and their wives and children were al undone." Despite Berkeley's misgivings, no one in Jamestown could see any option but to grant the commission.[52]

Even in the midst of tumultuous English factionalism, Algonquians used the assembly as an opportunity to safeguard the interests of their people. Cockacoeske attended to face accusations of Pamunkey disloyalty after their unsanctioned flight to the Great Dragon Swamp. In a performance of sovereign power that Northumberland County burgess Thomas Mathew remembered decades later, she wore a crown of glittering wampum and a fringed deerskin mantle, traditional ceremonial dress for a werowance yet legible to Europeans as the raiment of monarchy. Although not an imposing figure—Francis Moryson described her as "somewhat Plump of Body," with "a meane or indifferent stature"—Cockacoeske behaved like a queen. She strode with "a Comportment Gracefull to Admiration" and spoke "with grave Courtlike Gestures and a Majestick Air." Assuming the role of a grieving widow "with an earnest passionate Countenance as if Tears were ready to Gush out," she reminded the burgesses that her husband,

Totopotomoy, had given his life to defend Virginia from Rickahockan invaders in 1656, a loss for which she had received neither condolence nor compensation. Cockacoeske was flanked by her son, John West, a Pamunkey war captain who "hath been very active in the service of the English" against the Susquehannocks. His presence was a reminder that her family continued to fight on Virginia's behalf despite Volunteer persecution. Cockacoeske could not resist demands that she commit some of her warriors to serve as auxiliaries for the militia and under pressure relented to send twelve men as scouts. Nevertheless, the assembly agreed that the Pamunkeys could remain in the Great Dragon Swamp with the bulk of their warriors to protect the community. At a time when anti-Indian sentiment was cresting, it was a remarkable victory thanks to Cockacoeske's keen grasp on the emotional culture of English politics.[53]

For settlers, as well, emotional culture was at the forefront of the assembly. Some dissidents undoubtedly saw in the Volunteers an opportunity to advance programs of political reform or pursue their own personal ambitions, but most colonists were primarily interested in the safety of their homes and families. As burgesses struggled for compromise, Philip Ludwell reported that everyone was "desirouse to Finish their Buisiness, that they might be at their homes to secure their families and Estates from the murder and Rapine" of hostile Indians. We can surely assume that such sentiments expressed some of the heartfelt tenderness that men felt toward vulnerable wives and children, but they also expressed the hard realities of social control. For men wealthy enough to have "estates," it was not enough to secure their property from Indigenous raiders. They also had to keep unruly dependents in line. "Family," metaphorically speaking, included the enslaved people owned by the householder and the servants indentured to him. By law and by custom, these dependents were children of the patriarch, with a similar compact that subjects had with their sovereign: obedience for protection. Just as the government's failure to protect colonists justified the Volunteers' rebellion, a planter's failure to protect his dependents risked a household rebellion. Ludwell explained the double threat, writing that Virginia men suffered "the Fears of the Indians on our Borders, and our servants at home, who (If God prevent not their taking hold of this Great Advantage), must carry all beyond Remedy to Destruction." Expressions of concern for family were coded with the patriarch's need to ensure that laborers continued to hold them in fear, lest Indigenous violence sever the bonds of love and allow small-scale rebellions to cascade across the country.[54]

Indigenous affairs had forced colonists to convene the June assembly, and Indigenous actions forced them to dissolve it. On June 25 word reached

Jamestown that Native war parties had attacked settlements along the York River, forty miles behind the frontier and just twenty-three miles from the capital. No one knew whether this meant the new frontier fortifications had failed to repel Susquehannocks or the culprits were Algonquians within the colony's borders. The uncertainty forced rebels and loyalists in the State House into an uncomfortable common ground. Burgesses from New Kent County, a Volunteer stronghold close to the attacks, proclaimed their shock and demanded the assembly cut short so they could protect their families. Governor Berkeley likewise pressed the burgesses to conclude their business, expressing his "desire . . . to Goe home and see how his Familie did."[55]

Because the assembly ended in such haste, it left unresolved the political schism over the future of Indigenous peoples. The Volunteers scored several clear victories, including the long-sought commission that named Nathaniel Bacon "generall and commander in cheife" of a self-organized army. The "act for carrying on a warre against the barbarous Indians" doubled the size of the militia to one thousand men—fifty times the size of the force raised in Maryland—decommissioned the despised forts in Henrico, New Kent, and Rappahannock Counties, and redeployed their garrisons to protect frontier settlements. Plunder and slavery would finance this massive mobilization. The act allowed soldiers to "have the benefitt of all plunder either Indians or otherwise," and stipulated that "all Indians taken in warr be held and accounted slaves dureing life." This was the first time that Virginian law defined Native enslavement as a permanent condition. Another law eliminated the existing system of licensed Indian trade and declared "all trade and commerce with Indians is hereby utterly prohibited," including the arms and ammunition that tributaries were entitled to by treaty and needed to fight Susquehannocks. Finally, the assembly declared that Indian tributaries who left their towns were "enemies" and nullified their land rights. By sweeping away Virginia's alliances and encouraging settlers to see Native people as prey, these measures endorsed the Volunteers' jingoistic opposition to Indigenous peoples of all nations and inscribed anti-Indian sentiment into law.[56]

Yet the assembly's record demonstrates that not all colonists agreed with the Volunteers' anti-Indianism, perhaps in part because of Cockacoeske's striking appearance. The war act's preamble refuted the narrative that erased distinctions between different Native nations. It read, "wee are not altogether satisfied that all Indians are combined against us," and justice demanded that "we ought not to involve the innocent with the guiltie." Admittedly, it was not easy for tributaries to prove they were on the right side of that dividing line. According to the official criteria, unauthorized movements, refusal to disarm or surrender hostages on demand, or even speaking with "any Indian or Indians our present enemies, or Indians that shall hereafter become our enemies," was sufficient for the government to consider them belligerents. Even colonists who supported tributary alliances, such as Berkeley, had doubts about Algonquian allegiance. Perhaps that is why the act encouraged the use of military service to rebuild trust. Natives who enlisted as scouts and fighters were offered wages of twenty fathoms of wampum per month, as well as a bounty of one matchcoat for every Susquehannock captive. Counties such as Northumberland followed through, mobilizing "all the Indian men that are fitt for service" alongside its English militia. By affirming the value of Indigenous people to the colony's security and providing guidelines that allowed them to prove their fidelity, the war act rejected Volunteer arguments that all Indians were essentially alike.[57]

The June assembly did not settle any of the arguments dividing Virginians, English or Indigenous. It only ensured that the next confrontation would be harder to control. Pro-Berkeley burgesses passed an act to suppress "unlawfull assemblies and rebellions" that granted every government officer, from county constables to councilors of state, broad discretionary powers to crush any hint of civil unrest. They claimed that it was necessary "to inflict condigne punishment upon the offenders, which will conduce to the great safety and peace of this country, and enable us the better to defend ourselves against the barbarous and common enemie." In their zeal to protect the colony from insurrection, however, the act accomplished exactly what Berkeley had feared from the beginning: the empowerment of local agents to act without his instructions. By the end of the June assembly, the devolution of authority to county elites was the price of preserving unity against the scattered Susquehannocks and whatever Algonquians may have joined them.[58]

The first march of the Volunteers gave a taste of what power unmoored from leadership might look like. The assembly dissolved on June 25, the day that news of nearby raids reached the capital. The next morning, Volunteers marched toward the York River, anxious to finally confront their enemies with confidence that their government backed them. Nathaniel Bacon marched at their head but he was more follower than leader. The Volunteers' opponents were usually eager to cast Bacon as a charismatic commander, but Councilor Philip Ludwell portrayed him as a man swept along by the energy of the crowd, struggling to retain control over the forces he had unleashed. Ludwell wrote, "he is now marched up toward the place where the last mischeife was done . . . only to sattisfy his men who would else, many of them have left him." Most would have deserted if Bacon had not gone with them. Others did desert even with Bacon on the march: as soon as they received Berkeley's commission, many "staid at home att their own plantations to be secure and quiett . . . for self preservation against the Indians on the frontier." Protecting home and family from Susquehannocks and other Indians was the Volunteers' overriding motivation. They were loyal only to whatever authority allowed them to do so, whether it was the governor's or the rebels'. Any force that stood in their way would be ignored, circumvented, or smashed.[59]

As Virginians edged closer to civil war, the Susquehannocks were nowhere to be seen. They did not speak a single line, and yet in a way they had staged the entire drama. By the end of June 1676, the people of Gandastogue had transformed from a single community on the Potomac to a multitude of autonomous bands scattered across eastern North America. From Iroquoia to Albemarle, from the Ohio to the Delaware, small groups of Susquehannocks interacted with local colonists and Indigenous nations, pursuing the strategies they thought best able to make a future for their people. Some reached out in peace. Others brought war in their wake. The ramifications exacerbated ethnic tensions within colonial societies and encouraged challenges to governments who could not find them or stop them. In scattering, the force of Susquehannock influence paradoxically multiplied. Despite their small numbers, the ripple effects of their actions set in motion a series of political convulsions that gripped the English colonies. Even their shadows, or rumors of shadows, were enough to tip volatile colonies into a spiral of devolution and disorder.

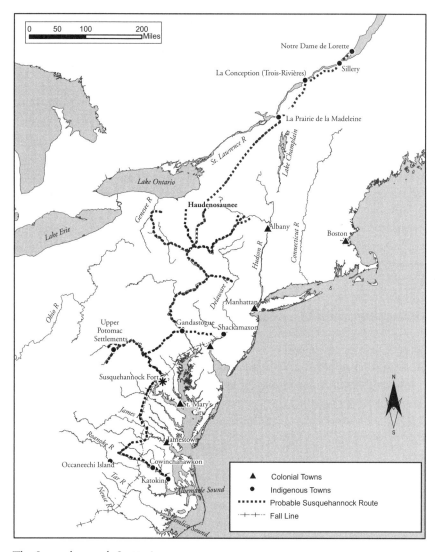

The Susquehannock Scattering

· 4 ·

THE CONTAGION
OF CONSPIRACY

As Philip Ludwell watched the Volunteers march away from Jamestown at the end of June 1676, he compared their rebellion to a disease. Bacon's rabble-rousing was "pleasant and sympathetique with the humers" of the masses because he said what frightened people wanted to hear. That was how the Volunteers' anti-Indian message "in an Instant Infected almost every corner of the Countrey." Though their military commission had averted crisis for the moment, Berkeley and the Virginia Council feared for the future, "perceiving the Disease to Grow Daungerouse and by its spreading, the Cure Difficult." This comparison of civil disorder to medical disorder was not limited to the conduct of colonists. The early stages of the Susquehannock-Virginia War, along with King Philip's War in New England, led colonial officials to describe Indigenous violence as a plague of rebellion spreading across the continent. "The infection of the Indians in New-England has dilated it selfe to the Merilanders and the Northern parts of Virginia," Berkeley had written shortly after the first wave of Susquehannock raids in February 1676. Barbados governor Jonathan Atkins, from his distant perch in the Caribbean, used the same language to describe both conflicts. He observed the "very great Damage done them dayly by the Indians . . . the infection of Rebellion extends it selfe as farre as Maryland and Virginia."[1]

Rebellion as pathology: it was an evocative metaphor. It conveyed to a metropolitan audience confusion about the causes of violence, uncertainty about how to halt its spread, and horror at its unstoppable advance. It also communicated the rebels' fundamental illegitimacy. According to prevailing political theory, the rising of subjects against their sovereign was a perversion of the organic state's healthy functioning. Thomas Hobbes described "the Infirmities . . . of a Common-wealth," which "resemble the diseases of a naturall body." Among them was "the Popularity of a potent Subject" because it led the people "away from their obedience to the Lawes, to follow a man, of whose vertues, and designs they have no knowledge." The idea of a virulent contagion obscured the complex causes of insurrection, eliding the many personal choices that led ordinary people to risk themselves and their families by taking up arms. Ludwell and Berkeley suggested that rebellion was an agent unto itself, spreading through the body politic as though rising from the pestilential miasmas that were thought to cause disease in the human body.[2]

The metaphor did, however, capture an important truth: insurrection tended to spread. In Berkeley's estimation, Anglo-Indian war was a contagion that spread of its own accord and led directly to civil unrest. Native "rebellion" against English colonizers infected colonists with a spirit of rebellion against their lawful governments. Indigenous violence and civil conflict were intertwined, each feeding the other. Synergistically, they metastasized. As outbreaks of disorder swept through New York, Maryland, Virginia, Carolina, and all the Indigenous nations surrounding them, rumors connected them into a single vast malignancy. The contagion, however, did not actually spread on its own. Using modern medical terminology that carries the metaphor further than any seventeenth-century writer, we might say that rebellion, like any communicable disease, required a vector. In this case, it was a form of communication very different from the susurration of rumors that shaped the early stages of the Time of Anarchy. The vector was conspiracy theory.[3]

Conspiracy theory was everywhere in early modern England. The normal functioning of politics in a monarchy could with some justice be considered a conspiracy: a small cabal of men densely connected by kinship and mutual interest—the king and his councilors—privately plotting to direct the course of national and international politics. Perhaps it should not be surprising, then, that the ambitious or disaffected pursued their political aspirations by scheming behind closed doors. The Tudor and Stuart eras were rife with real conspiracies, including the Ridolfi and Throckmorton Plots to assassinate Queen Elizabeth I, the Gunpowder Plot to blow up Parliament in 1605, and King Charles I's plan to seize London in the Army Plots of 1641. If the early modern English turned to conspiracy theory to understand contemporary politics, it was because they lived in a conspiratorial world. They carried this inclination with them to North America, where the language of conspiracy offered a handy explanation for breakdowns of law and order. When Gloucester County servants rose up against their masters in 1663, the Virginia Council blamed this "desperate Conspiracy" on a cadre of men that Robert Beverley described as "Oliverian Soldiers." Former Parliamentarians, holding on to the cause even after they were charged with treason and shipped to Virginia as convict laborers, "formed a villanous Plot to destroy their Masters." Rather than search for the roots of servant discontent in an exploitative society, it was simpler to blame a few bad apples, rotten to their republican cores, who spoiled the barrel. Such thinking may have been bad sociology but it was good politics. Denouncing one's opponents as conspirators stripped them of legitimacy so they could be isolated and destroyed.[4]

Virginia officials applied the same formula to the Volunteers, explaining away the movement by blaming a charismatic schemer. Berkeley wrote, without evident irony, "the whole country was in a most serene calme none suspecting the least suspicion of any troubles," until "a Young fellow one Bacon . . . infused into the People" sentiments that led to "this violent Rebellion." At first, the Volunteers seemed as good as their word. With commissions in hand, they left Berkeley's government alone and scoured the upper York River for Indian raiders throughout July 1676. However, reports about the results of their efforts were contradictory. According to John Cotton, the Volunteer rangers "put so much curage into the Planters" that colonists returned to their homes, free from fear for the first time since February. But William Sherwood had no confidence in courage when he claimed that the Volunteers, by diverting manpower from the frontier forts, were responsible for the massacre of at least one hundred settlers by enemy Indians. The confusion complicated Volunteer efforts to impress supplies for a second campaign around the falls of the James River. Toward the end of July, Gloucester County planters complained that Volunteers acted like unscrupulous freebooters. They took whatever they pleased, including munitions that householders needed to defend their own households, and threatened to kill any man who stood in their way. Volunteer abuse gave the Gloucester petitioners "just reason to fear of the Country in Gennerall" and they appealed to Berkeley "for the Security of our Familyes and Estates."[5]

Berkeley jumped to the conclusion that the Volunteer cause had been bogus all along, their anti-Indian rhetoric nothing but a cover for banditry. He nullified the military commission, claiming it had been extorted at gunpoint, and gathered a militia of loyalists. Berkeley's supporters insisted, "the Governor designed onely to raise a party to goe out against the Indians, and not against Bacon," merely planning to remedy the Volunteers' neglect of frontier defense. Some colonists suspected darker motives. With Berkeley denouncing the "tyrany and Usurpation of Nathaniel Bacon," it stretched credulity to believe he would allow armed Volunteers to ride back and forth across Virginia without interference. When Isaac Allerton, one of Berkeley's recruiters, rode into Gloucester County he found "few of the vulgar would follow us, saying wee would fight Bacon." Gloucester colonists professed no loyalty to Bacon and opposed him when they felt the Volunteers had become a source of fear that threatened their patriarchal rights and privileges. But when they learned that Bacon "was now advanceing against the common enemy" with a seemingly genuine commitment to protect the people, they refused to support Berkeley and "arose a Murmuring before his face 'Bacon Bacon Bacon.'"[6]

The foremost goal of most colonists was the defense of home and family. They did not trust Bacon, but they did not trust Berkeley either. Many believed Berkeley's followers had fabricated the Gloucester petition as a flimsy excuse to persecute a popular rival that was "contrived by a few and unknown to the Generality of that County." They warned the governor that armed conflict between factions would only give Indians more opportunities for slaughter, to the "ruing and destruction unto both." Berkeley pressed ahead anyway and gathered what men he could to confront the Volunteers, with disastrous results. The royal commissioners later explained, "the Glocester Petition . . . was the Ruine of the whole Colony, in Causing the Indian designe to recoyle in a Civil war upon the Colony." Berkeley's dogged pursuit of the Volunteers caused the Susquehannock-Virginia War to mutate into something even worse.[7]

Berkeley was a convenient target for critics, but much of the Volunteers' ire was cast toward the Green Spring men that made up his inner circle. This was a tried and true tactic. English conspiracy theorists often used the trope of the "evil councilors," depicting the monarch's advisors as cynical politicians secretly manipulating royal opinion toward sinister ends. Under the pretext that evil councilors had overswayed the sovereign, this trope allowed whatever faction happened to be out of power to oppose royal policies while still claiming loyalty to the monarch. Nathaniel Bacon formulated a colonial rendering of this theory. As Volunteers gathered for a rendezvous at the falls of the James in mid-July, he asserted "his Loyallty to his Prince, declaringe to them thatt his designe was noe other than meerly to serve his King and Country." The real problem was Berkeley and the Virginia Council, standing in for the king's advisers in America, who would not protect the king's subjects. The "negligence and coldnesse" of these councilors led them to callously disregard "the cryes of his Bretherens blood." Bacon insisted that the Volunteers were no rebels. They were honest servants of the people opposed by a clique of nefarious schemers subverting the commonwealth.[8]

Intimations of conspiracy turned the Volunteers' attention toward the government on the eve of their planned march against Native peoples. Bacon required his followers to take an oath of personal loyalty after rumors floated the possibility that spies had infiltrated the Volunteer camp. The oath emphasized the conspiratorial designs of Berkeley's faction, requiring adherents to control information and discover enemy secrets—not only the "Councills, Plotts and conspiracyes known of the Heathen," but also "any Plott or conspiracy" hatched by English partisans aimed at Bacon and the Volunteers. In a stirring speech, he argued that Virginia was in danger because Berkeley and his councilors seemed to care nothing for the common good and secretly pursued their own mysterious goals. Those goals must be discovered for the success of the war against Indians. "Lett us descend to know the Reasons why such proceedings are used against us," he finished, "that those whom they have raised for their defense, to preserve them against the fury of the Heathen, they should thus seeke to destroye, and to Betraye our lives whom they raised to preserve theirs." According to Bacon, insidious secrets concealed some terrible plot against the people. To win the wars against Susquehannocks and enemy Indians, they would first have to uncover the conspiracy.[9]

Conspiracy theory was more than a cognitive schema for understanding politics or a rhetorical tactic on partisan battlefields. It was also a form of narrative emplotment, with genre conventions that provided a framework for analysis of ongoing events. It can be easy to dismiss conspiracy theories, with their endlessly embroidered elaborations and the bizarre paranoia that drives them, as a form of mental pathology. However, conspiratorial thinking can be a useful way for people to diagnose social ills and suggest a course of treatment. In circumstances of such fear and confusion as colonists found themselves during the Time of Anarchy, when every breath of rumor seemed to complicate and mystify, the conspiracy narrative distilled and clarified. In this sense, conspiracy theory is the distorted mirror of rumor. Whereas rumors reflect an expanding web of interpretive possibilities, conspiracy theory represents an attempt to craft a coherent story out of chaos. The conspiracy narrative shifts the dissonance of many conflicting voices into the harmony of totalizing explanation. Most often, it is an explanation of how structures of power operate, why they have turned the world upside down, and how the righteous can act to restore order.[10]

After Berkeley's decision to gather an army and Bacon's resolution to confront the government, conspiracy theory acted as a lens that focused the scattered light of popular discontent into the incandescent singularity of insurrection. Berkeley's forces dwindled to a pitiful remnant of four loyalists who fled to the Eastern Shore. Hundreds of Volunteers occupied the Virginian heartland. On July 30, Bacon gathered his men at Middle Plantation and issued a "Declaration of the People" condemning Berkeley's misrule. The Declaration denounced the small group of oligarchs—a cabal of only twenty men, listed by name—as "wicked, and pernitious Councellors, Aiders and Assisters against the Commonalty." It used the oligarchs' financial interest in the Indian trade as a master key to explain Virginia's disaster. Despite Natives' "many Invasions Murthers and Robberies Committed upon us," the oligarchs "protected, favoured and Imboldened the Indians against his Majesties most Loyall subjects." Greed led Berkeley's clique to protect their Indigenous partners and turn a blind eye to the suffering of English colonists. The "unjust gaine" of the Indian trade, it concluded, meant the oligarchs had "Bartered and sould his Majesties Country and the lives of his Loyal Subjects to the Barbarous Heathen." Therefore, "the People" collectively claimed the mantle of authority and "in his Majesties name" declared Berkeley and his confederates "Traytors to the King and Countrey." All of the violence and disorder, the Declaration argued, was caused by a small group of evil-minded men. Their conspiratorial interest with the Indian enemy required an uprising for the people to save Virginia from ruin.[11]

Around the same time, Bacon issued a "manifesto concerning the Present troubles in Virginia," an incendiary denunciation of Native peoples for their part in the conspiracy. He claimed that unscrupulous merchants continued to trade with Indians despite the assembly's ban. Berkeley was not only complicit in this gun running, he clandestinely encouraged it to regain his monopoly. Indigenous trade partners, especially Pamunkeys and Appamattucks, thereby supplied themselves with guns and ammunition—weapons they inevitably turned against colonists. Bacon contended that tributary Indians, despite their status as subjects of the crown, "have bin for these Many years enemies to the King and Country, Robbers and Theeves and Invaders of his Majesties Right and our Interest and estates." The problem was that colonists could not distinguish one group of Indians from another. "Their Persons being difficultly distinguished or Known," he argued, "their many Nations Languages," and their knowledge of the legal system, allowed Natives to engage in "subterfuges such as makes us incapeable of prosecution." Effectively immune from the law, tributaries exploited their status as subjects with rights and protections to wage a covert war against the English. Bacon's solution was as simple as it was radical: "To Assert all those neighbour Indians as well as others to be Outlawed, wholly unqualified for the benefitt and Protection of the Law."[12]

This quasi-constitutional argument for the expulsion of Native peoples from the body politic was unprecedented in the history of English colonization in North America. Settlers had targeted specific nations during the bloody Anglo-Powhatan Wars, usually with the assistance of other Indigenous allies. Even the devastating destruction New England militias inflicted on Algonquians during King Philip's War was justified on the grounds that "rebellion" must be punished so the rebels could return to their proper place as subjected peoples. Bacon's Manifesto, by contrast, argued that Indigenous peoples were incapable of incorporation into England's empire. He therefore embraced charges leveled by his critics that the Volunteers' committed indiscriminate violence against tributary Indians. He proclaimed "our open and manifest aversion of all, not onely the Foreign but the protected and Darling Indians" beloved by Berkeley and the traitorous oligarchs. Bacon proudly advertised his plans for extermination, announcing "our Designe . . . to ruine and extirpate all Indians in Generall." The logic of conspiracy made the genocide of Native Americans into the apotheosis of the Volunteers' political project.[13]

The Declaration and Manifesto made anti-Indian sentiment central to rebellion. Bacon implied that Berkeley's regime had failed in its patriarchal obligation to protect English subjects precisely because it considered Indians subjects due the protection of the law. The government could recover its legitimacy only by fulfilling its duty to English subjects, which according to Bacon's logic meant declaring war on its Indian subjects. If Berkeley and his evil councilors refused to do so it only showed that their real allegiance was with the Indians. Such men were enemies of the people. Toppling the government thus became necessary not only to ensure that Volunteers could face down their Native enemies without a stab in the back from the smugglers supplying Indians with arms but also because it was the duty of all loyal subjects of the King. According to Bacon's conspiracy theory, rebellion against the government of Virginia was welded to the Indian wars: one could not be fought without the other.

Conspiracy theories, like infections, feed on communication. Narratives of conspiracy have a way of branching out to encompass all available information. By collapsing an otherwise unfathomable proliferation of contingencies into a singular story, it connects seemingly unrelated facts and transmutes plausible supposition into compelling certainty. Beyond clarifying the complicated and revealing the mysterious, it can also solve apparent paradoxes by laying bare hidden agendas and invisible machineries of power. In Virginia, the conspiracy theorists saw the ruling regime in collusion with enemy Indians and used Berkeley's relationships with tributary Indians as evidence. Maryland colonists similarly latched onto conspiracy theory as a rough and ready method for understanding communications between Natives and provincial leaders. Everyone knew the Calverts were talking to Indians. The question was: What were they saying to each other? In a time of war with shadowy belligerents, when everyone's loyalties were suspect, colonists had to ask how they should understand their leaders' attempts at diplomacy. How could they tell the difference between prudent statecraft and nefarious conspiracy?

As Maryland's proprietary party watched Virginia fall apart, they knew the unrest was ultimately rooted in Anglo-Indian violence and its emotional aftershocks. "To Our great Sorrow and greife," wrote Thomas Notley, acting as governor after Lord Baltimore sailed to England in June, "these Susquehannoughs have not only blowne the coales but made the fuel and the flame of that fire of troubles that now burnes in the breast and bowells of Our neighbours the Virginians." (The early modern English believed that the bowels, along with the heart, were the embodied location of emotions, although modern readers might be forgiven if the image of burning bowels elicits somewhat different feelings.) He and the rest of the council knew that Maryland must ensure peaceful relations between colonists and Indians if they wanted to avoid the same fate. In July the council expanded its protections for Algonquians, supplying forty militia to defend the Piscataways at Moyaone. Military regulations made assaulting any tributary Indian a capital crime and mandated severe punishment for even "abuse by words any of the said Indians." The council sent a strong signal to Algonquians that the government would protect them, even from rogue colonists. On August 17, they met with several Algonquian werowances to inform them that "there is a person called Collonel Bacon, who may perhaps come over into Maryland to annoy them and us." In case that "the Virginians doe come over without Our license," the Algonquians "may defend themselves." The Maryland government, in other words, ordered tributary Indians to repel English subjects from their sister colony with deadly force. It may have been a sensible precaution, but it was also the kind of baffling fact that caused conspiracy theories to flourish.[14]

Judging by the council's precautions, their defense of Algonquians did not go over well with the English populace. Notley, convening a council of war, announced that "the province is dayly threatened to be invaded by the Indians," and ordered colonists to gather in fortified plantations. However, more than ten men were forbidden in any location, "upon paine of being proceeded against as mutinous and Seditious persons gathered together with Force." Security was vital, in other words, but too much security would be interpreted as insurrection. The council further ordered the confiscation of privately held firearms for redistribution to commissioned militia. They knew that colonists would bitterly resent this measure so they added standing orders for all commanders to confront "any men in

Armes . . . who have not Commission from the Government." Popular discontent was surely fed by the suspicious concentration of those militia. Garrisons defended the Mattawoman and Piscataway towns, along with Mattapany, Lord Baltimore's plantation and the council's headquarters. Colonists apparently had to huddle together and fend for themselves while their leaders protected themselves and their Indians on the assumption that the people were the enemy.[15]

Luckily for the embattled rulers of Maryland, Susquehannocks in Gandastogue and Delaware wanted to negotiate. They reached out to Jacob My Friend to continue his role as the trusted broker between Maryland and Gandastogue. In July 1676, Susquehannocks, speaking through the man that Notley described as "Jacob Young Our old Interpreter," expressed their desire for "a peace with the English in Generall." Consistent with Conachoweedo's rejection of Edmund Andros's offer to mediate on their behalf, they designated Marylanders as "the principall Treators." Susquehannock diplomats suggested a conference in St. Mary's City and solicited a guarantee of safe conduct, with Jacob as their escort. The council grasped this proposal like a lifeline. In a letter to Lord Baltimore they wrote, "wee have considered the Overture of Peace made by the Susquehanough Indians . . . a blessing from God uphoped for." Following the Susquehannocks' lead, the council named Jacob the official intermediary, issued diplomatic passports, and prepared the ground for a peace council.[16]

Maryland's tributary Indians recoiled at the idea of peace with Gandastogue and scuttled this promising start. They had been on the front lines for months and they understood the cultural logic of mourning war. Unlike Maryland officials, who considered attacks on tributaries to be attacks on the province itself, Algonquians knew that Susquehannocks considered war against the English to be distinct from their wars against Indigenous nations. Algonquians saw the danger: knowingly or not, the Maryland government would sell them out, buying peace for settlers and abandoning tributaries to Susquehannock mercies. Therefore, at a meeting with the council on August 17, the Choptico headman Chotike unequivocally stated on behalf of the Algonquian leadership, "they are unwilling to have us make a peace with the Susquehanoughs." Instead he proposed an assault on Gandastogue, stating, "they will march with the English to the new Fort they have built, or otherwise to pursue the Susquehanoughs." Nothing came of this bold proposition, but the council's talks with tributaries seems to have stymied negotiations with the Susquehannocks.[17]

While the Calverts negotiated with Indigenous nations, simmering discontent reached a boiling point. In late August, disaffected colonists in the Clifts neighborhood, a stronghold of antiproprietary sentiment in Calvert

County, circulated a manifesto on "the Liberties of the Freemen of this Province." The details of their complaints are unknown because no copy of the circular survives, but the council described it as a "mutinous and seditious paper" that contained a blistering indictment of the proprietary regime. Their three major grievances were excessive taxation, restricted voting rights, and economic inequality, amounting to a condemnation of oligarchic rule. As with similar protests in Virginia, however, economic grievances were entangled with Anglo-Indian violence. The Clifts manifesto complained that the "expensive warre against the Sasquehannoughs" was paid for by a poll tax of 297 lbs. of tobacco—a heart-stopping twelve times the tax for the previous year. According to Governor Notley, this expenditure—not taxes in the abstract but the specific tax levied for the Susquehannock-Maryland War—"hath given occasion for malignant spir-itts to mutter." He explained, "the common people will never be brought to understand the just reason of a publicke charge, or will they ever believe that the expences for their own preservation." He predicted that this lack of understanding "may cause some of them to mutiny." Susquehannocks had placed so much pressure on Maryland's fragile political order that it threatened to break apart.[18]

Malignant spirits, muttering about taxes siphoned into the pockets of oligarchs under the cover of crisis, did indeed mutiny. On September 3, sixty men from the Clifts gathered under William Davies, John Pate, William Gent, and Giles Hasleham. They marched "with Force and Terror of Armes" toward Mattapany with the stated intent of forcing the government to fix the crooked political system that the Susquehannock-Maryland War had broken. Militia under the command of Henry Jowles blocked their path but could not disperse the disciplined ranks of rebels. Spooked by the armed standoff, the council abandoned Mattapany, proclaimed the leaders "mutinous and seditious persons," and offered a reward for their arrest. All of Davies's followers, however, were declared "good people" who had been "seduced and perswaded to joyne" the rebellion. Through this fiction that the ringleaders were conspirators who duped innocent people, the councilors hoped to rob Davies and his lieutenants of popular support.[19]

They need not have bothered. The Clifts men "dispersed themselves," deserting when it became clear that their show of force would not inspire a mass rising. Susquehannocks were not killing colonists, depriving Davies of the opportunity that Bacon had to claim the mantle of an Indian-fighting savior. While anxiety about the possible outbreak of Anglo-Indian violence was endemic, it was not powerful enough to galvanize full-scale insurrection. Jowles's militia captured Davies, Pate, and a handful of remaining followers, and the council hanged them as traitors. Notley justified the executions as strong medicine for a diseased body politic. "Never Body was more repleat with Malignancy and Frenzy then our people were," he wrote, "they wanted but a monstrous head to their monstrous body." He concluded, "since General Davis and Pate were hanged the Route hath been much amazed and apaled." With the conspirators dead, their decaying bodies a terror unto any aspiring demagogue, the council stemmed the contagion of rebellion.[20]

Conspiracy theory invites skeptics to view believers as extremists whose pathological ideas require an equally extreme response. When the skeptics are also agents of the state, it is easy to justify violent suppression—a response that paradoxically confirms the fears of the conspiratorially minded. But no matter how seemingly irrational, most conspiracy theories contain a seed of truth, and some contain more truth than they might at first appear. Conspiracy theorists are zealous in their efforts to connect the dots, obsessively accumulating facts because the evidence must be overwhelming to justify the grandeur of the conclusion. But the conclusion itself is often determined more by deeply embedded cultural formulas than by empirical investigation. In Maryland, no formula was more powerful than antipopery, the belief that Catholic overlords were covertly dedicated to the oppression of Protestants. Antipopery surged in both England and North America after 1673, when Parliament passed a Test Act barring "Popish Recusants" from office, which forced James, the Duke of York, to reveal his secret conversion to Catholicism. But the search for truth inevitably resulted in odd juxtapositions of seemingly contradictory facts, data that did not support the claim that all woes could be blamed on the Antichrist. Resolving those contradictions required interpretive leaps, resulting in unending elaborations of the theory. Eventually, through increasingly convoluted chains of argument, everything pointed back to the conspiracy. Rather than a defect, this was the source of conspiracy theory's peculiar power. By resolving irreconcilable antinomies and bundling the strands of divergent narratives into chimerical unity, anti-Catholic conspiracy theories purported to explain everything.[21]

In the wake of the failed Clifts uprising, popular discontent seethed even as armed resistance sputtered. Anonymous authors gave voice to that discontent in a manifesto titled "A Complaint from Heaven with a Huy and Crye and a Petition out of Virginia and Maryland," which argued that the wars of the Susquehannocks and the turmoil they unleashed were the work of a vast Catholic conspiracy. "Pope Jesuit determined to over turne Engeland, with feyer, Sword and distractions," they thundered, "and by the Maryland Papists, to drive us Protestants to Purgatory within owr selves

in America, with the help of the French Spirits from Canada." In painstaking detail, they condemned Lord Baltimore's regime for every sin con-
ventionally associated with popery: persecution, disloyalty, corruption, and
tyranny. Among the morass of accumulated examples since the colony's
founding, Baltimore's recent failure to protect the people from Indian
violence was a recurring theme. "The Kings Majesty hath intrusted the
Proprietary . . . to bee a good Steward to the Reallm of Engeland," so "the
Kings Subjects might live Secure from the incursion of the Indians and not
bee cut off and Massacrated." Because of his failure, "hee is guilty of the
late Murthers in Virginia and Maryland, and a great many of the Kings
Majesties Subjects lyves lost." Like their counterparts in Virginia, the authors evoked the suffering of families living under the threat of sudden and
violent death. They wrote, "the people must worke with their guns in the
feild with a perpetuall fear," and "som are cut off in the feild before they
see their enemy or can recover their houses, others are threatned in their
houses, men Weomen and Chillderen." The Calverts had abandoned any
pretense of protecting the people, preferring to line their pockets. "Christians Blood" was spilled, but Lord Baltimore "is glad . . . because it is his
Custom to exchainge the Kings Majesties Subjects, for furr." They concluded scornfully, "and thus wee live and goe like unto the Butchers Sheep
in the paster, and this is owr Rulers and Proprietarys Paternall Care."[22]

The authors of the Complaint gathered their grievances under the rubric
of Catholic misrule, which proffered a monocausal explanation for political
oppression and Indigenous violence. "Unmask the Vizard," they wrote with
a flourish, "and you will see a young Pope and a new Souveraigne pipe out
of his shell, and all the popish faction . . . bring their purpos step by step
to pass." Because the impulse toward tyranny originated from the Antichrist in Rome, the conspiracy spanned the globe. Jesuits "dispers themselves all over the Country," traveling in disguise with intent to "set the
Protestants at Odds, to propagate the Popes interest and Suppremacy in
America." These "blake Spirits" were natural traitors, and "hould a Secret Correspondency with the French pater Nostres" recruiting Indians for
a secret invasion from New France. "From Canada or Nova Franciæ over
the lake, into the Sinniko Indian Country amongst the Indians, Westerly
from Newyorke," Jesuits convinced Indians to invade Maryland, and "severall French cam downe in Indian apparrell amongst them." Indians were
involved somehow, though the authors' assertions were scattershot and inconsistent. Sometimes they implied that the Haudenosaunee were enemies
of Susquehannocks, other times adamant they were allies. They claimed
"the Piscattaway Indians hath invited the Sasquahana Indian to their Assistance," not merely conspirators but instigators "encourradged by their

own iff not a Popish Divell." Elsewhere, however, Algonquians were victims of Susquehannock hostility, yet still at fault for causing the war because "the Piskataway . . . Offended [the] Sasquahana Indians." These contradictions were overwhelmed by the palpable excitement of uncovering such a massive plot. The oppressive government of the Baltimore faction, Jesuit secret agents, shadowy Indian enemies—all of it was tied together as a diabolical assault on Protestant England that spanned from Europe to America.[23]

Nestled within this labyrinth of paranoid fantasy lay a kernel of insight. What seems at first glance like absurd histrionics was actually a fairly astute analysis of Atlantic world geopolitics in the 1670s. There *was* a growing schism between supporters of the Stuarts, who were attracted to French-style absolutist rule, and detractors known as Whigs, who anointed themselves the protectors of Protestant liberties. As the Society of Jesus's records testify, a Jesuit *did* travel incognito in 1674–1675, visiting "the whole of New England, Maryland, and Virginia" while "he was disguised," preaching in secret, and gathering clandestine converts among Protestant settlers. Missionaries *were* working to gain the trust of Haudenosaunee leaders to increase their influence over Iroquoia, and French coureurs des bois *did* accompany them on military expeditions. The governor of New France, Louis de Buade, comte de Frontenac, *was* trying to turn the Five Nations against the English, telling Mohawk sachems that Edmund Andros planned to betray them and destroy their nation. The Susquehannocks *were*, therefore, a fulcrum among the contending European and Indigenous powers. As Andros explained to Notley in September, "if some Course bee not speedily taken, they must all necessarily Submitt to the Maques [Mohawks], and Seniques, which passionately desire it, but might prove of a bad consequence" because the Susquehannocks would find "refuge with a grudge and rancour in their hearts." In other words, if the Haudenosaunee succeeded in absorbing the Susquehannocks, and the French succeeded in courting the Haudenosaunee, then the state of war between Gandastogue and Maryland could explode into an all-out Franco-Indian assault on English America that might tip the balance of power in Europe. These were not just plausible scenarios but actual projects whose outcomes were yet to be determined.[24]

The Complaint from Heaven is a sprawling document, twelve densely written manuscript pages of hysterical fantasy, incoherent narrative, and abysmal spelling even by seventeenth-century standards. It is admittedly a spectacularly unreliable source, which has led many careful historians to dismiss it outright. Others have found its malevolent grandeur too seductive to resist and have taken the manifesto at face value. The Complaint's merit, however, is not as an empirical record of political history so much as an expression of colonists' cognitive struggle to understand the large-scale forces shaping the future of the early modern world. Like Bacon's Declaration and Manifesto, the Complaint linked Anglo-Indian violence to oligarchical misrule, merging civil unrest and international war into a single existential threat. The authors wrote that the people "see themselves involved" in "a Miserable extreamity . . . with oppression and Warr from Within, and Hazard of life and Estate by Indians from without and at hom." Whatever its logical, or grammatical, shortcomings, the Complaint used conspiracy theory to grope toward an understanding of the unfolding Time of Anarchy. It elevated every householder's intimate fears to part a grand drama where the fate of England, its empire, and liberty itself—perhaps even God's divine plan in the Protestant battle against the forces of the Antichrist—all hung in the balance.[25]

Despite its remarkable ability to conjure clarity from chaos, conspiracy theory does not always create unity, even within the political faction it propels into action. Ambiguous or unrelated details get caught in its gravitational pull, interpreted according to conspiratorial logic. Disentangling any issue from the skein of the conspiracy becomes impossible, even when doing so would serve the interests of the theorists. Once unleashed, conspiracy theory has a way of feeding itself. Facts that seem to refute the theory can be mobilized to argue that the conspiracy is so far-reaching, the conspirators so powerful, that they can spread misinformation and suppress the truth. It trends naturally toward the radical and marginalizes moderates who question the extreme actions required to confront the conspirators. After all, if the adversary represents pure malevolence and poses an apocalyptic threat to the nation and its people, there can be only total victory or total defeat. The righteous cannot compromise with the devil, and anyone who suggests otherwise may be an enemy in disguise. The paradox of conspiracy theory is that its ideological completeness makes it a powerful tool for mobilizing support, yet that completeness also makes a movement built around it prone to factionalism, schism, and failure.[26]

Notwithstanding Nathaniel Bacon's populist pretensions, he never had anything close to unified public support. Many colonists held opinions similar to the Gloucester petitioners, prioritizing the defense of home and family over partisan struggles. The Lancaster militia refused to join Bacon's offensive because of "the Dayly affrights and feares of the Indians Dayly seene amongst us," which required them to stay close to home. Bacon's resort to conspiracy theory was partially a bid to give the Volunteer movement coherence. On August 3, Bacon held a convention at Middle Plantation. His followers used threats to oblige prominent planters to attend and locked them in the meeting house. After a fractious debate, the convention produced a "mischievous writing," as the royal commissioners described it, which argued that civil conflict was entirely the fault of Berkeley and his faction. The governor and his "evill Councellors," it read, "hath actually Commanded, fomented and stirred up the People . . . to Civill Warrs." Berkeley's treason forced the Volunteer military to abandon its struggle against Natives, enabling "the horrid outrages and Murders daily Committed in many parts of the Country by the Barbarous Enimy." Therefore, "it is Consistent to our Allegiance to his most sacred Majesty for us . . . to the uttermost of our power to oppose" Berkeley and his forces. The declaration transformed fear into outrage and mobilized that outrage to fuel the Volunteer movement. Signed by almost seventy leading men, it depicted Bacon as a lawfully commissioned general and Berkeley as a criminal subversive, turning a bombastic conspiracy theory into a platform for regime change. According to its inverted logic, the only way to maintain law and order in Virginia was to overthrow its government.[27]

The conspiracy theory framed Berkeley's attempts to suppress rebellion as proof of his villainous agenda. Government forces stripped forts of munitions so they would not fall into rebel hands, including the York River frontier fort whose arsenal was earmarked to combat Susquehannocks. According to John Cotton, Berkeley thus disarmed "the most conciderablest fortris in the countrey" and left the heartland around Jamestown open to Indigenous assault. From his headquarters at John Custis's Arlington estate in Northampton County, Berkeley managed to recruit only forty gentlemen, not nearly enough to match the hundreds of armed Volunteers. Instead he enlisted tributary Accomacs from the Eastern Shore, armed them with guns taken from the York fort, and prepared to send them against the rebels. This shocking news "did stager a grate many, otherways well inclined to Sir William." It was the nightmare scenario of wild conspiracy theories come true. Elizabeth Weldinge, a neighbor of Sarah and William Drummond, lamented "The Governor hath given the Accomac Armies free plunder," convinced that "we are all utterly undone . . . we shall all be made slaves." To English listeners saturated in the culture of antipopery, "slavery" was the consequence of arbitrary rule and the thirst for absolute power; for Virginians it also evoked the plight of growing numbers of enslaved Africans. Sarah Drummond, one of the most militant voices in the Volunteer movement, exploited these fears. She proclaimed that Berkeley, with five hundred Indians at his back, "has declared he will kill man woman and child, and give away what they had" to Indians as a reward for slaughtering colonists. In a society largely composed of indentured servants who labored under the thumb of rapacious oligarchs and former servants who scratched their way to freedom only to scramble for the oligarchs' scraps, this narrative tapped into visceral fears and resentments. For any colonist who would not be reduced to slavery, there was no other choice: they had to unseat the governor. In Drummond's hands, conspiracy theory was a tool for transferring anti-Indian sentiment into momentum for revolution.[28]

Despite its momentum, the Volunteer movement began to buckle under the weight of its own ideological commitments. If foreign Indians, tributary Indians, and the colonial government were actually a single enemy, the Volunteers had to wage war on three fronts. But leaders disagreed about which enemy was more dangerous. Some, including Bacon, wanted to focus on Indigenous enemies. However, his insistence that Indians were "all alike" and strident commitment to "ruine . . . all Manner of Trade and Commerce with them" alienated prominent Volunteers Sarah Grendon and William Byrd, who preferred to expand trade rather than destroy it. Some believed that reestablishing a functioning government should be the priority during a time of "such Great Confusion by the dayly Murder Rapines and Deprivations of the Barbarous Indians, and the People in all parts of the Country Crying out for help." Several Volunteer leaders argued that Berkeley could be isolated and ignored, and they sent orders for counties to elect burgesses for a revolutionary assembly on September 4. Others considered Berkeley the primary threat. Giles Bland, a royal agent who had clashed with Berkeley over customs duties, believed the Volunteers' resources should be devoted to naval supremacy, an invasion of the Eastern Shore, and the destruction of Berkeley's forces. A few had more grandiose visions. Sarah Drummond, representing a radical splinter of the Volunteer movement, went so far as to advocate the overthrow of the monarchy and the declaration of Virginian independence. In public meetings she proclaimed, "we can build ships and trade to any part of the world we pleased," and promised that "the child that is unborn shall have cause to rejoice for the good that will come yet by the rising of the country." Her republican spirit, however, clashed with the royalism of most Volunteers—including Bacon himself—who sent manifestos to England hoping to convince the king that they fought in his name.[29]

Although the Volunteers' conspiracy theory was far more elaborate than their opponents', Berkeley's faction mobilized the same rhetorical arsenal to destabilize the wobbly coalition of rebels. Officers of the nascent revolutionary government kidnapped the families of accused traitors and plundered their estates. Nicholas Spencer asserted that there was little difference between Bacon's rabble and the Indians he purported to oppose, "either can I say which is most to be feared, for as the Indians are A Barborous Enimie, so there is not less of savageness in the nature of most of his followers." William Sherwood argued that the Volunteers' real goal was not to protect the people but to profit by sowing chaos. He wrote that enemy Indians, "takeing advantage of these civill comotions, have comitted many horred murders . . . not onely in the fronteere Countys, but in the inward Countys," while Volunteers confiscated the weapons that householders needed to defend their families. Philip Ludwell, decrying the "violent pressures of unreasonable men," asserted this was part of a chilling conspiracy to take over the colony by a military coup. Bacon intentionally left the frontiers defenseless, allowing Indians to raze the country until the terrified people placed themselves in his hands. Government partisans inverted the Volunteer narrative but made the same argument: Indian raids and civil war were part of the same malign plot.[30]

The baroque extravagance of dueling conspiracy theories made it difficult for colonists to sort through competing claims to truth. John Cotton described the results of one propaganda campaign, writing that colonists "became so much destracted in there ressalutions, that they could not tell, at present, which way to turn them selves; while there tongues expressed no other language but what sounded forth feares, wishes, and execrations, as their apprehentions, or affections, dictated." Many fell to despair, "lookeing upon them selves as a people utterly undon, being equally exposed to the Governours displeasure, and the Indians bloody cruillties," while they struggled to keep from "drownding in the whirle poole of confuseion." While conspiracy theory mobilized some for political action, in others it produced only cognitive dismay.[31]

Faced with a narrative that presented a totalizing explanation for the chaos but mandated different solutions, the Volunteers broke into separate groups. Three hundred men under Giles Bland and William Carver launched a naval campaign against government holdouts on the Eastern Shore. Forces under Bacon marched toward the falls of the James River, "in prosecution of his first pretentions which were against the Occanechees and Susquahanoks." Another force, under Giles Brent Jr., patrolled the northern counties. Bacon switched direction mid-march toward the freshes of the York River, probably recognizing that a quick victory against tributary Algonquians would do more for his reputation than a trek beyond the frontier in search of elusive Susquehannocks. Conspiracy theory had done its work: no one dissented from the assumption that Algonquians were part of a general plot against the English. As the commissioners later wrote, "among the vulgar itt Matters not whether they be friends or foes soe they be Indians."[32]

Conspiracy theories always require an enemy other, an antagonist that serves as the antithesis of the theorists. The sprawling inclusiveness of the conspiracy often casts these others as figures of enormous influence. Some of those who come under the scrutiny of the conspiratorial gaze are indeed people in positions of authority: governors, proprietors, and oligarchs. The command of such men over the levers of political power is obvious; the theory merely embroiders their actual power with fantasies of its almost infinite reach. However, not all others are the grandees of society. Conspiratorial thinking often fixates on religious, national, or ethnic minorities who are among society's most disempowered members. In a terrible irony, the people supposed to be spectacularly powerful are actually marginalized and unprotected. In contrast to the secret puppeteers pulling the strings of history, whose commanders are perpetually beyond the grasp of crusading reformers, minorities live right next door, agonizingly vulnerable. When populist insurgents take aim at a far-reaching conspiracy, it is usually demonized others who become their victims.[33]

We might reasonably expect that colonists would identify people of African descent as the source of their fears. Fears of slave conspiracies were endemic in the sugar-growing islands of the Caribbean, where enslaved Africans outnumbered English colonists by as much as two to one. In 1675, authorities on Barbados preempted an alleged "damnable Designe . . . of the Negroes to destroy us all" by arresting, torturing, and executing dozens of suspects. Colonists harbored such fears because actual revolts were a fact of life. In early 1676, "rebellious Negroes" wreaked havoc on Jamaica and escaped into the northern mountains, forcing English militia to battle insurgent maroons. As the Time of Anarchy unfolded, seaborne traffic brought news of these uprisings and plotted uprisings to Virginia and elsewhere in the English Atlantic. It is therefore striking that no one in Virginia breathed a word of worry about black rebellion in 1676. Quite the opposite: both sides put guns into black hands. Berkeley declared that "all Sarvants"—presumably including servants of African descent—"should be set free" if they "would (in Arms) owne the Governours cause." Bacon upped the ante and "proclaimed liberty to all servants and negroes"—including enslaved Africans—if they fought for the Volunteers. There is no evidence of black flight from their plantations or reprisals against their masters, and no evidence that masters worried that there would be. In a moment when rumors made even the wildest plots seem plausible and everyone seemed to be conspiring against someone, no one on any side expressed the slightest concern about slave conspiracies. Instead, colonists fixated on the "protected and Darling Indians" who allegedly played the part of "honest quiet neighbours" as a mask for their barbarous intentions.[34]

Just as conspiracy theories coursed through English communities, we can safely assume that they coursed through Native communities. Unfortunately, the sources do not offer any glimpse of Indigenous forms of conspiracism. But the theory did not have to be that complicated. Unlike settlers, whose own imaginations were part of the problem, tributary Natives could not possibly doubt that powerful enemies were orchestrating their destruction when Nathaniel Bacon was broadcasting his genocidal intentions. Tributary Natives thus found themselves in an impossible bind. With rival factions claiming to be the legitimate regime, there was no way that they could prove their loyalty. Attempts to do so, such as Cockacoeske's contribution to the war effort against Susquehannocks or the Accomacs' support for Berkeley, only fed conspiratorial thinking that connected the government to a larger Indian plot. Attempts to aid the Volunteers likewise backfired, as the Occaneechis learned the hard way. Some Natives advocated armed resistance, but leaders such as Cockacoeske realized this would almost certainly lead to disaster and did everything in their power to restrain angry voices among their people. The royal commissioners wrote that she did "as much as she could to decline all occasion of offendinge the English, whome she ever soe much loved and reverenced." They went so far as to claim that she exhorted "her own Indians that if they found the English coming upon them that they should neither fire Gun nor draw an arrow upon them." The devolution of power among contending colonial factions left Algonquians with few options but to hide in the remote marshlands.[35]

The Volunteer invasion of the Great Dragon Swamp illustrates the harrowing precarity of tributary Algonquians. Swampy ground and torrential rains bogged down the Volunteers, leaving them hungry, wet, and miserable. On their own ground, Algonquians were able to escape the marauders, though not without cost. Pamunkey sentries warned one camp of approaching Volunteer scouts. Most Algonquians escaped, but Volunteers took an old woman and a child captive. When they forced the elder, a confidant of Cockacoeske, to serve as guide, she led them in circles for several days until Bacon realized the deception, killed her, and dumped her body in the waters. The Volunteers, "marchinge after this att Randome," stumbled upon a second camp, "where Severall Nations of the Indians laye," but again most Natives escaped. Only one Nanzatico woman, so malnourished that she could not walk, was taken captive. Bacon finally discovered the main Algonquian refuge, "a fine piece of Champion land" with open fields and scattered thickets. Algonquians scattered upon the Volunteers' approach but they were "followed by Bacon and his forces, Killinge and taking them Prisoners." Eight were cut down as they fled. The Volunteers took forty-five captives and plundered the nation's accumulated wealth: £700 worth of wampum, matchcoats, linens, and other treasures. Cockacoeske took the hand of a ten-year-old boy and ran, stumbling over the bodies of her kinfolk, heading deep into the marshes. Struck with terror and "fearinge their cruelty," the pair wandered for two weeks surviving on brackish water and the carcasses of wild turtles before they reunited with their community.[36]

The Algonquians' ruin gave Bacon the "victory" that he craved, and he cynically exploited their suffering as the civil war turned hot. The miserable slog through the Great Dragon Swamp had caused many Volunteers to desert, leaving only a core of 136 men who were "tyred, Murmuringe, Impatient, hunger starv'd, dissatisfied." Meanwhile, Berkeley's forces dismantled Bland's navy, took Jamestown, and defiantly reissued the proclamation that branded the Volunteers rebels. Bacon abandoned the frontier out of necessity and drummed up support by playing the part of a conqueror. Despite the low numbers of Indian casualties, "Bacon brag'd of many more to please and deceive the People, with a mighty Conquest." Colonists, "seeing the Indian Captives which they led along as in a shew of Triumph," flocked to his banner by the hundreds. This display of his patriarchal potency reportedly attracted "women telling him if he wanted assistance they would come themselves after him." The sight of Algonquians tied in halters, frightened and helpless, must have felt empowering to colonists who had spent months in fear of Indian attack. As rebel forces dug defensive earthworks for a siege of Jamestown, Volunteer captain William Cookeson wrote, "wee shewed them our Indian Captives upon the workes." Algonquians, lashed to the ramparts, stood beside a number of women, "all the prime mens wives, whose Husbands were with the Governour," who had been kidnapped to serve as human shields "upon the top of the smalle worke." The humiliation of loyalist women was meant to emasculate the men who could not protect them, just as the captive Algonquians demonstrated the government's impotence. The tableau drew a symbolic equivalence between English conspirators and Native enemies: if Berkeley and his faction insisted on defending their "Darling Indians," then the two would ultimately share the same fate.[37]

In the rebels' fleeting zenith, Volunteer forces captured Jamestown on September 19 and burned the town to prevent it from falling back into Berkeley's hands. However, weeks of wilderness marching and siege warfare in the heat and heavy rains took their toll. Bacon contracted typhus and died in October after a protracted period of delirium and diarrhea. As loyalists delighted to point out, the germ who spread the contagion of rebellion was himself consumed by disease after "god . . . infected his blood." The death of the Volunteers' charismatic leader led to the movement's fragmentation as "the faction began to fall into severall parties and opinions." Sarah Drummond remained committed to the doomed dream of an independent commonwealth. Her husband William Drummond lost influence by committing the sin of compromise, advocating reconciliation with Berkeley's faction. Giles Brent proved more opportunist than revolutionary, switching sides multiple times until his men deserted, "they being," explained John Cotton, "obliged to looke after their owne concernes and lives." Bacon's supposed successor, Joseph Ingram, never gained much popular support. Perhaps he lost the people's favor because he moved away from Bacon's extremist anti-Indian platform, ordering that Pamunkey captives be "restored to the Queen" and directing his lieutenants to make "full restitution of what they had plundered . . . from the Indians." With the Volunteers divided, government forces gradually gained the upper hand and isolated rebel garrisons throughout the colony. The few who remained committed to fighting the Indian-government conspiracy could not wage two wars at the same time and fell one by one.[38]

Rebels continued to fight for a multitude of causes, some intensely personal, others because they had nothing left to lose. For many of Virginia's servants and enslaved people, the rebellion offered their last hope of freedom. When Bacon promised liberty for military service, several hundred unfree people leapt at the chance. They proved to be the doomed rebellion's most desperate adherents. One of the last rebel garrisons, "foure hundred English and Negroes in Armes" at West Point, laid down their guns only after "they were all pardoned and freed from their Slavery." Another group of holdouts, twenty servants and eighty enslaved Africans, stood together until the duplicity of loyalist Thomas Grantham forced them to surrender rather than face certain death. They were all forced to return to their masters. At least one free man of African descent, a "Mulatto" man of property named Edward Lloyd, chose the Volunteer cause, and his family paid the price. Berkeley's officers imprisoned Lloyd and plundered his house. Two midwives testified that Berkeley's men "affrighted" his pregnant wife, who "forthwith fell in labour and in a most sad and Deplorable Condition dyed" with "a Child Still borne." It is difficult to say how many other black Virginians faced similar struggles. During the entire rebellion, these are the only slivers of evidence about people of African descent.[39]

To the very end of the rebellion, anti-Indigenous sentiment remained the heart of the Volunteer movement. For at least one colonist, the conviction that Indigenous peoples were an existential threat fueled a hatred that transcended the fear of death and even trumped any thought of family. When government troops laid siege to a rebel garrison commanded by Stephen Mannering, entreating him to surrender for his wife's sake, he responded, "God dam my wife." He fought, said Mannering as he stared down the enemy's guns, "to destroy the heathen, and if it were to doe againe he would doe it." The mixed-race garrison at West Point was also driven by opposition to Native peoples. Historians have often romanticized this moment of interracial resistance in the rebellion's fading light, assuming that it was an expression of solidarity among laboring peoples against exploitative masters. Their actions certainly demonstrate that they were willing to cooperate to achieve liberation, but scholars should not be too eager to see this standing together as a tragically lost opportunity. According to John Cotton, the men of the West Point garrison, both black and white, placed a condition on their surrender: that they "were still to be retained in Arms, if they so pleased, against the Indians." The sources are too slender to offer much insight into their motivations, and we might imagine that black Volunteers did not share English colonists' violent antipathy toward Native peoples. On the other hand, perhaps they did: black men and women would not have been spared the terror of Susquehannock raids and all of its effects. But whereas English fears were instrumental to mobilizing mass action, for people of African descent, personal feelings were less important than structural constraints. Any black man who wanted to take up Bacon's offer of freedom for military service, regardless of his opinion about Indigenous peoples, would have had to commit to the cause that animated the Volunteer movement from its inception: the destruction of the Indians. For the West Point garrison, that is what interracial solidarity meant. Their stipulation forces us to confront an uncomfortable feature of American settler colonialism: liberty and opportunity, for black people as well as white, were often predicated on Indigenous dispossession and disappearance.[40]

Conspiracy theory, like the contagion of rebellion that colonial authorities feared, did not respect boundaries. The conspiratorial fears that drove civil disorder and Anglo-Indian war in Virginia jumped along rivers, roads, and shipping lanes, spreading to neighboring colonies. During the passage, the supposed conspiracy mutated into forms that plugged into local political struggles. The Complaint from Heaven was written in Maryland and focused on longstanding grievances against the Calverts' proprietary rule, but the authors appropriated the energies driving rebellion in Virginia. They claimed to speak for the peoples of both colonies with a "petition out of Virginia and Maryland," and their indictment conflated the misrule of "the Barklian and Baltimorian Partys," as though the Chesapeake were governed by a single fell regime. They explained Berkeley's opposition to the Volunteers as the work of Jesuit secret agents, who "prevayled with the Virginians . . . by advising Sir Will Barkly." Lord Baltimore plotted with these collaborators to "Overturne Virginia" and "yoak the inhabitants" to his arbitrary rule, which only a rising in both colonies could prevent. The Complaint turned these separate outbreaks of civil disorder into a single struggle.[41]

Once news of the rebellion reached London, imperial officials created a cordon to contain the upheaval before it "spread its infection into the Neighbouring Plantations." Secretary of State Henry Coventry issued orders for governors to cease all traffic with Virginia "to prevent the Contagion of so bad an example in other Colonies" and the admiralty issued interdiction orders to ships of the royal navy. The embargo deepened an information blackout that already plagued Maryland, whose council could not even be sure of who was in charge of the Virginia government. In early August, Thomas Notley lamented, "our neighbours the Virginians are so embroyled with Domestick and intestine troubles besides the Indian Warr that Wee can have no correspondency with the Goverment there." Attempts to send messages to trusted sources failed, though news and rumor accompanied loyalist refugees. Thomas Ludwell reported, "most of the better sort are flying said to be retired to maryland or on board some shipps in potomeck river." Exiles no doubt carried plenty of alarming reports about Volunteer activities, which encouraged proprietary officials to believe the worst.[42]

The wisps of rumor that floated across the Potomac fed the Calvert faction's conspiratorial fears. On August 6, the council wrote to Lord Baltimore that Nathaniel Bacon "intends to embroyle your province in a Warr." The alleged plot centered on the rebel commander Giles Brent Jr., "a halfe Indian" son of Mary Kittamaquund, daughter of the Piscataway tayac during the time of Maryland's founding. Kittamaquund had lived in the Jesuit mission and received a Catholic education. At the age of eleven, she was married to Giles Brent Sr., an early member of Lord Baltimore's inner circle who later became a bitter rival. According to rumors, Brent intended to lead rebel forces across the river, not just to "kindle the fire" of the Volunteer cause but also to assert "his vaine title to his mothers Crowne and Scepter of Pascattaway"—in other words, to usurp Maryland by claiming his birthright as scion of the Piscataway royal family. There is no evidence that Brent harbored these ambitions, and the Calverts had a poor grasp of Algonquian matrilineal inheritance: Mary Kittamaquund derived no power from her tayac father and neither could her son. Nevertheless, the council believed that Brent's dynastic designs were tangled in a larger conspiracy. They charged that Bacon was manipulating the "young Giles Brent" to "make the pursuit of the Pascattaway Indians his pretence to enter" Maryland. Once Bacon rallied "all the needy and desperate persons" behind his anti-Indian crusade, he would overthrow the Calvert regime. They considered this scenario plausible enough to commission John Coode as commander of a small navy to patrol the Potomac and repel the "invasion of any Robbers, Pyrates, Spies, or others that shall attempt any thing against this his Lordships Province," and instructed ranger captains to oppose "any men in Armes" who did not possess "lycence from the Goverment of this Province to enter this province." While the Calverts braced for Susquehannock incursions and local insurrections, conspiracy theory led them to mobilize scarce resources to repulse invasions from Virginia.[43]

Conspiracy theory also spread the Time of Anarchy farther south, into the borderlands between Virginia and Albemarle. Fiercely independent colonists in Albemarle worried that William Berkeley, one of the eight Lords Proprietors of Carolina and the oligarch that most of them had crossed the Great Dismal Swamp to escape, would soon become their undisputed overlord. Between 1672 and 1674, Berkeley negotiated with the other Lords Proprietors to sell his share in the sugar-growing districts of southern Carolina for sole proprietorship of Albemarle. A campaign to subdue what he considered an unruly collection of runaways and pirates would inevitably have followed this transfer. Although the deal never went through, colonists prepared for resistance. In late 1675, antiproprietary partisan Patrick Jackson exchanged messages with William Drummond, former Albemarle governor and personal enemy of William Berkeley, to coordinate intercolonial opposition. Proprietary agent Thomas Miller publicly denounced Jackson. Miller's ally Thomas Eastchurch orchestrated a coup to depose the ruling governor, John Jenkins. In March 1676, antiproprietary forces led by Joanna Jenkins, George Durant, and John Culpeper, launched an "Action of Consperacy." They freed Jenkins, arrested Miller for "treasonable words," and forced Eastchurch to flee to England. Catching wind of the troubles, Berkeley ordered Albemarle colonists to send Miller "into Virginia for tryall before . . . Sir William Berkeley and Counsell." In June, the council acquitted Miller and allowed him to return to England. Despite this political defeat for antiproprietary forces, however, the chaotic state of the Virginia assembly allowed Culpeper to meet with Drummond in secret, pledge support for a Volunteer regime, and link the anti-Berkeley struggles in the two colonies.[44]

Intercolonial conspiracies became entangled in the Susquehannock scattering, with incendiary results. As civil war between Volunteers and government forces heated up in the summer of 1676, growing numbers of insurrectionists crossed the border. They built solidarity among colonists separated by geography but united in opposition to Berkeley's rule. Volunteer John Goode, in a confession after his surrender, claimed that Bacon declared his intention to combine the struggles of "Maryland, and Caro-

lina" to "cast off their Governours." After rebel fortunes waned and government troops picked off garrisons south of the James River, some Volunteers resolved to "retire to Roanoake . . . as a fit place to retire to for refuge"
and continue their armed struggle. Partisans traveling between Albemarle
refuges and Virginia battlefields, along trade paths between the Great
Dismal Swamp and the Chowan River, would have marched near the new
Susquehannock and Meherrin settlements on the eastern fringes of Chowanoke country. The sources offer few clues about what exactly happened.
Defeated rebels may have been angry, or afraid, or hungry for vengeance.
Perhaps they surprised Susquehannocks and Meherrins as they tended ripening fields of corn and angled for catfish and perch. Perhaps stealthy Indian sentries, determined to defend their new homes, ambushed militiamen
as they hefted heavy muskets through mud and clinked powder-filled ban-
doliers through the hushed fens. However it started, the result was what
proprietary agent Timothy Biggs called "a warr with the Indians."[45]

By late 1676, the Susquehannock-Virginia War had sprawled into the
southern borderlands and drawn other Indigenous nations into the conflict.
Chowanokes entered the war, either because Susquehannocks and Meherrins appealed for their protection or because settlers preemptively attacked them on the theory that all Natives were alike in their hostility. Just
as terrified colonists in Virginia suspected allied Indians of conspiracy and
antagonized them until their theories became reality, it is plausible that Albemarle colonists would have jumped to the conclusion that Chowanokes
were complicit in Susquehannock violence. Thomas Miller, who declined
to draw distinctions between Indigenous nations, later recalled, "the
Indians . . . in 76 had committed sundry murders and depredations upon
some of the inhabitants." Once Anglo-Indian violence erupted, fed by fear,
it spread according to its own viral logic. The Quaker traveler William
Edmundson wrote in his journal that Indians not only "did mischief and
murdered several," but also "haunted much in the wilderness between
Virginia and Carolina, so that scarce any durst travel that way unarmed."
The fighting lasted well into 1677.[46]

The Albemarle government, now in the hands of the antiproprietary faction headed by John Jenkins and Joanna Jenkins, could not remedy the
contagion of Anglo-Indian violence. Great distances between settlements—
in some cases twenty miles from one plantation to the next—made communication difficult and military coordination nearly impossible. John Jenkins was declared "Generalissime" but he lacked an effective army or a
legal commission from the Lords Proprietors. Combined with the series of
recent regime changes, many colonists were hesitant to follow an executive of poor efficacy and dubious legitimacy. Making matters worse, some

of Jenkins's supporters were wildcat traders with few scruples about smuggling "powder, shot and fire-armes" to "those Indian nations that are not . . . in amity with the English," leaving the colony desperately short of munitions. George Durant, whom his enemies described as "the most active and uncontrolable" of "all the factious persons in the Country" and the real power in the Jenkins regime, organized a convoy to sell the current crop of tobacco and return to supply "the Country with Arms and Amunition for their defence Against the Heathen." Unfortunately, his transatlantic journey took more than a year to complete. In the meantime, sporadic involvement with the civil war in Virginia heightened factional divisions in Albemarle. According to Thomas Miller the result was chaos. In the midst of an Indian war that should have united colonists, Albemarle was in "a miserable confusion by reason of Sundry factions amongst them."[47]

Conspiracy theory, despite its virulent spread in 1676, was not a universal malady. As the cases of Virginia, Maryland, and Albemarle demonstrate, rebellions occurred when longstanding discontents became entwined with the Susquehannock scattering. Yet New York managed to establish an effective quarantine against the contagion of violence despite fertile conditions for its spread. Colonists in the Delaware Valley had experienced four regime changes in twenty years, the most recent occurring in 1674 on the eve of the Time of Anarchy. Ethnic tensions divided English colonists from older waves of Dutch, Swedes, Finns, and Germans. The legacies of previous legal regimes created ample spaces for disputes over political jurisdictions, economic rights, and religious liberties. Natives under English rule watched as settlers in New England and the Chesapeake, convinced of a massive Indigenous conspiracy, turned on their Indian subjects, and naturally wondered if they would be next. Despite these volatile circumstances, Governor Edmund Andros managed the tensions between Natives and settlers, preventing fear, suspicion, and mistrust from spreading. New York's example shows that Anglo-Indian violence was a necessary factor in creating colonial crisis. The places where Indigenous peoples and English colonists remained at peace were the same places where conspiracy theories failed to gain traction and populist defiance faltered instead of spawning rebellion.[48]

Andros's proprietary regime encountered several challenges at the same time that conflicts in neighboring colonies reached epidemic proportions. In June 1676, disgruntled Dutch colonists on Manhattan spread rumors that King Charles II was dead and England was embroiled in civil war. Former WIC soldier Albert Hendricksz claimed "there would come ships here in short time from Holland to take this place" and transform it back to New Netherland. In Rensselaerswyck, Jacob Leisler and Jacob Milbourn denounced the Dutch Reformed minister Nicholaes van Rensselaer for heretical preaching, creating what Andros called "the great distraction" among the Dutch population. Because Andros had appointed van Rensselaer on the Duke of York's instructions, the confessional dispute was also a protest against English rule. In Albany, a crowd led by Jan Conell and Dirck Bradt staged a theatrical mockery of English officers, dressing up as the notorious Indian-killer Samuel Mosely and claiming their army of three hundred men would "drive away and kill the Indians on the river." In an ominous parallel to the Virginian Volunteers, whose antagonism to tributary Natives turned allies into enemies, the rioters' threats had "come to the ears of the Indians and caused a hasty departure or flight among them." In West Jersey, where overlapping patents and settlement by religious dissenters had fostered pugnacious resistance to proprietary authority since 1665, a Quaker coalition headed by John Fenwick crossed the line into open insurrection. Brandishing Indian deeds and a patent purchased from the former proprietor, Lord John Berkeley, he dispossessed prominent landholders near Salem. "Ryotously and Routously with Force and armes," Fenwick's followers "pulled down and destroyed some building and Dwelling." He then issued new land grants, ignoring patents issued by the Duke of York. Fenwick denied that Andros possessed any authority over West Jersey and effectively declared independence.[49]

Andros and his agents put down each of these challenges. In July, Hendricksz was arrested and tried for sedition. He recanted with the weak—and, according to eyewitnesses, false—excuse that he was so drunk he could not remember saying anything treasonous, "but was sorry if hee spake any such things." Andros applied carrot and stick to Leisler, demanding "suficient security" to guarantee good behavior, while Captain Thomas Delavall and local magistrates judiciously worked to "asuage and prevent all animosity" in the Dutch Reformed congregation. The Albany court prosecuted Conell and Bradt as "disturbers of the public peace, as concocters of lies and circulators of false rumors." The ringleaders admitted their guilt, claiming they intended only "to play some pranks" and "it was not done with such evil intention." The court's swift action reassured wary Natives that New York would stand by its promises of protection. Officers in New Castle arrested Fenwick and sent him to Manhattan for trial in January 1677. Despite Fenwick's vigorous resistance, insisting that only the king had the authority to judge the validity of his patent, his followers' direct action subsided in his absence.[50]

Susquehannock initiatives prompted a different sort of challenge from Andros's own subordinates. Susquehannock ambassadors, after making a peace offering to the Maryland government in July, extended their efforts toward leaders in the Delaware Valley. Ferrying messages through their friend Jacob, ambassadors invited Edmund Cantwell, deputy governor of New Castle, to meet near Palmers Island in August. Cantwell did not follow Andros's instructions to encourage Susquehannocks to become tributaries of New York and instead traveled secretly with Jacob to the mouth of the Susquehanna. The sachems "requested a peace and trade as formerly with the English"—the English, that is, in the Delaware Valley, a center of Susquehannock political and commercial energy throughout the seventeenth century, and not with the English of New York. Given the network of alliances in Delaware that had previously made Gandastogue a regional power, the sachems probably envisioned reviving intercultural trade as an important step toward securing Susquehannock independence. Cantwell, who was in such desperate financial straits from land speculation that he begged Andros for money "that I may once Com out of Debt," no doubt saw an opportunity for personal enrichment even if it meant subverting Andros's desire for a subordinate Susquehannock nation.[51]

Unfortunately for Cantwell, rumors of Anglo-Indian violence wrecked his schemes. Shortly after the Palmers Island meeting, Maryland trader Augustine Herrman wrote to Cantwell conveying "suspicion of a familyes being cutt off by the Indyans." Cantwell mobilized the militia and placed the region's inhabitants on guard, perhaps hoping to prevent colonists' fears from running amok. Rather than reassure anyone, it "gave an Alarum throughout the River." When the rumored killings turned out to be false, Andros castigated Cantwell for "making so rash an Alarum" and carelessly spreading panic. This incident is probably what alerted Andros to Cantwell's plot to broker a separate peace with the Susquehannocks. His response was swift and decisive. On September 23, Andros dissolved Delaware's government. He swept away existing institutions, replaced the legal code with the same "Duke's Laws" that governed New York, and reorganized the hodgepodge of localities into three court jurisdictions. Andros dismissed Cantwell in disgrace and appointed a new cast of officials, from John Collier as the new deputy governor down to local justices of the peace. One of their first acts was to replace skittish militiamen with professional soldiers, "not only for the Ease of the People, but also for the Reputation of the Government and Concidering that this is a frontier place." With governments everywhere falling because frontier people felt unprotected, reputation was everything.[52]

This intercolonial intrigue, with plots spanning from New York to Maryland, aimed to contain the potentially destabilizing influence of the Susquehannock scattering. Cantwell had inadvertently alerted Andros that cooperation between independent Susquehannocks and rogue colonists threatened his plans for a chain of Indian alliances. Andros's instructions to the newly appointed Collier illustrate how important he considered Susquehannocks to his vision. Out of six enumerated directives, four emphasized "The Suscahannaes are to bee [treated] also friendly, and some of them (as many as will) to come to mee," and coached Collier on diplomatic methods of minimizing Maryland's interference. In a letter to acting governor Notley, Andros argued that New York's control of peacemaking was in everyone's best interest. He had "some Interest with the Maques and Senniques, which can best deale with them," and therefore was in a position to offer "all assurances, for their future comport, and not any wayes to injure any English."[53]

Andros placed such a high priority on peace with the Susquehannocks because he understood, after watching every colony around him consumed by the ravages of rebellion and Anglo-Indian war, that even small incidents of violence could inflame long-simmering discontents. If the Susquehannock scattering had provoked fighting in New York, any of the minor revolts of 1676 might have spun out of control. Anglo-Indian bloodshed would have offered Hendricksz, Leisler, Conell, and Fenwick opportunities to play on colonists' fears and invoke the politics of patriarchal failure to challenge Andros's government, just as it had offered opportunities to Volunteers in Virginia. Any attempt Andros made to defuse the situation would likely have fed rumors of secret dealings, as dissidents had whispered of the Calverts in Maryland. His relationships with Native leaders and commitment to keeping diplomatic channels open would undoubtedly have spawned conspiracy theories that he was more loyal to Indians than colonists, allowing challengers to condemn him for cruelty, corruption, and arbitrary rule. In fact, that is exactly what happened a few years later, during King William's War (1688–1697), when Anglo-Indian violence spawned conspiracy theories and a rising tide of unrest that led to Andros's downfall and ultimately to revolution.[54]

Although conspiracy theory often propels conflict, if fashioned the right way it can also promote reconciliation. After the Restoration in 1660, Edward Hyde, Earl of Clarendon and favored councilor of King Charles II, explained the chaos of the recent civil war as the product of a conspiracy. "The number of those who really intended these prodigious alterations was very inconsiderable," he wrote in his multivolume history of the upheaval. With so few "really" implicated in wrongdoing, it was best for everyone to put the past behind them. In one of the first acts of his reign, Charles II issued an act of indemnity and oblivion that conveyed his wish "to bury all Seeds of future Discords and remembrance . . . as well in His owne Breast as in the Breasts of His Subjects one towards another." The king and his councilors asked all parties to suppress their anger, promoting national healing through a willful act of forgetting that rested on an official conspiracy theory. The king's agents in the colonies followed the same template.[55]

On January 29, 1677, a royal commission sailed into the Chesapeake at the head of an expeditionary force of a thousand red-coated troops. Berkeley's forces had crushed the rebellion's last remnants but the commissioners—Herbert Jeffreys, Sir John Berry, and Francis Moryson— still had a mandate to investigate the causes of the rebellion and restore order to the colony. In an address to the assembly convened in February, the commissioners lamented the malady that ravaged the body politic. Noting "the present distempered Condition and constitution of the generall Body of the People," they implored the burgesses "thoroughly to inspect and search fully into the depths, and yet hidden roote and sourse of this late Rebellious Distemper, that hath broke forth and beene so contagious and spreading over the whole Country." The commissioners charged the assembly "effectually to stanch and heale the fresh and bleeding Woundes these unnaturall Warrs and Rebellions have caused among you; that there may bee as few and small scars and markes remane." As imperial agents bearing a royal proclamation of indemnity and pardon, they emphasized the need for reconciliation.[56]

The commissioners' final report, "A True Narrative of the Rise, Progresse, and Cessation of the late Rebellion in Virginia," provided an official history of the insurrection. They claimed that their goal was to produce an objective narrative. They wrote in the introduction, "wee have imployed our best endeavours to informe ourselves . . . by the most knowing, credible and indifferent Persons" and "a strict Inquiry, observation, examination and the most probable impartial Reports." Everything else was thrown out because they "rejected whatever wee found or suspected to be false." The commissioners were not, of course, presenting an objective truth that already existed. They were creating a politically convenient narrative through the selection and arrangement of facts. Their history, like all histories, was an artifact constructed out of fragments of evidence, many of them contradictory, most of them inconsistent, and all of them colored by partisan bias. Their narrative, like all narratives, fashioned the chaos of recent events into a comprehensible plot. The plot they chose was a conspiracy theory.[57]

The commissioners' "True Narrative" took the shape of a parabolic arc: the beginning and end of a scheme that mapped onto the rise and fall of its mastermind, Nathaniel Bacon. He made an appealingly colorful villain: a rakish aristocrat running to America to escape the taint of scandal; an atheistic alchemist pursuing "mistique imployments" in the wilderness; an ambitious firebrand indulging a thirst for power by using Susquehannock raids as an excuse to raise an army and engineer a coup. Some of Bacon's followers "were deluded and drawn into Bacons Party," misled by cunningly crafted lies so they "knew not what they did." He swayed others through charismatic performance and seductive charm. Many more were intimidated into joining his ranks, only swearing allegiance to his cause "by threats and force and feare." According to the commissioners, the groundswell of support for the Volunteers was an illusion orchestrated by a conspiracy of Bacon and his confederates. Bacon's sudden death therefore spelled an end to his rebellion. The deceived, abused, and misguided colonists simply returned to their homes in peace. Through this framing, the commissioners distilled the complexity of the Susquehannock-Virginia War and the ensuing chaos into a magnificent clarity. Voiced in the demagogic thunder of Bacon's oratory and swallowed by a frenzied crowd, the dizzying array of political motivations that drove the Volunteers vanished through narrative magic, smoothed into a story of one man's fiendish pursuit of power.[58]

Like all good conspiracy theories, the one that made Bacon into a mastermind placed secrecy and lies at the heart of the story. According to the "True Narrative," Bacon plotted the course of the rebellion behind closed doors with a small group of "severall Gentlemen," who produced their declarations in the name of the commonalty in private spaces beyond public scrutiny. While building popular support for an extralegal Indian war, Bacon "pretended and boasted what great service he would doe for the Country in destroyinge the common Enimy." His lieutenants spread this propaganda and with "such like fair Frauds he subtily and Secretly insinuated by his owne Instruments over all the Country." These methods were particularly effective on the common people. The commissioners reported that Bacon "seduced the vulgar and most ignorant People . . . soe that their whole hearts and hopes were sett now upon Bacon." Ignoring the Volunteers' diversity and the complexity of their motivations, the commissioners reduced them to a uniformly lower-class rabble and feminized their political aspirations into quivers of excitement.[59]

In the aftermath of mass insurgency, this tidy story absolved an entire population that by any reasonable standard was guilty of treason. It also paved the way for reconciliation between bitterly opposed factions by placing defeated rebels and victorious loyalists on equal ground. The guilty were only a handful of black-hearted men, most of whom had died in the fighting or were court-martialed and hanged after their surrender. The thousands who supported them conveniently remained loyal subjects of the king and innocent victims of Bacon's machinations. The commissioners' conclusion was that the rebellion was the manufactured result of a single, solitary, evil genius, whose sinister ambitions had led the country to ruin. Their conspiracy theory transformed the messy tangle of Anglo-Indian war and popular uprising into *Bacon's* Rebellion.

The conspiratorial narrative is a structure of meaning that discerns patterns among chaos, conjuring agency where no clear agent actually exists. That is how it fuels popular politics and facilitates action even in the teeth of the maelstrom. As the commissioners' narrative demonstrates, however, conspiracy theory can also make agency disappear when the agents are so numerous or so powerful that they threaten to overthrow the ruling order. The conspirator-as-subject aggregates and simplifies, becoming the personification of the movement he supposedly directs. Speaking with a singular voice and acting with a singular will, he becomes imbued with a kind of power that ordinary people can never wield themselves. But the conspirator is also singularly vulnerable. Nathaniel Bacon's fall meant the disappearance of an entire movement. Conspiracy theory is a way for people to theorize about power, but we should remember that conspiracy can just as easily be a tool for power to contain its challengers.

Despite the elegance of the commissioners' narrative, however, they could not make the Time of Anarchy disappear. Conspiracy theory had catalyzed unrest into revolt, strained the various rebel factions to the breaking point, and spread insurrection across colonial borders. "Those [who] were resolved to stir up the people to sedition," lamented Berkeley in an evocatively mixed metaphor, "like a trayne of powder as it were in a moment it enfected not only Virginia but Maryland." The violence it unleashed had repercussions that reverberated long after belligerents laid down their arms. Philip Ludwell mused, "I think the Government of this place must for some years to Come be very toylesome, or very precariouse." Not even a powerful narrative could heal the bitter divisions between colonists. More to the point, that narrative did nothing to contain the political initiatives that Susquehannocks and other Indigenous peoples continued to pursue as settlers struggled to hold their fragile political orders together. Ludwell had his doubts about the diseased body politic's ability to survive. Even if "rough medicine be tymely applyed," he did not know "how the whole body will, without Great Difficulty, be preserved From a totall dissolution." As struggles for reconciliation took center stage in 1677, it soon became apparent that without some sort of quarantine the contagion of violence would continue its inexorable spread.[60]

· 5 ·

COVENANTS

THE ANONYMOUS AUTHORS OF THE *Complaint from Heaven* finished their conspiratorial screed with an ominous postscript. The defeat of Davies's uprising had dashed the people's hopes for liberation, but this was just the close of one chapter in a larger drama. "Now begins the Second part of the late Tragedy," they wrote. The plot of the second act revolved around the wars begun by Susquehannocks. They argued that "the Offended Susquahana Indians," who "the Sinnicoes have taken into their freindship and protection," were pressing their war against Maryland's tributary Indians. Lord Baltimore's insistence on standing by the Piscataways and other tributary Indians would inevitably drag colonists into the crossfire. They concluded that the proprietary party had "left the Country in fear and dangier of a longe destructive warr"—and that war was the perfect pretext to press men into service and commandeer supplies, "to make Ritch Officers . . . and poore planters." They concluded that "the Susquehan Indians hav ben intreated for a peace, but will make none," providing the perfect excuse for Lord Baltimore to implement absolutist tyranny.[1]

Despite the authors' many leaps in logic, they shrewdly captured an insight crucial to the Time of Anarchy: it all depended on the Susquehannocks. They needed their audience to understand this cardinal fact. Their petition was not addressed to fellow colonists but to "owr great Gratious Kinge and Souveraigne CHARLES the II, King of Engeland with his parliament." Their repeated insistence on the importance of Indigenous politics was a prelude to the proposed solution: abolition of Lord Baltimore's proprietary grant and direct royal rule. Hostile Indian nations and French confederates "connivinge with Maryland papists" were "surroundinge New England, New Yorke, New jursey and delowar." The existential threat required the king to bring "these several distinct Goverments to a better concord and amity in stead of enmity . . . which a Vice Roye or Governor Generallissimo from his Majesty would Reconcile, els as there is Civill Contention, so will it at laest breake out in a Civill Warr." The Complaint's authors, in other words, continued the quest to overthrow the Baltimore regime but with manifestos instead of muskets. Indigenous peoples were central to their scheme to reshape England's American empire through royal intervention.[2]

Though nothing came of the Complaint's proposals—Lord Baltimore's presence at court allowed him to fend off attacks against his proprietorship— they illustrate the moment's extraordinary fluidity. After the runaway disintegration of order in 1676, sweeping changes, for good or ill, seemed not just possible but imminent. The following year, Indigenous and English peoples in every place touched by the Time of Anarchy devoted their energies to projects aimed at restoring peace and reconstituting their polities. Empowered by the devolution of authority, leaders emerged from unexpected quarters and grasped the opportunity to reshape the order of things. Over the course of 1677, contending factions met in a series of conferences, each one centrally concerned with Indigenous peoples. The covenants they forged, and the struggles that shaped them, remade the boundaries of political communities across the eastern seaboard. However, some advocates for change championed projects so sweeping and so radical that they faced vocal and sometimes violent opposition. The task of rebuilding shattered structures of authority would turn out to be no less vicious than the chaos of 1676.[3]

In the first conference of 1677, the scattered Susquehannocks converged to decide the future of their nation. The new leaders that emerged after the 1675 siege had been gathering their dispersed kin since at least the summer of 1676. Edmund Cantwell observed that Susquehannocks had been "comming in" to the Delaware Valley throughout July. In August, the Maryland Council noted that Gandastogue-Susquehannocks "expect the remainder of their troopes, and as many of the Western Indians neer or beyond the Mountaines as they have been able to perswade to come to live with them." In addition to these Ohio-Susquehannocks, some Virginia-Susquehannocks heeded the call. Notley surmised that some of the Susquehannocks observed in the upper Chesapeake returned because "their hopes and Condition in Virginia . . . proves desperate." Not all Susquehannocks were simply returning home, however. In early 1677, "severall troops" of Susquehannocks had "come out of Virginia," but instead of returning to their homeland they "fled to the Senuques." Their surprising choice to willingly join with enemies indicated that reconstituting Gandastogue would not be a simple matter.[4]

The most important task facing the Susquehannock bands was negotiating an end to their wars with the Haudenosaunee. Their friend Jacob played a crucial role in laying the groundwork for this peace. The Maryland Council exhorted Jacob to gather the Susquehannocks "within the Bounds of the Province," hoping much like Andros in New York that they could restore stability by making Gandastogue into a tributary nation. Jacob accepted their passports but ignored their instructions. Instead, he set himself up as mediator between warring Indigenous nations and used his own judgment to secure the Susquehannocks' future. He "sought out the said Susquehannah Indians and found them," then traveled into Iroquoia "with great Hazard of his Life." He sent reports to the council that he was making slow but steady progress, but he devoted himself to accomplishing what Maryland's leaders most feared: a détente between Susquehannocks and Haudenosaunee. In December 1676, "Sennico and Susquehannoh Indians" had "a small encounter at Jacob Young's house," a trading post near Palmers Island. By his own account, Jacob "did Succour and Assist the Susquehannah Indians" while hosting this meeting, supplying at least twenty barrels of corn and prodigious quantities of meat. The meeting went well and both sides agreed to a larger conference for peace talks. In February 1677, the magistrates of New Castle observed "the Sasquehannos . . . passing by on the bakeside," traveling up the Delaware River. Their destination was the Lenape village of Shackamaxon, an international marketplace and political hub, a place of great ceremonial and diplomatic importance where ties among peoples were created and reinforced.[5]

The Shackamaxon conference was a meeting of Indigenous nations on Indigenous ground and it unfolded according to Indigenous agendas. Europeans arrived late and achieved nothing. On March 13, the Lenape headman Renowewan appeared before the nearby court at Upland to inform them, "att present a great number of Sinnico and other Indians" were at Shackamaxon, including "the Sasquehannos and these River Indians [Lenapes]." The conference had been going on for several weeks, long enough for "a great number" of Native leaders to congregate. Although Renowewan's proposition to the Upland Court was not recorded in its terse minutes, he apparently invited them to attend the conference "for the most quiet of the River." John Collier and Unami-speaking interpreter Israel Helm traveled to Shackamaxon on March 14 and stayed for five days. Unfortunately, Collier's narrow partisanship toward New York led him to squander this opportunity. Haudenosaunee delegates representing the Onondaga and Oneida nations offered to include Maryland in a general peace for the region. Collier, following Andros's instructions to focus on getting Susquehannocks under New York's control, curtly stated that Marylanders "would make warr or peace att their owne pleasure," and pressured the Susquehannocks to accept tributary status in New York. Rebuffed, the Indigenous delegates seem to have discounted the English as important players in the conference and Collier went home empty-handed.[6]

Though the Shackamaxon conference was a failure for colonial late-comers, the conference's primary purpose was not settling Anglo-Indian relations but establishing a new order among Indigenous nations. At Shack-amaxon, the scattered bands of Susquehannocks united for the first time in more than a year. A significant portion of the conference, it seems likely, involved reconnecting these groups, which had become largely autonomous after the murder of their senior sachems in 1675. That newfound autonomy, and the rise to prominence of new leaders such as Conachoweedo, resulted in conflicting visions of their nation's future. Among the attendees were two Susquehannocks from Virginia who had "fled to the Senuques," partici-pating as part of the Haudenosaunee delegation. Representing a new con-stituency we might call Iroquoia-Susquehannocks, these men advocated the position of their Haudenosaunee hosts: all the Susquehannock bands should coalesce in Iroquoia. The proposal was peaceful but it had a sharp edge. According to Renowewan, the Haudenosaunee's intention at Shackamaxon was to "fetch the Sasquehanno," willingly if possible but by force if neces-sary. Delaware-Susquehannocks, twenty-six families in all, rejected this ul-timatum and resolved to remain among their friends in Lenapehoking. The thirty families in Gandastogue, on the other hand, agreed to abandon their connadago and join their kinfolk in Iroquoia.[7]

Although the agreement was voluntary, the Susquehannocks' relocation turned violent. On the journey north, Haudenosaunee escorts began quar-relling. Jacob reported, "being of two severall Forts"—meaning the Onon-daga and Oneida towns—they argued about how they would parcel out the Susquehannocks. The "Susquehanoes were very much displeased," re-senting the violation of Shackamaxon's conciliatory spirit. They resisted the division of their people. In the ensuing fray, "some of them got away." The Haudenosaunee overpowered most, whom they bound and carried back to Iroquoia. The emotional culture of mourning war, shared by both Susquehannocks and Haudenosaunee, determined how the captives were treated. The Haudenosaunee killed none, Jacob explained to English au-thorities ignorant of Iroquoian customs, for "it is Judged" better "not to hurt them." Instead, "every one of the Forts strive what they can to get them to themselves," adopting the captives and converting Susquehannock enemies into people of the Longhouse.[8]

The covenants made at the Shackamaxon conference, and even its unexpectedly violent coda, marked an important shift in the relationships among Indigenous nations in the Northeast. The few who "got away" remained independent Susquehannocks of Gandastogue. Though much reduced in number, they continued their fight against the Haudenosaunee even when the cost was high. Delaware-Susquehannocks who resisted Haudenosaunee pressure at Shackamaxon became bound more tightly to Lenapes and Munsees. They resolved to stay in the Delaware Valley, transforming what had been a temporary refuge into a more permanent home. The Shackamaxon conference bought a lull in their hostilities with Iroquoia, but not a durable peace. Relations remained poised on a knife edge. Thomas Notley believed that the relationships among Haudenosaunee and Delaware Valley Indians would decide the future of the region, writing, "if those two Nations should warre upon each other" then Indigenous incursions into Maryland would inevitably follow. Those Susquehannocks who had been bound and carried from Shackamaxon joined, albeit unwillingly, the ranks of Iroquoia-Susquehannocks. As they struggled to make new homes among their captors, perhaps they found some solace as they reunited with friends and kin lost to captivity during the Susquehannock-Haudenosaunee wars. Despite their apparent defeat, the results of that struggle would dramatically reshape Indigenous nations and English colonies for years to come.[9]

Gandastogue was effectively partitioned along the kinship lines that had defined the varied destinations of groups in the scattering, turning temporary divisions into the seeds of new political communities. Although these transformations were just beginning in 1677, at the Shackamaxon conference Indigenous nations forged a covenant that reshaped the configurations of power in the mid-Atlantic. Renowewan attempted to include Europeans, but they played no part in the decisions made by Indigenous leaders and exerted no influence on the outcome. After Shackamaxon, every colonial effort to direct the course of events flowed within the channels of the new order that Natives had fashioned among themselves.

Far away from the struggles of Susquehannocks to reconstitute their community, Virginia settlers began an equally contentious process of reconstruction. Although armed resistance had been crushed by February 1677, only military force kept the peace. Governor Berkeley punished his foes without mercy, executing rebel leaders after courts-martial and ruining hated rivals by confiscating their estates. Oligarchs in government punished the "evil disposed servants" among the rebels by adding time to their contracts to make up for their masters' lost labor and plundered property, deepening the inequality in a deeply divided society. Talk of reducing rebel

servants to "slave[s] of the Colony" heralded worse to come. Rumblings
from the commonalty, whose political consciousness had been awakened
through participation in rebellious mass meetings and galvanized by the experience of shouldering muskets in company with other men, presaged a
renewed uprising the moment Berkeley's control faltered. The royal commissioners fretted that "the whole body of a Country lay tremblinge and
in panic" because "the number of the unconcerned in the late defection
were very soe few." They presented themselves with a velvet glove of
princely paternalism, issuing a proclamation of general amnesty to stifle rumors of retribution. But they did not hide their mailed fist: 1,094 royal
soldiers who occupied Virginia as though it were an enemy's country. The
force included thirty-six companies of crack troops from the Regiment of
Foot and the Coldstream Guards, among the best-trained and most loyal
soldiers in the Restoration Army, with proven experience quelling riots and
putting down "great tumults of disorderly persons." Across the Potomac,
acting governor Notley worried that only winter cold and naked oppression was keeping restive colonists under control. "There must be an
alteration . . . in the Government," he argued, "new men must be put in
power, the old ones will never agree with the common people, and if that
be not done, his Majestie in my opinion will never find a well setled Government in that Colony." Nothing short of a revolution would put an end
to endemic upheaval.[10]

Yet the nature of that revolution was sharply contested. Berkeley wanted
a revolution in the original sense of the word. "The wheele," Notley explained, "turned againe as wonderfully and swiftly," making a "revolution
in the Virginia affaires . . . in its whole progresse" and ending up where it
started: the undisputed dominance of the oligarchs in the Green Spring faction. Berkeley defended his draconian measures as necessary, justified, and
supported by legal precedent. He resented the royal commissioners' quest
for reconciliation as a challenge to his authority. The commissioners—led
by Herbert Jeffreys, captain in the king's household troops, and Sir John
Berry, an officer in the Royal Navy—represented a new thrust in Stuart imperialism, which groped toward the goal of bringing the fractious colonies
under centralized control. Colonial elites tenaciously defended their pre-
rogatives based on charter, custom, and the rights of Englishmen. Their
claims placed them in direct conflict with agents of a king who claimed to
be the "absolute Soveraigne" of the colonies with plenary power to "impose what forme of constitution both of Goverment and Lawes he pleaseth."
The royal commissioners, in a "Declaracion to his Majesties Loving Subjects," solicited grievances from each of the counties, which was part of
their instructions to find the causes of rebellion but was also a handy way

to collect ammunition in their battle against local elites. Through their grievances, disaffected colonists saw an opportunity to challenge Berkeley's government by appealing to imperial agents and continued to pursue the goal that had originally inspired the Volunteers' revolt: the exclusion of Indians from the body politic. The litigation of these grievances made Indigenous peoples central to the struggle over the new shape of the colonial order.[11]

Popular concerns about Indian violence had intensified as the rebellion came to an end. In January 1677, a wave of raids across the Northern Neck, which the commissioners believed to be the work of "the Suskahannocks and Doeggs," claimed the lives of sixteen families. Burgesses noted the "late murthers comitted by the barbarous Indians" in the northern counties, "which they dayly continue to comitt," and requested access to the royal arsenal and help from the king's troops. In April, Berkeley declaimed the "frequent incursions upon the frontier Plantations" and commanded militia under Sir Henry Chicheley to destroy Native warriors who were "lately gathered together into considerable bodyes and give daily suspition of doing more and greater mischiefs." The expedition was scratched as Berkeley and the commissioners squabbled over lines of authority, leaving frontier colonists unprotected. Given the opportunity to express themselves in solicited grievances, colonists made vivid emotional appeals that drew attention to their frightened and suffering families. In the hardest-hit neighborhoods of Rappahannock County, they wrote, "while wee are tending corne to feed our wives and children the Indians (if wee have no guard over us) would butcher us in our fields." They predicted "an Indian slaughter, which will undoubtedly befall us unless your honors send men to our assistance." The failure of Berkeley's militia, Volunteers, and now apparently even the imperial army to protect them left these colonists so helpless and frustrated they were dumbstruck. They wrote, "in a Word, our great feare, continuall Danger and Known wants are such that wee want words to express them." Their sense of unrelenting terror had not changed one jot since the first Susquehannock raids in 1675.[12]

Appealing to imperial compassion was a tactic to resurrect the Volunteer quest for a Virginia cleansed of Native peoples. Henrico County petitioners, echoing Nathaniel Bacon at his most strident, expressed their "desire and Request" for "Warr against all Indians in Generall." Lancaster colonists invoked the logic of patriarchal protection, insisting "the Warr against the Indians bee more speedily and effectually prosecuted," so that "all people may bee secured from all future feare and Damadges." They required protection because the existence of Indians in the colony presented a continual threat. Nansemond County petitioners invoked the perfidious effects of trade, explaining that "the favouring, and giving priviledges to some" Indian nations alienated those who were excluded, who "upon that pretence doe by a conspiracy or treachery destroy us." James City colonists blamed Berkeley's victorious faction, adding that "diverse covetous persons to advance themselves by trade with the Indians, have sold very great quantities of powder, shott, and ammunition to them . . . soe the Indians have bin therewith better provided then ourselves." The boldest added a conspiratorial flourish right out of Bacon's playbook. Henrico damned Berkeley's regime for its fidelity to tributary Indians, stating, "in favour of the monoppolists the people are betrayed to the perfidies of the mercyless Indians." There was only one solution. The Nansemond petitioners "desire . . . the destroying of all Indians, and that wee may have a warr with all nations and familyes whatsoever"—so that, a group of dissidents from Isle of Wight added, "wee may have once have done with them." These anti-Indian hardliners aimed to prove a simple equation to the commissioners: the existence of Indian subjects was a betrayal of English ones.[13]

County grievances illustrated the problem of administering an empire whose subjects came from multiple cultures and ethnicities. Petitioners from James City County questioned the loyalty of "our neighboring Indians," calling out their practice of "painting, and disfiguring themselves not to be knowne." Algonquians often dyed their skin both for practical reasons, such as repelling insects, and for ceremonial occasions. One such occasion was going to war. Normally warriors would use distinct designs, painting themselves half red and half black, further adorning their bodies with feathers, animal hair, and iridescent powder from pulverized shells. However, settlers reasoned, it would be easy for Algonquians to impersonate the aesthetics of foreign peoples, such as the Susquehannocks. Through "free accesse of the Indians amongst us," Algonquians gathered intelligence about English routines and vulnerabilities in colonial defenses. They could rise up at a moment's notice and massacre their neighbors. Disguised raiders washed English blood off their hands as easily as they washed off their war paint, blending back into their towns without leaving any evidence of their guilt. The James City colonists claimed they would be satisfied if "bounds be sett betweene us and them," reestablishing the segregated spaces mandated by the treaty of 1646. However, they pointed to the broader problem of cultural difference: every Indian that colonists encountered, no matter what they wore or how they looked, could be an enemy. Echoing Bacon's manifesto, they stated it was the Native body itself as much as Native actions that turned every plantation into a military frontier and left every colonist in a permanent state of fear.[14]

Ministers in the king's Privy Council and the Lords of Trade appreciated that Anglo-Indian violence was one of the chief causes of the colony's descent into civil war. Throughout 1676 they had been flooded with Virginian declarations and manifestos as the Volunteers rushed to convince faraway officials that their cause was just. The commissioners therefore understood the importance of managing popular anger, resentment, and fear directed toward the empire's Indigenous subjects. They claimed authority over Indian affairs, writing that "the sole Power of Peace and Warr are onely inherent to his Majesties Royall Prerogative." Wresting Indian policy away from Berkeley and the assembly accomplished their goal of transferring power from Jamestown to London. It also invested the Stuart imperial project in promoting coexistence between English and Indigenous subjects. The commissioners condemned Henrico's "wild request to have warr with all the Indians of a Continent" and warned colonists that their sentiments "shew their old mutinous humors, and in effect to desire new Bacons to head them." Whether or not they genuinely cared about the plight of Native peoples, imperial agents who wished to censure colonists for their sedition also needed to denounce the anti-Indianism at the core of the rebellion.[15]

Although the commissioners used their authority over Indian affairs to expand royal power, they hoped for local cooperation. Commissioner Francis Moryson, a Virginia colonist who had served as Berkeley's deputy in the 1660s, assured the governor that their purpose was to buttress rather than subvert his authority. The commissioners respected Berkeley's right to issue the call for an assembly to meet at Green Spring on February 20. Rather than give orders with the army of redcoats at their backs, they offered the burgesses an earnest exhortation to make peace with Virginia Natives in the spirit of honor, humanity, and loyalty to the king. The commissioners praised Berkeley's "equitable Policy and Prudence" in the "just and wise Peace" of 1646. They urged the burgesses to pursue the king's orders to restore peace with Virginia Indians and "joine your utmost endeavours with ours that it may be a truly good and just Peace (since such a one is like to be most secure and lasting)." The vision they outlined was modeled on the tributary system established under Berkeley's tenure. Enlarged from its local foundations and institutionalized under the king's aegis, it would be the blueprint for a multicultural empire.[16]

The commissioners made several practical arguments to silence the voices clamoring for Indian blood. They rebuked "that inconsiderate sort of men, who soe rashly and causelessly Cry up a Warr with, and seeme to wish and ayme at an utter Extirpation of the Indians." They noted that "perpetuall warr" required vast expenses, and therefore "a perpetuall tax on the Country," yet the men calling for it were "the first that Complain and Murmer at the Charge and Taxes that . . . attends such a Warr." As colonists from ten different counties complained, those taxes were one of the principal reasons that Susquehannock raids had tangled with economic hardship to spawn a general insurrection. Moreover, tributary Natives were vital to the colony's defense. These "amicable Indians," the commissioners argued, "are the best Guards to secure us on the Frontiers from the Incursions and suddaine Assaults of those other more Barbarous Indians of the Continent, who never can be brought to keepe a Peace with us, But will still continue our most Implacable and Mortall Enemies." Inverting the logic of anti-Indian grievances, they argued it was vital to retain tributary loyalty precisely because the Susquehannock-Virginia War was ongoing. The more that the "daylie Murders and Depradations" of the Susquehannocks were "upon us, the more earnestly it inforces this Argument for a Peace with the Frontier Indians." The bottom line was that Virginia colonists had to "consider and understand theire owne security and interest." That meant distinguishing Indian friends from Indian enemies.[17]

The commissioners amplified their appeals to reason with emotional rhetoric. Addressing the "unreasonable sort of men" who authored rabidly anti-Indian sentiments, the commissioners implored them "to lay their handes on their hearts, and seriously Consider" why they felt such rage. Could their vindictive wrath, the commissioners wondered, be anything other than "base Ingratitude" toward the loyal Indians who guarded the frontiers? Or was it something darker, "a nameless Prodigie of Infatuation and mere madnesse" that drove them to hate and kill without cause? Such madness had been ruinous. It brought not only Anglo-Indian war but also civil war between colonists. "Like men devoyd of reason, Religion, Loyaltie, or Humanitie, wee were murdering, Burning, Plundering, and Ruining one another, without remorse or Consideration," they lamented, "Which shames us, and makes us become a Reproach and a By word to these more Moral Heathens." Therefore, the commissioners urged "that you endeavour to gaine and preserve a good and just Peace and Correspondence with your Indian Neighbours, That they may not hold up their handes, and cry out against you, nor call you unjust and perfidious." This was the same kind of language, laced with pathos and designed to inspire solidarity, that settlers had used to describe English men and women. Applying that language to Native peoples, the commissioners reversed the moral calculus that had come to prevail in 1676. Although rebels and loyalists had justified violence by wrapping themselves in the mantle of righteous victimization, it was actually the defenseless Natives of Virginia who were the innocents deserving protection. By calling on colonists to empathize with the suffering of Indian neighbors, the commissioners included Indigenous peoples in the moral community of the English empire.[18]

The burgesses were unmoved and the assembly disappointed the commissioners' hopes for reconciliation. They did, at least, reject the most radically anti-Indian proposals on the table. The assembly allowed the nations expelled from their towns by vigilantes to "safely retorne to, and abide in theire townes" as "freinde Indians." However, this gesture was accompanied by an erosion of legal protections for tributary Natives and an official endorsement of Indigenous slavery. Berkeley himself granted a petition to keep "an Indian Girle which was taken by Mr Bacon and his party in his late March against the Indians," demonstrating that he had all but abandoned his previous commitment to amicable relations. Under his guidance, the assembly allowed soldiers to "reteyne and keepe all such Indian Slaves, or other Indian goods, as they either have taken, or hereafter shall take, to theire owne proper use for theire Better Encouragement to such service." By paying future soldiers with enslaved captives, they adopted the Volunteers' model of financing war through human plunder. This incentive for future Anglo-Indian violence was accompanied by sweeping away regulations on arms trafficking, including with "freinds and neighbour Indians." The Indigenous slave trade had a well-established pattern of exchanging guns for captives, so this was an invitation to expand slaving through the use of Native partners. The assembly strengthened this connection in October 1677. One act legalized the unlimited trade of goods, including guns and ammunition, with Indians from any nation so long as the exchange took place at designated markets such as Fort Henry. Ending monopolies on arms dealing and eroding prohibitions on human trafficking meant that Indian trade networks were back in business, accompanied by a ruthless level of competition and an increasingly precarious position for all Native peoples.[19]

The commissioners believed that these steps toward Indigenous exclusion would enflame Anglo-Indian tensions, delaying the peace mandated by the king and placing the whole colony in further danger of war and rebellion. They considered Indian relations the key to restoring order and bringing the colony more closely in line with the king's designs. They lamented the setback to "that most important affaire of the Indian Peace, the breach and want whereof had soe apparently involved that Collony into such misery, daily dred, heavy taxes, and occasioned such generall dissatisfaction among your Majesties Subjects, and was the ground of the Rebellion itselfe." Yet, they reported to Whitehall, neither "Sir William Berkeley nor the Assembly made not the least stepp, offer towards, or Progresse in it." The commissioners had proffered a practical vision in which Native peoples were a vital part of a multicultural empire by aiding in the protection of English subjects. Their proposals had been trampled in the rush to decide whether it was better to enslave Indians or annihilate them.[20]

The commissioners expressed their dismay in their official history, the "True Narrative." Ventriloquizing the voice of the Virginian commonalty, they wrote, "the People expostulate and saye, how shall wee know our enimyes from our friends, are not the Indians all of a Colour." The remark stands out because seventeenth-century Europeans had not yet developed the rigid categorization of humans according to skin color that came to be known as "race." But it is difficult not to interpret this as a signifier of racial thinking, a brief hint that the reconfiguration of political community hammered out at Green Spring mapped on to the indelible color of Native American skin. Admittedly, their meaning is somewhat ambiguous. Perhaps they meant the Indians' "colour" as a metaphorical flag of allegiance, a turn of phrase to describe popular conspiracy theories about far-reaching Indigenous coalitions. Perhaps it echoed petitioners' worries about what was on Indian skin rather than the skin itself, because "itt was Impossible to distinguish one nation from another, they being deformed with Paint of many Colors." But maybe it was exactly what it sounds like to modern ears: the experimental use of a new language to describe differences between English and Indians, blurring the distinctions among Indigenous nations, groping toward an exclusionary new way of conceptualizing who could be a subject of the king. Even though Bacon was dead, his belief that something essential in the nature of Native peoples disqualified them from membership in the English empire did not die with him.[21]

While colonists argued over the fate of Indians, the Virginians with the most at stake—Indigenous peoples—did not sit idly by. The most prominent voice belonged to Cockacoeske, the Pamunkey weroansqua. She responded to the commissioners' call for grievances in the same way that English colonists did: by submitting a list of complaints and requests on behalf of the people she represented as loyal subjects of the crown. She petitioned to have Pamunkey lands restored, "alleaging her leaving her towne was occationed through her feare of the Rebell Bacon and his Complices." Many settlers relied on similar excuses. Defeated rebels claimed Bacon intimidated them into disloyalty, disavowing the rebellious actions they had committed at gunpoint, while loyalists emphasized that marauding rebels had forced them into flight. Using emotional rhetoric to place herself on the same level as English partisans allowed her to extract concessions from the assembly. Burgesses limited compulsory military assistance and promised that Pamunkey fighters would enjoy the same right to plunder as English militia. Attempts to redeem enslaved Pamunkeys failed, perhaps because they "were disposed of by Sir William Berkeley," who revealed he was no friend of the "Darling Indians" by selling them for a tidy profit. However, she managed to obtain restrictions on how long colonists could "entertain"—that is, employ—Pamunkey laborers without her signed consent and thus mitigated the danger of them slipping into debt, servitude, and slavery. Cockacoeske took an active part in the struggle to shape the new colonial order by engaging in the politics of grievance alongside other Virginians.[22]

Cockacoeske seized on the possibilities offered by the intrusion of imperial power. It helped that one of the royal commissioners was Francis Moryson, with whom she had a close relationship. The two had become acquainted during Moryson's tenure as acting governor in the early 1660s, a period during which, according to Robert Beverley, "all the Indian Affairs [were] settled." While acting as the colony's agent in London in 1676, Moryson was preoccupied by the plight of the "queen of Pomonky scince she was driven off of her land by Bacon." He repeatedly referred to Cockacoeske as he sought to shape the imperial response to the rebellion, highlighting the necessity of "a strict instruction to the Commissioners to doe the pomonky Indians justice," especially by securing their land rights. The two corresponded with unusual warmth and intimacy. Native-produced letters are extraordinarily rare in the seventeenth-century Chesapeake, but Cockacoeske—much like a queen—dictated letters to her secretary. Addressing him as "good Netop," the Algonquian word for friend, she wrote with poignant yearning and loneliness, "you have allwayes been my friend Soe I hope you will Still Continue, for I have none to confide in . . . save yourselfe, nor any friends here." In early 1677, she and Moryson shared a frustration with Berkeley and the burgesses, who had offered no meaningful restitution to the Volunteers' victims, seemed indifferent toward the king's command to produce a peace treaty, and made little effort to enact structural reforms to prevent future Anglo-Indian violence. She wanted a new order that would protect the rights and privileges of her people. The king across the sea wanted a new order that would bring unruly colonists to heel and Moryson was his instrument. This was her moment of opportunity.[23]

Cockacoeske initiated diplomatic talks with the commissioners as the assembly rumbled to a close in March 1677. Nicholas Spencer observed, "our Indians . . . solicited a peace," and on March 27 the commissioners reported to Whitehall that representatives from the Pamunkey, Nansemond, Appamattuck, and Nottoway nations had signified "theire readynesse to enter into a firme League of Peace with the English." The commissioners admitted how much influence Cockacoeske had over the process. Negotiations, especially hammering out the new relationship between tributary nations and the colonial government, proceeded "as she desired." Cockacoeske was instrumental in securing the cooperation of other Indigenous leaders in the peace process. She "not onely came in herself," the commissioners wrote, 'but brought in severall scattered Nations of Indians." The commissioners succeeded in removing the major impediment, Governor Berkeley. Complaining that Berkeley, preoccupied by a spree of "illegal and arbitrary proceedings," had not "made the least step himselfe towards . . . a good and Honorable Peace with the Indians," Herbert Jeffreys proclaimed himself governor and forced Berkeley to sail back to England to answer allegations of misconduct. All the pieces were in place for a treaty conference at Middle Plantation.[24]

Native leaders performed their status as subjects of King Charles II in ways the English were sure to understand: through expressions of love. Cockacoeske wrote to Moryson, "findinge the Great Kinge of England to be my very good friend, as also my reale Defender," she promised "I shall pay as much Loyalty as any of his English Sujects" and to "posess those Neighbor Indians of mine, and others, to be of the Same minde and affections to his Majestie, as I am." Other Native leaders were even more flamboyant in their royalism. The weroansqua of the Weyanokes had reason to hate the English; Bacon had enslaved her adolescent brother and Berkeley had carried him to England, never to be seen again. Nevertheless, she introduced herself to the commissioners by asking the name of the English queen. They answered Catherine of Braganza. She then "charged all her people to remember that shee had taken to her selfe the name of Queene Catherine which shee often repeated and seemed very proud of the honor of soe great a name." It was a common Algonquian practice to take new names at turning points in their lives, and the name they chose was always a marker of the transformation's significance. The weroansqua Catherine performed her new identity as a proclamation of affection for King Charles and happiness to be an English subject.[25]

In complementary fashion, the commissioners arranged the ceremonies at the Treaty of Middle Plantation to symbolically affirm Virginia Indians' status as subjects of the sovereign patriarch King Charles II. The treaty signing ceremony was scheduled for May 29: Charles II's birthday, the day of his restoration to the throne, and a holy day on which all English subjects swore an oath from the *Book of Common Prayer* that asserted his divine right to rule as "our dread Sovereign Lord." In a new courthouse that Jeffreys had ordered built and "fitted for this occasion," tributary leaders were admitted behind the bar where they knelt, proclaimed their fealty to Charles II, and signed the treaty. After Jeffreys added his signature, each of the "Indian Kings and Queenes" received it from his hand "as from His Majesties" and reverently kissed it as an object of power. The thoroughly English service concluded at sunset with volleys of cannon fire and "generall acclamations of Joy." The signing ceremony, the commissioners reported, "celebrate[d] his Majesties Birthday and Restauration with this good work of concluding the Peace with the Indians," symbolically uniting Natives and colonists in their shared subjection to the king.[26]

The text of the treaty was unequivocal: Indians were subjects entitled to rights and protections that flowed from their subordination to the sovereign. The first article read, "The Respective Indian Kings and Queens doe from henceforth acknowledge to have their immediate Dependency on, and owne all subjection to, the great King of England, our now dread Soveraigne." Their rights to "lands and Possessions" were "in such sort and in as free and firme manner as others his Majesties Subjects have." The treaty guaranteed that "the said Indians be well secured and defended in their persons, goods and propertyes against all hurts and Injuryes of the English," with promises that crimes committed by colonists against Indians would be punished "as the Lawes of England or this Country permit." These explicit enumerations of Indigenous rights were great victories for Cockacoeske and other Native leaders, and imperial officials took pains to ensure that Virginia colonists would respect them. By order of the Privy Council the treaty was "printed, and Copyes sent into Virginia, for the better publication and observance thereof." Settlers were put on notice that the Baconian logic of Indian exclusion had been repudiated "by his Majesties Command." King Charles II had endorsed the treaty and decreed that tributary Indians were members of his empire.[27]

The Treaty of Middle Plantation was designed to solve the problems inherent in a multicultural commonwealth. It acknowledged that economic desperation was the cause of petty crimes that became the flashpoint for violence and it recognized that small provocations could spiral into war and rebellion. One article explained,

> by the Mutuall discontents, Complaints, Jealousyes and fears of English and Indians, occasioned by the violent Intrusions of divers English into their Lands, forcing the Indians by way of Revenge to kill the Cattle and Hogs of the English, whereby offence and Injurys being given and done on both sides, the peace of this his Majesties Colony hath been much disturbed and the late unhappy Rebellion by this meanes (in a great measure) begun and fomented which hath involved this Country into soe much Ruine and Misery.

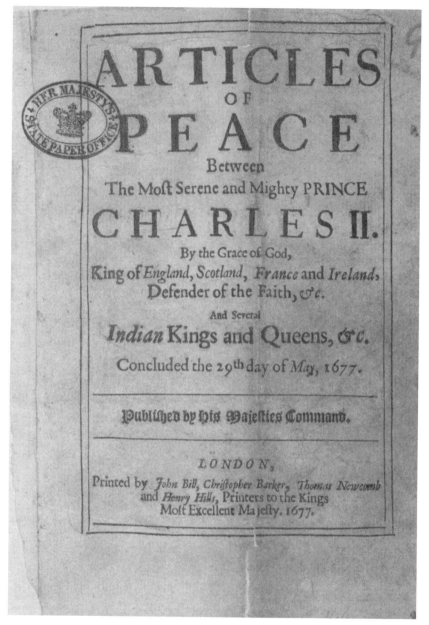

ARTICLES
OF
PEACE

Between
The Moſt Serene and Mighty PRINCE

CHARLES II.

By the Grace of God,
King of *England*, *Scotland*, *France* and *Ireland*,
Defender of the Faith, *&c.*

And Several

Indian Kings and Queens, *&c.*

Concluded the 29th day of *May*, 1677.

Publiſhed by His Majeſties Command.

LONDON,
Printed by *John Bill*, *Chriſtopher Barker*, *Thomas Newcomb*
and *Henry Hills*, Printers to the Kings
Moſt Excellent Majeſty. 1677.

Title page of the Treaty of Middle Plantation, printed for circulation in Virginia.
The National Archives of the United Kingdom.

Accordingly, the treaty included reforms to ensure that Natives could enjoy a secure place in colonial society. Articles assigned land to nations which had been dispossessed, gave Indians rights to fish, hunt, and gather wild plants "not usefull to the English" even on privately owned land, and forbade English colonists from settling within three miles of any Indian town. The treaty also contained several provisions aimed at curtailing Indigenous slavery. It required colonists to obtain licenses to employ Indian laborers, mandated that contracts for Native indenture be identical to those governing English servants, exempted tributaries from imprisonment for debt to eliminate peonage, and stated that Indians "shall not bee sold as slaves." These protections closely paralleled Cockacoeske's grievances and created a shield against conditions that forced Natives to choose between meek disappearance or violent resistance.[28]

Cockacoeske's influence over the treaty was reflected by its most ambitious accomplishment: reconstitution of the fragmented Powhatan nations. Before 1677, the relationship of tributary nations to each other had been ambiguous but in practice each governed its own affairs. Article 12 of the Treaty of Middle Plantation established their commensurate status as equals, "except the Queene of Pamunkey, to whom several scattered Nations doe now againe owne their ancient Subjection . . . and are to keep and observe the same towards the said Queene in all things as her Subjects, as well as towards the English." The Pamunkeys, in other words, were recreated as a chiefdom of composite sovereignty, owing tribute to King Charles II but owed tribute by other Indigenous nations in Virginia. Despite the supposed antiquity of this subjection, it was actually a new order among Indigenous nations. Article 12 required the Algonquian nations to "come in, and plant themselves under her Power and Government," granting Cockacoeske the authority to redistribute refugee populations as she saw fit. Article 18 established a legal framework for intra-Native disputes, mandating that the governor would arbitrate "any Discord or breach of peace happening to arise between any of the Indians in amity with the English." This provision effectively enlisted imperial power to enforce Cockacoeske's authority over Indigenous rivals. The commissioners considered this elevation of her power to be in the colony's best interest. Substituting one central authority for a multitude of dispersed ones made Indigenous peoples easier to rule, and there was no better ruler for the job than the weroansqua whom they described as "a faithfull frend and lover of the English." The commissioners' imperial mandate and Cockacoeske's ambitions intersected in this new Pamunkey paramount chiefdom, which invested the colonial government in defending Cockacoeske and her successors.[29]

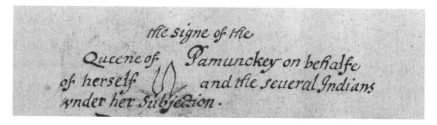

Cockacoeske's signature on the Treaty of Middle Plantation. "Articles of Peace between King Charles the Second and the several Indian Kings and Queens," 29 May 1677. The National Archives of the United Kingdom.

On paper, the Treaty of Middle Plantation looked like a significant achievement for both sides. Cockacoeske revived the embattled Indigenous nations of Virginia into a united chiefdom, and the commissioners created a legal framework for a multicultural English empire. It built on the Treaty of 1646 and the 1662 statutory reforms intended by Moryson to provide some protections to Indians. The 1677 treaty codified this patchwork of regulations into a system, which could in time be expanded to encompass all the Native nations under English rule. The treaty made headlines in the *London Gazette,* and the commissioners were enthusiastic about its prospects for success. They reported to Whitehall, "this good peace with the Indians, which wee trust allso is like to be a long and lastinge one," would not only improve Anglo-Indian relations but also promote stability because it would spare "the people of Virginia from the great charge they formerly underwent and damage sustained by reason of a warr with the Indians, beinge now made sensible how much peace with them is their safe security and Interest." Virginia Natives also saw promise in the treaty. Before the ink was dry, Perecuta of the Appamattucks signaled his desire to add his signature. "Severall Nations" more, including "such as were never Before in Amity with the English," expressed interest by the end of the year. By 1680 Nansemonds, Nanzaticos, Portobaccos, Monacans, and Saponis had officially signed on. Offered an opportunity to certify their status as subjects under the English king, who would forever be obligated to protect them from men like Nathaniel Bacon, Natives took the leap.[30]

Unfortunately for Natives, settlers, and imperials alike, the treaty's architecture had a structural flaw. As the commissioners claimed, some colonists did see security in the new order. But others continued to view Indians with an antipathy that ranged from moderate to murderous, resisted the idea that Indians were fellow subjects, and nursed resentments against the authorities that enforced the treaty. It had Indigenous detractors as well, particularly those left out of the negotiations. Chickahominies, who had never paid tribute to the Powhatans and remained independent up to the collapse of the paramountcy in 1646, resented being placed under Cockacoeske's subjection without their consent and resisted her pretensions to authority. The danger of such a dispute was apparent to the colony's secretary, Thomas Ludwell. Conflict between Pamunkeys and other Indian nations "will for ever Keep our peace in hazard of being broken," he wrote, because the treaty obligated the government to mediate between Indigenous disputants. If the government supported Cockacoeske, then her enemies would take up arms against the English. If the government decided against her, then she would accuse them of breaking the treaty, with the same result: taking up arms against the English. Ludwell was not overly worried about the military power of tributary nations, but he did fear the contagion they could unleash. He concluded, "in the present Condition of the Country such a warr would Certainely Hazard a new Rebellion." The covenant formed at Middle Plantation ensured that Indigenous politics would continue to be a destabilizing force in the new order.[31]

Not everyone was interested in talking peace in 1677. The twin scourges of Anglo-Indian war and civil disorder persisted in Albemarle even as Virginia lurched toward reconstruction. Rather than admit defeat, ragged remnants of the Volunteers took advantage of the impassable swamps to evade Virginia militia and imperial troops. The assembly asserted that the Albemarle government encouraged these partisans by "receiving such as are fledd from hence for theire treason and Rebellion." Native fighters took advantage of the porous border, threatening the Southside counties. They "often offer Injuryes," the burgesses complained, "and are allwayes ready to receive such of our enemyes who Fly from us." The lack of regular communication between Albemarle and Virginia, exacerbated by Natives ambushing colonists on the major transportation corridors, amplified Virginians' belief in the severity of the crisis. Jeffreys thought the situation so volatile that he stationed a company of royal troops in Nansemond and Isle of Wight Counties.[32]

In Albemarle, there was little compromise in the ongoing dispute between feuding factions. The antiproprietary partisans led by Jenkins had lost the ability to govern. Miller's deputy Henry Hudson testified, "the Government . . . lay in a tumultuous confusion," which paralyzed the people and left them incapable of organizing a force to fight the Chowanokes and Susquehannocks. New England merchants, on whom Albemarle colonists were economically dependent and to whom they were heavily indebted, exploited their predicament. "There being A warr with the Indians," merchants threatened to raise prices unless colonists rejected the customs duties mandated by the Navigation Acts. This would fatten the merchants' bottom line even as it prodded Albemarle settlers to risk "faction and Rebellion" to continue the flow of supplies necessary for their war against Indigenous peoples. Timothy Biggs reported, "the people were very mutunous and reviled and threatened the Members of the Counsell that were for settleing the said duty," turning against the Jenkins government. As in Virginia and Maryland, the financial burden of waging war against Native peoples exacerbated the political crisis.[33]

Proprietary forces took advantage of the upheaval to regain power. In July 1677, Thomas Miller, who had fled to England the previous year and convinced the Lords Proprietors that the Jenkins government must be brought to heel, returned to Albemarle. He carried a commission and papers certifying Thomas Eastchurch as governor of the province and Miller as his deputy. Despite "great abuse and affronts"—Patrick White publicly assaulted him and threatened to "freely run his knife . . . into the said Miller"—he exercised his executive authority to convene an assembly. He presented his credentials and a letter from the Lords Proprietors that forgave colonists their illegal support for the Volunteers because of "the apprehensions you had of Sir William Berkeley's being sole Proprietor." Miller convinced the assembly to abandon the failed antiproprietary faction with the promise of victory, pledging he would not rest until he had "reduced the Indians." According to Miller's account, he "brought the people . . . to a reasonable good conformity to his Majestyes and the Lords Proprietors Laws and authority and (as then seemed) to the generall satisfaction of the inhabitants." The combination of populist promises to protect the people, like those Bacon had offered, and a commission that gave him a stamp of legitimacy, which Bacon fatally lacked, induced the assembly to accept Miller's leadership.[34]

English and Indigenous belligerents in Albemarle fought until one side admitted defeat. Miller rallied the militia and marched northwest into Chowanoke country. On their way they passed Bennetts Creek, location of the settlements of Meherrins and Albemarle-Susquehannocks, "the Rebelious Indians of Virginia." According to settlers' later recollections, "open war was made upon the said Indians." Despite their strength—Chowanokes could put as many as one hundred warriors in the field—the Albemarle militia were victorious "by Gods assistance though not without the loss of many men." After a decisive defeat at Katoking, the main Chowanoke town, they were "wholly subdued."[35]

In Albemarle, the English brought peace with the sword, dictating terms to their Indigenous enemies without the messy compromises that negotiations entailed. Unfortunately for the victors, Thomas Miller's defeat of the Chowanokes and their allies did not bring harmony to fractious colonists. Peace allowed them to remember why they despised proprietary rule. Miller prosecuted Jenkins and his followers for mismanaging the war, issuing stiff fines for their negligence and barring them from holding office. Under his directive, the assembly that met in November 1677—purged of most antiproprietary settlers—levied an extraordinarily high tax to pay for the recent war. Miller found that even military success was not enough to maintain popular support. As in Maryland and Virginia, settlers had a ready stock of grievances against Miller and the Lords Proprietors he represented, but it was the fiscal strain of waging war against Indigenous peoples that caused the government to lose its legitimacy.[36]

Despite the Susquehannock and Chowanoke defeat, war with Indigenous peoples broke the Albemarle government. On December 1, 1677, George Durant's convoy finally returned from England with the munitions he purchased to battle Natives, putting an arsenal in the hands of the antiproprietary faction. With no more Indians to fight, they used it to overthrow Miller's regime instead. Rebels in the Pasquotank precinct proclaimed Miller a traitor, fanned out into surrounding areas, and arrested proprietary agents. A "Juncto"—known afterward principally by the secretary who drafted its proclamations, John Culpeper—"elected a parliament" and declared itself independent of proprietary rule. The revolutionary assembly openly rejected "his Majestys proclamations and Lords Proprietors authority" and brazenly proclaimed that if the Lords Proprietors themselves came to Albemarle they would be tried for treason against the people. The guns originally intended to fight Chowanokes and Susquehannocks became the guns propelling a revolution.[37]

Indigenous peoples remade their communities by finding new possibilities despite the chaos and violence of settler politics. Albemarle stripped Chowanokes of most of their territory, forcing them onto a small reservation. Susquehannocks and Meherrins migrated north, resettling on land at the mouth of the Meherrin River that had once belonged to the Chowanoke nation and now was claimed by Virginia. They founded a new town, "planted corne and built Cabbins on the Chowanacke old fields." A number of Chowanokes came with them, preferring independence as part of a multinational community rather than subjection to their conquerors. This new community, constituting itself after a series of violent dispossessions and

forced migrations, chose to distance itself from Albemarle settlers preoccupied with their latest round of rebellion. Instead they chose to pursue the
opportunities created by Cockacoeske and the new imperial power in the
Chesapeake. In 1680, Ununtsquero and Horohannah, both listed as a "cheife
man of the Maherians," signed the Treaty of Middle Plantation, formally
accepting subjection to King Charles II. The Meherrins' two signatures suggest that leaders of more than one people may have been involved in the
decision to sign on to the imperial covenant and end their long journey of
violence and dislocation.[38]

The final covenant of 1677 was forged at Albany, where Indigenous and
colonial powers contended for influence over the mid-Atlantic. The future
of the Susquehannock people, which remained in flux after Shackamaxon,
was at the center of their struggles. Onondagas and Oneidas had scored a
great coup by dividing the Gandastogue-Susquehannocks among themselves, opening an opportunity for them to take a leading role among the
League nations. Mohawks, however, opposed that ambition. Mohawk
leaders had pursued a more prominent role in Haudenosaunee politics since
the 1650s, using their geographical position as the symbolic eastern door
of the League's Longhouse to claim a privileged position in relations with
European colonists based in Albany. Mohawk leaders had struggled to convince the scattered Susquehannocks to join them instead of the western
nations, and they continued to pursue this goal in 1677. This struggle
among Haudenosaunee nations for influence shaped the possibilities and
limitations of colonial diplomacy as they sought to make peace with the
Susquehannocks.[39]
    Like the Haudenosaunee, colonial leaders were emphatic about the
Susquehannocks' importance in deciding the region's future. The crisis of
1676 had taught them that even a handful of raiders from a scattered
nation could spark the fires of rebellion. They positively trembled at the
prospect that Susquehannocks might involve more powerful Indigenous
peoples, especially the League of Five Nations, with its population of ten
thousand, including two thousand warriors. New York governor Edmund Andros repeatedly warned his counterparts in Maryland that a
Susquehannock-Haudenosaunee rapprochement would be disastrous.
Maryland officials were painfully aware that they had never formally ended
the state of war between their province and Iroquoia. Violence had only
temporarily abated as Haudenosaunee forces pursued others targets, so it
was imperative to make peace before they made common cause. Acting governor Thomas Notley resolved to "take all imaginable care to be at peace
with both the Sennico and Susquahannock . . . being both Nations the

bloodiest people in all these parts of America." On April 30 he instructed Henry Coursey, a loyal member of the council, to arrange peace talks with the Haudenosaunee at Albany. This became a landmark conference in which English and Indian ambassadors, meeting to determine the future of Gandastogue and its people, reshaped the geopolitics of eastern North America.[40]

Prospects for peace were complicated by power struggles among the colonies. The Calverts hoped that peace with Iroquoia would enhance Maryland's power relative to its neighbors. Coursey's commission directed him to include Virginia in the peace treaty, claiming loftily that it was their duty as "brethren and fellow subjects." They artfully omitted the obvious implication that speaking for Virginia in an international council was an assertion of dominance. The Virginians apparently did not appreciate the presumption. When Notley invited Virginia to participate in the conference as a silent partner, Governor Jeffreys, focused on his own bid for imperial leadership through the Treaty of Middle Plantation, did not bother to respond. Moreover, Maryland's ambitions were constrained by their ignorance of "the true state of the Susquesahannohs." Notley could not even say for sure "if that there be such a Nation," and if there was, whether they had the "capacity to treat by themselves" or if the Haudenosaunee now spoke for them. Coursey was dependent on Andros and his subordinates for this vital intelligence. Andros, however, had his own agenda: using Indian affairs to cement New York's place as the center of the Stuarts' American empire. He had made great strides toward this goal in cooperation with Mohawks, encouraging nations shattered by King Philip's War to coalesce under Mohawk protection and ensuring that Albany was the center of their orbit. To complete this vision, however, he needed the Susquehannocks under the wing of either the New York government or Mohawk sachems. He ceaselessly badgered his subordinates to bring the Susquehannocks to New York, or failing that—despite his disingenuous warning that a Susquehannock alliance with the Haudenosaunee would be disastrous—"to get them to the Masoques [Mohawks]." With each colony making a play to become the center of Indian affairs, the peace conference was also a contest and intercolonial cooperation a chimera.[41]

Amid these layers of international intrigue, Jacob My Friend quietly stepped in to orchestrate the 1677 Albany conference. When Jacob received word of Coursey's mission, he started preparing the ground. By his account, Jacob "did find out and Speak with the said Siniquo Indians," traveling for the second time in six months to the country of his enemies at "great Hazard of his Life." He then met with the remaining Susquehannocks in Gandastogue and convinced one to accompany him. Coursey met this "young

Indian" and "talked with [him] at Jacob Youngs." The young Gandastogue-
Susquehannock told Coursey that his people had been "hunting to make a
present to you for peace," gathering furs to present as a diplomatic gift.
Jacob also introduced Coursey to Delaware-Susquehannocks, "4 Susqua-
hanoes and with them the emperor of the Delaware bay Indians"—probably the venerable peacemaker Renowewan—who were "all inclining to a
peace." Jacob, knowing that Andros was determined to relocate the
Delaware-Susquehannocks, helped convince them and their Lenape hosts
to travel to Albany and join the general peace. He coached Coursey on
everything from New Yorkers' diplomatic schemes to the protocols of Iroquoian diplomacy. Coursey recognized that Jacob was indispensable to his
mission, reporting to Notley, "what truth is to be had is from him and none
else." His advice, knowledge, and linguistic skills made it "a necessity to
carry Jacob Young along with me without whom I cann doe nothing."
Coursey was satisfied that this work would keep Maryland safe, but Jacob,
from his unique position, was pursuing a much more ambitious agenda:
achieving reconciliation among the scattered Susquehannocks, Lenapes, Iroquoia, Maryland, and New York, all in one elegant swoop.[42]

Jacob's plans ran afoul of Andros's determination to remain in command
of Anglo-Iroquois diplomacy. Coursey, as his instructions authorized and
exigency demanded, appealed to Andros for assistance in bringing Haudenosaunee delegates to the table. Andros obliged and sent wampum to each
of the Five Nations for a meeting at Albany. His price was a drastic revi-
sion of Coursey's diplomatic strategy. The Maryland Council had drafted
preliminary proposals for Coursey to deliver at Albany, a blustery attempt
to turn Maryland into a colonial hegemon. The draft claimed Maryland's
right to speak for all the English colonies, blamed the "near destroyed"
Susquehannocks for the recent wars, and threatened to bring the full might
of the English empire against Iroquoia unless the Five Nations kept the
Susquehannocks in line. Under pressure from Andros—Lord Baltimore later
castigated him for the "great obstruction he had given Colonel Coursey in
his Negotiation at Fort Albany"—Coursey cut the saber rattling that might
offend Haudenosaunee diplomats, scrapped his claim to speak for all colonies, and added a new acknowledgment that Albany was the proper site
for future councils. When Coursey met with Onondaga and Oneida delegates on July 20, his proposals were a shadow of what the Maryland
Council had suggested, and more in line with Andros's agenda than
Jacob's.[43]

In contrast to the Treaty of Middle Plantation, for which Native leaders
followed English protocols and participated in English ceremonies to assert their membership in the English world, diplomatic exchanges at Al-

bany were Indigenous in their idiom. The convener of a treaty council would typically begin with a ceremonial cleansing of weariness and anger and exhortations for calm thoughts and peaceful feelings. They gave long, carefully structured orations that recited shared histories and proposed future relationships, each of which would be sealed with a gift of wampum or other objects of power. The other side would deliver their replies on the following day, after adjourning for an evening of public festivities and allowing all parties plenty of time for private discussion. Coursey did his best to adapt to these customs when he met with eight Haudenosaunee ambassadors, and likely dozens of other Native attendees, in the crowded Albany courthouse. Although "through mistakes some discontents or injuries may have happened between us," he began, employing the vague passive voice eternally beloved by politicians, now "we are willing that all what is past be buryed, and forgott." He made only one tepid request: that the Haudenosaunee "tak[e] care . . . that your Indians nor none liveing among yow or Coming through your Country do for the future injure any of our persons, Pascattoway or other our Indians liveing with us." Beyond this anodyne commitment to peaceableness, Coursey merely suggested that in case of any future violent incidents, they should meet at Albany to resolve their differences before resorting to war.[44]

Onondaga spokesman Garakontié seized on Coursey's weak play to shape the conference's agenda. A shrewd politician who cultivated ties with both New France and New York to bolster the Onondaga nation's leadership, Garakontié used selective forgetting and creative invention to conjure a new geopolitical landscape. In his response the following day, he intoned, "we desire now, that all which is past may be buried in Oblivion, and doe make now an Absolute Covenant of peace, which we shall bind with a Chain." The chain, linking peoples together in friendship, was a common Haudenosaunee diplomatic metaphor; they had "joined together with chains" to various European and Indigenous groups in the seventeenth century. Now Garakontié forged a new chain between Onondaga and Maryland. Beyond this grand gesture, his speeches were focused more on assertion than concession. He vaguely promised, "we shall not injure or doe any Damage to the People of Maryland or Virginia," but made no such promise about tributary Algonquians and warned colonists to stay out of the way while Onondaga warriors were "fighting against the Susquehannohs." He did "acknowledge that we have killed off your Christians and Indians," but placed the blame on "Jacob Young alias my Friend," who "was a great occasion thereof." As Indigenous orators often did to emphasize the significance of their words, he repeated the charge in a second speech. Garakontié "again rehearse[d] that Jacob Young was a great Leader and Captain against them, whereby the warrs have been continued." Jacob, who was standing by Coursey's side as interpreter, must have squirmed as he listened. Through this accusation, Garakontié placed blame for the history of violence on Jacob and the Susquehannocks, even as he urged forgetting and reconciliation through his "Covenant of peace."[45]

Swerisse, the Oneida spokesman, revealed the intra-League politics behind Garakontié's rhetoric. Though in years past the Oneida nation had deferentially acknowledged the Mohawks as "uncles," Swerisse referred to the Onondaga nation as "fathers" of the Oneidas. Among the matrilineal Haudenosaunee, a father was not as powerful a figure to a child as an uncle, but Swerisse's deference to Garakontié nevertheless suggested political realignments in Iroquoia. Swerisse made similarly vague promises to keep the peace in the future, but he claimed "never to have killed any Christians," blamed Maryland colonists for inciting violence, and absolved Oneidas of any responsibility to make restitution for attacks against Algonquian tributaries. However, these public pronouncements were a prelude to more conciliatory conversations in private. As the Onondaga sachem Othonoenis later related, "after that the Propositions were ended in . . . the Court house" Jacob and Coursey met with the Onondaga delegation in Coursey's quarters. Offering "presents of Strung wampum by Jacob Young alias my frind"—Coursey was merely an observer here—the Marylanders proposed a follow-up meeting at Onondaga rather than Albany. Such a conference appealed to both parties: establishing a diplomatic center outside of Mohawk or New York's control would increase Maryland's power among the colonies and Onondaga's among the Five Nations. Jacob, making a personal gesture toward reconciliation, proposed to give heft to the chain that Garakontié had forged from words.[46]

The second phase of the conference began on August 4, when Mohawk ambassadors met with Coursey. Their spokesman, Canondondawe, asserted the primacy of the Mohawk–New York axis. "The Covenant that is betwixt the Governor Generall and us in Inviolable," he stated, "yea so strong that if the very Thunder should breake upon the Covenant Chain it would not break it asunder." With this pronouncement, Canondondawe transformed Garakontié's chain, one of many binding the Haudenosaunee to other peoples, into a singular Covenant Chain whose central links were New York and the Mohawk nation. Three times Canondondawe emphasized Albany's symbolic importance, and he strenuously urged Coursey never to meet with the other four Haudenosaunee nations anywhere else. He gladly extended the chain of friendship to embrace Maryland and Virginia so long as they recognized that Andros would always be the primary mediator and Haudenosaunee would meet only when "his Honor . . . grant yow the priviledge for to speak with us here." Canondondawe even honored the personal service that Marylanders did when they "beheaded the Sachem of the Susquahanohs named Achnaetsachawey," who had captured his two sons. (Little can be said about Achnaetsachawey, who is not mentioned in any previous or subsequent source, but Canondondawe's statement that Marylanders executed him suggests that he may have been of the five sachems murdered during the 1675 siege of the Susquehannock connadago.) Magnanimity cost him little; the Mohawks, their attentions fixed firmly to the east, had few historical entanglements with the southern colonies. His motivation was less to heal an existing breach with the English than to claim control of the relationship itself. Wresting the covenant away from Garakontié, Canondondawe elevated the Covenant Chain to greater importance.[47]

On August 22, a full month after the conference began, Seneca and Cayuga ambassadors finally met with Coursey. Attawachrett spoke for the Cayugas, who acknowledged the Senecas as their metaphorical uncles. In two speeches he explained, "our Resolution was taken together," so the Seneca spokesman Adondarechaa's words represented both nations. Adondarechaa acknowledged the long war between Maryland and the Senecas but disavowed any real enmity. He explained that violence against colonists had occurred because of "their Entertaineing of those Indians that were our Enemies," referring to the old alliance between Maryland and Gandastogue. He reciprocated Coursey's spirit of forgetting past strife. "We thank yow that yow doe bury and forgett all former discontents or injuries as we doe the same," he said, "and never more to be remembred." Adondarechaa endorsed the Mohawks' primacy in matters of the League's foreign policy with the English. He rehearsed, "we have alwaies had a firm Covenant with this Government," meaning New York, so therefore "lett that which yow have proposed to us be as fast and firm as the Covenant we have with the Governor Generall," Edmund Andros. The Senecas and Cayugas accepted, and induced Coursey to accept as well, that New York and the Mohawks were the central links in the Covenant Chain that tied the League and English America together.[48]

Knowledge of these exchanges has come down to the twenty-first century because the English secretary Robert Livingston wrote summaries of every speech. There was another meeting, however, that left no records because no settlers were present. Lenapes and Delaware-Susquehannocks did not speak in any of the documented proceedings, but they were present in Albany. Coursey noted that "two of their chiefe men with all haste" followed him to Albany, and he considered the peace agreements to include Lenapes (later known as Delawares). When Notley published news of the conference's success, he proclaimed peace with "the Sinnondowannes, Cajouges, Onnondages, Onneydes, Maques, and Mattawass or Delaware Indians."

Later generations of Indigenous leaders recalled this conference as the moment when Lenapes and Haudenosaunee ended years of bitter fighting and when Delawares were "made women" by accepting a position as honored mediators and keepers of the peace. The immediate effects were unmistakable: Haudenosaunee wars with both Susquehannocks and Lenapes ceased. The one violent incident that occurred in late 1677 involved Oneida warriors who had not yet heard news of the peace and immediately made restitution, "the better to keep the Covenant." The Delaware-Susquehannocks remained on the Schuylkill without interference, the last of the Gandastogue-Susquehannocks voluntarily moved to Iroquoia, and the Susquehannocks who had forcibly migrated to Iroquoia stayed in their new homes. It appears that Indigenous ambassadors held their own conference alongside the Anglo-Iroquois meetings at Albany, and among themselves ratified the state of affairs created by the Shackamaxon conference.[49]

The 1677 Albany conference was both a great success and a great failure. It began a process by which many chains linking the Five Nations and European colonies became a singular Covenant Chain, a process that would continue for several years. Even if Haudenosaunee delegates promised little of substance to Coursey, the inclusion of Maryland and Virginia in the chain was a significant accomplishment. It created a channel of communications and a space for diplomacy, allowing representatives to meet in Albany, address each other as brothers, and resolve future crises. Within the League, the Senecas' acceptance of Albany as the central site of an alliance with the English colonies began to heal a decades-long rift between the Mohawks and the other four nations, a process that would ultimately strengthen Iroquoia as a whole. These accomplishments were the result of a conference whose primary purpose was to address the danger that the Susquehannock nation posed to regional stability.

Yet there were weak links in the chain that arose from fundamental miscommunications about the fate of the Susquehannock nation. Marylanders assumed that the conference hammered the final nail in Gandastogue's coffin. Notley's happy proclamation conspicuously failed to mention the Susquehannocks, an erasure that signaled the Calverts' line after 1677: the Susquehannock nation no longer existed. Maryland had "near destroyed them" and the Haudenosaunee had finished the task by absorbing the survivors. They were now effectively Haudenosaunee and subject to their hosts. That was why Coursey had tried to include the colony's tributary Indians in the covenant, asking capaciously that League sachems promise to restrain "your Indians" as well as those "liveing among yow or Coming through your Country" from violence. The premise of this demand, unfortunately, fundamentally misunderstood the nature of Haudenosaunee diplomacy. Known as kaswentha, this tradition did not enact international relations through a binding set of agreements in the style of European treaties, which were impossible to enforce in a consensus-based political system. Rather, it reflected a commitment to maintaining a forum for arbitration but assumed all parties would continue to pursue their own independent paths. One of those parties was the Susquehannock people. All the League spokesmen committed their own people to peace, but none of them made such a promise on behalf of the Susquehannocks who lived among them. Jacob was distraught at the conference's failure to secure a clear agreement about Susquehannocks. According to Coursey, Jacob said "if he had known . . . that the Susquehannahs had not to have been Included in that Peace," he would "rather have given 20000 lbs. Tobacco than have Come" to Albany. Perhaps he foresaw the blood that would flow from this failure.[50]

As important as the Albany conference was to all the peoples involved, the misunderstandings it engendered meant that the wars of the Susquehannocks were far from over. None of the covenants forged in 1677 brought satisfactory conclusions to the conflicts they were supposed to end. As any Susquehannock might have observed, only cool heads and a commitment to consensus could produce a lasting peace. In contrast, peacemaking efforts in 1677 were emotionally charged and bitterly contested, even after the seals were stamped and gifts exchanged. Instead of healing the wounds of war, the new orders established by these agreements merely redrew the battle lines. All their covenants were brittle. As the covenants fractured, a new and bloody chapter of the Time of Anarchy began.

· 6 ·

CAPTURING IROQUOIA

THE ONE HUNDRED SUSQUEHANNOCKS carried into Iroquoia might have been expected to disappear. Most Europeans assumed their story was over. In 1677, a Jesuit wrote that the Haudenosaunee "have at Last succeeded in Exterminating the Andastoguetz [Susquehannocks]." It was not an unreasonable description given the traditional practices of mourning war. Requickening ceremonies were designed to assimilate foreign peoples by submerging their old identities and replacing them with new identities as members of Haudenosaunee communities. An Onondaga elder, speaking to ethnographers in the nineteenth century, compared captives to "a body cut into parts and scattered around," explaining that his ancestors "scattered their prisoners, and sunk and destroyed their nationality, and built up their own." Rather than disappearance, though, Susquehannocks experienced an astonishing resurgence. In a matter of months, Susquehannock leaders achieved status and influence in Iroquoia. They became war chiefs who led Haudenosaunee men into battle. Even more incredible, they directed the Haudenosaunee toward targets of their choosing: English colonists and Algonquians in the Chesapeake. In the process of adopting Susquehannocks, the League nations also adopted the Susquehannocks' enmities. As a Haudenosaunee ambassador explained in 1679, the "nations with whom the Susquehannohs lived" had not initially been hostile, "but by the insinuation and instigation of the Susquehannocks . . . they are now become all One." Haudenosaunee warriors had captured the Susquehannocks, but somehow the Susquehannocks captured Iroquoia.[1]

However rough their passage, Susquehannocks did not arrive in an entirely strange country. Captives had been flowing from Gandastogue to Iroquoia since the 1650s, sometimes in ones and twos, sometimes by the hundreds. The Haudenosaunee had executed some to expiate their grief, but adopted others as Seneca, Cayuga, Onondaga, Oneida, and Mohawk. According to scholar Richard Hill Sr. (Tuscarora), foreigners who came to Iroquoia "abided by Haudenosaunee cultural protocols," and "did not abandon their own traditional ways but added a cultural affiliation with the Haudenosaunee." Susquehannocks, whose culture embraced connections with foreigners and whose politics created networks of kinship and alliance, were well equipped to make the transition. The hundreds or thousands of relatives already in Iroquoia would have welcomed them. These men and women neither shed their Susquehannock skin in favor of a new identity nor stubbornly resisted the influence of their adopted communities. They reinvented themselves, becoming new people without losing who they had been, remaining fully Susquehannock even as they became one people with the Haudenosaunee. Out from this new layer of being sprang an extraordinary strength.[2]

The Susquehannocks' layered identities allowed them to wield a peculiar sort of power that the English were not prepared to counter or even understand. Because settlers assumed they had been destroyed, they could hide in plain sight, exercising political influence on their supposed captors while evading English demands for accountability. They used that influence to carry on the wars that started in 1675, which in their eyes had not ended. Susquehannock-inspired raids began in 1678 and quickly became an onslaught, shredding the fragile covenants between colonists and tributary Natives and threatening to bring unstable colonial regimes crashing back into indiscriminate violence and civil war. Colonists only gradually came to understand that what they thought to be the remnant of a ruined nation could unleash the full force of the Haudenosaunee on the peoples of the Chesapeake.[3]

Susquehannock captives regained their power with astonishing speed. As early as 1678, rumors circulating among Chesapeake Indigenous nations suggested that they had become players in League politics. Piscataway messengers informed the Maryland Council of "the Common Rumor that the Sinnequo Indians (by Instigation of the Remaineing part of the Susquesahannoughs now amongst them) are Designed to come downe and make warr upon the Pascattoway Indians toward the Latter End of this Summer." The news flew further south as well. "In Virginia there was a rumor that the Sinnequos did designe this next fall to scoure the heads of those Rivers," the council recorded. Tributary Algonquians took the rumors seriously: the "Pascattoway Indians doe verily beleive" that raiders were coming. Piscataways did not say how they acquired this intelligence or why they believed it credible. Nevertheless, word spread that Susquehannocks intended to continue their war against Algonquians in Maryland and Virginia, and they were bringing their friends with them. Edmund Andros noted that the region was "much allarmed with rumours of war," even New Yorkers who so far had been spared Indigenous attack. He could not bring himself to believe the Haudenosaunee would turn to violence without pretext, "having been always very good and faithfull to this Government and kind to all Christians a this side." He had to admit, though, that they had become increasingly aggressive since the Albany conference.[4]

Tidings of war were unwelcome amid colonial turmoil. Struggles for power and autonomy gained a new immediacy among tributary nations after the covenants of 1677. Cockacoeske brandished the Treaty of Middle Plantation to assert a degree of authority that no Indigenous leader had exercised since the days of Opechancanough. She demanded that werowances recognize her supremacy, exacted tribute, and forcibly relocated women and children to bolster the Pamunkey population. Constructing a powerful and assertive Pamunkey chiefdom came at the expense of its neighbors. After moving whole nations, she sold their land to settlers. If she was thinking along the same lines as leaders such as Metacom and the saunkskwa (female sachem) Weetamoo in New England, she may have intended the profits to finance diplomatic coalition building with other Native nations, as well as stockpiling arms and ammunition for self-defense. But several nations resisted her pretensions to Powhatan power, and insisted, wrote secretary Thomas Ludwell, that "they intended noe such subjection by those Articles." Cockacoeske complained to Francis Moryson, "I am very much dissatisfied about the Rappahannacks, but espetially about the Chickahomineys." Chickahominy resistance began with quiet disobedience but escalated to diplomatic insults, assassination, and preparations for war. Werowances of other nations submitted to Cockacoeske, but their capitulation caused internal rifts. Ludwell reported, "most of the young men of several townes" were "discontented at their new subjection to that Queen which they say was consented to by their old men against their wills." Ambitious young leaders gathered supporters and formed separate bands, who "lye off in parties in the woods and will not come in, which renders our peace insecure." The royal commissioners had hoped that elevating Cockacoeske would clarify the lines of authority among Indigenous nations, but instead it had created a proliferation of aggrieved and unstable new political units.[5]

Colonial governments could not avoid involvement in these Indigenous disputes. Cockacoeske dragged the Chickahominies into the General Court, calling on the English to enforce their subjection as per the treaty. But the treaty obligated the government to protect all tributary nations, which allowed the Chickahominy manguy (chief) to argue that it must protect his people from Pamunkey aggression. The problem for officials was that arbitration was bound to leave someone unsatisfied. If the governor decided in favor of the Pamunkey, Ludwell explained, then the indignant loser would "run to armes" against the English. If instead he ruled against the Pamunkey then Cockacoeske "would have looked on it as a breach of the Articles and our danger would have been as great." Colonists who bore no love for Indians rankled at being placed in this dilemma and did not conceal their contempt for Indigenous lives. Ludwell fumed, "I never thought it the Interest of this Colony to hinder them from Cutting each others throats." It did not take long for Natives opposed to Cockacoeske to turn their anger on the English supporting her. In early 1678, tributaries killed five colonists on an outlying plantation. Werowances dutifully delivered the killers to the English for trial and execution, but only at the cost of enraging their own people. "All our young Indians," Ludwell lamented, "seem reddy for another warr." By March, the powder keg, primed by rogue tributaries unhappy with their leaders' covenants, seemed ready to explode.[6]

Maryland was no less volatile. Colonists believed the demise of the Susquehannock nation to mean that their territory was free for the taking and began moving into the Susquehanna Valley. Delaware-Susquehannocks took violent measures to defend their homeland. Assailants, "pretending that most of the Land" in the lower Susquehanna Valley "doth properly belong to them," killed cattle to drive the squatters away and then killed three colonists as they slept on the bank of the river. Relations with Algonquians also frayed. In early February, Eastern Shore Algonquians murdered the Williams family at Wicomico. Investigation by Somerset County sheriff Thomas Walker suggested the killers were "Pocaptaps party," a splinter group of Nanticokes following an aspiring young leader. Notley stated, "I am of opinion that Pocatap is the murtherer or the cause thereof and that no Susquahannoh is there." But this was cold comfort in the face of hostility from allied Natives. Nanticoke headman Unnacokassimon claimed the true killer was Krawacom, a Checonessek from Delaware Bay. When confronted by three hundred militia and Western Shore Indians, Unnacokassimon offered the angry English two Nanticokes to be "sacrificed for their Satisfaction" and agreed to accept tributary status. Krawacom was arrested but escaped from prison, crossed the Potomac, and took refuge among Rappahannocks, sparking fears of hostile Indigenous coalitions. Even as rumblings of a coming offensive from Iroquoia drifted through the Chesapeake, Natives and settlers were as divided and acrimonious as ever.[7]

The incursions began with the first stirrings of spring. In March five hundred "Northern Indians" came south, hitting piedmont Siouan groups such as the Manahoacs. In July they killed two Rappahannock women as they picked wild blackberries, as well as an English family in the York Valley. The attacks were unexpected and the assailants unknown. When the raiders set up an armed camp in "the Old Susquehannoh Fort," however, it seemed to confirm suspicions that Susquehannocks were behind the attacks. The raiders tore through the Potomac Valley in August and by this time Piscataways were adamant about their identities. Tayac Nicotaughsen informed the Maryland Council, "some of their Indians" were "lately killed" by "Senniquo and Susquahannoh Indians." Their goal, tributary scouts told Thomas Ludwell, was "takeing revenge on some of our neighbor Indians for injuries don them," and ultimately "the destruction of severall of those Indians under our protection."[8]

War parties striking out from the ruins of the Susquehannock connadago spread terror through Virginia and Maryland. The raids, wrote Ludwell, "hath put all our fronteers in a fear." The Pamunkey interpreter Cornelius Dabney similarly reported that "the Forreigne Indians viz the Senecaes [had] put our Indians into a feare." Mutual terror and accumulated grievances made it difficult for Algonquians and English to find common cause. Colonists found new reasons to resent the Treaty of Middle Plantation. Jeffreys, noting that the raiders in York Valley slipped by tributary sentries, admonished "our Neighbour Indians for their neglect" and reminded them they were "obliged by the Articles of Peace to be watchfull and keep out Rangers and prevent such mischeifs." Ludwell was certain the treaty would cost English lives, because "if we protect our Indians as wee are obliged by those articles wee must have a warr with their enemies." In Maryland, English suspicions were more visceral than legalistic. In August a group of painted Indians murdered the Cunningham family in Charles County. Mrs. Cunningham, who survived a blow to the head from a tomahawk which caused severe brain damage, lingered for several days before dying of her wound. Based on her mute gestures, many colonists believed it was the work of rogue Piscataways. Tributary werowances expressed shock at the accusation, proclaiming "the English had been their greatest Friends . . . and if Once they should breake with them, they must certainly be most miserable expecting nothing but Death." The council suspected that Piscataway claims of Susquehannock attacks were only "rumor," false news to cover their own violent actions, but their mistrust alienated Maryland's most important allies in the middle of a foreign invasion.[9]

Colonial fears led to a spiral of preemptive violence and retaliation. In August, a party of two hundred Oneidas, on their way back from a raid on southern Siouans, approached English farmsteads near the falls of the James River to gather provisions. Driven by panic, colonists "deserted their plantations and Flying lower downe, gave the alarme to the people as they went." Henrico County scrambled a troop of forty-six cavalry to confront the Oneidas. Lacking an Iroquoian-speaking interpreter, however, they only managed to provoke the Oneidas by shouting and pointing loaded guns in their direction. The surprised raiders readied for battle, which the militia interpreted as evidence of a planned ambush and opened fire. Oneidas fired back, killing the English commanders. Both sides withdrew in a hail of gunfire, suffering several casualties. The militia killed two warriors and took one woman captive, claiming her as plunder, enslaving her, and selling her to planters in Bermuda. The furious Oneidas harried English settlements on their way home, taking captive the women and children of the Proktor and Thackeray families.[10]

Adding to colonial fear and confusion, south of Albemarle the Tuscaroras began to stir. Ludwell noted unconfirmed reports that a Tuscarora war party had "attempted but without successe" a plantation in Southside Virginia. According to Jeffreys, this was only one of many circulating rumors about Indian attacks. Continual invasions throughout the year "hath struck a very great terror both into our English on the Frontiers as well as our owne Neighbour Indians," he wrote, "which Causes them to raise divers strange reports." He acknowledged rumors that Tuscaroras "committed these murthers," but also "by all the intelligence that I can have . . . by any of our out runing Indians, I cannot finde any certainty of this at all." Scanty Albemarle records make it difficult to confirm or deny the reports, though one tidbit suggests that they might have been true. One colonist was tried by the Higher Court in 1679 for embezzling the province's arms and ammunitions, which left it defenseless "when the Cuntrey was in a feare of a war with the Indians." The rumors, moreover, were not implausible. Since 1663, Albemarle colonists had generally abided by a treaty with the Tuscaroras that forbade settlement south of the Sound or west of the Chowan River. When proprietary governors broke this promise in 1666, Tuscaroras had responded with raids to drive the interlopers away. Most colonists learned their lesson, but the Lords Proprietors issued orders to expand settlement toward the Neuse and Pamlico Rivers and Thomas Miller would likely have followed them. He and Eastchurch had authorized new settlements after their coup in 1675, forcing the Jenkins government to evict the settlers in order to keep the terms of the treaty. If, as seems likely, Miller broke the treaty again in 1677 by expanding settlement into Tuscarora territory, they may have struck back in 1678. Even if all the rumors were wind, stories of Tuscarora war parties added to colonists' bewildering sense of being attacked from every direction by Indians of many nations.[11]

Ripple effects from raids, and rumors of raids, ramified through colonial communities and inspired calls for action. Josias Fendall, inveterate opponent of the Baltimore regime and neighbor of the murdered Cunninghams, campaigned for election as a Charles County assemblyman on a one-plank platform that Nathaniel Bacon would have admired: "that were he Commander of the County Troope he would Destroy all the Indians." Jeffreys noted that Oneida attacks in Henrico "hath very much alarumed the whole Country." No doubt thinking of the disaster that came from Berkeley's failure to assuage the people's fears, Jeffreys made a show of imperial force. He personally led "my owne Redcoates, and a considerable number of Horse to give encouragement to those poore distressed people," demonstrating that the government would protect them. He made similar promises to tributary Natives, having "ordred all our Neighbour Indians to infort themselves" and "assured them to give them imediat succour my self." The best his army could do, though, was catch a lone Oneida warrior unawares, carry him to Jamestown, and execute him for murder.[12]

By autumn 1678, Susquehannock and Haudenosaunee attacks had tipped the Chesapeake colonies dangerously close to a general crisis. A raid on the Piscataways resulted in several casualties and the loss of most of their arsenal. The Maryland Council issued a province-wide alert ordering military readiness for an imminent invasion, but dithered between rearming its Piscataway allies and going to war against them if it turned out they had been responsible for the Cunningham murders. Virginia convened an emergency assembly, where it became clear that raids had inflamed public opinion against Indians. Colonists were enraged that Oneidas had taken English captives to Iroquoia and trusted tributary Indians less than ever. The suspicious actions of Maryland Algonquians and spike in anti-Indian sentiment among Maryland colonists gave them "great reason to suspect a generall ill designe amongst all the Indians." Knowing that if the captives were not returned soon the government would face unruly anti-Indian violence, Jeffreys wrote to the newly knighted Sir Edmund Andros asking for help. Failing that, the council had few options but a quixotic invasion of Iroquoia.[13]

The coming winter gave the colonies a desperately needed reprieve. After a last burst of attacks against the Appamattuck town, Occaneechi Island, and several other Siouan nations, Susquehannock and Haudenosaunee warriors returned home. Settler fears subsided as frontier violence ebbed. The Maryland assembly noted, "now the leaves are Dropping off the Trees, and the weather like to be cold," so "the Inhabitants of those parts have not the same Reason to be afrayd of the Indians." In December, Virginians could happily affirm Secretary Coventry's hope that "your feare of the Indians are by this time quieted." But the spring brought new reasons to be afraid.[14]

Despite the cloud of uncertainty that hung over these northern raiders, with every clash producing new flights of rumor about their identity and motivations, their targets were precisely chosen. Manahoacs and nearby Siouans were part of the Occaneechis' tributary network, many of whom had helped the Occaneechis massacre a band of Susquehannocks in 1676. The Rappahannocks inhabited the territory where Susquehannock warriors had intruded in early 1676, while Pamunkey and Appamattuck warriors had mobilized to repulse them. Piscataways had been at the 1675 siege of the Susquehannock connadago, killed and captured Susquehannocks after their breakout, and advocated warring on the Susquehannocks unto destruction. If viewed as Haudenosaunee actions, the 1678 raids represented a sudden departure in foreign policy. But if one gave credence to the rumors, sightings, and circumstantial evidence connecting Susquehannocks to these attacks, it was just a continuation of previous struggles. When Henry Chicheley, writing as acting governor after Jeffreys's death in December 1678, described "our late troubles and distractions with the frequent incursions of Indians *for three years last past*," he was signaling his recognition that the flurry of moccasined feet down the Great Warpath was part of an unfinished war between Susquehannocks and their enemies.[15]

The ravaged Susquehannock nation had revived itself in Iroquoia as captives rapidly settled into new homes. They were probably aided by kinfolk who had been incorporated into the Haudenosaunee in earlier decades. One tantalizing piece of material evidence—a woven carrying strap—suggests that their path may have been smoothed by cultural affinity with their captors. Like many Native peoples, Susquehannocks used carrying straps to help bear heavy loads by distributing weight along the spine, decorating this utilitarian object with designs meaningful to its makers. The pattern woven into this strap, a series of stepwise slashes, was similar to the patterns of Oneida wampum belts, objects that symbolized sincerity and friendship. The craft of the strap attests to the cultural similarities between Susquehannocks and Oneida, expressed through aesthetics, that may have made their captivity easier to navigate. In March 1679, a Seneca envoy detailed the social result to Maryland colonists. Meeting with the council in Notley Hall, he drew a map of Iroquoia by setting kernels of corn on the table, each designating a major Haudenosaunee settlement. Susquehannocks, he explained, lived in the middle two nations, Oneida and Onondaga. Far from degraded prisoners or laboring slaves, "the Susquehannocks

Susquehannock Carrying Strap. Courtesy of Skokloster Castle, Sweden.

goe from Towne to Towne peaceably as Friends," traveling to the other
Haudenosaunee nations whenever they wished. Haudenosaunee, who considered freedom of movement one of the core attributes of sovereignty,
would not have allowed Susquehannocks such mobility unless they had
achieved some degree of autonomy and political status within the League.[16]

The Seneca envoy portrayed a Susquehannock nation that was, somehow
at once, both a discrete nation within the League and one subsumed by the
Five Nations. Indigenous polities sometimes absorbed entire nations as subordinates, but Susquehannocks in Iroquoia seem to have enjoyed both
greater integration and greater autonomy than would be expected from this
relationship. The amphibious quality of being both Susquehannock and
Haudenosaunee without contradiction was the source of much colonial
confusion. They were still, as Algonquian intelligence had suggested in early
1678, a cohesive entity. Thomas Ludwell described Virginia's assailants as
"those six powerfull nations who goe under the comon name of the Se-
neckaes," as though the League had simply added Gandastogue intact. Yet
their division between Onondagas and Oneidas encouraged the view that
captives had been assimilated as Haudenosaunee and that Gandastogue was
no more. In fact, the envoy explained, both were true. Their nation both
did and did not exist; they could truthfully identify as Susquehannock, or
Oneida or Onondaga, as they pleased, depending on the circumstances.
They reveled in the power this camouflage gave them. The envoy said, "the

Susquehannocks laugh and jeare at the English saying they cann doe what mischief they please for that the English cannot see them." The Susquehannocks' perplexing duality allowed them to evade the grasp of colonial authorities, rendering the English blind, unbalanced, and reactive to a power they could hardly perceive, much less understand.[17]

According to later generations of Susquehannock descendants, this amphibiousness was remarkably persistent. In the nineteenth century, several citizens of the Oneida Nation appeared in a Pennsylvania courtroom to claim ownership of land that belonged to them by their Susquehannock descent. Despite having lived in Oneida country for generations, they identified as "heirs and descendants from and of the tribe of Conestoga Indians," using an Anglicized spelling of Gandastogue. These political identities were not mutually exclusive. They asserted that forced migration and amalgamation with Haudenosaunee did not deprive them of their territorial rights. These multiple identifications have continued into the twenty-first century. Ethnographers researching Indigenous peoples in modern Pennsylvania interviewed an anonymous informant who was a Seneca citizen with Susquehannock ancestry. They explained that in their community "many people have Susquehannock blood. . . . They hid with people they knew would protect them." Living in Iroquoia did not diminish their sense of being Susquehannock, nor did their Susquehannock identification diminish their belonging to the Seneca Nation. "They will say, 'We're Susquehannock' until something goes down on the Seneca Reservation, and then, 'Oh, we're Seneca.'" Iroquoia-Susquehannocks may not have been quite this comfortable with multiplicity in 1679, so soon after their incorporation. But then again, it should not be surprising that such a shift was possible for the people of Gandastogue, for whom flexible connections with foreigners was a constitutive feature of social and political belonging.[18]

The envoy revealed that a shared emotional culture and common practices of mourning war allowed Susquehannocks to influence the Haudenosaunee. They were "of such a turbulent bloody mind that they will never cease Doeing mischiefe both to the English and Pascattoway Indians soe long as a man of them is left alive." He related a story in which Susquehannocks spoke in a League council—a remarkable feat in itself because subordinate nations did not have the right to speak on their own behalf in League councils, especially in foreign affairs; that power belonged to their adoptive nations. Nevertheless, "the Greate man of the Susquehannocks made a Speech," said the envoy, "that he was pretty well Satisfied with the Revenge he had taken of the Virginians." With his kin avenged, he turned his sights elsewhere, "and now did intend to fall upon the Pascattoway Indians and the English in Maryland." The sachem's fury is palpable, even

through layers of time and translation. "The said Greate man of the Susquehannocks . . . Declared that he would never have any peace with the English, or the Pascattoway, Choptico, or any other Indians whatsoever on
the South Side of Potapsco to whom he will never cease to Doe all the mischiefe he cann." The sachem focused on targets who had wronged him
and his kin; "those on the other side of Potapsco they have noe prejudice
against them haveing never received any injury from them." He, and others
like him, kindled "the same bloody mind" among Oneidas and Onondagas,
who joined the mourning war "by the insinuation and instigation of the
Susquehannocks," with whom "they are now become all One." The envoy
distilled a complex cultural transformation into a simple message: Oneidas
and Onondagas were raiding the Chesapeake, Susquehannocks captains
were behind the raids, and their hostility was directed at the peoples who
had betrayed them.[19]

The envoy's revelation of Susquehannock influence on the League was
bad news for colonists, but his story included other troubling details. He
claimed that Virginia Algonquians had rendered "help and assistance" to
the raiders. The story corroborated rumors about tributary treachery that
had blown through settler communities since 1676 and added to the tensions between colonists and tributaries. When the envoy finished speaking,
Nicotaughsen petitioned Lord Baltimore for guns and ammunition, complaining that his people were "daily expecting their Enemy to fall upon
them." Awkwardly, though, it turned out a rogue Piscataway named Wassetass and his followers were the ones guilty of the Cunningham murders.
Rumors circulated that Wassetass's men were moving openly in Moyaone,
the Piscataway town, suggesting the complicity of the larger nation. The
council launched an investigation, which Nicotaughsen stonewalled. The
councilors decided it was "convenient to apprehend" two random Piscataway men and executed the scapegoats without trial. This crude solution
allowed them to proclaim that justice had been done, but it must have
enraged the Piscataway community. Anglo-Indian relations continued to
deteriorate even as colonial authorities received reliable intelligence that
another Susquehannock assault was coming.[20]

It came in spring. In April 1679, Susquehannock and Haudenosaunee
war parties struck Siouans in the piedmont as well as Algonquians in the
Potomac and Rappahannock Valleys. Ten Rappahannock County militia
stumbled into a shootout with a much larger force, escaping with 50 percent
casualties. The stinging defeat, wrote the traveler John Banister, "has
alarmed us, and we are in a posture of defence, daily expecting them." By
May, there was news of almost continual raids. Philip Ludwell was rattled
when the raiders, including "some Susquehannoes who have Alwaies been

our irreconcileable Enemies," pitched camp just above the falls of the James River—the same location that Susquehannocks had used to launch attacks on the Tidewater in 1676. Frontier settlers, with "great suspitions" the invaders planned on "comitting greater" attacks in the summer, fled their plantations. In June, raiders were "lately seene lurking about the Plantations" in Baltimore County, Maryland, inspiring "feares and jealousies in the Inhabitants" and provoking flight toward the coast. Rumors from the rugged Virginia-Albemarle borderlands spoke of Indian war parties—Susquehannock, Haudenosaunee, or Tuscarora, depending on who told the tale—picking off isolated plantations.[21]

The volume of these rumors amplified as they spread, spawning variations that reached a shrieking pitch in Whitehall. The repeated phrase "fears and jealousies" was a trigger for anyone in early modern England, a shorthand for hysterical anti-Catholicism. Its use to describe Native conspirators put Indians in the same conceptual category as disloyal lords who chose popery over patriotism, diabolical Jesuits in disguise, and wild Irish thirsting for English blood. Embroidered tales of Indigenous power drove home the point. Captain Ridge of the *Hopewell* informed the Lords of Trade and Plantations it "was reported to him" that "a body of eight or ten thousand Indians assembled about Blackwater [River] upon the Northern borders of Carolina, which gave great terror to the people." On July 28 the London newspaper *Domestick Intelligence* reported Indian attacks so severe that colonists could no longer travel from one plantation to the next. "It has been usual of late years for them to Commit the like," it told the English public, and "if not timely supprest, it is to be feared may have an ill influence upon the Affairs of that Countrey." By the summer of 1679, anyone in a London coffeehouse could tell you the Indian wars in America were worse than ever.[22]

The colonies did not have an effective military solution. The Privy Council recalled most of its redcoats in 1678, leaving only one hundred royal soldiers in Virginia. But knowledgeable colonists doubted that imperial troops were a match for the skirmishing tactics of Indigenous warriors. "The Indians waye of fighting," wrote Francis Moryson to men who had only ever warred on European battlefields, "is only by way of Surprize, soe that all our offensive warr is butt a huntinge of them as wolves and not fighting with them as men." Soldiers trained to square off against Spanish tercios and French musketeers could not protect colonists. "We may feele them once a week and not see them once a yeare," Moryson added, "they will burne a lone howse or two tonight, and be forty miles off tomorrow." Short of invading Iroquoia and torching its crops—the militia's viciously successful strategy for subduing Powhatans in earlier wars—the only option was bulking up defenses. The Virginia assembly ordered a new series of forts with permanent garrisons at the heads of the major rivers, farther into the interior than any previous fortifications.[23]

Those who had experienced the stealth and speed of Susquehannock warriors in 1676, and who had launched a rebellion with antifort slogans on their lips, were probably not impressed by the prospect of building even more stationary bastions. The cost, moreover, was ruinous. Upkeep of the new forts increased the poll tax by 47 lbs. of tobacco, on top of the already unprecedented high of 116 lbs. for regular expenses, an even higher total than the amount that had tipped chronic discontent into insurrectionary fury in 1676. There was no question that the Maryland government could sustain even this questionable effort. With neither imperial troops on hand nor the financial resources to maintain permanent garrisons, they ordered a company of twenty rangers to patrol the province's northern frontier. This small band stood little chance of even discovering an impending attack much less matching muskets with hundreds of Susquehannock and Haudenosaunee fighters.[24]

Colonial leaders realized that diplomacy was their only chance to end the violence. The Virginia government, recognizing Edmund Andros's special relationship with the Mohawks, called upon his help. Unfortunately, Andros discovered that the Oneida woman that Virginians had enslaved was the granddaughter of Swerisse, the respected sachem who had spoken on behalf of his nation at the 1677 Albany conference. Andros used his Mohawk contacts to redeem three of the captive English, but Swerisse refused to return the remaining woman and two children until his granddaughter, "for whoes loss he is much troubled," was returned. The best Andros could do was convince the Oneidas and Onondagas to talk with Virginia representatives in Albany. As Lord Baltimore observed, the actions of "some indiscreet or rather mad men" in Virginia had made this mess and only Virginia could clean it up. Andros's agents in Albany, assisted by Mohawk sachems, laid the groundwork for a conference by distributing gifts of wampum to the Five Nations. In the meantime, the Virginians arranged an embassy to attend the treaty council and raced to track down and buy back an Oneida woman from a sugar plantation somewhere in Bermuda.[25]

Virginian ambassador William Kendall met with Mohawk sachems in Albany on September 25, 1679. The first direct contact between Virginians and Mohawks, it was a cordial meeting. Mohawk warriors had not been involved in any of the southern raids, and Andros had coached Kendall to give copious gifts and perform ceremonies to "keep the Inviolable chayn clear and clene, meaning the Covenant chayne." Kendall's meeting with

Onondaga and Oneida representatives from October 30 to November 1 was less friendly. He accused Oneidas of breaking their covenant and threatened imperial retaliation. He warned, "your Actions . . . are Sufficient Reasones to Induce us to a Violent war against you which might Engage all our Confederatt English neighbours, subjects to our great king Charles." It was a bluff—Kendall had no authority to make such a threat when the Haudenosaunee viewed Andros as the English spokesman—but one calculated to make his propositions more palatable. Because they had agreed to return two of the remaining three English captives, Kendall said, "we are therefore willing and have and doe forgive all the Dammages you have done our Poeple (thogh very great)." He insisted, however, that "you nor any Liveing amongst you or comeing from you, for the future doe not offend or molest our Poeple or Indians Liveing amongst us." *Any living amongst you,* as so often in the colonists' fuzzily inclusive legalism, referred to Susquehannocks, the mysteriously powerful captives who Kendall demanded the Haudenosaunee keep on a leash.[26]

Onondaga and Oneida leaders affirmed their alliance and apologized for the recent violence, but placed the onus on Virginians to prevent future altercations. The Oneida spokesman Doganitajendachquo intoned, "lett all that which is Passed not only be forgotten but be Buryed in a Pitt of oblivion," so that the covenant forged in 1677 could "be kept Inviolably as a fast chayen, which is keept smooth bright and shyning like silver or gold." The Onondaga spokesman Garakontié dodged responsibility for recent raids with the perennially convenient excuse that elders could not control young men out for blood. A smallpox epidemic had ripped through their communities in 1678, unleashing a flood of grief and inciting mourning wars. "All our Indians," he explained, "have been distracted or without there Senses in Committing of this fact against the Christians in Virginia, for it is done without our order and against our will." Doganitajendachquo blamed the violence on colonists who refused to offer the hospitality due to friends. In 1677 Coursey had guaranteed the Haudenosaunee right to "freely come towards your Plantations, when wee went out a fighting to our Indian Enemyes to Refresh our Selfs if wee wer a hungry." Doganitajendachquo argued that Oneida attacks were the inevitable result when colonists brandished guns instead of offering corn. The best way to avoid violence, he admonished Kendall, was to "lett us have Victalls when wee goe a fighting against our foresaid Enemys." As for the Susquehannocks tacitly implicated by Kendall—they no longer existed. Doganitajendachquo said, "the Susquehannes are all destroyed, for which wee Return you many thanks." In a conciliatory spirit, he gave the English credit for annihilating the Susquehannocks, so nothing further needed to be done.[27]

Kendall's attempt to redeem the last remaining English captive revealed the Susquehannocks' ambiguous but potent status in Iroquoia. When Kendall asked for the return of the "Christian Girle of our Parts with you," Doganitajendachquo said he would return her if he could, "but that lyes not in our Power." He explained, "shee is brought there by dispersed Indians Called Canistoges or Susquehannes, and not taken by our Nation." The girl was now in the custody of a "Squae [squaw]"—a Susquehannock woman, in all likelihood a matron—who did not want to let her go. Perhaps, as happened in mourning wars, the woman had adopted the girl to replace a deceased relative and the two had developed an emotional bond. The Seneca envoy to Maryland had earlier mentioned that the "English which were taken . . . are become all one Indians with themselves." Perhaps the girl did not want to return any more than the matron wanted to let her go; when given the chance to return, many European captives, particularly women, chose to remain with their new kin instead. Doganitajendachquo promised "the Sachims shall sitt about it, and doe there endevour" to convince the Susquehannock to return the English girl, "and be glad when shee shall have attained to her liberty." But Oneida sachems could not compel the matron's consent, and the decision was in her hands. Doganitajendachquo was obviously dismayed by his inability to meet Kendall's demand, giving the enormously valuable gift of a twenty-row wampum belt in recompense. Yet he revealed the Susquehannocks' amphibious state of being at once "all destroyed," merely "dispersed Indians" instead of a nation, yet still possessing the sovereign power to defy the wishes of their supposed captors even when international peace hung in the balance.[28]

The wrangling over Swerisse's granddaughter and the English girl, while superficially similar in each side's determination to redeem them, illuminates the different roles that captivity played in each society—roles that were in the midst of dramatic change. Among the Haudenosaunee, captivity was less an economic institution than a social one. Although captives did perform labor, especially during an initial probationary period, the ceremonial process of requickening transformed foreigners into members of the community. Traditionally, Haudenosaunee had expected captives to abandon natal affiliations and embrace their new identity. However, the sheer volume of captives produced by midcentury mourning wars promoted tolerance of something less than total assimilation, as a Jesuit missionary observed of ostensibly captive Wendats in 1656. "They retain their own customs and peculiar usages," he reported, "and live apart from the Iroquois, satisfied to be united with them in good feeling and friendship." Susquehannocks who arrived en masse in 1677 shared some version of this experience, retaining aspects of their society and culture but also uniting with the Haudenosaunee. Changing practices did not diminish the importance of captivity in constituting the nation. In the aftermath of death—such as the epidemic that struck Oneida country in 1678—it repaired the social fabric, healed grief, and restored peace. Women and girls were preferred because they were less likely to resist than men and more likely to accept their new status. As female captives became Haudenosaunee wives, they gave birth to children who ensured the future of the nation. That is why all the captives that Susquehannocks and Oneidas took in 1678 were female, and perhaps one of the reasons why a Susquehannock matron might not want to let her Christian girl go.[29]

Among Virginia colonists, by contrast, forms of Indigenous captivity were becoming chattel slavery. For most of the century, Indian captives taken in "just wars" had been servants or apprentices bound for limited periods of time, ostensibly for the purpose of converting them to English culture and "civility." Their status remained legally ambiguous even as the laws governing black slavery progressively tightened. But the innovations that made Indian bodies into a financial reward for military service eroded earlier goals of cultural conversion in favor of economic considerations. While the law clearly defined Indian captives as servants in 1670, colonists debated the status of new captives in 1677 and in 1678 the justices of Charles City County granted a petition to keep "an Indian boy . . . as a slave for life." Such ad hoc decisions became provincial policy in 1682, when a statute defined all Indian captives as slaves. In contrast to the Iroquoian goal of social integration, Native captives such as the enslaved Oneida woman were alienated from colonial life. They were turned into commodities, their bodies made fungible and disposable, their personhood reduced to labor that could be exploited for profit. Because control of one's dependents was central to masculine identity, mastery over chattel slaves became increasingly fundamental to patriarchal privilege. Female slaves were especially valuable because, according to English ethnic stereotypes, they were "drudges" accustomed to menial labor. They were as valuable for their reproductive capacities as their productive ones, bearing children who could be as ruthlessly exploited as their parents. That is perhaps why colonists in 1678 executed the Oneida man they captured but sold the Oneida woman to a Bermuda planter, and her indistinguishability from any other laboring woman was the reason she was easy to buy back.[30]

With Swerisse's granddaughter on a ship to North America and the Oneida promise to work on redeeming the English girl, the results of the 1679 Albany conference were apparently satisfactory. Mohawks strengthened their links with the southern colonies, Onondagas and Oneidas reminded the English of their obligations, and Kendall received apologies for past wrongs and vague promises for future good behavior. In February 1680, Andros wrote to Whitehall with a sunny view of the accomplishment. He beamed that he had "concluded an Honorable Peace between the Indians and Christians of Virginia and Maryland," thus resolving the crisis. Andros should have known better. Between the end of the conference in November and his letter in February, the snows fell and warriors sheathed their knives for the winter. But, no matter what colonists thought they had accomplished in Albany, Susquehannocks and their Haudenosaunee allies had no intention of keeping them sheathed after the thaw.[31]

Susquehannock power grew each year, and so did the intensity of their assaults. Successful raids netted captives, causing the nation's numbers to swell. In 1677, Jacob had reported about one hundred Susquehannock captives carried north to Onondaga and Oneida. By 1681, according to a Haudenosaunee ambassador, Susquehannocks numbered roughly four hundred people living among all five League nations. In other words, the population identifying as Susquehannock quadrupled in just four years, a demographic explosion made possible by the absorption of Siouan and Algonquian captives. Unrelenting raids depleted the defenders' manpower while augmenting the attacking forces, giving Susquehannock mourning wars greater reach with every passing season. In 1680, Piscataways reported, "the Susquehannohs told them that they would have revenge for their greate men killed [in] the late warr and that they expected to have their Indians taken by us to be restored." It is not surprising that Susquehannocks would desire to soothe their grief for the dead by killing and capturing the enemies responsible, or that they would want to make their communities whole by redeeming captive kin. It is perhaps more surprising, though, that the women and men who had been carried into bondage into Iroquoia in 1677 were, by 1680, able to enlist hundreds of Haudenosaunee allies to their cause.[32]

Raids gained steam from another unexpected fuel: the captives themselves. Susquehannocks were not the only captives in Iroquoia who retained connections to their natal identities. The Seneca envoy who had provided colonists with vital intelligence about Susquehannocks in Iroquoia was born Anacostank, one of the smaller Potomac nations historically affiliated with the Piscataway chiefdom. Captured and adopted by the Senecas, he now identified with both nations. He said, "he had received soe much civility and kindness from them [Senecas] that he did long to see them as much as his owne Friends," but nevertheless considered his visit to the Chesapeake to be "Comeing home." While this envoy came on a diplomatic errand, other requickened Algonquians spearheaded assaults on their former countrymen. In 1681, Haudenosaunee war captains negotiating with Maryland militia commanders explained, with apparent exasperation, that the latest raid on the Piscataways "was not altogether as their greate men pleased." What seemed to be Haudenosaunee hostility was actually the work of "some which they had tooke Prisoners from the Pascattowayes" who "came now with them," intent on going "into the Fort to fetch out their Relations." In a striking parallel to Susquehannock experiences a few years earlier, Piscataway captives were harnessing their captors' military power to retrieve their kin, with the apparent goal of reconstituting their communities among the Haudenosaunee. The diffusion of like-minded Algonquians throughout Iroquoia added momentum to the Susquehannocks' wars.[33]

Colonists were confused by this desire to violently "fetch" relatives, but it may have been a reasonable goal within the emotional culture of mourning war. Despite the coercion and violence inherent in the process of capture and requickening, some modern Haudenosaunee emphasize that it was a voluntary choice for foreigners to embrace their new identities and the political allegiance that came with it. According to the twentieth-century Cayuga Chief Jacob Thomas, "any nation or individual from outside," by learning the ways of the Great Law of Peace, "would discipline their minds and spirits to obey and honour the wishes of the Council of the League." One way that captives might discipline themselves—that is, to demonstrate their loyalty to the Longhouse—would be to lead raids against their former people. Such raids might also reflect the efforts of captives to co-opt Haudenosaunee mourning wars for their own purposes. For Natives weary of the slow violence of life under the rule of English colonizers, the prospect of finding shelter under the Haudenosaunee Tree of Peace might have been attractive, inspiring bold action to reunite friends and family. Because kinship was the basis for political belonging, those kin were the sinews of power. Gathering old kin in a new country, even if by force, could allow unproven and ambitious leaders to rapidly enhance their political influence. By leading raids against their natal communities, in other words, captives could make the best of a bad situation by simultaneously performing Haudenosaunee identity, reviving their communities, and reshaping the country of their captors.[34]

The complex politics in Iroquoia stoked the fires of war. In spring 1680, Susquehannock and Haudenosaunee warriors escalated from lightning raids to assaults on fortified positions. In early May, three hundred "Sinniquo and Susquehannoh Indians" laid siege to Moyaone, building a fort five hundred yards from the Piscataways' palisades to cut off their escape. Tayac Nicotaughsen and his councilors tried to negotiate. The antagonists "severall times discoursed with each other," but refused any possibility of rapprochement. Piscataways fought, losing two men but forcing the attackers to lift the siege. By the time the Maryland Council scrambled the militia to assist, the raiders had melted away, but Piscataways believed they would return with reinforcements. Small parties of Susquehannocks and Haudenosaunee foraged for provisions in colonial settlements, expecting the English to provide hospitality as friends in the covenant. When colonists fled or refused, warriors rummaged through houses, slaughtered livestock for food, and sometimes plundered guns, clothing, and other valuables. Piscataway informants claimed that during the siege Susquehannock warriors "severall times asked where the English men were on the Pascattoway side," suggesting that direct attacks on colonists would swiftly follow.[35]

The attackers' boldness caused "great terror and amazement of the English Inhabitants in those parts not knowing what their Designe may be." As frontier colonists fled, panic mutated from fear of the invaders into fear of their targets. Negotiations between Nicotaughsen and enemy captains, conducted beyond range of colonists' observation and known only from Native reports, engendered suspicion that the tayac might be so desperate he would switch allegiance. Militia captain Randolph Brandt, who arrived with a squadron of twenty men too late to catch the attackers, wrote, "I very much doubt our Indians," and concluded that "if they are not Countenanced they will submitt to the Senniquo." Amid rising tensions, rogue colonists—possibly traveling Virginians—murdered a prominent Piscataway in a drunken altercation on the banks of Aquia Creek. Indigenous men in warpaint who claimed to be Senecas but "spoke in the Pascattoway tongue" accosted settlers in Anne Arundel County. They could have been Piscataways angry about the murder, requickened Algonquians on the hunt, or bilingual Haudenosaunee; there was no way for colonists to tell. Rumors spread that tributary fighters had already joined the Susquehannock side.[36]

While Marylanders struggled to hold together, Virginians had a reprieve. Nicholas Spencer, appointed colonial secretary after Thomas Ludwell's death, tentatively reported they had "made as firme a peace with the Northern Indians as with Indians can bee concluded." Susquehannocks and their allies concentrated their forces on the Potomac and, according to the Dutch traveler Jasper Danckaerts, went "south to make war against the Indians of Carolina, beyond Virginia." Although colonists received only vague reports of the raids in 1680, intelligence about 1681 incursions into the southern piedmont detailed the devastating results. By summer they had "taken the Occonogee Iseland" and captured "the King and many of his Indians." Haudenosaunee made up the bulk of the forces, but there was no mistaking who led the charge. Spencer wrote, "the remaynng part of the Susquehanas . . . were the movers of the Senacoes to their late South-erne Expedition, with whom it is to be feared we shall be Infested whilst any Susquahanas are Liveing amongst them." What Bacon and his Volun-teers had failed to do in 1676, Susquehannocks accomplished five years later. The surviving Occaneechis migrated west into the Appalachians in search of refuge from further assault. Despite the scale of this onslaught, the battles occurred far beyond Virginia's borders. From the northern fron-tier, William Fitzhugh wrote, "we are at present very quiet from our In-dian Enemies." The raiders left Tidewater colonists and Algonquians alone, apparently respecting the covenant they made with Kendall.[37]

Unfortunately, even without the catalyst of foreign invasion, the bad blood between colonists who had come to see all Indians as enemies and tributaries who rejected the new colonial order sparked a new round of violence. Breakaway bands dedicated to resisting Cockacoeske and her imperial backers gathered their forces. In early 1680, a party of dissident Chickahominies killed an English family near the falls of the James. Militia and loyal tributaries tracked down the party's settlement, slaughtered its men, and enslaved the women and children. This was only one of many groups, however, and they were prepared to fight against overwhelming odds. "Severall Townes are united and prepareing for Warr," wrote Spencer, "which if not Timely stopt will Certainely fly into a Nationall Warr."[38]

The return of English captives from Iroquoia, carrying reports that Virginia Algonquians "have been seen to be amongst them," enflamed public opinion and led to extralegal violence. These rumors encouraged dark speculation that Haudenosaunee raids had been "induced by the Neighbor Indians in amity with us," or even that raiders who seemed to be Haude-nosaunee were Algonquians in disguise, "the ill assured Neighbour Or pretended forreigne Indians." Acting governor Chicheley, hoping to broker a cease-fire, called upon Abraham Wood to arrange a convocation of tributary leaders in Jamestown. Unfortunately, "the clandestine designes of some Indian traders" sabotaged the talks. William Byrd, former Volun-teer leader and pioneering Indian slaver, ambushed the ambassadors, "destroying . . . seven Indian men after surrender, and bringing away twelve women and children captives." The toxic cocktail of laws rewarding mili-tary service with human plunder, the growing might of Indian slave traders, and stewing ethnic hatred proved far more compelling than the prospect of peace. The result, which struck the assembly as a cruel injustice, was entirely predictable: "new disturbances made by the Indians Swollen to the greater Magnitude."[39]

Byrd's brazen attack on Algonquian leaders at Jamestown points toward the surging importance of the Indian slave trade. It grew in part because of changing English attitudes about Indigenous slavery, but the shift was only possible because of Susquehannock attacks against their Indigenous enemies. The Occaneechis had held a stranglehold on the southeastern road network from the strategic crossroads of Occaneechi Island. When Susquehannock assault forced the Occaneechis west, it created a vacuum of power. Ambitious and aggressive colonists swarmed into the interior after the assembly lifted all restrictions on Indian trade in 1680. William Byrd rapidly made inroads as far as Cherokee country, managing a small army of traders willing to brave the danger of the newly opened roads. Cadwallader Jones, who parlayed his reputation as an Indian-fighter into command of the Rappahannock River fort, spearheaded new slaving routes with breathtaking speed. By 1682 his network stretched from the Delaware Bay to what is currently central Georgia, gobbling up "indyan children Prisoners." These organized enterprises were accompanied by a stream of wildcat traders, which Byrd described as a "great number of Idle Persons goeing out to trucke and trade amongst the Indians," who left little trace in the records. Despite the danger, many men thought the prospect of growing rich by enslaving Indians tempting enough to risk it.[40]

Ripple effects of Susquehannock victory over the Occaneechis contributed to the entrenchment of Indigenous slavery. Occaneechi power had not only restrained the scale of Virginia's slaving, but had also created a geographic partition separating the trade networks of Virginia and Carolina. After 1681, the Southeast became a free-for-all as competing factions in both colonies established partnerships with any Native group willing to sell captives. In Carolina, the Lords Proprietors forbade Indigenous slaving in the interests of international stability, but their efforts foundered on the self-interested defiance of colonists, including officials who were supposed to enforce their orders. Carolinian slavers based out of Charles Town were ruthless, partnering with and then betraying one Native group after another, even arming those who raided Virginia. Nations such as the Westos, Yamasees, and Tuscaroras raided as far as the Gulf coast for captives to sell in Charles Town, Albemarle, and Rappahannock. Albemarle planters claimed an increasing number of enslaved Natives as "headrights" that entitled them to fifty acres of land, using the slave trade as fuel for both territorial expansion and capital accumulation. The phenomenon was not confined to the South. Native groups as far north as the upper Delaware Valley Minisinks participated in raids on Indigenous mission communities in Spanish Florida. William Byrd corresponded with merchant and New York City mayor Stephanus van Cortlandt to purchase "wampum . . . large, even, and well strung," so he could trade it to Tuscaroras for enslaved Indians. In 1679, New York, which stipulated that "all Indyans here, are free and not slaves, nor can bee forct to bee servants," made exceptions for those "brought from the Bay of Campechio"—the Gulf of Mexico—"and other foreign parts." The bloody boom in this trade was made possible by the combination of colonial contempt for Indigenous life, insatiable demand for plantation labor, and the Susquehannocks' opening of the interior transportation network.[41]

With the slave trade wreaking havoc on everyone as it enriched only a few, Maryland authorities sought to calm internal tensions, but vitriolic cleavages hamstrung their efforts. In 1680, Nicotaughsen complained that his people were "oppressed by the Sinniquo and Susquehannohs," and pressed the Maryland Council for militia and weapons to aid in their defense. The council instead pushed for their removal to the Eastern Shore under protection of the more populous Nanticokes. The tayac countered with a proposal out of Cockacoeske's playbook: "if the Lordshipp will order the neighbouring Indians (viz) Mattawomans, Chopticos etc up to Piscattoway they will keepe their ground and maintaine their Fort against their Enemies." It made military sense to consolidate tributary forces, but it would also use English power to place several nations under Piscataway authority, essentially reconstituting the old Piscataway paramount chiefdom. Mattawomans and Chopticos, led by the werowance Maquata, declared they "will not remoove but will Defend their Interest to their utmost power." He suspected, with good reason, that "by their goeing thither they should be dispossessed of their Lands," and "alleadgeth the Eastern Shore Indians are as much their Enemies as the Susquehannohs." While tributary nations tussled over security, autonomy, and power, dragging the government into the middle, an increasing number of settlers saw nothing but the menace that Indians posed. John Waterton, justice of the peace of Anne Arundel County, gathered an extralegal volunteer squad "to see if we can find the Indians," proclaiming he acted "for the Countrey Service." Militia captain George Wells raced to inform the council of this "rash unadvised Actions of foolish people," condemning "him and those of his Company who are forward to their owne ruine to create an Enemy."[42]

Virginian infighting was equally venomous. When the new royal governor, Thomas Lord Culpeper, arrived in June he attempted to shore up the Treaty of Middle Plantation. Francis Moryson had suggested each treaty signatory should be gifted a robe of royal purple and a gilded crown, "to import that they Actually as well as confessarily hold these their very Crownes from your Majestie." The Lords of Trade agreed, throwing in luxurious gifts such as a hat of white beaver fur and band of silver, a gold-hilted sword and pair of inlaid pistols for John West, and a wardrobe of silk and velvet gowns fit for a season at the king's court. The gifts pleased

Cockacoeske and Queen Catherine, and apparently helped soothe raw nerves among tributaries. "Our Indians," Spencer reported, "this summer have been, of a peaceable and quiett demeanor." Yet the council sputtered with rage. Not bothering to hide their loathing for the king's Indian subjects, they howled that "such Marks of Dignity as Coronets . . . ought not to be prostituted to such mean persons." Councilors argued that the gifts would be interpreted as weakness, "they esteeming presents to be the effects of fear," would cause jealousy among the nations who did not receive gifts, and would only drag colonists deeper into disputes between squabbling tributaries. The assembly stated, "many Murthers and depradations hav[e] been done upon his Majesties Subjects Since the peace was made," but that was only to be expected "according to the faithless and Savage Nature of those people." The whole Treaty of Middle Planation, they concluded, was sheer folly.[43]

Reeling under foreign assault, with alliances between English and Indians ready to crack, the colonies fell back on costly and ineffective military solutions. Maryland militia, with or without legal commissions, rode back and forth across the frontier in search of rampaging Susquehannocks, treacherous Piscataways, or both. But they always seemed one step behind the elusive raiders. When John Waterton's volunteers, marching "to the releife of those who had for fear deserted their houses," finally tracked down a small band of raiders, "what Indians were Discovered escaped their hands." Piscataways continued to stymie the government's plans for their removal, but despite rumors of tributary collusion with the enemy the council had little choice but to send shipments of ammunition to the people bearing the brunt of the fighting.[44]

The Virginia government stuck to its network of manned fortifications, but the exorbitant expense was impossible to maintain in the midst of an economic crisis brought about by low tobacco prices. Spencer reported, "if tobacco should Continue soe meane in its Value as it is, and the Countrey engaged in a Warr," then the colony "will not be Able to support it selfe." With military spending "too chargeable for the greate poverty of the inhabitants of this country" but also "deemed of an absolute necessity," the assembly privatized security. They reduced garrisons to skeleton crews of twenty men and outsourced provisioning to contractors. The burgesses empowered "undertakers" to create militarized frontier enclaves to defend against incursions. Even with these measures, however, the sprawling expanse of Virginia settlements meant there were "no meanes nor wayes Possible for defence, and by the Country held in Continuall feares and Apprehensions of Indian Warrs." As inflexible military spending on fortifications of dubious value threatened to ruin the colony, fear of sudden attack was institutionalized as part of daily life. Laws required men to re-main armed for war at all times, even when attending Sunday services. Lest such desperate measures provoke whispers that the government was not protecting its people, the assembly also stiffened the fine for "raising false and scandalous reports" to a brutal £500 sterling.[45]

In the rising heat of 1680's summer, Susquehannocks and Haudenosaunee launched another wave of attacks on Potomac Algonquians. In early June, Piscataways informed Maryland commanders that "Susquehannohs and Sinniquos . . . have killed seaven of their men." Nicotaughsen, "haveing great feares and jealousies of the Sinniquo and Susquehannoh Indians their professed enemies," came to the painful conclusion that it was more impor-tant to save his people from raiders than his land from squatters. The council allowed the Piscataways to relocate to Zekiah, a swampy tract of land owned by the Calverts, where they hastily threw up houses and pali-sades. By the end of the month raiders were probing Mattawoman terri-tory and sweeping Zekiah swamp, prompting worries that Mattawomans would run out of powder and Piscataways would be discovered before they had time to complete their fortifications. As tributaries retreated, Natives of unknown identity assaulted settlers on the Gunpowder and Bush Rivers in Baltimore County. George Wells, studying their route and noting it was different from the paths usually traveled by Haudenosaunee, concluded, "it does not appear to be the Sinniquos as I feared at first." Rather, "it is some Susquehannohs fled from the Sinniquo Army," rogues who were probably also "those that did the mischief for the severall before goeing yeares in the same River." But there was no way to be sure and there was little he could do except urge his dragoons on another fruitless chase.[46]

As Anglo-Indian violence consumed the Chesapeake colonies, Jacob My Friend stepped in. The Maryland government had asked him to intervene as soon as they received credible intelligence that the attackers were Susque-hannock. In 1678, Jacob made contact with the men camped in the ruins of Gandastogue, opening a line of communication that he built upon in 1680. As raiders harried Zekiah swamp and the northern frontier in June, he advised Captain Wells how to "speake with their great men before the fire blaze out" into "an Intestine Warr." Jacob warned that they would likely launch more attacks in July or August. He suggested that "some person that understands the language" should be stationed at the trading post of Anthony Demondidier, which sat astride the main overland route between the Susquehanna River and the Potomac, to hail the war captains as they passed. He was, the council stated without hesitation, "the fittest man they cann think" for the job, "being a person that understands well the language of the said Indians." They commissioned him as the province's envoy, instructing him to meet with incoming Susquehannocks at Demondidier's post, convince their leaders to parlay, and escort the Indian embassy to a meeting with Lord Baltimore.[47]

What happened next is difficult to determine, as it must be reconstructed from accusations that surfaced during Jacob's indictment for treason and his spirited defense. According to Jacob's testimony, in early September he learned that a large party of Oneidas was gathering at the falls of the Susquehanna River. As per his instructions, he immediately sent gifts to their captains as an invitation to travel to Spesutie Island, where they met with Baltimore County magistrates George Wells and Henry Johnson. Speaking through Jacob as an interpreter, the officers proposed that the Oneidas return home and send diplomats to St. Mary's City for a meeting with Lord Baltimore and the council. According to the charges against him, however, Jacob learned about the Oneida gathering almost as soon as they camped at the Susquehanna falls in the beginning of August. Ignoring his instructions, he invited the Oneida captains to his trading post, gave a gift of duffels, and proposed the Oneidas "go home and fetch an Army." On their return, he promised, "Jacob would be ready in Arms to Assist the said Onneide Indians in Invading this Province in Order to destroy the Pisscattaway Indians." Only after forming this secret pact did Jacob inform Wells and Johnson and go through the farce of pretending to arrange a conference.[48]

Either Jacob fulfilled his commission to the letter or he hatched a conspiracy to betray the province. But which story is true? Jacob had convincing alibis, including several witnesses who placed him at his Delaware home at the time he supposedly held this clandestine meeting. On the other hand, the case against Jacob was based on the word of the Oneida sachem Tekanistapendacquo, whose testimony would naturally carry some weight. The question gets more complicated if, as circumstantial evidence suggests, the "Oneidas" in question were actually Iroquoia-Susquehannocks. They had come as members of war parties that Piscataway informants identified as both Haudenosaunee and Susquehannock. Their movements were more consistent with Susquehannock habits than Haudenosaunee. Whereas Haudenosaunee typically gathered at the forks of the Susquehanna River, this group camped seventy miles farther south at the falls of the river, a well-established rendezvous point for Susquehannocks. During their conference with Wells and Johnson, these "Oneidas" accepted a pass of safe passage and promised to travel to St. Mary's City. Rather than travel on Western Shore highways frequented by Haudenosaunee, they went down Eastern Shore paths, through lands that Susquehannocks had claimed in

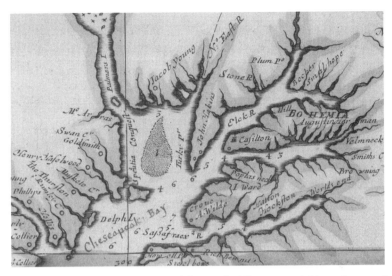

Jacob My Friend's trading post. Detail from John Thornton, *A Map of some of the south and east bounds of Pennsylvania in America* (London, 1681). Courtesy of the John Carter Brown Library at Brown University.

their 1652 treaty of friendship with Maryland. Instead of heading to St. Mary's, they cut a swathe of destruction through Maryland, brandishing their diplomatic badge all the while. Perhaps, like other Susquehannocks in Iroquoia, they committed their mischief as they laughed and jeered at the English, who could not after all see them.[49]

Whether Jacob met with Oneidas in secret, and whether those Oneidas were once people of Gandastogue, this much is certain: the meeting on Spesutie Island did not pave the road to peace. After a visit to Jacob's trading post for a bout of drinking and carousing, the war parties returned to Iroquoia. But they did not send ambassadors to St. Mary's City. In fact, they did not even wait until spring to launch their next attack. Far from accepting Maryland's olive branch, they escalated their wars to unprecedented intensity.

These raiders from the north disoriented colonial observers and crippled their attempts to respond. The English lacked the information to see, and the tools to understand, the dynamics of mourning war, captivity, and requickening. The protean identities of assimilated peoples confounded colonists who, even in the best circumstances, had trouble telling Indians apart. The insurgent politics of incorporated nations, who wielded obscure forms of influence on their hosts, rendered Indigenous agendas inscrutable. Lord Baltimore's 1682 exchange with Anthony Brockholls, acting governor of New York during Andros's absence, exemplifies the colonial dilemma. Baltimore asked Brockholls for help in ending the violence committed by "Northern Indians," using this vague catch-all because he could not be sure which nations were responsible. Brockholls replied, "the Northerne Indians whom you Charge to have been the Actors of those Mischeifs are soe Numerous, farr, Distant and of soe many Severall Nations that I know not whom to Aske Sattisfaction of."[50]

Susquehannocks, a small remnant of a seemingly broken nation held captive far from home, should not have been able to reduce colonial governors to helpless frustration. But they did. They survived decades of grinding war, agonizing demographic collapse, betrayal of colonial allies, and finally, capture and forced incorporation by the Haudenosaunee. Yet in Iroquoia they managed much more than survival. They leapt back from the edge of extinction, acquired prestige and power among their hosts, and harnessed the League's military energies to pursue their own political goals—all in less than two years. The flow of captives during decades of mourning war paved the way for this transformation. What had seemed to be the slow withering of the Susquehannock nation was also the gradual flowering of a network of kin within Iroquoia. The influx of captives after Shackamaxon galvanized this network and engineered a rise so rapid, and so complete, that Susquehannock leaders exercised an influence on their captors wildly out of proportion to their numbers. Under the resulting onslaught, the colonies sank into fiscal crisis, military paralysis, and ethnic infighting. They were unable even to grasp, much less to battle, the elusive leviathan of Susquehannock power. After 1680, the strength of that leviathan only grew.

· 7 ·

SUSQUEHANNOCK RESURGENCE
AND COLONIAL CRISIS

In 1681, four years after the Albany conference first joined Maryland and Iroquoia in a covenant of friendship, the Susquehannocks' wars raged with no end in sight. Tributary nations were steadily ground down, tensions between settlers and Algonquians regularly flared up, and colonial militaries were both expensive and ineffective. Although there had been only a handful of English casualties, authorities behaved as though the province stood on the brink of disaster. Lord Baltimore, in a speech to an assembly convened to address the crisis, belied the enormity of the danger. Their task, he told the representatives in the Lower House, was to find a way to renew the 1677 treaty with the Haudenosaunee, "to rid the Province, of these Susquehannahs and other Mixt Nations that come Yearly down and infest both Maryland and Virginia." Ending the wars spearheaded by Susquehannock captains was "the only Sure foundation upon which Our future Peace and Tranquility must Depend." The danger was not limited to foreign raiders or rogue tributaries; Anglo-Indian war threatened to provoke insurrection. Baltimore argued that Susquehannock violence allowed "great Licence and Liberty [that] Severall Wicked Malicious Persons give themselves in broaching Lyes and false Stories which greatly Disquiet all good People." The smallest incident could give rise to "another Rebellion on foot in this Province."[1]

The pattern Lord Baltimore described was a feedback loop between Anglo-Indian violence and colonial crisis. The pressure on the colonies' fragile political orders had been building for years. The fierce rivalries that erupted in 1676 had been buried by the covenants of 1677, but they were not forgotten. As waves of Indigenous assault crashed against the colonies, factional conflicts resurfaced and gained a vicious new energy. Disputes among settlers pushed relations with Native tributaries to the breaking point, and in the process entrenched the improvised racial thinking that emerged from earlier emergencies. The danger of rebellion, the specter of ethnic violence, and the deeper societal changes that they engendered were a consequence of the pervasive experience of warfare. Because, as Baltimore indicated, the waves of attack were unrelenting. Susquehannocks and their coalition of "Mixt Nations" came with the spring and left in autumn, but they always returned. Their appearances can seem scattershot or random in the colonial records, which sporadically mention Indigenous attacks amid reams of paper on personal disputes, tobacco economics, and squabbles over boundary lines. In actuality, Susquehannock-led raids were devastatingly regular. As Philip Ludwell explained after the pattern had become apparent, "Northern Indians" prompted by "some Susqehannoes" scoured the frontiers on a rhythmic cycle "according to their Annuall Custome." Considering the seasonal pattern of Indigenous warfare—and indeed, the seasonal patterns everywhere before the invention of oil, rubber, and mechanized steel—fighting was constant between 1678 and 1685.[2]

Susquehannocks were at the center of the maelstrom. Becoming powers again from within Iroquoia, their recovery pushed the English colonies toward disorder. The cycle of violence combined all the forces that drove earlier phases of the Time of Anarchy. Susquehannock attacks, guided by the emotional logic of mourning war, spread terror, and terror undermined the patriarchal social order. Colonial uncertainty about the identities of attackers fueled fear, and rumor thrived in its wake. As colonists struggled to grasp the agents directing this violence, conspiracy theories proliferated. Localized disputes transformed into grandiose struggles against extravagant evil, aggravating political cleavages among colonists and their Native neighbors. The Susquehannocks' ability to capture not only Haudenosaunee power, but also the energies of Algonquian captives, added energy to each new round of raids. As political grievances and economic discontent fused with regular waves of carnage on the frontier, racial hatred and the contagion of rebellion gathered a terrible momentum. The Susquehannocks, in resurgence, became a force that kept the English colonies perpetually on the edge of crisis.

The destructive spiral of Anglo-Indian violence after 1677 occurred in the midst of turbulent factionalism among colonists. Although Governor Jeffreys ousted Sir William Berkeley, the Green Spring faction did not flinch from doing battle, as Councilor James Bray put it, "in Defence of the Rights Priviledges and Honor" of the oligarchs. After Berkeley died during his journey to England, his widow Lady Frances Culpeper Berkeley led the faction in ruthlessly suppressing defeated rebels such as Sarah Drummond. When Jeffreys defended repentant rebels in pursuit of reconciliation, Philip Ludwell, who married Lady Berkeley in 1680, vilified Jeffreys as "a Pittifull little fellow with a Perrewigg" and publicly denounced his government as "rule by an Arbitrary power." Jeffreys, recognizing the challenge to the Stuart mission of imperial centralization—and, no doubt, the dangerous language of antipopery encoded in the word "arbitrary"—complained to Whitehall that his own council was a "Caball" whose members "endeavour To Avoid his Majestyes Authority." Meanwhile, former rebels recovered political office and spouted unrepentant sedition. Newly politicized "young freemen" caused "great disorders of elections" by demanding voting rights, tax relief, and a voice in reforming the deep injustices in their society. Rebel women such as Elizabeth Regan "fomented manye Malignant and rebellious Words tending to Sedition." Lady Berkeley, in a poignant letter written to her husband when she had not yet received news of his death, was certain that unless "a few more examples should be made . . . there will be no face of Goverment hear."[3]

Jeffreys's death in December 1678 left the Green Spring faction ascendant, but their dominance left colonists with "a great deal of ill bloud among them, and makes them look upon one another as enemies." The garrison of royal soldiers, intended to bring order and bolster imperial rule, only made things worse. The troops expressed sharp dissatisfaction with the government's failure to quarter and provision them, reportedly shouting, "hang the Governor and God damn those Counsellors." Acting governor Chicheley marched the soldiers up the James River "to Keepe in Awe some of The Late Rebells who Then were Somewhat Mutinous," but the soldiers threatened to mutiny themselves. The old Volunteers were waiting in the wings, and authorities feared that discontented imperial troops would "Joyne with the old party to disturb our Peace."[4]

Upheaval in Albemarle fueled fears of renewed rebellion. Thomas Eastchurch, the commissioned governor for whom Thomas Miller was a deputy, arrived in Virginia in December 1677 and found his province in "open Rebellion." Revolutionary leaders mitigated their antimonarchical fervor and acknowledged "our selves to be his Majesties Faithfull Subjects in all Respects," but they refused to recognize proprietary authority and declined to pay the customs duties mandated by the Navigation Acts. They denounced Miller, "who was Illegally sent here [as] President by Thomas Eastchurch," and scoffed at Eastchurch's claim to legitimate rule over Albemarle, "his Government as he pretends it." Eastchurch emphasized the danger of the Albemarle insurrection spreading northward, warning of "the Dangerous Consequence of this Rebellion to Virginia as well as Albemarle, if it be not

Speedily Quasht." Albemarle had been a haven for fleeing Volunteers, who would leap at the chance to reignite their struggle. Lady Berkeley reported that "40 of the Rogues that wear run to the Southward" had mounted a sortie into Virginia, capturing a member of the council before falling into drinking and raucous partying that "alaramed all that part of the Counterie." Secretary Thomas Ludwell acknowledged, "we must have an eye to them lest our people doe from that sparke take fire againe." The rebellion was alive, Virginians thought, and could spread in an instant.[5]

Eastchurch's illness and death in February 1678 stalled any action. The revolutionaries formed their own council, courts, and assembly, ruling themselves and "despiseing all Authority but Their Owne." By the end of 1679, their new government was up and running, to the fury and frustration of Virginia officials. Albemarle, fumed Virginia governor Thomas Lord Culpeper in 1681, "is the Sinke of America, the Refuge of our Renegadoes, and till in better order, Dangerous to us." Although Whitehall debated sending military forces "to reduce that Countrey into obedience," the Lords Proprietors chose the cheaper option of sending a new governor, Seth Sothel. Unfortunately, Sothel was captured en route by Algerine privateers and sold into slavery in North Africa. The Lords Proprietors quietly allowed the troublesome province to govern itself despite complaints of its detrimental effects on other colonies. When Sothel finally took up his post in 1683, after ransom from captivity, he ignored orders from the Lords Proprietors to prosecute rebels and instead installed several of them as his councilors. His confiscation of four thousand acres belonging to Lady Berkeley may have initially gratified the revolutionaries, but it did not advertise to anyone that law and order had returned to Albemarle. Sothel then used corrupt appointees to the county court to imprison political opponents, both revolutionary leaders such as George Durant and proprietary agents such as Timothy Biggs. Viewed from Jamestown or London, it seemed that Albemarle had traded the anarchy of revolution for the kind of arbitrary rule that every good English subject hated and feared.[6]

Transatlantic turmoil fed instability in Maryland, giving new life to conspiracy theories linking the Calverts' Catholicism to Indigenous violence. In 1678, England was rocked by the Popish Plot, a supposed conspiracy to assassinate King Charles II and install his Catholic brother James on the throne. Whigs in Parliament fulminated about secret cabals of papists controlling the levers of state and Jesuit secret agents preparing the way for a French invasion. Their calls to exclude James—and any other Catholic—from ever holding the crown provoked the most serious political crisis the realm had faced since the Restoration. English antipopery reached such a fevered pitch that peers in the House of Lords bandied about accusations that members of the English nobility were sponsoring a Jesuit infiltration of Virginia. Because a circle of Irish lords were purported to be the ring-leaders behind the Popish Plot, Protestants in Maryland considered Lord Baltimore—whose lands and manor were in Leinster County, Ireland—an obvious suspect. In 1679, news broke that hostilities between England and France had flared up in Europe, prompting fears of war and suspicions that English Catholics would stand with their coreligionists rather than their countrymen.[7]

As "report of the troubles in England" and dubious "news of a French war" percolated through English America, they conjured associations with black-robed Jesuits and their Indigenous converts. The traveler Jasper Danckaerts claimed that Jesuits lived in every Indian town from the Chesapeake to Canada. The missionary "teaches and advises the Indians," who "begin to listen to them too much; so much so, that some people in Virginia and Maryland as well as in New Netherland [New York], have been apprehensive lest there might be an outbreak" of Franco-Indian attackers. Colonists needed little prodding to assume the worst. Authorities in Virginia believed that "some of our Indians intend more mischeife (that is the young men) . . . if there be a warr with france." Josias Fendall, having already made himself popular by pledging to destroy all Indians if given the chance, took advantage of the fear and suspicion. He spread rumors that Parliament had revoked the Calverts' charter because of their complicity in the Popish Plot, and that the navy was sailing to Maryland to oust the proprietary regime. According to several witnesses, he told anyone who would listen that he would gladly save Parliament the trouble, "for if they will but send two or three Lines to me" he would overthrow Lord Baltimore with the help of forty good Protestant men from the Clifts.[8]

Civil strife unfolded amid a backdrop of implacable Indigenous hostility. Susquehannock-led raids struck the frontiers each spring and summer without fail, the sine curve of their approach and retreat mapping onto the ebb and flow of colonial disorder. Susquehannock raids caused only a small number of English casualties, and in military terms never posed a threat to the colonies' survival. Yet they placed pressure on regimes whose fault lines were already showing such severe signs of strain that they threatened to crack open. A 1680 incident demonstrated that even without direct attacks on colonists, the sort that caused demands for action and denunciations of governments, the regularity of Susquehannock raids could bring simmering discontents to a boil. With the costs of frontier defense spiraling, in 1679 the Virginia assembly replaced militia with royal soldiers and submitted a hopeless petition for the crown to deduct military expenditures from quit-rents. Unfortunately, the king wanted his empire to generate revenue, not deplete it, which was all the more imperative as he faced a hostile Parliament which believed that paying for soldiers meant funding tyranny. Far from supporting the colonial military, the royal treasury did not even pay the troops on time. Indebted soldiers became so unruly they mounted a minor mutiny in August 1680, after which the assembly no longer trusted them to guard the arsenal at Middle Plantation. Yet they could not cut military spending even as tobacco profits dried up. "The late intestine divisions of this your Majesties Colony of Virginia," complained the assembly, "together with the charge of tedious warr with the Indians who dayly make incursions, and sometimes murders upon us, have reduced us to a poore and distressed estate." According to Thomas Ludwell, "another warr," whether with tributary nations or foreign invaders, "would bring on great disorders if not another Rebellion amongst us." The colony was so volatile, he warned, that Anglo-Indian violence could tip the people into insurrection at any moment.[9]

The plan that Jacob put into motion with the Susquehannocks in 1680 would bring an end to the Time of Anarchy by bringing satisfaction to the raiders and safety to colonists, solving the problem from both sides. First, Susquehannocks and Haudenosaunee would deliver a shattering blow against the weaker tributary nations. The magnitude of the assault would strike fear into the remaining Algonquians, exacerbate their demands on the colonial government for protection, and generate rumors that the surprise attack must have been caused by someone's betrayal. Next, a double-cross: under the guise of negotiating a truce, Haudenosaunee envoys would coerce the Piscataways into betraying the English to save themselves from destruction. Word would leak to colonial authorities, causing them to suspect their own allies of treachery, which would amplify the chorus from extremists that all Indians were enemies. The raiders' ability to camouflage themselves, sowing confusion and doubt among colonists, would ratchet up the tension. Conflict between settlers and tributary Natives would escalate to the level that civil disorder threatened to erupt, as the predictable pattern had played out for the previous six years. Then the endgame: the Haudenosaunee would swoop in with a solution, proposing that the English allow them to destroy the tributary nations. Further raids would be unnecessary, peace would come to the region, and colonists could live confident in their security both from foreign attackers and enemies within.

Jacob would have disavowed his role in concocting such plan, of course, but if we approach the scenario with a detective's eye there is no denying that he had means, motive, and opportunity. As a veteran diplomat, he had developed influence among Indigenous nations and Maryland settlers. He had deep connections with Susquehannocks, and in the process of brokering peace between them and the Haudenosaunee he had built links with leaders in Iroquoia. He knew the tenor of colonial politics as well as any Marylander, using his privileged position as interpreter to move in the Calverts' inner circle. As a resident of the northern frontier, he also had his ear to the ground and understood the impact of Native violence on frightened settlers. His motivations included a personal grudge against tributary Algonquians, probably due to their past attacks on Susquehannocks as well as the danger they continued to pose to colonists. Jacob repeatedly grumbled to councilors that they should not be protecting the Piscataways and mused that colonists would be better off if the Haudenosaunee destroyed them. Shattering the tributary Algonquians would, in one blow, give his Susquehannock kin their revenge, allow his new Haudenosaunee associates to finish their mourning war, and bring stability to his English neighbors. Finally, he had the perfect opportunity to propose his plan when Susquehannocks and Oneidas passed along the road where the council commissioned him to engage the raiders in diplomatic talks. The course of events mapped onto Jacob's longstanding desires and his unique capabilities.[10]

We need not, however, attribute to Jacob an uncanny ability to mastermind such a convoluted plot. It was probably as much improvised as orchestrated, a series of opportunistic uses of rumor and conspiracy. Moreover, Jacob's plans were almost certainly collaborative efforts with his Susquehannock kin, and we should not discount the possibility that Susquehannock captains and matrons were the plotters and Jacob merely their instrument. Nevertheless, as subsequent events make clear, there is no question that Jacob was a crucial actor in the drama. The evidence for his role as a conspirator is, admittedly, circumstantial. But treating Jacob as a key player in a plan hatched with Susquehannocks explains much about the Haudenosaunee's sudden changes in strategy and tactics that would otherwise be inexplicable.

Whether or not Jacob suggested that raiders "go home and fetch an Army," as the treason charges alleged, that is exactly what they did. Up to this point, only Onondagas and Oneidas had participated in raids on the Chesapeake, while the other League nations directed their attentions elsewhere. In 1681, Susquehannocks were observed in Cayuga country for the first time, including "the chiefe of them," and they convinced the Cayugas to join them. They also recruited several other nations, including the Doegs, who had made common cause with Susquehannocks after the 1675 incident with Thomas Mathew's hogs. This coalition's campaign marked a radical departure from the familiar raiding pattern. Instead of spring, they launched their assault in February 1681, during the coldest months of winter. Like the 1676 raids on Virginia, it took place just after the Midwinter Ceremony, when dreams could determine momentous courses of action. They switched targets from Piscataways to the Mattawoman town on the Potomac. Caught without warning, the Mattawomans were practically defenseless. Algonquians reported that "most of the Mattawoman Indians had been lately Surprised and cutt off by the Susquehannohs." Although the headman Maquata and a few others escaped, raiders took the majority of the Mattawomans back to Iroquoia as captives. In a single swift stroke, the nation was nearly annihilated.[11]

The Susquehannock coalition's crushing victory provoked panic among Maryland's tributary nations. Tayac Nicotaughsen called on Lord Baltimore's patriarchal obligation to protect his subjects, hoping to leverage the crisis to the Piscataways' favor. He told the council that the near destruction of the Mattawomans "hath struck such dread and terror" in all the tributaries that "they are in continuall feares and jealousies of being alike surprised and cutt off." Therefore, they "expect and crave protection from his Lordshipp" as guaranteed by treaty. He claimed that because "the Susquehannohs were a common Enemy alike to them all," the other nations wished to gather in the Piscataways' fortified town in Zekiah Swamp for their protection. The council obliged by ordering the survivors to relocate to Zekiah and designated the Piscataway town as the entrepot for shipments of food and armaments. Other tributary headmen, however, resented Nicotaughsen's presumption to speak for them. They used the same emotional rhetoric of patriarchal obligation to resist. Maquata and Ababco, the Choptank headman, met with Lord Baltimore and "pitifully sett forth to him the distressed condition they were in being in continuall expectation of their Enemies approach and being Surprised and cutt off by them." They refused to move to Zekiah and demanded assistance, telling Baltimore they "did therefore expect to be protected by the English." The Algonquians' fear caused dissension among tributaries and placed Maryland's government in the middle of their squabbles.[12]

In early summer, the Susquehannock coalition launched an even larger offensive. Two hundred raiders slipped through the frontier without Maryland rangers even noticing. According to Jacob, their intent was "by presents to endeavour to draw the Pascattoways with them, but if they cannot to destroy them." The pretense of negotiations elicited hopeful support from Maquata, who escorted them to Zekiah fort. The talks, however, were just a ruse to cloak the centerpiece of the Susquehannock plan. The raiders sent representatives to speak with Nicotaughsen. The mood, according to militia commanders who arrived toward the end of the conference, was convivial. Speakers exchanged speeches and ritual gifts of wampum. Piscataways mingled with their adversaries "and much friendship past betweene them." During this conference, a Haudenosaunee ambassador later claimed, the Piscataways "joined with the Susquehannohs to destroy the Anondago [Onondaga] Indians." In other words, Susquehannock captains proposed an alliance with the Piscataways against the Onondaga nation. Nicotaughsen, under tremendous pressure as two hundred enemy warriors stood ready to pounce, accepted the Susquehannock proposal as the price of survival. As soon as he did, the Susquehannocks abandoned their ruse, broke the peace, and took over a dozen astonished Piscataways captive as they withdrew.[13]

Maquata, horrified at the Susquehannocks' duplicity and Nicotaughsen's capitulation, immediately understood what had happened. The Susquehannock demand for Piscataway cooperation against the Onondagas was an absurdity; Susquehannocks had lived peaceably in Onondaga country for years. By accepting this proposal, however, Nicotaughsen gave Susquehannock leaders a tool to sway League politics. They would return to Iroquoia with an incendiary tale to tell, featuring the Piscataway nation's underhanded plot to tear apart the Great Peace of the Longhouse. Maquata explained that Susquehannocks "have served them two crooked tricks," first, by pretending peace to get Algonquians to lower their guard and second, by deceiving them into an agreement that would unite the fractious Haudenosaunee nations against them. Surely "they will come with a greater party ere long," he predicted, not only to Zekiah but also "greate Companys of these Indians downe amongst the Plantations" where they would menace English colonists.[14]

While tributary nations braced for more "Indian Stormes," colonists expressed more suspicion than solidarity. In another tactical shift, the raiders avoided colonial settlements to prevent accidental violence, depriving English governments of their usual source of outrage. Virginia officials congratulated themselves for keeping the frontiers "peaceable and Quiett" through their network of fortifications, but Natives knew the quiet was strategic. When the Maryland Council tried to weasel out of protecting the Mattawomans by arguing that neighboring settlers would defend them, Maquata scoffed, "the English very well knew that the Enemie would not disturb the English, but sought onely their [Algonquian] lives without any injury" to colonists. Lulled by an artificial hush behind the frontier, colonists were therefore distrustful when tributary nations mobilized to defend against coalition attacks. In early May, Eastern Shore settlers reported signals that Nanticokes were going to war, sending women and children to hidden refuges and mobilizing large parties for unknown purposes. Virginia secretary Nicholas Spencer observed that "neighbouring Indians dayly Expect an Attacke" and were "makinge unusuall Preparations for marches," but there was no way to tell if they intended to repel Susquehannock raiders or massacre unsuspecting English.[15]

The politicking of tributary leaders, desperate and running out of options, made a bad situation worse by sparking settler fears of Indigenous conspiracy. Maquata told the council that Piscataways "were the Chiefe meanes of the Damage he had lately susteined from the northern Indians in cutting off his Fort." Nicotaughsen had "sold him as well as the English" to the enemy's wrath. To prove this charge, Maquata produced an informant named Passanucohanse; the English referred to him by the derisive nickname Jackanapes, early modern slang for a monkey or trickster. Passanucohanse was born Mattawoman, captured in the coalition's winter assault, requickened as a Cayuga, and sent into the field against his friends and family, then escaped during the height of the summer campaign. He claimed that Piscataways were forming a secret alliance against the English. As evidence, he claimed that Nicotaughsen had circulated an axe wrapped in a wampum belt, signifying war, to Nanticokes in Maryland and Nanzaticos in Virginia before sending it on to Iroquoia, where Passanucohanse had seen it himself. There is no way to know what Passanucohanse's motives were in telling this unlikely story of Piscataway conspiracy, but his confusing identity—a captive bringing intelligence who came as a warrior with the enemy—did not reassure colonial authorities. Militia identified other Mattawomans, some of whom they knew personally, among the forces besieging Zekiah town, further adding to the cloud of uncertainty. Settlers, bewildered by the camouflage of captives and the labyrinth of Indigenous intrigue, succumbed to "great terror and confusion," trusting no one and suspecting all their allies of collusion.[16]

When summer incursions of unprecedented size resulted in a few frontier settlements being plundered for provisions, the visceral power of fear crystallized colonial suspicions. Well-informed colonists such as Nicholas Spencer, who got most of his information from Algonquian allies on the northern frontier, knew "the late Insolencies and Injuries" were unquestionably the work of "the Senacoes in their passing and Repassing from the Northward to the Southward." Unfortunately, other colonists were not so discerning. Small incidents piled up: a party of Chicacoans arguing with their English neighbors; livestock slaughtered and left to rot out of anger and contempt; armed and suspicious Native men approaching English plantations; Indians of uncertain identity, painted for war, haunting the Chesapeake borderlands. Settlers "in most parts of the Country," observed Spencer, were "not without feares and Jealousies of the Indians Intentions."

Fears and jealousies: a formulaic phrase that captured an increasingly formulaic tangle of ethnic stereotypes about dangerous Native peoples and dark fantasies of the violence they could unleash.[17]

In the fervid environment created by the Susquehannock coalition's raids, a group of unknown attackers killed the Potter family at Point Lookout, a finger of land jutting into the Chesapeake south of St. Mary's City. Settlers of various stripes blamed almost every possible Indigenous nation. The Potters' neighbors accused a rogue Nanticoke known by the picaresque name Robin Hood. St. Mary's militia arrested several Chopticos living nearby. The Choptico suspects claimed that Nanzaticos from Virginia were the killers. Virginians knew the Nanzaticos were nowhere near the scene of the crime and, completing the circle of accusation, assumed it must be Nanticokes. Most Algonquians believed "it is the Sinniquos and Susquehannocks," who had been spotted canoeing down the Potomac, prompting tributary demands for more guns and powder to fight them off. The Maryland Council ordered an investigation that dragged on for months, producing reams of depositions that could not clearly establish any of the pertinent facts, adding up to nothing but a sharp static of shady allegations and dubious alibis. Colonists cut through the interpretive difficulty by lumping all Indians together and treating them with automatic suspicion. The council authorized militia to confront any group of Indians they encountered and kill on sight any who did not immediately wave a white flag of surrender, to spare colonists the "dread and terror" of encountering Native peoples. When settlers and Algonquians needed to stand together, they were at each other's throats. The plan was working perfectly.[18]

Ripple effects from the 1681 raids pushed colonists to the breaking point as rumor and conspiracy theory did their work. Investigators noted that the Potter family had lived in a thickly populated region far from the frontier and had their throats slit, "a way of Killing never knowne from Indians." Their chilling conclusion was that "they were murdered by Christians." The Calvert regime was sending munitions to embattled tributary nations, causing some to whisper, with feeling if not a firm grasp of forensic anatomy, "noe wonder then the English had their throats cutt when the Proprietary gave them powder and shott for that purpose." A garbled story circulated that the Susquehannock coalition included requickened Mattawomans who boasted of "two French amongst them and that they marry with them and are all one with them," a pointed reminder that Catholics and Indians were really the same enemy. Thomas Truman, who had become a hero to those nursing anti-Indian sentiments, noted a sudden exodus of Catholic priests from the colony, with the dark implication that they would make natural coordinators between the Calverts and their Jesuit masters in New France. In Charles County, Josias Fendall proclaimed openly what many had been murmuring: "the Papists and Indians joined together" in a fiendish coalition that combined Susquehannocks, Haudenosaunee, tributary Algonquians, and Calvert supporters, who "together had a mind to destroy all the Protestants."[19]

The contagion jumped the Potomac. Fendall and his confederate, John Coode, crossed the border to drum up support. They stopped by every dock and landing in northern Virginia with tales of grandiose malevolence and a stirring call to action. They even tried to recruit Nicholas Spencer, a member of the Virginia Council, who summed up their theory as "so Irrationall a Conjecture that its Senaco Indians by the Instigation of the Jesuits in Canada, and the Procurement of the Lord Baltemore to cut off most of the Protestants of Maryland." Spencer urged them to cease their rabble-rousing. Their story was, he wrote with derision, a "wilde and gross Apprehension," but fears of papist plots in Europe and Indians closer to home meant this conspiracy theory "seized the Inhabitants of Virginia." John Wynn of New Kent County testified that colonists were so terrified of the forces arrayed against them that "they were forced to keepe watch and ward night and Day expecting every houre to be cutt off by the Papists and Indians together." Following Fendall's lead, Protestants argued that "wee must stand upon our owne Defence," organizing extralegal militias to destroy the Indian threat. While they were at it, added Coode, they might as well "overturn the Government," decapitate the Calvert regime, and drive Catholics out of North America.[20]

The Calverts rushed to stamp out this fire before it could spread. At the end of June Chancellor Philip Calvert called an assembly and proclaimed that the "urgent and weighty occasions and affaires relateing to the state and wellfare of this our Province (now every way alarmed by Forreigne Indians)" were so urgent that there was no time to hold elections. The legislators voted in during the relative calm of autumn 1678 would take their seats again. Perhaps, as rumors suggested, the Calverts recalled the disastrous assemblies of 1676, in which frightened voters sent conspiracy theorists and aspiring strongmen to the state house. Philip Ludwell noted, "the Generall discourse" was that the Calverts feared Fendall and Coode promoting insurrection while wearing the mantle of public service, and therefore wanted "to take them off From acting as burgesses in their next assembly." Baltimore did not rest with half measures. In mid-July, officers arrested Fendall and Coode in the dead of night and hauled them before the council on charges of seditious speech and attempted mutiny. Chancellor Calvert made a proclamation strengthening the bans on "spreading falce Rumors and reports," which were "alwaies a growing Evill that seldom ends otherwise then in distruction of the publick peace" and were more important than ever "now in this time of Danger by the Incursions of Foreigne Indians, when the minds of People ought to be most united." The council hoped that disorder would subside with the ringleaders under lock and key and promises of severe punishment for anyone else with loose lips.[21]

Their hopes were in vain, because nothing spawns rumors faster than commandments for silence from on high. In the summer of 1681, chatter about Natives and Catholics became the center of social life in the province, much of it focused on a rumor of fantastic implausibility. An Indian traveler, the story went, stopped by an English farmstead carrying ribbon-wrapped papers in a silk grass basket. Asking to stay the night, he cheerfully explained that Lord Baltimore had "sent a Packett of letters to the Sinniquos," whose Jesuit allies would read the letters to them, proposing "for them to come and cutt off the Protestants." The story turned out to have originated with Daniel Mathena, a notorious drunk who spent too much time at the tavern and liked to tell tall tales in his cups. He had been repeating this same story since 1679 without anyone giving it credence. In 1681, it suddenly seemed more believable. Colonists retelling the story generated fanciful spin-offs, such as a boy searching for a lost horse who found an Indian scout boasting, "those English called the Romans and the Sinniquos are to joine together and kill all the Protestants." That colonists who once dismissed such tales as farcical might now find them frightening indicates how the constant background buzz of terror led colonists to consider Indians of any kind too dangerous to tolerate.[22]

The dissemination of these rumors illustrates the thin line between sociability and sedition. Some people spreading them, such as Fendall and Coode, deliberately stoked popular fears to build a political movement. But many, perhaps most, colonists spread them because the story was just too juicy not to talk about. It was the sensation of the moment and everyone had an opinion. Men attending a recreational horse race hosted by James Rumsey debated the rumors, some admitting that the basket of letters terrified them, while others discounted the story as "very idle." The same conversation took over the neighborhood's next church meeting. "One Day at Church before it begann," recalled Rumsey, "the Report of his Lordshipps furnishing the Indians with powder and shott . . . was the generall discourse amongst the people." Many were skeptical, but everyone had heard the rumors and everyone retold them in the process of discussion. As it turned out, one of the men principally responsible for spreading Mathena's story, John Tyrling, stated, "he could not give any creditt to it." In fact, he believed that Mathena's story was stupid and irresponsible, angrily announcing "that the said Mathena and those who reported it after him ought to be whipped." But there was no way to dispute the rumors without inadvertently speeding them along. Ironically, arguing that the story was incredible and denouncing its tellers as dangerous malcontents only accelerated the spread of rumors to an intoxicating velocity.[23]

In July 1681, excited chatter about conspiracies kickstarted an uprising. Militia lieutenant George Godfrey appeared in the taverns where outraged drinkers told and retold stories of Indians with baskets of murderous letters. He urged his fellow Protestants to "goe downe and Demand Captain Fendall," who would take command of the military and make good his promise to "destroy all the Indians." On July 18, Godfrey and forty followers marched toward St. Mary's City, but their campaign was an ignominious repeat of Davies's failed uprising in 1676. John Coode had boasted that when it came to the moment of supreme crisis, ten thousand Protestants would answer the call. However, because the Susquehannock coalition had withdrawn in June and left the frontiers quiet, the dissidents failed to recruit more than a handful of men. Government militia quickly dispersed this small group and arrested Godfrey. Lord Baltimore, satisfied that armed insurrection had been prevented, wrote to Whitehall, "Had not these three persons been secured in time you would soon have heard of another Bacon."[24]

Although the uprising fizzled, the groundswell of opposition to Calvert rule and the conspiracy theories pervading public discourse did not. "If a man may Judge the hearts of people by their language," Nicholas Spencer wrote philosophically, "they are sett against the government with much bitternesse." Many assumed the Calverts would use the uprising as an excuse to persecute Protestants and tighten their grip on power. Word spread that Protestant militia were laying down arms in passive mutiny rather than serve under Catholic commanders, preferring to face the Indians on their own rather than fight for the tyrants conspiring with those Indians. Philip Ludwell believed that Maryland colonists, caught in the grip of "their intestine distractions," were "ready to breake Forth into Acts of Violence," which weakened the colony's defenses against Indigenous incursions. Lord Baltimore was convinced that Virginians were supporting dissidents in a plot to undermine his rule, blind to the danger that "a defection in my Government may raise an other Bacon in Virginia the people there being as ripe and readdy for another Rebellion as ever they were." Baltimore, the victim of so much conspiracy theorizing, could not help but indulge in it himself.[25]

As the Chesapeake colonies teetered on the verge of crisis, in late summer the Susquehannock coalition launched its largest offensive yet. Maquata's fears were prescient: Susquehannocks told Onondaga sachems of the Piscataways' plot against them, and outraged Onondagas convinced the Haudenosaunee to "joyne together in order to assist one another" and destroy the Piscataways. The formidable Mohawks, as well as Mahicans, Catskills, and Esopus—Gandastogue's allies in the Hudson Valley during the 1660s—joined the coalition's "mixt nations" of Onondagas, Oneidas, Cayugas, Doegs, and requickened Algonquians. It was clear to all that Susquehannocks were leading the fight. According to the Choptico werowance Chotike, "the maine reason" for the invasion "is that the Pascattoway Indians haveing formerly had warrs with the Susquehannohs, the Susquehannohs haveing mixed themselves with the Sinniquos have Engaged them in their Quarrell." Advance parties scouted Zekiah Swamp in early August, using the ripened corn to cover their approaches. Between three and six hundred warriors followed, poised to deliver a killing blow. Within a week, Piscataway warriors were desperately short of powder and shot from repelling probes.[26]

It was time for Jacob and his confederates to execute the final stage of their plan. Shock waves from successive coalition offensives in 1681 had undermined solidarity between colonists and their Algonquian allies. Now, they hoped, the Calverts might be ready to sacrifice their tributaries if it brought peace to the province. On August 22, Jacob escorted coalition spokesmen to meet with Lord Baltimore and his advisors in St. Mary's City. Colonial secretaries described them as Oneida and Onondaga, but they may have been Iroquoia-Susquehannocks. One hint was their presence in Maryland and proposal for regular councils at St. Mary's, rather than Albany, which Haudenosaunee diplomats insisted was the appropriate place for talks. Moreover, their demands included the construction of a trading post on the Susquehanna, replacing the old factory on Palmers Island, to facilitate the free flow of arms and ammunition. Haudenosaunee used the more convenient arms markets in Albany, but Susquehannocks had long relied on sources from Maryland. Finally, they demanded the return of all Susquehannocks held captive in Maryland, without mentioning the rest of the Five Nations. Militia captain Randolph Brandt, considering this circumstantial evidence, concluded, "those Indians I treated with are not reall Sinniquos." If indeed they were Iroquoia-Susquehannocks, their ability to speak "in behalf of the rest of the Northern Indians" indicates both the strength of their political influence and their leadership in the campaign.[27]

The two envoys assured the council that they "desire the English not to feare any thing for they will not molest them," and made an emotional appeal for the English to embrace peace. Presenting a belt of wampum, they stated "the English should not entertaine evil thoughts but to take out the badd and putt in good thoughts in their minds." While they urged the English toward peace, they also stated their intention to eradicate Maryland's tributary nations. "They are now goeing after the Pascattoway Indians," the envoys announced, and "will now see if they cann make an end of them." The Nanticokes would be next, then the smaller nations, and all the rest. Reminding Lord Baltimore that Piscataways had been secretly plotting against the English, the envoys asked him to give this war his blessing. Better yet, Maryland should assist by ceasing to arm and provision the Piscataways so that troublesome Algonquians "shall never disturb the English more." In his position as interpreter, Jacob made the pitch he had been preparing to give for more than a year. He asked the council to see that Algonquians were the real enemy, and that accepting their destruction would allow friendship with the Haudenosaunee, and the "many Susquesahannohs amongst them," to take root.[28]

The gambit almost succeeded. Jacob made a pointed observation that Piscataways were faithless allies, claiming "the Northern Indians told him" that the Piscataways' defection had been prevented only by the surveillance of Captain Brandt's rangers. The council interrogated one werowance after another, who trotted out extravagant stories of Piscataways circulating axes wrapped in wampum and proposing war against the English to every Indian nation from Delaware to Iroquoia. The envoys offered to escort Henry Coursey and William Stevens through the war zone in Zekiah Swamp so they could speak with other captains, stipulating "Jacob Young may accompany them thereto to Satisfie the whole troope."[29]

When Coursey and Stevens met the captains on August 28, however, the plan unraveled. Haudenosaunee warriors had just fallen in a skirmish, and the captains' blood was up. When Coursey and Stevens inquired whether it was true that Piscataways had circulated war belts, the sachems dismissed the matter as unimportant compared to Piscataway fighters "killing one of the Present Troope," which had "aggravated the matter." Coursey and Stevens responded with angry demands that they explain why they had broken a promise made at Albany to leave the Piscataways alone. When it became clear that Marylanders considered attacks on Piscataways to be an affront to the English, the Haudenosaunee lost interest in further talk. The captains adjourned for the night, promising to reconvene the next day. Instead, they launched an assault on the Piscataways under cover of darkness, with "a great many Gunns shott in the night," killing one and taking seventeen captive. By dawn, coalition forces had dispersed into smaller raiding parties. As they made their way back to Iroquoia, they picked up an additional eleven Piscataway captives and liberated an enslaved Susquehannock "at worke in the Shopp" of the tanner Henry Hawkins. For Jacob and the Susquehannocks, it was a minor victory but a defeat of the larger design to turn Maryland against its tributaries.[30]

As the Susquehannock coalition withdrew from the Chesapeake for the winter, the colonies had a chance to catch their breath. Maryland's assembly met in contentious debates about the present crises, but they fought with rhetorical grandstanding rather than guns. The provincial court exiled Fendall to Virginia and sentenced Godfrey to death, giving Lord Baltimore the chance to placate rabid conspiracy theorists by commuting his sentence to life in prison. Coode was found not guilty, his sedition excused as over-zealous toasts given at taverns and dinner parties, and was admonished "to love your quiet better then your Jest." The Virginia Council noted, "all apprehensions, Jealousies and fears of troubles" were "att present dissipated and laid aside, by the retiring of our common and domestick enemies the Indians." However, the seasonal pattern of violence had become too familiar for anyone to believe they would not return. In January 1682, travelers in Albany observed "Sinniquos" stocking up on powder and shot, freely admitting they "intended for to come for Maryland at the Spring of the yeare . . . and Demand the Pascattoway Indians." Jacob's plan to unite settlers with the Susquehannock coalition had failed, just as Maryland's diplomacy and Virginia's fortifications had failed. Something had to be done, or the Chesapeake would remain locked in a cycle of Anglo-Indian violence and fantastical revolts against the leaders helpless to stop it.[31]

While the colonies were locked in perpetual short-term crisis, deeper changes took root. In the midst of regular Susquehannock-led raids, the system of racialized plantation slavery that would become a hallmark of eighteenth-century society was taking shape. England's participation in the Atlantic slave trade surged after 1672, when King Charles II rechartered the Royal African Company. Thanks to enthusiastic Stuart sponsorship of black slavery, the supply of enslaved Africans rose and their price fell. Between 1670 and 1690 the black populations of Virginia and Maryland more than doubled, growing from a small portion of the labor force to almost 50 percent of unfree workers. Dwindling immigration by indentured servants, who found better opportunities in England, amplified the importance of black workers to the tobacco economy. Accordingly, the planters who served as justices in the county governments and burgesses in the assembly passed piecemeal legislation that made slavery more difficult to escape. As enslaved Africans rose in demographic prevalence and economic significance, the oligarchs ensured that chattel slavery closed on black men and women like a vise.[32]

Indigenous slavery surged during these same years, due in large part to upheavals stemming from the Time of Anarchy. Unlike the Atlantic trade, however, which was controlled by a small number of well-connected merchants who put the majority of Africans in the hands of the richest planters, the Native slave trade was more democratically distributed. By 1690, only 10 percent of small planters owned enslaved laborers, but in frontier counties such as Henrico more than half of those slaves were Indigenous. For many aspiring patriarchs in Virginia, the gateway to wealth and power was through the exploitation of Native laborers, providing a strong incentive to expand the interior trade. A 1682 law in Virginia stipulated that "all Indians which shall hereafter be sold by our neighbouring Indians, or any other trafiqueing with us as for slaves are hereby adjudged, deemed and taken . . . to be slaves." As English slaving networks spread their tendrils through the Southeast and the numbers of Indigenous slaves swelled, lawmakers promoted the trade's expansion and made slavery a permanent condition.[33]

The legal subordination of Africans and Indians gradually eroded the distinctions between the two groups, correlating darker skin and servile status. A 1680 law restricting the mobility of enslaved people applied to "any negroe *or other slave.*" When Indigenous enslavement was proclaimed a perpetual and heritable condition in 1682, it established an equivalence between all imported "Negroes Moors, Mollattoes or Indians" and declared Native women and black women taxable at the same rate, making them fiscally identical. These legal innovations painted both Native Americans and Africans with the brush of racialized slavery. By the time Virginia enacted its first comprehensive code of slave laws in 1705, the legislation used the catch-all category "negros, mulattos, or Indians." It was a natural step for the English to imagine people of color as different in ways more fundamental than legal status. Colonists abandoned their efforts to convert Africans and Indians to Christianity—ostensibly a great cause that had animated English overseas expansion in the first place—and came to see them as hereditary heathens whose souls were incapable of salvation. The corollary of the equation of dark skin with slavery was the association of whiteness with English liberty, and patriarchal manhood with the mastery of chattel slaves defined by their race.[34]

Generations of scholars have explored the gradual changes in colonists' thinking about the people they pressed into bondage, probing the ways that the exploitation of black and Indigenous laborers constructed patriarchal authority and white supremacy. Few, however, have appreciated that these racial divides sharpened in an atmosphere of perpetual terror—not merely anxiety about servile uprising, but fear of foreign invaders who could not be stopped and conspirators plotting to aid them.[35]

By 1679, Susquehannock-led raids had caused Indian-fearing to become a fact of life in the Chesapeake colonies, and those fears shaped the legal regime regulating black and Native peoples. When the Virginia assembly increased surveillance of Indigenous bodies, requiring tributary Algonquians to disarm and submit to interrogation upon demand "to the end wee may the better know them from our enemies," it was in the midst of "sundry murthers, rapines, and many depredations lately committed" by raiders from the north. In 1680, the assembly forbade "any negroe or other slave" from bearing arms or leaving their plantations without a permit and authorized the use of deadly force against runaway Africans and Indians. It passed amid rising tensions between settlers and tributary Natives that someone as well informed as Nicholas Spencer believed "will Certainely fly into a Nationall Warr." Such a war brought with it, as always, the danger of domestic insurrection. While English masters watched African and Indian laborers toil on their plantations and used the law to push them ever more tightly under their thumbs, they could not escape the "greate terror and amazement" that came with the constant threat of sudden and unpredictable Susquehannock violence.[36]

The growing number of enslaved Africans made a "nationall Warr" frightening in a way that colonists in North America had never faced before. The 1682 assembly met while "many of the people in divers parts of the Countrey are in great feare and dread of the Forreigne Indians speedy comeing downe amongst us," the burgesses noted, "as for some years past they have annually done." Unless the government did something, "our neighbour Indians will submitt themselves to and joyne with them, which if soe will in all likelyhood prove ruinous to this whole Countrey." Reports from northern Virginia claimed that "the Forreigne Indians" had established a fortified camp at the falls of the Potomac, and several "negros Runnaways was taken by them." These enslaved Africans may have been welcomed as equals or, more likely, treated as captives; the sources are too scanty to say. From a colonial point of view, it did not matter. Afro-Indigenous maroon communities already existed in the Caribbean, where English settlers came to fear and hate them. Their creation in North America was an alarming signal of interracial solidarity that might herald an uprising among people of color to aid the invading Susquehannock coalition. Thus, the 1682 laws restricting African and Indian rights, and the racial thinking they expressed, did not reflect the tightening grip of a confident elite, but the fragile grasp of embattled patriarchs. The plantation complex and the system of racial subordination that would come to define the eighteenth-century South took shape amid a war against Indigenous powers that English colonists, despite their pretensions to mastery, could not seem to control.[37]

By 1682, the cycle of violence had become depressingly regular, the circuit between Indigenous power and colonial disorder painfully clear. Even when raids hit tributary Indians rather than settlers, they inspired fear and challenged the masculinity of English men unable to protect dependent women and children. Colonists invoked the patriarchal compact of sovereign and subject to demand protection. The attackers' flexible identities, combined with colonists' inability or unwillingness to distinguish between different groups of Indigenous peoples, inspired racial thinking that branded all Indians as enemies and spawned rumors that allied Indians were the true authors of the violence. Settlers and tributaries therefore called on governments to protect them from each other, a double-bind that authorities could neither avoid nor fulfill. Paradoxically, either furnishing assistance to tributaries or attempting diplomacy with the raiders raised suspicions that authorities were colluding with the perpetrators of violence. The discontented and opportunistic did not hesitate to hone blunt suspicion into the sharp edge of conspiracy theory to subvert, or even overthrow, what they saw as perfidious regimes. Rumbles of insurrection made the colonies more vulnerable to further attacks and, completing the circuit, colonists themselves more nervous and prone to panic.

After five years of continual assault, colonial authorities finally began to grasp the politics of captivity and assimilation that kicked this cycle into overdrive. Virginia burgesses noted that foreign raiders were terrifying enough, but they faced the added "dayly dread and horror of our neighbour Indians joyning with them." Failure to provide protection would encourage tributary defection to the enemy for their own self-preservation, and therefore they "are justly to be dreaded if we doe not protect them from the Senecaes." Unfortunately, and maddeningly, peacemaking was also likely to provoke tributary defection out of concern that colonial governments would sell them out. Spencer explained, "our neighbour Indians will not repose any confidence in such treatyes, saying to treat with those northern Indians, is either to offer themselves as sacrifices or at least to become their Vassalls," and they were better off negotiating their own terms for relocation to Iroquoia. While European feudal terminology such as "vassal" did not accurately capture the dynamics of Iroquoian captivity, Maryland Councilors understood the danger of allies transforming into enemies. "If we abandon our Friend Indians here we shall not onely force them to submitt to their Northern Enemyes," they stated, "but to Incorporate with them, and soe not onely considerably strengthen them." Failing to abide by treaty obligations to protect tributary Natives would not only bolster Iroquoia's manpower, "but also add a party who will spurr them on to breake the peace in reveinge of our breach of Articles and Deserting them." They had learned, at least on some crude level, that when the victors in mourning war adopted the defeated, they also assumed the enmities harbored by their new kin, "as wee see the small remnant of the Susquesah-annohs have done."[38]

The evidence suggesting that Susquehannocks were the fuel propelling this cycle was so overwhelming by 1682 that colonists no longer bothered to qualify their statements with any degree of uncertainty. Nicholas Spencer, conveying intelligence from Native tributaries who escaped from captivity in Iroquoia, wrote, "the Indians who committ these spoyles and Injuries, are some Susquehannaes amongst the Senecaes and dayly provoke them to Ill acts." Susquehannocks were not merely provocateurs, he knew, but leaders. They "are the occasion of the warr between Senecaes and our Indians, which they never use to doe, but alwayes marcht to the northward, and still would If they were not sett on this way by the Susquehannaes." Neither their power nor their determination was to be underestimated. "Soe long as one of that nation lives," Algonquians told him, "wee are not to expect peace."[39]

As everyone expected, the Susquehannock coalition returned to war as the frosts receded. The Maryland government tried to prepare, but nerves were still frayed from the convulsions of 1681. Some colonists dared to openly advocate a coup against the Calverts. Anti-Indigenous sentiment was so pervasive the council felt the need to remind militia commanders that they were not to interpret their commissions as a license "upon any slight or frivolous occasion or out of a humour to create a warr by killing any Indian they meete." Only six dragoons could be spared to patrol the expected invasion route "betweene the head of the Pottuxen River and the branches thereabouts up to the Susquehannogh Fort," an opening over seventy miles wide. The militia did not even slow the invaders down. The Chesapeake frontier became a vast war zone as raiders struck Piscataways in Zekiah, Nanticokes on the Eastern Shore, Nanzaticos in the Northern Neck, and Pamunkeys in York Valley. Despite the lack of attacks on settlers, as usual panic spilled over into English neighborhoods.[40]

Virginia was ripe for disaster. Glutted markets and depressed tobacco prices had ruined the plantation economy. Pressure had been building for a one-year cessation of tobacco planting to drive up the price through artificial scarcity. Royal officials, under orders not to cut into the king's customs revenue, repeatedly squelched the proposal and even prevented the assembly from meeting to silence calls for economic relief. Rich and poor planters alike sank into debt, uniting them in a rare and dangerous form of disaffection shared across class lines. In April, a faction of burgesses led by Robert Beverley issued a strident demand for a cessation, arguing that failure to enact this fiscal measure would activate the circuit between Indian violence and colonial rebellion. Debt, taxes, and the exorbitant cost of frontier defense, he argued, had reduced the people to a "miserable and lost Condition." The royal soldiers, who were supposed to ameliorate the financial burden of securing the border, were among the poorest, most indebted, and most unruly. Rumors that the king had ordered the soldiers demobilized without back pay only made them more intractable. The soldiers were more likely to join "with the discontents of the people" than hold the line against foreign Indians, and thus "occasion the hazard if not utter Ruine of this his Majesties Countrey and people." Despite this warning that the smallest incident of Anglo-Indian violence could tip popular discontent into insurrection, Lieutenant Governor Henry Chicheley prorogued the assembly. News of a new round of Indian attacks reached Jamestown the same day.[41]

On May 1, a "Parcell of Riotous persons" launched a "strange insurrection," what Nicholas Spencer described as passing "a Law of Cessation of their own makeing." Hundreds of planters in Gloucester County destroyed their own tobacco crops and those of nearby plantations. The riots spread to New Kent, Middlesex, and Rappahannock Counties—all areas close to the recent Indigenous raids. Imperial troops, as predicted, joined the insurrection rather than putting it down. When militia patrols started ranging the countryside, rioters destroyed tobacco fields by night. As militia arrested men, "ill disposed women" defiantly picked up scythes and joined the riot. Spencer observed the contagious quality of disorder. The crowd grew as colonists went from plantation to plantation convincing the masters to join them, "by this the infection soe spread, that . . . It was to be feared, it would soon difuse itselfe over the whole body." Rumors of the expanding malignancy flew north. Lord Baltimore, worried that the exiled Fendall would hijack the riot into a Protestant crusade against Catholics, described the proceedings as "evill practises of some ungoverned people tending very much to the same design of that of the late rebell there Bacon."[42]

The Virginia government pacified the rioters through regular patrols and promises of economic relief, convincing them that they had made their point and had more to gain from negotiated reforms than revolutionary violence. By the beginning of June, the crisis had passed. According to Spencer, only one thing saved Virginia from outright rebellion: "our Indians," he wrote, "this summer as yet have not given any occasions of ill apprehensions." He added, with a visible sigh of relief, "(I thank God)."[43]

The range and power of the Susquehannock coalition could not be contained by any single colony. The contagious nature of rebellion affected them all. Colonial officials came to understand that the fortunes of England's colonies were bound together. "Wee shall soone be involved in the same

Fate," predicted Thomas Lord Culpeper in 1681. What to do about it, however, was not obvious. According to Edmund Andros, the colonies' dismal record in 1675–1676 illustrated the need for royal control of Indian policy. This is not surprising coming from a devoted imperial agent; Andros went on to cite Anglo-Indian violence as evidence that representative institutions were inferior to autocratic ones, arguing that both negotiating with and fighting Indians "cannot bee managed by such popular Governments." But even colonists came to see the value of a heavier royal hand if it would end the torrent of frontier violence. In 1676, the anonymous authors of the Complaint from Heaven begged for "a Vice Roye or Governor Generallissimo" to bring "these several distinct Governments to a better concord and amity." This notion of a consolidated viceroyalty eventually came to fruition when James II created the Dominion of New England in 1686. However, short of this sweeping reorganization of the colonies in contempt of their governments, there was little that could be done from London. In 1681, the Lords of Trade conceded that "peace and Warr . . . with the Indians" was, by the powers in their colonial charters, "left to the discretion of every distinct Governor." The best they could do was urge colonial leaders to coordinate their Indian policies with "the participation and consent of one another."[44]

The growing desire for intercolonial cooperation ironically hindered convergence because each government promoted itself as the best repository for supreme authority over Indigenous affairs. Andros and his agents defended their special relationship with the Mohawks to ensure that colonies could talk to the Haudenosaunee only through New York's governor, to whom the Haudenosaunee gave the name "Corlaer." The Calverts persisted in their attempts to displace Corlaer and establish a new place for treaty councils outside Albany, and they presumed to speak on behalf of Virginia. Virginian governors made the same play, revising the Treaty of Middle Plantation to include Maryland without consulting the Calverts. They reasoned that Virginia was the only royally governed colony and therefore the best advocate for imperial centralization. In 1681, Thomas Lord Culpeper argued that Indian policy should proceed only "by the knowledge and Approbation of the Gouvernor and Councell of Virginia." While everyone saw the benefits of intercolonial coordination, each imagined a hierarchy with themselves at the top. The result, as Andros sagely predicted, "so long as each petty colony hath or assumes absolute power of peace and warr," each interfered with the Indian affairs of its neighbors, sabotaging diplomacy and compromising security.[45]

Divisions among English colonies worsened with the creation of Pennsylvania in 1682. Charles II bestowed this proprietary colony on William

Penn to pay off an enormous debt, carving it out of territories also claimed by Maryland and New York and ordering those colonists to "yeald all due obedience, to the said william penn." The king's brother, James, dutifully yielded. Lord Baltimore, however, had struggled to fend off challenges to his proprietary for years, and he resented losing the Delaware Valley at, so to speak, the stroke of a pen. In August 1681, he proclaimed his right to ownership of the St. Jones district, then under the administration of New York, and prepared to occupy it before Penn's grant could take effect. Local magistrates wrote in a panic to Manhattan, "we do expect" Baltimore "every Day to Come and Subdew us with Force and Arms to Bring us under him." It was a fair concern. In 1673 Maryland militia had invaded the Whorekill district for the same reason, burning the homes of anyone who refused to recognize Calvert rule.[46]

Penn presented himself in a conciliatory fashion; in fact, he did everyone a favor by purchasing John Fenwick's patent to New Jersey to prevent him from raising any further trouble. His colony's boundary with Maryland was, however, announced as "to be determined," and taking possession of contested ground inevitably invited contention. In September 1681, William Markham, Pennsylvania's first governor, circulated William Penn's command to the St. Jones colonists that "none of you pay any more Taxes or Sessments by any order or law of Maryland." Antiproprietary colonists across northern Maryland refused to pay taxes, either hoping to transfer their allegiance or opportunistically spiting the Calverts. Condemning this "peece of Sedition," Baltimore deplored Penn's encouragement of anarchy, "the people," he wrote, "hopeing they shall suddenly be under noe Government." In his zeal to enforce order, unfortunately, he sent militia to New Castle—by right part of Pennsylvania but claimed as "Baltimore's Country." Baltimore's men threw the local sheriff in the river and threatened to slaughter cattle belonging to a widow for eating grass growing in Lord Baltimore's soil, adding to the chaos in what local resident William Welch called an "unlawful Riotous Assembly in Terrour of the people."[47]

The struggle between Maryland and Pennsylvania depended on the fate of the Susquehannock people. Penn laid the groundwork for his colony in the midst of the Time of Anarchy. He had learned from the bloodletting in New England and the Chesapeake that the goodwill of Native people was essential to colonial stability. He therefore made it a priority to secure Indigenous title to the land granted by his royal charter. In October 1681, before he arrived on American shores, Penn instructed his agents to "buy Land of the true Owners which I thinke is the Susquehanna People." This became more important when Penn realized that his province lacked any natural harbors, having been deceived by inaccuracies in the best European maps. Unless Penn could claim an outlet to the Atlantic, Pennsylvania would be, as he admitted morosely, "but a dead lump of earth." Baltimore and his agents did their best to ensure that a dead lump was all Pennsylvania would ever be. Maryland Surveyor General George Talbot told Penn, "the Susquehannoks and theire Country were Conquered by the Marylanders at great Expence of blood and money and the Susquehanohs are now noe Nation." Therefore, ownership of the Susquehanna Valley "is Invested in my Lord by right of Conquest." Since Penn planned to use Indian deeds to buttress his claim, the Calverts dusted off the idea they had first floated in 1677: the Susquehannocks were no longer a nation with the power to sell land to anyone.[48]

Baltimore's right-of-conquest argument held little water, however, while his province was scrambling to counter Susquehannock raids every year. Word reached Maryland in the summer of 1682 that three separate war parties were heading toward the Chesapeake. Reliable intelligence suggested that "some of the Troopes are Comanded by the Susquehannocks," who planned to "bear their designes against the Christians." Before the year was out, raiders had captured more than fifty Piscataways and fifty Choptanks, killing several colonists and plundering their homes before retiring. The Maryland Council etched its acid frustration into vellum, condemning the Susquehannocks, who "never faile to kill all English when ever they are the greater number in any party, and make us feele the effects of warr though they live under the shelter of nations that pretend a peace with us." Baltimore's battle with Penn added a new layer of urgency to the imperative of ending, once and for all, the Susquehannocks' wars.[49]

Desperation prompted the Calverts, awash in a quagmire of conspiracies real and imagined, to venture an audacious conspiracy of their own. Passanucohanse, the Mattawoman who had shared stories about the Piscataways' treachery in 1681, suggested a solution to the Susquehannocks' neverending raids. "For a smale sattisfaction," he claimed, "the senecaes would deliver up all the susquehannaes to the english." Better yet, "the hope is that if the senecaes will be hired to deliver them up, they will alsoe be hired to destroy them." The scheme to buy Haudenosaunee mercenaries required finesse, Passanucohanse stressed, because if Susquehannocks sniffed out the plot they would "indeavor a Flight, and then become Feiercer enemies." The council jumped on the suggestion. It commissioned Henry Coursey to return to Albany with Philemon Lloyd, to discover "if those Northern nations would be hired to cutt off the remnant of the Susquehannohs." Though traveling as diplomats, their clandestine mission was to "purchase the peace of the Province by extinguishing that Vipers brood." It was a feeble ploy. Giving so much credit to Passanucohanse's

Pennsylvania's founders had little knowledge about the mid-Atlantic beyond the coastline, but they knew that the Susquehanna River would be the province's artery into the continental interior. John Thornton, *A Map of some of the south and east bounds of Pennsylvania in America* (London, 1681). Courtesy of the John Carter Brown Library at Brown University.

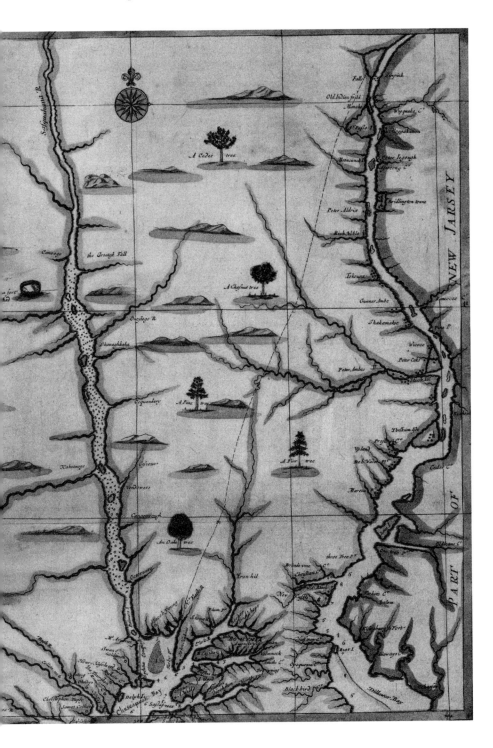

story was more wishful thinking than shrewd realpolitik. By 1682, however, the Calverts were reduced to grasping at straws.[50]

At a 1682 conference in Albany, Maryland's weakness was apparent in
the way that Haudenosaunee ambassadors casually disposed of its best efforts. On August 3, Coursey and Lloyd met with Senecas, the one Haudenosaunee nation that had yet to participate in raids on the Chesapeake.
Offering thanks for the Senecas faithfully keeping their covenant with
Maryland, Coursey and Lloyd proposed that future meetings, held so "the
Chain of Friendship may be kept bright and strong," should take place in
a new location: Jacob Young's trading post. They thought it was a clever
way to stifle Penn's claims to the Susquehanna Valley, undermine the
Mohawk–New York axis, and offer the Senecas a market outside of Albany.
The Senecas, motivated by intensifying wars in the west and deteriorating
relations with New France, were intent on solidarity with the other League
nations and strengthening their alliance with New York. The orator Adondarechaa, who had spoken with Coursey in the same space five years earlier,
stated that the proper meeting place was Albany and the proper mediator
was Corlaer. In his speeches, he continued the rhetorical transformation of
plural "covenants" and "chains" binding individual colonies to the Haudenosaunee nations into a singular Covenant Chain. Senecas, he asserted,
"desire that the Chain of the Covenant may never be broken but be kept
clear and held fast on both sides," and included "your Friend Indians especially the Piscatowayes Indians in the Covenant Chain." He promised to
"forbid . . . all Indians of other Nations living amongst us, to break the
Covenant," allaying Maryland's concerns about Susquehannocks. Adondarechaa's repeated stress on the unitary Covenant Chain binding Iroquoia
and English America at Albany continued the evolution of the Anglo-
Haudenosaunee relationship.[51]

The council between Coursey, Lloyd, and representatives from the other
League nations was not so cordial. Abandoning any hope of a sly proposal
for the Haudenosaunee to sell out the Susquehannocks, the Marylanders
gave a hard-edged ultimatum. They accused the Haudenosaunee of breaking
the covenant they had forged five years earlier. If the Haudenosaunee failed
to admit their "evill actions" and provide recompense, "wee shall make
warr upon you in your own Country, and . . . reduce you to the same Condition and want, as other Indian Nations that have broke their faiths with
Christians." Characteristically, the Haudenosaunee admitted fault but
denied responsibility. Odianne, speaking on behalf of Mohawks and Onondagas, said their warriors had been "drunk in their Capacity, voyd of understanding and out of their sences, when they committed that evill in your
Country." Mourning war was regrettable but unavoidable. The Oneida

Tekanistapendacquo, speaking on behalf of Oneidas and Cayugas, apologized for the violence and expressed "desire that the harm done may be dugg into the ground, and do wipe off the Tears and the blood." The Haudenosaunee speeches were entirely in the spirit of kaswentha diplomacy that maintained a forum for restoring peace but allowed independent action for all parties. To the English, however, it was an exasperating set of answers that blamed violence on uncontrollable young men and their deranged emotions, suggesting that little would change in the future. Each nation offered a wampum belt, laying it at the feet of the Maryland envoys so "the Mischeifs done may be forgott and forgiven . . . and may not remain in the heart." Disgusted, Coursey and Lloyd left the gifts lying in the dust, refusing to cover the dead.[52]

Albany magistrates intervened to cool the Marylanders' tempers, allowing the ambassadors to try again the next day. Coursey and Lloyd, stepping back from grandiose threats they could not possibly carry out, demanded five hundred beaver skins for property damages and extradition of the 1681 expedition's leaders as restitution for "the Blood of our people." The Haudenosaunee politely demurred, pleading poverty and the war captains' death in combat. However, they offered to recall the war parties currently in the Chesapeake and promised to end the attacks against Maryland's tributary Natives. "Wee do take the Piscatoway Indians, and all your Freind Indians fast in our Covenant," Onondaga spokesman Tackaniennondi stated, the first time the Haudenosaunee explicitly included tributaries in the covenant. It filled the fatal omission in the 1677 Albany treaty and held out the hope of a permanent cessation of violence, a major victory for Coursey and Lloyd. Even more importantly, the Haudenosaunee spokesmen spoke not of multiple covenants with English colonies, but one Covenant Chain with all of them. Tekanistapendacquo concluded grandly, "wee do make the Covenant Chain fast and clear like gold wherein Corleir and they of Maryland and Virginia and wee are linked." With increasing consistency, the Haudenosaunee began to link their separate agreements with different colonies in a single chain.[53]

The conference might have ended there, but Coursey and Lloyd asked a question no one expected to hear. "Wee are told that some Christian hath stirred you up to make warr upon the Piscatoway Indians, and promised to deliver them up to you," they said. If it was true, they wanted to know who it was. Tekanistapendacquo gave a shocking answer. He said, "about 2 years ago a troop of ten Onneydes were at the house of Jacob Young," where he planned the 1681 invasion of Zekiah Swamp. Jacob told them, "go home and fetch an army of your people," gave a gift of duffels, and promised, "wee shall all be at arms and then destroy them and deliver them into your hands." Tekanistapendacquo hesitated to offer this information, stating, "wee should nott have told itt if you had nott made such sharp enquiry." Surely he understood the revelation of this conspiracy would have consequences for Jacob. Perhaps that is why he emphasized that Jacob intended to serve the interests of both Haudenosaunee and English. Jacob had said that colonists "suffer great damages by these Indians because you make warr upon them in our Country." Therefore, destroying the Piscataways would bring captives to Iroquoia and security to Maryland. As far as Coursey and Lloyd were concerned, however, the conclusion was inescapable: the years of war that had ravaged the Chesapeake frontiers, brought tributary nations to the brink of destruction, and kept colonial societies on the edge of insurrection, had all been orchestrated by Jacob My Friend.[54]

The Marylanders politely accepted Tekanistapendacquo's answer. The conference concluded with ritual promises to "let the Chain wherein Corleir, that is the Governor of New York, and they of Maryland and Virginia and wee are lock't, be kept fast and inviolable upon both sides." Two weeks later, as soon as Coursey and Lloyd arrived back in Maryland, Lord Baltimore ordered Jacob's arrest.[55]

The 1682 Albany conference was convened to end Anglo-Indian violence caused by Susquehannock provocateurs, but it resolved nothing on that point. Susquehannocks did not even appear, much less speak. Delegates occasionally referenced "nations living amongst us," but did not address the matter directly. Marylanders never tried to get the Haudenosaunee on board with Baltimore's farcical conspiracy to exterminate the Susquehannocks. Nor did the conference successfully end Anglo-Indian violence. Although Haudenosaunee orators were coming to speak of the Covenant Chain as an alliance that linked all the League nations to all the English colonies, in 1682 the transformation was incomplete. They may have paid lip service to Virginia's place as a link in that chain, but Virginians did not appear in Albany to confirm the peace and no one promised anything about Virginia's tributary nations. After four years of following the Susquehannocks, Onondagas, Oneidas, and others had plenty of motivation for pursuing glory, revenge, and healing through combat with southern Indians. With every trip they gained more experience with previously unfamiliar paths; each warrior who fell provided reasons to return. In 1683, and for years afterward, Haudenosaunee warriors carried out their seasonal raids to the south. Yet something was different after the 1682 Albany conference: Susquehannock captains no longer led the way.

It is impossible to say with any certainty what changed. The sources provide clues only in the negative. From 1677 to 1682, English documents record an endless barrage of Susquehannock sightings. Some were wisps of rumor, others uncertain reports, only a precious few reliable intelligence. They ran the gamut from fearful speculation by ignorant settlers to eye-witness reports by Native informants. But every spring and every summer, the news was the same: the Susquehannocks are coming. Then, suddenly and without comment, all mention of Susquehannocks stopped. The available evidence suggests that if Susquehannocks went south after 1682, they did so with knives sheathed and guns holstered. The tide receded, and Susquehannocks ceased to be the force driving the spiral of international war and colonial upheaval that defined the Time of Anarchy.

Susquehannocks, an elusive presence in the archive even under the best of circumstances, did not explain their reasons for this change in behavior. Rival Haudenosaunee leaders might have eclipsed them in influence, or perhaps the increasing belligerence of French officials shifted the weight of League politics. Maybe they were tired of unending war. Perhaps they felt like the Susquehannock sachem when he had proclaimed, "he was pretty well Satisfied with the Revenge he had taken." Or, just possibly, the wars ended because Susquehannocks made a peace with their Indigenous enemies without settlers even noticing.[56]

In 1685, a Piscataway named Isaack reported that "greate men of the nation of Sinnico Indians called Sachochinagheti" had come to the edges of Maryland to make peace with his people. But were they in fact Haudenosaunee? Their leaders, "Sinnico Warr Captains and Chiefe Commanders," said that they spoke on behalf of "their owne proper nation called the Sachochinagheti Nation." The Sachochinagheti appellation is a mystery, for this is the only time it ever appears in any documents, but it certainly is strange that they formed a "nation" within the Haudenosaunee and there is no other record of its association with the League. The only other people that English sources described as a nation among the League during this period were Susquehannock. Moreover, they acted strangely for Haudeno-saunee. The delegation came south, in direct contradiction of repeated insistence by ambassadors that Albany was the only proper place for council treaties. They announced that "they would stay upon Susquehannah River to wayte an answer," and camped in the same places that Susquehannock-led parties had chosen for years, in what once was Gandastogue's heart-land. This circumstantial evidence suggests that the Sachochinagheti may have been Iroquoia-Susquehannocks.[57]

Sachagacagency, the spokesman for this enigmatic delegation, conveyed his desire for peace with colonists and Indians in Maryland. He repeated it seven times, each time accompanied by gifts of wampum and beaver pelts to emphasize the depth of his sincerity. The spokesman stated, "there was in them noe rancour, noe malice" because "they had taken a medicine soe wholesome that it had purged them of all venome whatever." Now "their breasts were filled with comfort . . . they were now at quiett, at rest, and peace of mind." Sachagacagency stated that his people were "satisfied of the greate friendship betweene the English and them" and "the Pascattoway Indians, and all other Indians in these parts." Emotional balance had been restored. They were ready for the wars to end.[58]

Even if the conjectural identification of the Sachochinagheti with Susquehannocks is mistaken, there are many other reasons why the people of Gandastogue might have counted themselves satisfied and ready to embrace peace. They had found homes in Iroquoia, autonomous but connected to the web of kinship and reciprocity that animated Haudenosaunee life. They united old allies and made common cause with former enemies, rising from the ashes of defeat to become a force that shook the ground of eastern North America. They devastated Algonquians in Maryland, leaving the Mattawomans on the verge of annihilation and other nations severely weakened. Virginia's nations were so ravaged that in 1683 one official noted, "severall Nations are Extinct: and som are Runn away, and others soe wasted that they joyne 2 or 3 Togither to make one." Susquehannock-led raids forced the Occaneechis to abandon the island from which they ruled the southern trade paths. While their enemies withered under this onslaught, a new Susquehannock nation grew in size and strength. In 1682 the population of people who called themselves Susquehannock, whether by birth or adoption, was higher than it had been in 1675, on the eve of their terrible ordeal.[59]

Despite their apparent disappearance, Susquehannocks charted a new course for their people the same way they had earlier in the century: by inviting multiple groups of foreigners into their homeland and profiting from connections to them all. In 1683, the sachems Machaloha and Kekelappan granted overlapping tracts of land at the mouth of the Susquehanna River to William Penn. The territory, which included Jacob's trading post, was both Gandastogue's strategic outlet and Penn's gateway to Atlantic commerce. Historians have often assumed that Machaloha and Kekelappan were Lenapes with no right to the Susquehanna Valley, characterizing these grants as convenient frauds that served the interests of both parties. But Penn knew who he was dealing with. He wanted to acquire "nothing less than what was the Susquehannah Claim," he wrote. So he sent his agents among the Lenape because "the remaineder of the Susquahannahs, who are right Owners thereof, are amongst them." Penn got a solid claim to the Susquehanna out of the deal, crippling his Maryland rivals. Susquehannocks got a fresh start with newcomers who seemed eager for peaceful trade and anxious to avoid conflict. "I have great love and regard towards

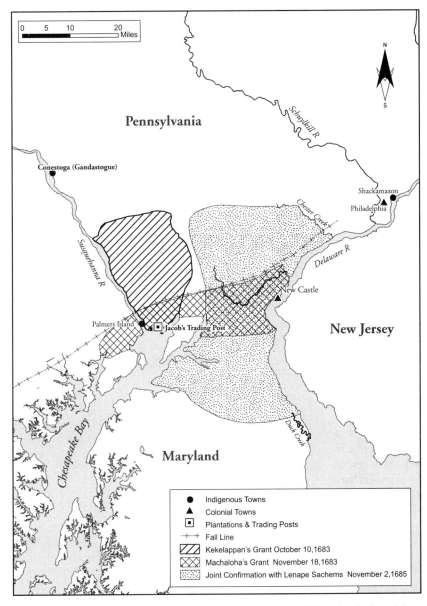

Delaware-Susquehannock Land Grants to William Penn. Although scholars debate the ethnic identity and political affiliation of the Indigenous proprietors, the land in question was the same territory that Susquehannock sachems had previously granted to Maryland, New Sweden, and New Netherland in the 1650s.

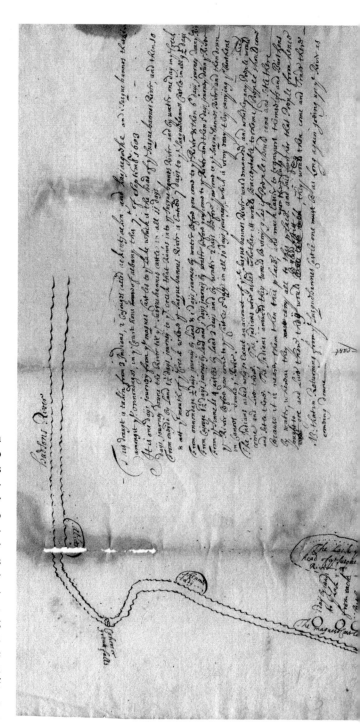

The Susquehanna River and routes to Iroquoia. Cayugas and Susquehannocks enticed New York colonists to settle the Susquehanna Valley by describing its rich soils and easy access to Haudenosaunee fur traders. "Settlements along the Sesquehanna River, 1683." The Gilder Lehrman Institute of American History, GLC03107.01923.

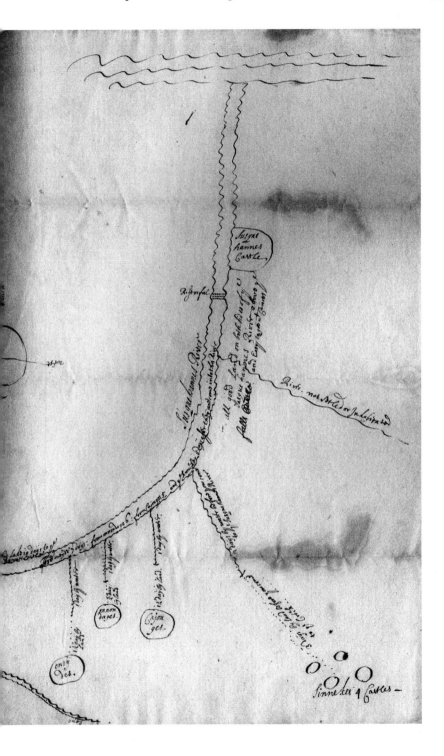

you," wrote Penn in his letter to the sachems, "and I desire to Winn and gain your Love and freindship by a kind, just and peaceable life."[60]

Susquehannocks also embraced New Yorkers. In September 1683—within three days of Kekelappan's sale to Penn—two Cayugas accompanied "a susquehannes that Lives amongst the onnondages" to the Albany court-house, where they invited colonists into the upper Susquehanna Valley. They stated, "they would be verry glad if People should come and Setle there because it is nearer them" and easier to trade without an arduous journey. Therefore, New York colonists "ought to goe and Live there, they would be gladd off itt." The following year, Cayugas and Onondagas jointly claimed they were the owners of "the Susquehanne River which we wonn with the sword." Using a right-of-conquest argument legible to the English— an argument that historians agree was a diplomatic fiction—they conveyed the Valley to the new Corleir, Andros's successor, Thomas Dongan. The grant sealed New York's alliance with Iroquoia, but also served Susquehan-nock interests. Susquehannocks thereafter enjoyed not only the protection of the League, but also alliances with two English colonies, both of which were eager to revive the fur trade in their old heartland. Perhaps, from a Susquehannock point of view, it seemed like it might be possible to revive the glory days when Gandastogue prospered at the crossroads of empires.[61]

So when the seasons turned from the autumn of 1682 to the winter of 1683, Susquehannocks put down their guns. Their long fight was over, and so were the wars that had propelled the Time of Anarchy. Despite years of blood and exile and unfathomable loss, they had, after a fashion, won.

EPILOGUE

Susquehannock intervention saved their friend Jacob's life, but they could not save him from captivity. In 1682, after Susquehannock messengers threatened to avenge Jacob if he was executed, the Maryland assembly decided it was too dangerous to bring him to trial. Instead, they left him over the winter in the St. Mary's City prison, an unheated stone blockhouse, clapped in chains of cold iron. Jacob denied all of the charges leveled against him. He denied gathering the Susquehannocks after their scattering or providing them with aid and shelter. He denied hatching a conspiracy with Oneidas to lead them as a war captain against the Piscataways. He rehearsed every faithful service he had done for Maryland: every danger he had braved and every privation endured, every time he had traveled into Indigenous territories "with Great hazard of his Life, meerly to procure the peace Safety and Wellfare of this Province." Jacob even denied his kinship to the Susquehannock people. He denied marrying a Susquehannock woman, fathering Susquehannock children, or any bond of love tying him to their nation, stating that he "utterly denyeth that he ever Alienated . . . his Affection from the Lord Proprietary." Jacob, alias My Friend, swore that he loved and feared his patriarchal lord, the Baron Baltimore, just like an English subject should.[1]

Jacob spent the next year in a jail cell with rotten food, ragged clothes, and a bed of filthy straw. One friend testified to his suffering, complaining to the assembly that Jacob was "sick and weake being all over his body broken out with boyles and sores." Anna Young, Jacob's wife, came to his defense. She was an English woman whom Jacob presumably married after the death of his Susquehannock wife, whose nationality allowed Jacob to father English children and strengthen his affective ties to the province to which he declared allegiance. We can only guess how she reacted to the stunning charges leveled against her husband, whether she knew about his previous marriage to a Native woman, or if she believed his disavowal. For her and so many other women in early America, the documents reveal little. Nonetheless, she acted as many English women did by petitioning on behalf of her husband. Anna Young supplicated the assembly to "pitty and Comisserate her Husbands Condition," protesting that "his long Imprisonment" had strained her aging husband nearly to the breaking point, leaving him "much Deminnished." The assembly finally brought Jacob to the bar in October 1683. It took them only one afternoon to convict him on all charges.[2]

Still, Susquehannock power cast a shadow over the proceedings. After protracted bickering between the councilors of the Upper House and the representatives of the Lower House, the assembly declined to pass the death sentence that such egregious crimes warranted. Instead, they issued a fine of £1,000—an enormous sum at a time when £30 was a comfortable annual income for a planter—as well as the costs of his imprisonment, over 11,000 lbs. of tobacco. Jacob, in debt because his incarceration left him unable to attend to his business affairs, begged to have the fines reduced if he promised to leave Maryland. The assembly agreed and issued an order that "Jacob Young will forthwith Depart this Province and go for Holland" and "never returne into Any part of America." It seemed a fitting punishment for a man whose greatest crime was betraying his English allegiance. In November 1683, Jacob was banished from Maryland.[3]

As convicted mastermind, Jacob My Friend played the same role in Maryland that Nathaniel Bacon had in Virginia. In the aftermath of Bacon's Rebellion, all parties found that they could agree on one thing: the insurrection was orchestrated by a villainous conductor who was solely responsible for the destruction that it wrought. Collective embrace of this conspiracy theory erased everyone's guilt and paved the way for reconciliation. In the same way, once everyone agreed that Jacob had been pulling the strings all along, the Baltimore circle, Protestant dissidents, Algonquian tributaries, and Haudenosaunee warriors could all put down their weapons. Jacob's betrayal absolved the Calverts for the devastation of tributary Natives and the popular discontent that repeatedly brought the province to the brink of the revolution. And if the invasions were a Susquehannock initiative led by the adopted Susquehannock Jacob, then the Haudenosaunee bore no responsibility either. Jacob could absorb all the guilt and slink away to Europe—unharmed, to appease the watchful Susquehannocks—while the new Albany agreement had a chance to take hold. According to the conspiracy theory that sacrificed Jacob to consecrate a new peace settlement, the Time of Anarchy—and the Susquehannock resurgence that fueled it—was engineered by one man who turned out to be no friend at all.[4]

By the end of Jacob's trial, the Time of Anarchy was coming to an end. Although brief in the long sweep of early American history, the decade between 1675 and 1685 was transformative. The Time of Anarchy encompassed a torrent that crashed through eastern North America and ripped societies apart. It left wreckage in its wake, yet the forces unleashed were not merely destructive. In the Time of Anarchy's aftermath, the flows of power moved in new channels. Susquehannock actions—and their unpredictable ramifications as those actions rippled through colonial societies—reordered Anglo-Indian relations in four ways: the forging of the Covenant Chain; the dramatic expansion of the Native slave trade; the acceleration of racial thinking and racialized slavery; and the imperial reconstruction of the tributary system. These constituted a revolution in Anglo-Indian relations with lasting consequences for Indigenous peoples and the course of English colonization. Taken together, they were the Time of Anarchy's most important legacies.

The Covenant Chain was hammered out in the series of Albany councils dedicated to ending the wars of the Susquehannocks. The breakthrough at the 1682 conference solidified in 1685, when Indigenous diplomats from Maryland and Virginia met directly with counterparts from Iroquoia to make, as a Seneca spokesman put it, "the Renewed Covenant . . . better and stronger." The Susquehannock disposition of territory to New York and Pennsylvania helped settle the boundaries between English and Haudenosaunee spheres of influence. "Minquas Country," the old Dutch term for Gandastogue still used by cartographers, became a shorthand for the limits of the empire's western reaches. Beyond that limit, Haudenosaunee raiders traversed the Great Warpath through the Appalachian valleys, well away from colonial plantations and tributary towns. Instead of striking toward the coast, they went north to raid New France and its Native allies and south toward Indigenous nations without links to the English colonies. In the following decades, these mourning wars would have serious consequences for the Haudenosaunee. Nevertheless, the Covenant Chain represented the opening of new possibilities for peaceful coexistence with the English, particularly in New York and Pennsylvania.[5]

In the spirit of Indigenous understandings of international relations, the Covenant Chain was not a treaty written on paper in ink, no matter how much settlers would have liked it to be. It was the linking of peoples who

had previously been strangers, creating an ongoing relationship that required maintenance. Haudenosaunee orators frequently referred to recurring councils, with their ritual declarations of friendship and mutual
exchange of gifts, as a brightening of the chain, freeing it from the rust
that accumulated with time and cleaning the mud and blood that sullied it
because of bad feelings and rash actions. The dynamic alliance symbolized
by the Covenant Chain structured the relationship between the English colonies and the Haudenosaunee—and because of Iroquoia's power and influence, Indigenous nations across the Northeast—for most of the next
century.[6]

While the Covenant Chain fostered new opportunities for Anglo-Indian
coexistence in the mid-Atlantic, in the South those possibilities were violently foreclosed by the growing Native slave trade. This too was a development shaped by Susquehannock action, even if it was one that they did
not intend. Before the Time of Anarchy, small numbers of Virginia merchants and the Occaneechi chiefdom had controlled the trade, cooperating
to perpetuate a slaving monopoly that was highly lucrative but limited in
scope. Susquehannock-led assaults forced the Occaneechis to evacuate their
island stronghold in 1681, which left the road networks through the Appalachians open to contestation. With the floodgates open, English slavers
poured into the west, funneling Native captives into colonial slave markets.
Merchants from Virginia and Carolina armed any Indians willing to sell
them slaves, and many southern nations responded eagerly as guns became
an indispensable tool for survival. Making matters worse, Haudenosaunee
came from the north along the open paths, pummeling southern nations to
bring captives back to Iroquoia.[7]

Natives faced a stark choice between acting as predators or becoming
prey. The traditional imperatives of captive taking—communal healing and
the coercive making of new kin—became entangled with the market logic
of human commodification. While Native peoples did not simply abandon
their practices of captivity for capitalist ones, the necessity of replenishing
military supplies meant that it was vital to stay in the black on the brutal
ledgers of English slavers. Those who failed to do so found that English
merchants had few qualms about enslaving business partners who fell into
debt or became more trouble than they were worth. Small nations shattered under the onslaught. Refugees sought the protection of more powerful
neighbors. Coalescent communities gradually created confederations capable of repelling northern raiders and resisting the insatiable hunger of
the plantation machine. The violence of the slave trade reverberated across
the Southeast well into the eighteenth century, reshaping the social and political contours of the region.[8]

As the Indigenous slave trade metastasized, racial divides sharpened, diminishing possibilities for meaningful coexistence. Growing numbers of enslaved Natives forcibly marched along inland paths, joined by growing numbers of enslaved Africans packed into ships sailing across the saltwater, gradually replaced servants of European descent as the majority of the labor force in the South. For colonists, the lived experience of mastery was an important part of coming to see laboring people of color as inferior, and that experience helped build the complex of ideas and attitudes that we call "race." The power of issuing orders and wielding the whip; close proximity to bodies caked with dirt and sweat after a day's work in the humid heat, and the satisfaction of judging them disgusting; the ability to prey on women who could not say no, and to profit from selling their children; the easy leap to thinking that these qualities made human beings unworthy of respect or even empathy—these were visceral, sensory, and emotional experiences inextricable from the entrenchment of racism. But alongside this empowering sense of mastery, colonists had to contend with the radically disempowering experience of Anglo-Indian warfare.[9]

The construction of slavery's machinery of exploitation, and the ideological shifts that made that machinery seem as natural and necessary as sunshine and oxygen, took place in the middle of an ongoing war with Susquehannocks and their allies. Colonists, believing they faced enemies on all sides and desperate to protect themselves and their families, struggled to tell the difference between Native friends and Native enemies. In the midst of terrible danger—or at least what they convinced themselves was terrible danger—a mixture of embattled masculinity, cognitive fatigue, and growing hatred led some colonists to stop trying to tell them apart. Nathaniel Bacon and his fellow Volunteers willfully ignored the diversity of Indigenous peoples, flattening distinctions between them and arguing that all Indians were essentially alike. The syllogism then completed itself: if some Indians were enemies, and all Indians were the same, then all Indians were enemies, including those who claimed to be fellow subjects of the king. Bacon's ideological innovation mapped English terror onto Native bodies, experimenting with new ideas about the meanings of bodily difference to forge the hot iron of Indian-fearing into the cold steel of Indian-hating. The Indians are all of a color, the Volunteers had cried; they could be massacred with impunity and transformed from terrifying people into exploitable things. The few that remained could be pushed aside or forced away so that settlers could forget that Native people existed at all.[10]

The racial thinking that emerged during Bacon's Rebellion was a major factor causing the system governing Native subjects to implode, resulting in a civil war between settlers and Algonquians who were both subjects of the Crown. Despite the rights and protections that tributaries enjoyed on paper, they were devastated by the enemies that surrounded them, both foreign raiders such as Susquehannocks and the English neighbors who refused to consider them friends. They died in combat, took flight to remote holdfasts, suffered from diseases that ran rampant in conditions of crowding and malnutrition, were captured by Iroquoians and enslaved by colonists. By the Time of Anarchy's end, this pulverizing violence had depopulated a vast swath of Native homelands in the coastal Chesapeake. When governors such as Sir William Berkeley stood by Indians in the belief that they could be valuable members of colonial society, men like Bacon rose to overthrow them. The administrators who followed learned that they could earn the loyalty of Indian-hating settlers by ignoring Indigenous rights. In the last years of the seventeenth century, governors of Virginia, Maryland, and other colonies increasingly adopted policies that eroded Native sovereignty, undermined their economies, encouraged their dispossession, and pressured them to migrate west. If such policies fell short of the Volunteers' enthusiastic calls for genocide, they nevertheless fostered circumstances that made it easy for Indigenous peoples to die.[11]

Coastal Algonquians survived this onslaught in large part because of the opportunities they created for themselves amid colonial upheaval. In cooperation with royal officials, who supported tributary Natives to further their own agenda of imperial centralization, Indigenous leaders helped build a new tributary system from the ruins of the old. The 1677 Treaty of Middle Plantation, whose architecture bore the imprint of the Pamunkey weroansqua Cockacoeske, was a crucial tool in their struggle. Cockacoeske designed it to reconstitute the old Powhatan paramount chiefdom under the aegis of the English empire, an innovative political form that served both imperial and Indigenous interests. If her actual achievement fell short of that design, it should not detract from the importance of the attempt. The fact that she pursued such an ambition at all shows that Algonquians envisioned an Indigenous future and struggled to make it real. The legal protections enshrined in the treaty did not have as much force as Cockacoeske might have hoped, but they nevertheless established a framework for the imperial governance of Indian affairs that subsequent generations of Indigenous leaders used to weather the storms of settler colonialism. Werowances observed the treaty's ceremonial obligation to present the governor of Virginia with tribute every year, and they continued to do so even after the colony rebelled against its king and became a state in a new republic. When the Pamunkey tribal nation achieved federal recognition in 2015, the unbroken relationship established by the Treaty of Middle Plantation was essential to the success of their case. In 2017, recognition of the Chickahominy, Eastern Chickahominy, Upper Mattaponi, Rappahannock, Monacan, and Nansemond tribal nations followed, paving the way for a revitalization that has only just begun.[12]

The human nexus for these continental shifts was the Susquehannock people. Viewed from New York or Philadelphia, they might have seemed like a sideshow in the forging of the Covenant Chain; viewed from Jamestown or Charles Town, only bit players in the expansion of the Indigenous slave trade. They seem marginal because colonial archives contain only glimpses of their actions, and those glimpses privilege a colonial gaze that obscures the deep connections between the changing shape of Anglo-Indian relations in different regions. The view from Gandastogue illuminates those connections and brings into focus the ways that northern diplomacy and southern violence, divisive racial thinking and imperial centralization, all developed in concert. The revolution in Anglo-Indian affairs was shaped by Susquehannock hands and forged in the fire of Gandastogue's violent rebirth.

Although the shape of Anglo-Indian relations changed on a grand scale during the Time of Anarchy, it was not geopolitics that caused Maryland burgesses to shrink from Susquehannock threats. When they declared it was "absolutly unsafe for the Province to bring the said Jacob to Tryall," they recognized that even a small spark of Susquehannock violence could ignite the powder keg of popular discontent, sending them back into the maelstrom of Anglo-Indian war and rebellion. The Time of Anarchy put this tangled relationship between Indigenous power and colonial violence, and the emotional cultures that gave it explosive force, into stark relief.[13]

The cycle was clear. Grief motivated Susquehannock raids as warriors sought to heal the trauma of lost kin by ravaging the bodies of their enemies, striving to strike terror into the hearts of survivors. Fear led Virginia colonists to demand that their government fulfill its patriarchal obligations as protector, arousing resentment when the government refused or failed. Rumors of violence spawned conspiracy theories that led men such as Nathaniel Bacon to transmute helpless fear into avenging fury, lashing out against Native allies and then challenging the government that insisted on protecting them. This circuit between Anglo-Indian violence, Indian-fearing, and insurrection was direct, unambiguous, and obvious to everyone who experienced it. As royal commissioners Sir John Berry and Francis Moryson wrote, "by the Mutuall discontents, Complaints, Jealousyes and fears of English and Indians . . . the peace of this his Majesties Colony hath been much disturbed and the late unhappy Rebellion by this meanes (in a great measure) begun and fomented which hath involved this Country into soe much Ruine and Misery." As central authorities splintered, even minor incidents provoked new rounds of crisis. This pattern played out over and over again during the Time of Anarchy, first in Virginia, but then in Maryland, and then Albemarle—everywhere, in fact, that Susquehannocks took the offensive.[14]

It may seem paradoxical that the actions of a few Susquehannocks could have such an outsized impact, but in fact this is one of the most important lessons from the Time of Anarchy. The power of politicized emotions to turn intimate tragedies into mass movements allowed even small groups of raiders and vigilantes to drag whole nations to war. The relationship between Anglo-Indian violence and colonial disorder meant that initiative rested on the margins, far from the centers of power. It was not a well-organized group of insurgents that spun Indian raids into Bacon's Rebellion, nor an Indigenous empire that convulsed the colonies for a decade. It was, instead, improvised ensembles of terrified settlers and scattered bands of mourning refugees.

In the end, the structure of Susquehannock social and political organization that George Alsop derided as mere "Anarchy" was not a weakness, but a strength. Their flexible, decentralized networks of kinship alliances allowed fractured communities to reconstitute themselves and harness hidden sources of power. They did not need great chiefs to command this process. One matron's dream could lead embattled Susquehannocks from Iroquoia to Albemarle to mobilize the power of allies and turn it against their enemies. When Susquehannocks unleashed that power, they triggered the rebellions that Thomas Lord Culpeper lamented as "our Time of Anarchy." In doing so they revealed that the English empire in America, which looked so imposing on paper, was fragile enough to tear itself apart. Its governments may have claimed absolute dominion over people and territory, but it was ultimately composed of individual families, and the foremost loyalty of those families was to each other. Individually and in groups, they defied governors, proprietors, and kings. A single planter's anger over a beloved servant's death might start a chain reaction causing an entire colony to tumble into crisis. The Time of Anarchy was, so to speak, governed by this irony of power. Often enough, it was the weakest and most precarious actors who shaped the future of North America.[15]

This is not the end of the story. As the Time of Anarchy came to a close, Susquehannocks began migrating back to their homeland. By 1687, small parties had established seasonal camps in the Susquehanna Valley, hunting and trading with the merchants of Philadelphia. Cayuga spokesmen called them "antient Inhabitants of Susquehanne butt belonging to our Castle," and there was "one born Cayouger" among their ranks. By 1690, they had rebuilt their old connadago and drew others from Iroquoia. That year a group of Onondagas came to St. Mary's City and informed the council that they were pioneers of a southern migration by members of all the League nations, who "came from their own country . . . to settle among the Susquahanough Indians here, upon the Susquahanough River." The new settlement's leaders conveyed their desire to "confirme the former League of Friendship" with Maryland. Barely a decade after captive Susquehannocks were dragged to Iroquoia by force, they had gained not only the liberty to return to their homeland but also the power to convince former captors to leave their homelands and join them.[16]

Their friend Jacob, who quietly moved to Pennsylvania instead of sailing back to the Netherlands, did his part. In 1684, William Penn wrote from Philadelphia that "Jacob Young" was "lately with me, and severall Indians" to share information about Susquehanna Valley geography and fur trading routes along the Schuylkill River. These Indians—most likely the Delaware-Susquehannocks who settled at the "Susquehannah Indian Town" on the Schuylkill in 1676—worked with Jacob to make Pennsylvania a home for both Natives and settlers. Within a few years, Jacob had patched up relations with the Maryland government. Few colonists had more experience with the "northern Indians" than Jacob, and he was invited to retake his position as interpreter. By 1692, he became so indispensable that the council hesitated to make decisions about Indian affairs without his advice. A decade after his treason trial, it formally recognized the "many Good Services Mr Jacob Young hath done and performed to this Province." One of those services was maintaining the relationship between Maryland and the new community of Susquehannocks and Haudenosaunee.[17]

The community gathered kin from the wide expanse of the Susquehannock scattering. In 1693, Jacob escorted two ambassadors, one Susquehannock and the other Shawnee, to meet with the Maryland Council. They had sojourned for years to the south and as far west as the French Fort Saint Louis on the Illinois River, befriending Shawnees and sharing hardships against mutual enemies in the lower Ohio Valley. Now, tired of wandering and war, they wished to "settle *upon their own Land* at the Susquehannoh Fort and to be taken and treated as Friends." These Ohio-Susquehannocks and their Shawnee companions joined the Haudenosaunee and Susquehannocks from Iroquoia. Demanding recognition of their land rights and undiminished sovereignty, they declared the refounding of Gandastogue.[18]

New friends were joined by former enemies. Seasonal trappers sent regular trading parties to the Potomac to build ties with the Piscataways and

other Algonquians. In 1693, Susquehannock leaders invited them to move
to the Susquehanna Valley. In a council with Lenape and Pennsylvania representatives, "Kyanharro and Oriteo, two Susquehanna Indians," recited
the hardships suffered by the "kyanisse Indians." (Kyanisse was a rendering
of Ganawese, the Iroquoian word for Maryland Algonquians, which was
Anglicized as Conoy.) Kyanharro spoke in a language that Susquehannock-
speaking interpreters could not understand, and his name shared the same
root as kyanisse, suggesting that he may have been born Algonquian and
requickened as a Susquehannock with a name that advertised his heritage.
Using the language of kinship, he promised that he would protect the
Conoys, stating, "you are of my blood; I cannot denie you, but must receive you." He exhorted the Pennsylvania Council to treat Conoys with
the same love and kindness they had shown toward Susquehannocks. The
Conoys left Maryland and eventually founded a new town north of the
Susquehannock settlement. In the early decades of the eighteenth century,
they were followed by other peoples who once had clashed with Gandastogue: Nanticokes and coastal Algonquians escaping settler encroachment
and unfriendly governors, Occaneechis and other Siouans fleeing incessant
raids, and Tuscaroras defeated in war with Carolina colonists. They all became part of the communities gathering in the Susquehanna Valley.[19]

Gandastogue—the place that English writers spelled "Conestoga"—
thrived on the booming waters of the Susquehanna. For half a century
after its refounding, Gandastogue sat at the crossroads of a growing regional trade. Shawnees, with widely dispersed networks of kin in the rich
hunting grounds of the Ohio Valley, brought furs to Pennsylvania trading
posts through Delaware-Susquehannocks, the "Skoolkill Indians" that
Conestogas called "our Cousens still tho you live a little Further From us
then you did." Philadelphia merchants eagerly traded furs for wool and
cloth, glass and iron, guns and plenty of powder. Conestoga was the magnet
for Indigenous migrants of many nations and was the most important site
for diplomatic relations between the "Susquehanna Indians" and the colony
of Pennsylvania. Conestoga Town was a community of over 150 Susquehannocks and "Senecas" from all five of the Haudenosaunee nations.
Nearby, a town called Minguannan, where Machaloha and his people lived,
was home to two hundred "Delaware Indians," and a thousand more lived
along Brandywine and Chester Creeks. It is likely that among them were
Delaware-Susquehannocks drawn by the gravity of their reconstituted
kin. Another community a few miles south of Conestoga Town housed
around one hundred Shawnees who came to the valley with the Ohio-
Susquehannocks. In 1701 Conestoga's headman, Connodaghtoh, "King

of the Sasquehannah Minquays or Conestogo Indians," spoke not only for his people but also for other Indians of the Susquehanna Valley. In a treaty council with William Penn, Connodaghtoh stated that his people and Pennsylvania colonists "shall forever hereafter be as one Head and One Heart, and live in true Friendship and Amity as one People." Like their ancestors who built a network of kin and allies flung across eastern North America, the Conestogas' new nation would be a motley confederation of diverse peoples. Their relations were maintained by the cultivation of calm thoughts and good feelings, their unity built through the tireless, persistent, painstaking search for consensus. As Connodaghtoh promised, that same process would also link them to the colonists of Pennsylvania and guide their steps into a shared future.[20]

If we watch this rebirth with a teleological eye, knowing that Conestoga's economy would shrink as the fur trade declined and that the cauldron of eighteenth-century imperial war would ultimately consume it, we miss something vital about this moment. The Susquehannock people had been betrayed and massacred, displaced and pursued, captured and enslaved. To survive they had been forced to choose from a small set of hard options. Yet despite this history of suffering, the people of Conestoga expressed a defiant optimism. The Susquehannocks who came from the west in 1693 had been "reduced to a small number," their spokesman admitted sadly, but now there was a fledgling generation, "as it were newly grown up." The people who made up the multiethnic political community of greater Conestoga were women and "lusty young men" who came of age after the dark days of the Time of Anarchy. One of those men manifested his hope as an indelible work of art. Using the fine metal tools available from colonial merchants, he carved a moose antler into a decorative comb for a matron to tuck into her hair on formal occasions such as diplomatic councils. It depicted two men, one a Susquehannock wearing the sort of European-style frock coat that traders brought to Conestoga, the other a colonist wearing the brimmed hat of a Quaker. They are lean and confident, standing equal. They face each other, Indigenous and settler mirror images. Their arms are raised, as if in friendship, their hands merged in the dividing line of the comb's frame. They do not quite touch, but their reciprocal reach conveys a universe of possibility.[21]

Twenty-five years after the Susquehannock people scattered across the continent, after years of war with their enemies and struggles among themselves, they were gathered again in their homeland. No matter the pronouncements of would-be colonial conquerors, Gandastogue had never died. It was a nation composed of kin bound by webs that stretched across

Hair comb from Conestoga. Courtesy of the Metropolitan Museum of Art, New York, the Charles and Valerie Diker Collection of Native American Art, Gift of Charles and Valerie Diker, 2019.

the divisions of culture, language, and territory. It survived because its people remained connected to each other and wove new strands of contact with Natives and settlers around them. It thrived for a generation after its rebirth because of the young men and women who had grown up and wanted a new beginning. They did not know what the future held, any more than the rest of us. But they were determined to fight for it.[22]

Abbreviations

Notes

Acknowledgments

Index

· ABBREVIATIONS ·

Journals

AHR	*American Historical Review*
EAS	*Early American Studies*
JAH	*Journal of American History*
JSH	*Journal of Southern History*
MHM	*Maryland Historical Magazine*
NCHR	*North Carolina Historical Review*
NYH	*New York History*
PAPS	*Proceedings of the American Philosophical Society*
PMHB	*Pennsylvania Magazine of History and Biography*
VMHB	*Virginia Magazine of History and Biography*
WMQ	*William and Mary Quarterly*

Manuscripts

Beinecke Library	James Marshall and Marie-Louise Osborn Collection, Beinecke Rare Book and Manuscript Library, Yale University, New Haven, Connecticut
Bodleian Library	Weston Library, Special Collections, Bodleian Libraries, University of Oxford
British Library	British Library, London
Codrington Library	Codrington Library, All Souls College, University of Oxford
Coventry Papers	Henry Coventry Papers, Longleat House, Library of the Marquess of Bath, Wiltshire (microfilm copy, 95 reels, ACLS British Manuscripts Project, Washington, DC, 1900–1990)
DHS	Delaware Historical Society, Wilmington, Delaware

HSP	Historical Society of Pennsylvania, Philadelphia, Pennsylvania
Huntington	Huntington Library, San Marino, California
LoC	Library of Congress, Washington, DC
LVA	Library of Virginia, Richmond, Virginia
MSA	Maryland State Archives, Annapolis, Maryland
NCSA	North Carolina State Archives, Raleigh, North Carolina
Newberry Library	Edward E. Ayer Collection, Newberry Library, Chicago, Illinois
NJHS	New Jersey Historical Society, Newark, New Jersey
NYPL	New York Public Library, New York City, New York
Pratt Library	Hugh H. Young Collection of Colonial Maryland Papers, Special Collections Department, Enoch Pratt Free Library, Baltimore, Maryland
PSA	Pennsylvania State Archives, Harrisburg, Pennsylvania
Rockefeller Library	John D. Rockefeller Jr. Library, Williamsburg, Virginia
Small Library	Albert and Shirley Small Special Collections Library, University of Virginia, Charlottesville, Virginia
TNA	The National Archives of the United Kingdom
	ADM: Admiralty Series
	CO: Colonial Office Series
	LC: Lord Chamberlain's Accounts Series
	PC: Privy Council Series
	SP: State Papers, Domestic Series
	WO: War Office Series
VHS	Virginia Historical Society, Richmond, Virginia

Printed Sources

Andrews, *Narratives*	Charles M. Andrews, ed., *Narratives of the Insurrections, 1675–1690*. New York: Charles Scribner's Sons, 1915.
Andros Papers	Peter R. Christoph and Florence A. Christoph, eds., *The Andros Papers: Files of the Provincial Secretary of New York During the Administration of Governor Sir Edmund Andros, 1674–1680*. 3 vols. New York: Syracuse University Press, 1989.
Archives of Maryland	William Hand Browne, et al., eds., *Archives of Maryland*. 72 vols. Baltimore: Maryland Historical Society, 1883–1972.
CRNC	William L. Saunders, ed., *Colonial Records of North Carolina*. 10 vols. Raleigh, NC: P. M. Hale, 1886–1890.
DRCHSNJ	William A. Whitehead, ed., *Documents Relating to the Colonial History of the State of New Jersey*. 33 vols. Newark, NJ: Daily Advertiser Printing House, 1880–1928.

DRCHSNY E. B. O'Callaghan, ed., *Documents Relative to the Colonial History of the State of New York.* 15 vols. Albany, NY: Weed, Parsons, 1853–1887.

EJCCV H. R. McIlwaine and Wilmer Lee Hall, eds., *Executive Journals of the Council of Colonial Virginia.* 6 vols. Richmond: Virginia State Library, 1925–1966.

Hening, *Statutes* William Waller Hening, ed., *The Statutes at Large: Being a Collection of All the Laws of Virginia, from the First Session of the Legislature, in the Year 1619.* 13 vols. Richmond, VA, 1809–1823.

Jesuit Relations Reuben Gold Thwaites, ed., *The Jesuit Relations and Allied Documents: Travels and Explorations of the Jesuit Missionaries in New France, 1610–1791.* 73 vols. Cleveland, OH: Burroughs Brothers, 1896–1901.

JHBV H. R. McIlwaine, ed., *Journals of the House of Burgesses of Virginia.* 13 vols. Richmond: Virginia State Library, 1905–1915.

LIR Lawrence H. Leder, ed., *The Livingston Indian Records, 1666–1723.* Gettysburg: Pennsylvania Historical Association, 1956.

LJCCV H. R. McIlwaine, ed., *Legislative Journals of the Councils of Colonial Virginia.* 3 vols. Richmond: Colonial Press, Everett Waddey, 1918.

MCARS Arnold J. F. van Laer, ed., *Minutes of the Court of Albany, Rensselaerswyck and Schenectady.* 3 vols. Albany: University of the State of New York, 1926–1932.

MCGCCV H. R. McIlwaine, ed., *Minutes of the Council and General Court of Colonial Virginia, 1622–1632, 1670–1676.* Richmond: Colonial Press, Everett Waddey, 1924.

MECPNY Victor Hugo Paltsits, ed., *Minutes of the Executive Council of the Province of New York: Administration of Francis Lovelace, 1668–1673.* 2 vols. Albany, NY: J. B. Lyon, 1910.

NYHM *(Delaware Dutch)* Charles T. Gehring, ed. and trans., *Delaware Papers (Dutch Period): A Collection of Documents Pertaining to the Regulation of Affairs on the South River of New Netherland, 1648–1664.* New York Historical Manuscripts, vols. 18–19. Baltimore: Genealogical Publishing Company, 1981.

NYHM *(Delaware English)* Charles T. Gehring, ed., *Delaware Papers (English Period): A Collection of Documents Pertaining to the Regulation of Affairs on the Delaware, 1664–1682.* New York Historical Manuscripts, vols. 20–21. Baltimore: Genealogical Publishing Company, 1977.

NYHM
(General Entries) Peter R. Christoph and Florence A. Christoph, eds., *Books of General Entries of the Colony of New York.* New York Historical Manuscripts: English. 2 vols., Baltimore: Genealogical Publishing Company, 1982.

Pennsylvania Archives Samuel Hazard, et al., eds., *Pennsylvania Archives.* 138 vols. 1852–1935.

PSWB Warren M. Billings, ed., *The Papers of Sir William Berkeley, 1605–1677.* Richmond: Library of Virginia, 2007.

PWP Richard S. Dunn and Mary Maples Dunn, eds., *The Papers of William Penn.* 5 vols. Philadelphia: University of Pennsylvania Press, 1981–1987.

RCNCD Colonial Society of Pennsylvania, *Records of the Court of New Castle on Delaware.* 2 vols. Lancaster, PA: Wickersham Printing Company, 1904–1935.

RCUP Edward Armstrong, ed., *The Record of the Court at Upland: in Pennsylvania. 1676 to 1681.* Philadelphia: J. B. Lippincott & Co., for the Historical Society of Pennsylvania, 1860.

RVCL Susan Myra Kingsbury, ed., *Records of the Virginia Company of London.* 4 vols. Washington, DC: Government Printing Office, 1906–1935.

[Sherwood],
"Virginias Deploured
Condition" [William Sherwood], "Virginias Deploured Condition (1676)." In *Collections of the Massachusetts Historical Society,* 4th ser., vol. 9, 162–176. Boston: Massachusetts Historical Society, 1876.

Wiseman's Book *Samuel Wiseman's "Book of Record": The Official Account of Bacon's Rebellion in Virginia.* Edited by Michael Leroy Oberg. Lanham, MD: Lexington, 2005.

· NOTES ·

Prologue

1. "Reports of Conferences between Lord Baltimore and William Penn, and Their Agents, 1682, 1683, 1684," in *Narratives of Early Maryland, 1633–1684,* ed. Clayton Colman Hall (New York: Charles Scribner's Sons, 1910), 440. Given the Susquehannocks' importance in the seventeenth century, the specialist literature is surprisingly sparse. The last study devoted to their history was published more than half a century ago: Francis Jennings, "Glory, Death, and Transfiguration: The Susquehannock Indians in the Seventeenth Century," *PAPS* 112, no. 1 (1968): 15–53. For broader historical studies with a significant focus on the Susquehannocks, see J. Frederick Fausz, "Merging and Emerging Worlds: Anglo-Indian Interest Groups and the Development of the Seventeenth-Century Chesapeake," in *Colonial Chesapeake Society,* ed. Lois Green Carr, Philip D. Morgan, and Jean B. Russo (Chapel Hill: University of North Carolina Press, 1988), 47–98; Francis Jennings, *The Ambiguous Iroquois Empire: The Covenant Chain Confederation of Indian Tribes with English Colonies from Its Beginnings to the Lancaster Treaty of 1744* (New York: W. W. Norton, 1984); Matthew Kruer, "Bloody Minds and Peoples Undone: Emotion, Family, and Political Order in the Susquehannock-Virginia War," *WMQ* 74, no. 3 (2017): 401–436; James D. Rice, "Bacon's Rebellion in Indian Country," *JAH* 101, no. 3 (2014), 726–750; Cynthia J. Van Zandt, *Brothers among Nations: The Pursuit of Intercultural Alliances in Early America, 1580–1660* (New York: Oxford University Press, 2008), 116–136, 166–186. In contrast to the scant historical scholarship, archaeologists have produced a rich body of work on the Susquehannocks and their neighbors. For overviews of this sizable literature, see Barry C. Kent, *Susquehanna's Indians* (1984; Harrisburg: Pennsylvania Historical and Museum Commission, 2001); Paul A. Raber, ed., *The Susquehannocks: New Perspectives on Settlement and Cultural Identity* (University Park: Pennsylvania State University Press, 2019). For outdated but still valuable studies, see also Donald A. Cadzow, ed., *Archaeological Studies of the Susquehannock Indians of Pennsylvania* (Harrisburg: Pennsylvania Historical Commission, 1936); John Witthoft and W. Fred Kinsey III, eds., *Susquehannock Miscellany* (Harrisburg: Pennsylvania Historical and Museum Commission, 1959).

2. For a character sketch of Jacob focusing mostly on proprietary politics in Maryland, see Francis Jennings, "Jacob Young: Indian Trader and Interpreter," in *Struggle and Survival in Colonial America,* ed. David G. Sweet and Gary B. Nash (Berkeley: University of California Press, 1981), 347–361. On intercultural brokers, see Juliana Barr, *Peace Came in the Form of a Woman: Indians and Spaniards in the Texas Borderlands* (Chapel Hill: University of North Carolina Press, 2007); James F. Brooks, *Captives and Cousins: Slavery, Kinship, and Community in the Southwest Borderlands* (Chapel Hill: University of North Carolina Press, 2002); J. Frederick Fausz, "Middlemen in Peace and War: Virginia's Earliest Indian Interpreters, 1608–1632," *VMHB* 95, no. 1 (1987): 41–64; Nancy L. Hagedorn, "'Faithful, Knowing, and Prudent': Andrew Montour as Interpreter and Cultural Broker, 1740–1772," in *Between Indian and White Worlds: The Cultural Broker,* ed. Margaret Connell Szasz (Norman: University of Oklahoma Press, 1994), 44–60; James H. Merrell, *Into the American Woods: Negotiators on the Pennsylvania Frontier* (New York: W. W. Norton, 1999). Jacob went by many different surnames—presumably including a Susquehannock name by which he was known among his kin by marriage—and it is not clear which he would have preferred, so I refer to him by his first name or by his alias Jacob My Friend throughout this book.

3. *DRCHSNY,* 12:317; *Archives of Maryland,* 7:370. Aside from these two oblique references nothing else is known about the Susquehannock woman who married Jacob, including her name, familial origins or social standing, reasons for marrying a Dutch man, thoughts and feelings about navigating the space between two cultures, and her ultimate fate. Neither is there any evidence that speaks to the lives of their children. On intercultural intimacy and fur trade marriages, see Clara Sue Kidwell, "Indian Women as Cultural Mediators," *Ethnohistory* 39, no. 2 (1992): 97–107; Susan Sleeper-Smith, *Indian Women and French Men: Rethinking Cultural Encounter in the Western Great Lakes* (Amherst: University of Massachusetts Press, 2001); Susanah Shaw Romney, *New Netherland Connections: Intimate Networks and Atlantic Ties in Seventeenth-Century America* (Chapel Hill: University of North Carolina Press, 2014), 122–190; Sylvia Van Kirk, *Many Tender Ties: Women in Fur-Trade Society, 1670–1870* (Norman: University of Oklahoma Press, 1980).

4. *Archives of Maryland,* 7:348, 371–372, 383–384.

5. *Archives of Maryland,* 7:398–399.

6. For the most comprehensive studies of Bacon's Rebellion, see James D. Rice, *Tales from a Revolution: Bacon's Rebellion and the Transformation of Early America* (New York: Oxford University Press, 2012); Wilcomb E. Washburn, *The Governor and the Rebel: A History of Bacon's Rebellion in Virginia* (Chapel Hill: University of North Carolina Press, 1957). For the most important works on Bacon's Rebellion more generally, see Bernard Bailyn, "Politics and Social Structure in Virginia," in *Seventeenth-Century America: Essays in Colonial History,* ed. James Morton Smith (Chapel Hill: University of North Carolina Press, 1959), 90–115; Warren M. Billings, "The Causes of Bacon's Rebellion: Some Suggestions," *VMHB* 78, no. 4 (1970): 409–435; Kathleen M. Brown, *Good Wives, Nasty Wenches, and Anxious Patriarchs: Gender, Race, and Power in Colonial Virginia* (Chapel Hill: University of North Carolina Press, 1996), 137–186; Edmund S. Morgan, *American Slavery, American Freedom: The Ordeal of Colonial Virginia* (1975; repr. ed., New York: W. W. Norton, 2003), 215–292; Brent Tarter, "Bacon's Rebellion, the Grievances of the People, and the Political Culture of Seventeenth-Century Virginia," *VMHB* 119, no. 1 (2011): 2–41; Peter Thompson, "The Thief, the Householder, and the Commons: Languages of Class in Seventeenth-Century Virginia," *WMQ* 63, no. 2.

(2006): 253–280; Susan Westbury, "Women in Bacon's Rebellion," in *Southern Women: Histories and Identities,* ed. Virginia Bernhard et al. (Columbia: University of Missouri Press, 1992), 30–46. On the Maryland uprisings, see Rice, *Tales from a Revolution,* 81–83, 148–160; Antoinette Sutto, *Loyal Protestants and Dangerous Papists: Maryland and the Politics of Religion in the English Atlantic, 1630–1690* (Charlottesville: University of Virginia Press, 2015), 129–158. On disruptions in New York, New Jersey, and Delaware, see John M. Murrin, "English Rights as Ethnic Aggression: The English Conquest, the Charter of Liberties of 1683, and Leisler's Rebellion in New York," in *Authority and Resistance in Early New York,* ed. William Pencak and Conrad Edick Wright (New York: New-York Historical Society, 1988), 56–94; Brendan McConville, *These Daring Disturbers of the Public Peace: The Struggle for Property and Power in Early New Jersey* (Ithaca, NY: Cornell University Press, 1999), 18–19; Donna Merwick, "Becoming English: Anglo-Dutch Conflict in the 1670s in Albany, New York," *NYH* 62, no. 4 (1981): 389–414. On Culpeper's Rebellion, see Noeleen McIlvenna, *A Very Mutinous People: The Struggle for North Carolina, 1660–1713* (Chapel Hill: University of North Carolina Press, 2009), 46–70; Mattie Erma E. Parker, "Legal Aspects of 'Culpeper's Rebellion,'" *NCHR* 45, no. 2 (1968): 111–127; Hugh F. Rankin, *Upheaval in Albemarle: The Story of Culpeper's Rebellion, 1675–1689* (Raleigh, NC: Carolina Charter Tercentenary Commission, 1962).

7. For a general account of Indigenous conflicts during this period, see Jennings, *Ambiguous Iroquois Empire,* 113–142. In Virginia, see Rice, "Bacon's Rebellion in Indian Country," 730–734; Ethan A. Schmidt, *The Divided Dominion: Social Conflict and Indian Hatred in Early Virginia* (Boulder: University Press of Colorado, 2015), 149–176; Kristalyn Marie Shefveland, *Anglo-Native Virginia: Trade, Conversion, and Indian Slavery in the Old Dominion, 1646–1722* (Athens: University of Georgia Press, 2016), 44–60. In Maryland, see Francis Jennings, "Indians and Frontiers in Seventeenth-Century Maryland," in *Early Maryland in a Wider World,* ed. David B. Quinn (Detroit, MI: Wayne State University Press, 1982), 216–241; James D. Rice, *Nature and History in the Potomac Country: From Hunter-Gatherers to the Age of Jefferson* (Baltimore: Johns Hopkins University Press, 2009), 143–160. In Albemarle, see Lars C. Adams, "'Sundry Murders and Depredations': A Closer Look at the Chowan River War, 1676–1677," *NCHR* 90, no. 2 (2013): 149–172.

   This book does not include analysis of King Philip's War, which was contemporaneous with these conflicts but driven by forces distinctive to New England. I have not discovered any evidence that the Anglo-Indian violence of King Philip's War was directly connected to other outbreaks of violence west of the Hudson River, though I would not be surprised if the question rewarded further study. Important works on King Philip's War include Lisa Brooks, *Our Beloved Kin: A New History of King Philip's War* (New Haven, CT: Yale University Press, 2018); James D. Drake, *King Philip's War: Civil War in New England, 1675–1676* (Amherst: University of Massachusetts Press, 1999); Douglas Edward Leach, *Flintlock and Tomahawk: New England in King Philip's War* (New York: Macmillan, 1958); Daniel R. Mandell, *King Philip's War: Colonial Expansion, Native Resistance, and the End of Indian Sovereignty* (Baltimore: Johns Hopkins University Press, 2010). For an excellent study on the relationship between Anglo-Indian violence and challenges to colonial authority, see Jenny Hale Pulsipher, *Subjects unto the Same King: Indians, English, and the Contest for Authority in Colonial New England* (Philadelphia: University of Pennsylvania Press, 2005).

8. Several important studies have made intercolonial or cross-regional connections: April Lee Hatfield, *Atlantic Virginia: Intercolonial Relations in the Seventeenth Century* (Philadelphia: University of Pennsylvania Press, 2004), 191–218; Michael Leroy Oberg, *Dominion and Civility: English Imperialism and Native America, 1585–1685* (Ithaca, NY: Cornell University Press, 1999), 113–228; Rice, "Bacon's Rebellion in Indian Country," 726–750; Stephen Saunders Webb, *1676: The End of American Independence* (New York: Alfred A. Knopf, 1984). However, even when these studies pay careful attention to the active role of Native peoples, they retain a conceptual framework derived from a colonial point of view: focusing on "Bacon's Rebellion" rhetorically places Virginia colonists at the center of a fundamentally decentralized cascade of conflicts. This book builds on the work of these pioneering historians, but argues that the various events among which they draw connections are better conceived as a single event framed around Indigenous spaces.

9. George Alsop, *A Character of the Province of Mary-Land* (London, 1666), 60–61; Lord Culpeper to [Sir Leoline Jenkins?], 20 March 1683, TNA CO 1/51/68, fol. 171v. Alsop's pamphlet is available in a modern compilation whose editors censored "coarse and vulgar" sections, including scatological humor, to protect the delicate sensibilities of early twentieth-century readers; Clayton Colman Hall, ed., *Narratives of Early Maryland, 337.*

10. Peter Kropotkin, *Mutual Aid: A Factor of Evolution* (New York: McClure, Philips and Co., 1902); Marcel Mauss, *The Gift: The Form and Reason for Exchange in Archaic Societies,* trans. W. D. Halls (New York: W. W. Norton, 1990); Franklin Rosemont, "Karl Marx and the Iroquois," *Arsenal/Surrealist Subversion* no. 4 (1989): 201–213 (republished at https://libcom.org/library/karl-marx-iroquois -franklin-rosemont [7 July 2009]); Pierre Clastres, *Society against the State: Essays in Political Anthropology,* trans. Robert Hurley and Abe Stein (New York: Zone Books, 1987); David Graeber, *Fragments of an Anarchist Anthropology* (Chicago: Prickly Paradigm, 2004), 84–86; Taiaiake Alfred, *Wasáse: Indigenous Pathways of Action and Freedom* (Peterborough: Broadview, 2005); Joanne Barker, *Native Acts: Law, Recognition, and Cultural Authenticity* (Durham, NC: Duke University Press, 2011); Glen Coulthard, *Red Skin, White Masks: Rejecting the Colonial Politics of Recognition* (Minneapolis: University of Minnesota Press, 2014); Nick Estes, *Our History Is the Future: Standing Rock versus the Dakota Access Pipeline, and the Long Tradition of Indigenous Resistance* (New York: Verso, 2019); J. Kēhaulani Kauanui, *Paradoxes of Hawaiian Sovereignty: Land, Sex, and the Colonial Politics of State Nationalism* (Durham, NC: Duke University Press, 2018); Audra Simpson, *Mohawk Interruptus: Political Life Across the Borders of Settler States* (Durham, NC: Duke University Press, 2014), 106–107, 193–194; Leanne Betasamosake Simpson, *As We Have Always Done: Indigenous Freedom through Radical Resistance* (Minneapolis: University of Minnesota Press, 2017); Kim TallBear, "Making Love and Relations Beyond Settler Sex and Family," in *Making Kin Not Population,* ed. Adele E. Clarke and Donna Haraway (Chicago: Prickly Paradigm, 2018), 145–164.

11. James C. Scott, *The Art of Not Being Governed: An Anarchist History of Upland Southeast Asia* (New Haven, CT: Yale University Press, 2009). Anarchist histories are a useful way to put two very different strands of scholarship, both important in this book, in conversation. A focus on the constituent elements of political order unites both recent studies of Indigenous societies, which emphasize kinship-based politics as a source of flexibility, resilience, and power, and studies of family in the

Atlantic world, which emphasize households as the constitutive unit of empire; Julia Adams, *The Familial State: Ruling Families and Merchant Capitalism in Early Modern Europe* (Ithaca, NY: Cornell University Press, 2005); Barr, *Peace Came in the Form of a Woman;* Heidi Bohaker, "*Nindoodemag:* The Significance of Algonquian Kinship Networks in the Eastern Great Lakes Region, 1600–1701," *WMQ* 63, no. 1 (2006): 23–52; Raymond J. DeMallie, "Kinship: The Foundation for Native American Society," in *Studying Native America: Problems and Prospects,* ed. Russell Thornton (Madison: University of Wisconsin Press, 1998), 306–356; Julie Hardwick, Sarah M. S. Pearsall, and Karin Wulf, "Introduction: Centering Families in Atlantic Histories," *WMQ* 70, no. 2 (2013): 205–224; Anne F. Hyde, *Empires, Nations, and Families: A New History of the North American West, 1800–1860* (Lincoln: University of Nebraska Press, 2011); Sami Lakomäki, *Gathering Together: The Shawnee People through Diaspora and Nationhood, 1600–1870* (New Haven, CT: Yale University Press, 2014); Jacob F. Lee, *Masters of the Middle Waters: Indian Nations and Colonial Ambitions along the Mississippi* (Cambridge, MA: Belknap Press of Harvard University Press, 2019); Jennifer L. Palmer, *Intimate Bonds: Family and Slavery in the French Atlantic* (Philadelphia: University of Pennsylvania Press, 2016); Sarah M. S. Pearsall, *Atlantic Families: Lives and Letters in the Later Eighteenth Century* (New York: Oxford University Press, 2008); Bryan C. Rindfleisch, *George Galphin's Intimate Empire: The Creek Indians, Family, and Colonialism in Early America* (Tuscaloosa: University of Alabama Press, 2019); Romney, *New Netherland Connections;* Kathleen Wilson, "Rethinking the Colonial State: Family, Gender, and Governmentality in Eighteenth-Century British Frontiers," *AHR* 116, no. 5 (2011): 1294–1322; Michael Witgen, *An Infinity of Nations: How the Native New World Shaped Early North America* (Philadelphia: University of Pennsylvania Press, 2012).

12. John Fanning Watson, "Travelling Notes of J. F. Watson: Trip to Harrisburgh &c - Jany 1835," [pp. 36–37], Watson Family Papers, Winterthur Library, Winterthur, DE; Jasmine Gollup, "Tracking the Susquehannocks: 'Proto-Susquehannock' Sites in the Upper Susquehanna Valley," in Raber, *Susquehannocks,* 26–27. The few sources that purport to describe Susquehannock spiritual beliefs and practices were produced by colonists in eighteenth-century Conestoga, a town founded by Susquehannock descendants. However, Conestoga was a multiethnic community that included Haudenosaunees, Shawnees, and Lenapes (Delawares). Colonists' descriptions of identifiably Lenape ceremonies and their use of Algonquian words for supernatural beings suggest that we should not assume these eighteenth-century observations of the Conestogas accurately describe seventeenth-century Susquehannock spirituality; Tobias Eric Biörck, *The Planting of the Swedish Church in America,* trans. Ira Oliver Nothstein (Rock Island, IL: Augustana College Library, 1943), 32–35; *A Speech Deliver'd by an Indian Chief, In Reply to a Sermon Preached by a Swedish Missionary* . . . (London, 1753), Newberry Library; C. A. Weslager, "Susquehannock Indian Religion from an Old Document," *Journal of the Washington Academy of Sciences* 36, no. 9 (1946): 302–305. On the 1763 massacre of the Conestogas, see Kevin Kenny, *Peaceable Kingdom Lost: The Paxton Boys and the Destruction of William Penn's Holy Experiment* (New York: Oxford University Press, 2009); Lee Francis 4, Weshoyot Alvitre, and Will Fenton, *Ghost River: The Fall and Rise of the Conestoga* (Philadelphia: Library Company of Philadelphia, 2019). Although the Susquehannock polity was destroyed, many people of Susquehannock descent continue to live in Pennsylvania and among other tribal nations; David J. Minderhout and Jessica D. Dowsett, "Our Stories, Our

Future: The Eastern Delaware Nations Oral History Project," *Society for Applied Anthropology* 32, no. 1 (2010): 32–37.

13. On representational violence and erasure, see Ned Blackhawk, *Violence Over the Land: Indians and Empires in the Early American West* (Cambridge, MA: Harvard University Press, 2006); Jean M. O'Brien, *Firsting and Lasting: Writing Indians out of Existence in New England* (Minneapolis: University of Minnesota Press, 2010).

14. Jean M. O'Brien, "Historical Sources and Methods in Indigenous Studies: Touching on the Past, Looking to the Future," in *Sources and Methods in Indigenous Studies,* ed. Chris Andersen and Jean M. O'Brien (New York: Routledge, 2017), 15–22; Alyssa Mt. Pleasant, Caroline Wigginton, and Kelly Wisecup, "Materials and Methods in Native American and Indigenous Studies: Completing the Turn," *WMQ* 75, no. 2 (2018): 207–236. On ethnohistory, the intersection of anthropological and historical methods, see Bruce G. Trigger, "Ethnohistory: Problems and Prospects," *Ethnohistory* 29, no. 1 (1982): 1–19; James Axtell, "The Ethnohistory of Native America," in *Rethinking American Indian History,* ed. Donald L. Fixico (Albuquerque: University of New Mexico Press, 1997), 11–27; Sebastian Felix Braun, ed., *Transforming Ethnohistories: Narrative, Meaning, and Community* (Norman: University of Oklahoma Press, 2013). On centering Native histories, see Ned Blackhawk, "Look How Far We've Come: How American Indian History Changed the Study of American History in the 1990s," *OAH Magazine of History* 19, no. 6 (2005): 13–17; Lisa Brooks, *The Common Pot: The Recovery of Native Space in the Northeast* (Minneapolis: University of Minnesota Press, 2008); "Forum: Colonial Historians and American Indians," *WMQ* 69, no. 3 (2012): 451–540; Susan Sleeper-Smith et al., eds., *Why You Can't Teach United States History without American Indians* (Chapel Hill: University of North Carolina Press, 2015).

15. Brown, *Good Wives;* Morgan, *American Slavery.* For other strong arguments based on class conflict, see Theodore W. Allen, *The Invention of the White Race,* 2 vols. (New York: Verso, 1994–1997); T. H. Breen, "A Changing Labor Force and Race Relations in Virginia, 1660–1710," *Journal of Social History* 7, no. 1 (1973): 3–25; Anthony S. Parent Jr., *Foul Means: The Formation of a Slave Society in Virginia, 1660–1740* (Chapel Hill: University of North Carolina Press, 2003), 141–162. The argument that the eruption of class conflict during Bacon's Rebellion stimulated planters to embrace racial slavery has been enormously influential and remains the dominant narrative decades after its initial formulation, a staple of virtually every college textbook and undergraduate lecture course. However, scholars should be more cautious about perpetuating it than we typically are, because neither of the historians most frequently associated with it, Kathleen Brown and Edmund Morgan, actually makes the reductive equation that Bacon's Rebellion equals racial slavery. Moreover, recent scholarship has shown that the math does not add up. Prosopographical analysis reveals no significant correlation between wealth or social class in determining the sides that colonists chose and no clear geographical division between coastal and frontier colonists; John Harold Sprinkle Jr., "Loyalists and Baconians: The Participants in Bacon's Rebellion in Virginia, 1676–1677" (PhD diss., College of William and Mary, 1992). Wealthy planters preferred enslaved black labor virtually from the start; the switch from servant to enslaved labor was accelerated by declining servant immigration in the late seventeenth century, and the surge in black populations—not just in Virginia but everywhere in English America and the Caribbean—was the result of the crown's aggressive promotion of the Atlantic slave trade; John C. Coombs, "The Phases of Conversion: A New Chronology for the Rise of Slavery in Early Virginia," *WMQ* 68, no. 3 (2011): 332–360;

Lorena S. Walsh, *Motives of Honor, Pleasure, and Profit: Plantation Management in the Colonial Chesapeake, 1607–1763* (Chapel Hill: University of North Carolina Press, 2010); Allan Kulikoff, *Tobacco and Slaves: The Development of Southern Cultures in the Chesapeake, 1680–1800* (Chapel Hill: University of North Carolina Press, 1986), 37–44; Russell R. Menard, "From Servants to Slaves: The Transformation of the Chesapeake Labor System," *Southern Studies* 16, no. 4 (1977): 355–390; Holly Brewer, "Slavery, Sovereignty, and 'Inheritable Blood': Reconsidering John Locke and the Origins of American Slavery," *AHR* 122, no. 4 (2017): 1038–1078; Abigail L. Swingen, *Competing Visions of Empire: Labor, Slavery, and the Origins of the British Atlantic Empire* (New Haven, CT: Yale University Press, 2015).

16. On Indigenous power in early America, see Matthew R. Bahar, *Storm of the Sea: Indians and Empires in the Atlantic's Age of Sail* (New York: Oxford University Press, 2019); Barr, *Peace Came in the Form of a Woman*; Alejandra Dubcovsky, *Informed Power: Communication in the Early American South* (Cambridge, MA: Harvard University Press, 2016); Kathleen DuVal, *The Native Ground: Indians and Colonists in the Heart of the Continent* (Philadelphia: University of Pennsylvania Press, 2006); Pekka Hämäläinen, *The Comanche Empire* (New Haven, CT: Yale University Press, 2008); Pekka Hämäläinen, *Lakota America: A New History of Indigenous Power* (New Haven, CT: Yale University Press, 2019); Lakomäki, *Gathering Together*; Lee, *Masters of the Middle Waters*; Robert Michael Morrissey, *Empire by Collaboration: Indians, Colonists, and Governments in Colonial Illinois Country* (Philadelphia: University of Pennsylvania Press, 2015); Witgen, *Infinity of Nations*. Much of this literature either builds on or challenges Richard White's pioneering work on spaces where neither Indians nor Europeans were able to dominate the other, and thus mutually shaped the wrenching and often violent transformation of early America; Richard White, *The Middle Ground: Indians, Empires, and Republics in the Great Lakes Region, 1650–1815* (Cambridge: Cambridge University Press, 1991). For pioneering work on the power of small Indigenous nations, see Elizabeth Ellis, "Petite Nation with Powerful Networks: The Tunicas in the Eighteenth Century," *Louisiana History* 58, no. 2 (2017): 133–178.

17. On early modern empires as contingent, contested, and negotiated entities, see Lauren Benton, *A Search for Sovereignty: Law and Geography in European Empires, 1400–1900* (Cambridge: Cambridge University Press, 2010); Christine Daniels and Michael V. Kennedy, eds., *Negotiated Empires: Centers and Peripheries in the Americas, 1500–1820* (New York: Routledge, 2002); Elizabeth Mancke, "Empire and State," in *The British Atlantic World, 1500–1800*, ed. David Armitage and Michael J. Braddick (2002; 2nd ed., New York: Palgrave MacMillan, 2009), 193–213; Patrick Spero, *Frontier Country: The Politics of War in Early Pennsylvania* (Philadelphia: University of Pennsylvania Press, 2016).

1. The Struggle for Order in Gandastogue and English America

1. John Smith, "The Proceedings of the English Colonie in Virginia, . . . (1612)," in *The Complete Works of Captain John Smith, 1580–1631*, ed. Philip L. Barbour (3 vols.; Chapel Hill: University of North Carolina Press, 1986), 1:231–232.

2. [John Cotton], "The History of Bacon's and Ingram's Rebellion, 1676," in Andrews, *Narratives*, 49; *Archives of Maryland*, 15:239; "Charles City County Grievances 1676," *VMHB* 3, no. 2 (1895): 137.

3. Matthew Kruer, "Bloody Minds and Peoples Undone: Emotion, Family, and Political Order in the Susquehannock-Virginia War," *WMQ* 74, no. 3 (2017): 401–436. To

understand the relationship between the internal experience of individuals, which is essentially unknowable, and the linguistic articulation of emotions that results in written and oral sources, on which all scholars rely, I draw upon William Reddy's concept of "emotional regimes," culturally specific frameworks for the experience and expression of emotion, which I refer to as "emotional cultures"; William M. Reddy, *The Navigation of Feeling: A Framework for the History of Emotions* (Cambridge: Cambridge University Press, 2001), esp. 54–111. For important works in the history of emotions, see Nicole Eustace, *Passion Is the Gale: Emotion, Power, and the Coming of the American Revolution* (Chapel Hill: University of North Carolina Press, 2008); Susan C. Karant-Nunn, *The Reformation of Feeling: Shaping the Religious Emotions in Early Modern Germany* (New York: Oxford University Press, 2010); Stephanie Olsen and Rob Boddice, "Styling Emotions History," *Journal of Social History* 51, no. 3 (2018): 476–487; Jan Plamper, *The History of Emotions: An Introduction,* trans. Keith Tribe (Oxford: Oxford University Press, 2015); Barbara H. Rosenwein, *Emotional Communities in the Early Middle Ages* (Ithaca, NY: Cornell University Press, 2006); Carol Z. Stearns and Peter N. Stearns, "Emotionology: Clarifying the History of Emotions and Emotional Standards," *AHR* 90, no. 4 (1985): 813–836.

4. Sara Ahmed, *The Cultural Politics of Emotion* (New York: Routledge, 2004); Lauren Berlant, "The Epistemology of State Emotion," in *Dissent in Dangerous Times,* ed. Austin Sarat (Ann Arbor: University of Michigan Press, 2005), 46–78; Nicole Eustace, "Emotion and Political Change," in *Doing Emotions History,* ed. Susan J. Matt and Peter N. Stearns (Urbana: University of Illinois Press, 2014), 163–183; Jeff Goodwin, James M. Jasper, and Francesca Polletta, eds., *Passionate Politics: Emotions and Social Movements* (Chicago: University of Chicago Press, 2001).

5. *Jesuit Relations,* 54:75; Barry C. Kent, *Susquehanna's Indians* (1984; Harrisburg: Pennsylvania Historical and Museum Commission, 2001), 13–18; Jasmine Gollup, "Tracking the Susquehannocks: 'Proto-Susquehannock' Sites in the Upper Susquehanna River Valley," in *The Susquehannocks: New Perspectives on Settlement and Cultural Identity,* ed. Paul A. Raber (University Park: Pennsylvania State University Press, 2019), 19–39; Christopher T. Espenshade, "Peri-Susquehannock Pottery of the Tioga River Area, Pennsylvania and New York," *Pennsylvania Archaeologist* 84, no. 1 (2014): 46–61; April M. Beisaw, "Environmental History of the Susquehanna Valley around the Time of European Contact," *Pennsylvania History* 79, no. 4 (2012): 366–376; James T. Herbstritt, "Becoming Susquehannock: The West Branch and North Branch Traditions," in Raber, *Susquehannocks,* 41–69.

6. George Alsop, *A Character of the Province of Mary-Land* (London, 1666), 61–62; John Laurence Creese, "Emotion Work and the Archaeology of Consensus: The Northern Iroquoian Case," *World Archaeology* 48, no. 1 (2016): 14–34; Kent, *Susquehanna's Indians,* 354, 360–363; Lisa M. Lauria, "Public Kettles, Private Pots: The Materiality of Seventeenth-Century Susquehannock Cooking Vessels," in Raber, *Susquehannocks,* 102–104; Sharon D. White, "To Secure a Lasting Peace: A Diachronic Analysis of Seventeenth-Century Susquehannock Political and Economic Strategies" (PhD diss., Pennsylvania State University, 2001), 49–52, 56.

7. George E. Gifford Jr. and Marion Tinling, "A Relation of a Voyage to the Head of the Bay," *The Historian* 20, no. 3 (1958): 350; [Anonymous], "Relation of Maryland," in *Narratives of Early Maryland, 1633–1684,* ed. Clayton Colman Hall (New York: Charles Scribner's Sons, 1910), 74; Daniel K. Richter, "War and Culture: The Iroquois Experience," *WMQ* 40, no. 4 (1983): 528–559; Kruer, "Bloody Minds," 407–411. On Haudenosaunee condolence rituals, see Matthew Dennis, *Cultivating*

a Landscape of Peace: Iroquois-European Encounters in Seventeenth-Century America (Ithaca, NY: Cornell University Press, 1993), 77–85, 102–105.

8. Kent, *Susquehanna's Indians,* 18–21, 143–144, 313–314; John Witthoft, "Ancestry of the Susquehannocks," in *Susquehannock Miscellany,* ed. John Witthoft and W. Fred Kinsey III (Harrisburg: Pennsylvania Historical and Museum Commission, 1959), 22–26; Henry Heisey, "An Interpretation of Shenks Ferry Ceramics," *Pennsylvania Archaeologist* 41, no. 4 (1971): 44–70; Ira F. Smith III and Jeffrey R. Graybill, "A Report on the Shenks Ferry and Susquehannock Components at the Funk Site, Lancaster County, Pennsylvania," *Man in the Northeast* 13 (1977): 45–65; Robert Wall and Heather Lapham, "Material Culture of the Contact Period in the Upper Potomac Valley: Chronological and Cultural Implications," *Archaeology of Eastern North America* 31 (2003): 153–154, 158–161, 170–171; April M. Beisaw, "Untangling Susquehannock Multiple Burials" (Report submitted to the Pennsylvania Historical and Museum Commission, 2008), 6, 9–10, 14–16; Lauria, "Public Kettles, Private Pots," 112–113. On the influence that captives wield over their host societies, see Catherine M. Cameron, *Captives: How Stolen People Changed the World* (Lincoln: University of Nebraska Press, 2016), 133–162.

9. Martha L. Sempowski, "Early Historic Exchange Between the Seneca and the Susquehannock," in *Proceedings of the 1992 People to People Conference,* ed. Charles F. Hayes III (Rochester, NY: Rochester Museum and Science Center, 1994), 51–64; Richmond E. Myers, "The Story of Transportation on the Susquehanna," *NYH* 29, no. 2 (1948): 158–159; Paul A. W. Wallace, "Historic Indian Paths of Pennsylvania," *PMHB* 76, no. 4 (1952): 411–439; Kent, *Susquehanna's Indians,* 165–171; Angela M. Haas, "Wampum as Hypertext: An American Indian Intellectual Tradition of Multimedia Theory and Practice," *Studies in American Indian Literatures* 19, no. 4 (2007): 77–100; Penelope Myrtle Kelsey, *Reading the Wampum: Essays on Hodinöhsö:ni' Visual Code and Epistemological Recovery* (Syracuse, NY: Syracuse University Press, 2014), xi–xxvii; George S. Snyderman, "The Functions of Wampum," *PAPS* 98, no. 6 (1954): 469–494.

10. "From the 'Korte Historiael Ende Journaels Aenteyckeninge,' by David Pietersz de Vries, 1633–1643 (1655)," in *Narratives of New Netherland, 1609–1664,* ed. J. Franklin Jameson (New York: Charles Scribner's Sons, 1909), 224; April M. Beisaw, "Memory, Identity, and NAGPRA in the Northeastern United States," *American Anthropologist* 112, no. 2 (2010): 244–256; Kent, *Susquehanna's Indians,* 347–348; Erik R. Seeman, *The Huron-Wendat Feast of the Dead: Indian-European Encounters in Early North America* (Baltimore: Johns Hopkins University Press, 2011).

11. John Smith, "A Map of Virginia. With a Description of the Countrey, the Commodities, People, Government and Religion (1612)," in *Complete Works,* 1:149; Smith, "Proceedings of the English," in *Complete Works,* 1:231–232; April M. Beisaw, "Stress and Shifting Identities in the Susquehanna Valley around the Time of European Arrival," in Raber, *Susquehannocks,* 73–90; Lisa M. Lauria, "Mythical Giants of the Chesapeake: An Evaluation of the Archaeological Construction of 'Susquehannock,'" *Journal of Middle Atlantic Archaeology* 20 (2004): 21–28. On the concept of nodes and networks to describe Indigenous political formations, see Sami Lakomäki, *Gathering Together: The Shawnee People through Diaspora and Nationhood, 1600–1870* (New Haven, CT: Yale University Press, 2014).

12. Smith, "Map of Virginia," in *Complete Works,* 1:149–150; Smith, "Proceedings of the English," in *Complete Works,* 1:231–232; Marshall Joseph Becker, "Susquehannock Stature: Evidence that They Were a 'Gyant-Like People,'" in Raber, *Susquehannocks,* 159–181. On European views of Native Americans through the lens of

European antiquity, see Raymond M. Brod, "The Art of Persuasion: John Smith's *New England* and *Virginia* Maps," *Historical Geography* 24, nos. 1–2 (1995): 96–99; Hugh Honour, *The New Golden Land: European Images of America from the Discoveries to the Present Time* (New York: Pantheon, 1976).

13. William Gouge, *Of Domesticall Duties: Eight Treatises* (London, 1622), 14; James I, *The True Lawe of Free Monarchies, or The Reciprock and Mutuall Duty Betwixt a Free King and His Naturall Subjects* (London, 1603), D3; James I, *Basilikon Doron, or His Majesties Instructions to His Dearest Sonne, Henry the Prince* (London, 1603), 2; James Harrington, *The Common-Wealth of Oceana* (London, 1656), 62; Susan Dwyer Amussen, *An Ordered Society: Gender and Class in Early Modern England* (1988; New York: Columbia University Press, 1993), 34–66 (esp. 36–39); Holly Brewer, *By Birth or Consent: Children, Law, and the Anglo-American Revolution in Authority* (Chapel Hill: University of North Carolina Press, 2005), 17–44 (esp. 20–23); Kathleen M. Brown, *Good Wives, Nasty Wenches, and Anxious Patriarchs: Gender, Race, and Power in Colonial Virginia* (Chapel Hill: University of North Carolina Press, 1996), 13–17; Mary Beth Norton, *Founding Mothers and Fathers: Gendered Power and the Forming of American Society* (New York: Alfred A. Knopf, 1996); Gordon J. Schochet, *Patriarchalism in Political Thought: The Authoritarian Family and Political Speculation and Attitudes Especially in Seventeenth-Century England* (Oxford: Blackwell, 1975); J. P. Sommerville, *Royalists and Patriots: Politics and Ideology in England, 1603–1640* (1986; 2nd ed., London: Longman, 1999), 29–36. On the popular endorsement of patriarchal theory, see Gordon J. Schochet, "Patriarchalism, Politics and Mass Attitudes in Stuart England," *Historical Journal* 12, no. 3 (1969): 413–441.

14. John Dod and Robert Cleaver, *A Godly Forme of Houshold Government, For the Ordering of Private Families . . .* (1598; repr., London, 1630), Aa5; Thomas Hobbes, *Leviathan or The Matter, Forme and Power of a Common-Wealth Ecclesiasticall and Civill* (1651), chap. 43, para. 4; Sir Robert Filmer, *Patriarcha and Other Writings,* ed. Johann P. Sommerville (Cambridge: Cambridge University Press, 1991), 12; James I, *Basilikon Doron,* 25; Samuel Johnson, *A Dictionary of the English Language . . . ,* vol. 2 (London, 1755), s.v. "Love"; Hening, *Statutes,* 1:57, 100; Melanie Perreault, "'To Fear and to Love Us': Intercultural Violence in the English Atlantic," *Journal of World History* 17, no. 1 (2006): 71–93; Judith M. Richards, "Love and a Female Monarch: The Case of Elizabeth Tudor," *Journal of British Studies* 38, no. 2 (1999): 133–160.

15. Gouge, *Of Domesticall Duties,* 8, 128; Dod and Cleaver, *Godly Forme of Houshold Government,* Y8v; Kruer, "Bloody Minds," 409–412; Susan Dwyer Amussen, "Punishment, Discipline, and Power: The Social Meanings of Violence in Early Modern England," *Journal of British Studies* 34, no. 1 (1995): 3–5, 12–18; Ronald Schecter, "Conceptions of Terror in the European Enlightenment," in *Facing Fear: The History of an Emotion in Global Perspective,* ed. Michael Laffan and Max Weiss (Princeton, NJ: Princeton University Press, 2012), 31–53. On love and fear in the eighteenth-century British Empire, see Brendan McConville, *The King's Three Faces: The Rise and Fall of Royal America, 1688–1776* (Chapel Hill: University of North Carolina Press, 2006), 106–119.

16. William Crashaw, *A Sermon Preached in London Before the Right Honourable the Lord Lawarre . . .* (London, 1610), E4v; "Lawes Divine, Morall, and Martiall, 1612," in *The Old Dominion in the Seventeenth Century: A Documentary History of Virginia, 1606–1700,* ed. Warren M. Billings (1975; rev. ed., Chapel Hill: University of North Carolina Press, 2007), 35–40; Mark Nicholls, ed., "George Per-

cy's 'Trewe Relacyon': A Primary Source for the Jamestown Settlement," *VMHB* 113, no. 3 (2005): 261–262; Hening, *Statutes*, 1:67; Edmund S. Morgan, *American Slavery, American Freedom: The Ordeal of Colonial Virginia* (1975; repr. ed., New York: W. W. Norton, 2003), 60, 79–90.

17. Thomas Harriot, *A Briefe and True Report of the New Found Land of Virginia* (London, 1590), 29; Samuel M. Bemiss, *The Three Charters of the Virginia Company of London*, Jamestown 350th Anniversary Historical Booklets, no. 4 (Williamsburg: Virginia 350th Anniversary Celebration Corporation, 1957), 54; R[obert] J[ohnson], "Nova Britannia: Offering Most Excellent Fruites by Planting in Virginia," in *Tracts and Other Papers Relating Principally to the Origin, Settlement, and Progress of the Colonies in North America: From the Discovery of the Country to the Year 1776*, ed. Peter Force (4 vols.; Washington, DC: 1836–1846), vol. 1, doc. 6, p. 14; *RVCL*, 1:311; Crashaw, *Sermon Preached in London*, Hr; Nicholls, "George Percy's 'Trewe Relacyon,'" 231; Ken MacMillan, "Benign and Benevolent Conquest? The Ideology of Elizabethan Atlantic Expansion Revisited," *EAS* 9, no. 1 (2011): 32–72; Perreault, "'To Feare and to Love Us,'" 81–87.

18. Martin D. Gallivan, *James River Chiefdoms: The Rise of Social Inequality in the Chesapeake* (Lincoln: University of Nebraska Press, 2003); Frederic W. Gleach, *Powhatan's World and Colonial Virginia: A Conflict of Cultures* (Lincoln: University of Nebraska Press, 1997), 22–60, 115–122; Helen C. Rountree, *Pocahontas, Powhatan, Opechancanough: Three Indian Lives Changed by Jamestown* (Charlottesville: University of Virginia Press, 2005), 25–52, 82–85; Margaret Holmes Williamson, *Powhatan Lords of Life and Death: Command and Consent in Seventeenth-Century Virginia* (Lincoln: University of Nebraska Press, 2003), 47–72; Dr. Linwood "Little Bear" Custalow and Angela L. Daniel "Silver Star," *The True Story of Pocahontas: The Other Side of History* (Golden, CO: Fulcrum, 2007), 18–21; Smith, "A True Relation of Such Occurrences and Accidents of Note, as Hath Hapned in Virginia . . . (1608)," in *Complete Works*, 1:57; Smith, "The Generall Historie of Virginia, New-England, and the Summer Isles . . . (1624)," in *Complete Works*, 2:196–197.

19. William Strachey, *The Historie of Travell into Virginia Britania*, ed. Louis B. Wright and Virginia Freund (London: Printed for the Hakluyt Society, 1953), 24; Custalow and "Silver Star," *True Story*, 64–65; Camilla Townsend, *Pocahontas and the Powhatan Dilemma* (New York: Hill and Wang, 2004), 124–134; *JHBV*, 1:22; *RVCL*, 4:38, 58, 73; J. Frederick Fausz, "An 'Abundance of Blood Shed on Both Sides': England's First Indian War, 1609–1614," *VMHB* 98, no. 1 (1990): 3–56.

20. *RVCL*, 3:672; Ralph Hamor, *A True Discourse of the Present Estate of Virginia . . .*, (London, 1615), 11–12; Smith, "Generall Historie," in *Complete Works*, 2:246–247; J. Frederick Fausz, "The Powhatan Uprising of 1622: A Historical Study of Ethnocentrism and Cultural Conflict" (PhD diss., College of William and Mary, 1977); Dylan Ruediger, "'Neither Utterly to Reject Them, Nor Yet to Drawe Them to Come In': Tributary Subordination and Settler Colonialism in Virginia," *EAS* 18, no. 1 (2020): 1–31. Scholars debate the appropriate words to describe these episodes of mass violence, which is complicated because both *ethnic cleansing* and *genocide* are twentieth-century juridical creations designed for legal standards of proof and the prosecution of perpetrators in international courts. For recent overviews of these sensitive issues, see Benjamin Madley, "Reexamining the American Genocide Debate: Meaning, Historiography, and New Methods," *AHR* 120, no. 1 (2015): 98–139; Jeffrey Ostler, *Surviving Genocide: Native Nations and the United States from the American Revolution to Bleeding Kansas* (New Haven, CT: Yale

University Press, 2019). I agree with the scholars who argue that genocide is the appropriate term.

21. Hening, *Statutes*, 1:292–293, 323; "Some Recently Discovered Extracts from the List Minutes of the Virginia Council and General Court, 1642–1645," *WMQ* 20, no. 1 (1940): 67; William L. Shea, "Virginia at War, 1644–1646," *Military Affairs* 41, no. 3 (1977): 142–147.

22. *Archives of Maryland*, 3:66, 5:159–161, 231–232; [Cotton], "Bacon's and Ingram's Rebellion," 49; J. Frederick Fausz, "Merging and Emerging Worlds: Anglo-Indian Interest Groups and the Development of the Seventeenth-Century Chesapeake," in *Colonial Chesapeake Society*, ed. Lois Green Carr, Philip D. Morgan, and Jean B. Russo (Chapel Hill: University of North Carolina Press, 1988), 59–63; Cynthia J. Van Zandt, *Brothers among Nations: The Pursuit of Intercultural Alliances in Early America, 1580–1660* (New York: Oxford University Press, 2008), 116–136.

23. "Letter of Isaack Rasières to the Directors of the Amsterdam Chamber of the West India Company," in *Documents Relating to New Netherland, 1624–1626, in the Henry E. Huntington Library,* trans. and ed. A. J. F. van Laer (San Marino, CA: Henry E. Huntington Library and Art Gallery, 1924), 211; David Pietersz de Vries, "From the 'Korte Historiael,'" in *Narratives of Early Pennsylvania, West New Jersey, and Delaware, 1630–1707,* ed. Albert Cook Myers (New York: Charles Scribner's Sons, 1912), 24; Beauchamp Plantagenet, *A Description of the Province of New Albion* (1648), 20; "Affidavit of Four Men from the *Key of Calmar*, 1638," in *Narratives of Early Pennsylvania*, 87; *NYHM (Delaware Dutch)*, 1–2, 9; A. R. Dunlap and C. A. Weslager, "More Missing Evidence: Two Depositions by Early Swedish Settlers," *PMHB* 91, no. 1 (1967): 38; John E. Guilday, Paul W. Parmalee, and Donald P. Tanner, "Aboriginal Butchering Techniques at the Eschelman Site (36 La 12), Lancaster County, Pennsylvania," *Pennsylvania Archaeologist* 32, no. 2 (1962): 59–83; Gary S. Webster, "Susquehannock Animal Economy," *North American Archaeologist* 6, no. 1 (1984–1985): 41–62; *Map of New Castle Upon Delaware as William Penn Saw It,* Map Collection, HSP; Gunlög Fur, *Colonialism in the Margins: Cultural Encounters in New Sweden and Lapland* (Leiden: Brill, 2006), 139–170; Amy C. Schutt, *Peoples of the River Valleys: The Odyssey of the Delaware Indians* (Philadelphia: University of Pennsylvania Press, 2007), 51–56; Jean R. Soderlund, *Lenape Country: Delaware Valley Society Before William Penn* (Philadelphia: University of Pennsylvania Press, 2015), 42–44, 55–58; Mark L. Thompson, *The Contest for the Delaware Valley: Allegiance, Identity, and Empire in the Seventeenth Century* (Baton Rouge: Louisiana State University Press, 2013), 35–81; Wallace, "Historic Indian Paths," 433.

24. *Jesuit Relations*, 30:85–87, 253; *Archives of Maryland*, 3:420–421; David J. Sorg, "Lost Tribes of the Susquehanna," *Pennsylvania Archaeologist* 74, no. 2 (2004): 68; Augustine Herrman, *Virginia and Maryland As it is Planted and Inhabited this present year 1670* (London, 1673), Geography and Map Division, LoC; Smith, "Proceedings of the English," in *Complete Works*, 1:232; William C. Johnson, "The Protohistoric Monongahela and the Case for an Iroquois Connection," in *Societies in Eclipse: Archaeology of the Eastern Woodlands Indians, A.D. 1400–1700,* ed. David S. Brose, C. Wesley Cowan, and Robert C. Mainfort Jr. (Washington, DC: Smithsonian Institution Press, 2001), 81; Marilyn C. Stewart, "A Proto-Susquehannock Cemetery near Nichols, Tioga County, New York," *Bulletin, Journal of the New York State Archaeological Association* 58 (1973): 1–21; Stellan Dahlgren and Hans Norman, eds., *The Rise and Fall of New Sweden: Governor Johan Risingh's Journal, 1654–1655, in Its Historical Context,* trans. Marie Clark Nelson (Stockholm, Sweden: Almqvist and Wiksell International, 1988), 237.

25. *Archives of Maryland,* 1:23, 3:64–66, 5:226; Fausz, "Merging and Emerging Worlds," 72–73; James D. Rice, *Nature and History in the Potomac Country: From Hunter-Gatherers to the Age of Jefferson* (Baltimore: Johns Hopkins University Press, 2009), 100–102.

26. *Archives of Maryland,* 1:271–272.

27. "Extracts from the Annual Letters of the English Province of the Society of Jesus," in *Narratives of Early Maryland,* 127–128, 135–136; Father Andrew White, "A Briefe Relation of the Voyage unto Maryland, 1634" in *Narratives of Early Maryland,* 42; *Archives of Maryland,* 2:15, 25; Wayne E. Clark and Helen C. Rountree, "The Powhatans and the Maryland Mainland," in *Powhatan Foreign Relations, 1500–1722,* ed. Helen C. Rountree (Charlottesville: University of Virginia Press, 1993), 112–135; Rice, *Nature and History,* 47–70; Rebecca Seib and Helen C. Rountree, *Indians of Southern Maryland* (Baltimore: Maryland Historical Society, 2014), 55–82; Gabrielle Astra Tayac, "'To Speak with One Voice': Supra-Tribal American Indian Collective Identity Incorporation among the Piscataway, 1500–1998" (PhD diss., Harvard University, 1999), 109–113, 116–121.

28. Sir John Harvey to Sec. Windebank, 14 July 1635, TNA CO 1/8/73, fols. 195r–195v; *Archives of Maryland,* 1:196–198, 3:64, 102–103, 116–117, 119–122; "Extracts from the Annual Letters," in *Narratives of Early Maryland,* 136; Fausz, "Merging and Emerging Worlds," 71–78; Russell R. Menard, "Maryland's 'Time of Troubles': Sources of Political Disorder in Early St. Mary's," *MHM* 76, no. 2 (1981): 124–140; J. Mills Thornton III, "The Thrusting out of Governor Harvey: A Seventeenth-Century Rebellion," *VMHB* 76, no. 1 (1968): 11–26.

29. *Archives of Maryland,* 1:265, 3:165. On the English Civil Wars, see Michael Braddick, *God's Fury, England's Fire: A New History of the English Civil Wars* (London: Allen Lane, 2008); Christopher Hill, *The World Turned Upside Down: Radical Ideas during the English Revolution* (New York: Viking, 1972); Jonathan Scott, *England's Troubles: Seventeenth-Century English Political Instability in European Context* (Cambridge: Cambridge University Press, 2000). On the Civil Wars in Atlantic context, see John Donoghue, *Fire Under the Ashes: An Atlantic History of the English Revolution* (Chicago: University of Chicago Press, 2013); Carla Gardina Pestana, *The English Atlantic in an Age of Revolution, 1640–1661* (Cambridge, MA: Harvard University Press, 2004); Timothy B. Riordan, *The Plundering Time: Maryland and the English Civil War, 1645–1646* (Baltimore: Maryland Historical Society, 2004). On anti-Catholicism, see Peter Lake, "Anti-Popery: The Structure of a Prejudice," in *Conflict in Early Stuart England: Studies in Religion and Politics, 1603–1642,* ed. Richard Cust and Ann Hughes (London: Longman, 1989), 72–106; Arthur F. Marotti, *Religious Ideology and Cultural Fantasy: Catholic and Anti-Catholic Discourses in Early Modern England* (Notre Dame, IN: University of Notre Dame Press, 2005); Dennis M. Moran, "Anti-Catholicism in Early Maryland Politics: The Puritan Influence," *Records of the American Catholic Historical Society of Philadelphia* 61, no. 3 (1950): 139–154.

30. *Archives of Maryland,* 3:279; Leonard Strong, *Babylon's Fall* (1655), in *Narratives of Early Maryland,* 242; Owen Stanwood, *The Empire Reformed: English America in the Age of the Glorious Revolution* (Philadelphia: University of Pennsylvania Press, 2011), 54–81; Antoinette Sutto, *Loyal Protestants and Dangerous Papists: Maryland and the Politics of Religion in the English Atlantic, 1630–1690* (Charlottesville: University of Virginia Press, 2015).

31. Hening, *Statutes,* 1:360; *JHBV,* 1:76–77; *PSWB,* 96; Ann Hughes, *Gender and the English Revolution* (New York: Routledge, 2012), 122–124; Warren M. Billings, *Sir William Berkeley and the Forging of Colonial Virginia* (Baton Rouge: Louisiana

State University Press, 2004), 106–108; David L. Smith, "'Our fears surpass our hopes': Virginian Reactions to the Execution of Charles I (1649–1652)," in *Fear and the Shaping of Early American Societies,* ed. Lauric Henneton and L. H. Roper (Leiden: Brill, 2016), 137–159. Berkeley's views were common among royalists; Sommerville, *Royalists and Patriots,* 37–43.

32. *Archives of Maryland,* 3:277–278. On English friendship, see Naomi Tadmor, *Family and Friends in Eighteenth-Century England: Household, Kinship, and Patronage* (Cambridge: Cambridge University Press, 2001). On Iroquoian friendship, see Gregory D. Smithers, "'Our Hands and Hearts Are Joined Together': Friendship, Colonialism, and the Cherokee People in Early America," *Journal of Social History* 50, no. 4 (2017): 609–629.

33. *MECPNY,* 1:45–48, 339–341; *Pennsylvania Archives,* 2nd ser., 5:263, 266. Other documented multiethnic sachems include the Hackensack war captain Achipoor Minquaes and Mantes sachems Siscohoka and Mechekyralames; Robert Steven Grumet, "'We Are Not So Great Fools': Changes in Upper Delawaran Socio-Political Life, 1630–1758" (PhD diss., Rutgers University, 1979), 112–114; Amandus Johnson, *The Swedish Settlements on the Delaware: Their History and Relation to the Indians, Dutch, and English, 1638–1664* (Philadelphia: University of Pennsylvania Press, 1911), 332. Europeans engaged in endless disputes over Indigenous ownership of Delaware Valley land and the legality of various purchases. For an attempt to parse these complex and legally abstruse controversies with the goal of determining the "true" owners, see Francis Jennings, "Glory, Death, and Transfiguration: The Susquehannock Indians in the Seventeenth Century," *PAPS* 112, no. 1 (1968): 50–53. On the complexity of Indigenous hybrid identities, see Matthew Liebmann, "Postcolonial Cultural Affiliation: Essentialism, Hybridity, and NAGPRA," in *Archaeology and the Postcolonial Critique,* ed. Matthew Liebmann and Uzma Z. Rizvi (Lanham, MD: AltaMira, 2008), 73–90.

34. *Pennsylvania Archives,* 2nd ser., 5:266; *Archives of Maryland,* 3:277; Dahlgren and Norman, *Rise and Fall of New Sweden,* 239.

35. Dahlgren and Norman, *Rise and Fall of New Sweden,* 197, 239; Van Zandt, *Brothers among Nations,* 167–170, 182; Fur, *Colonialism in the Margins,* 100–138; Tom Arne Midtrød, "Native American Landholding in the Colonial Hudson Valley," *Native American Culture and Research Journal* 37, no. 1 (2013): 79–104; Schutt, *Peoples of the River Valleys,* 31–40.

36. *Jesuit Relations,* 35:193, 37:97, 38:191, 41:21, 45:243; Jon Parmenter, *The Edge of the Woods: Iroquoia, 1534–1701* (East Lansing: Michigan State University Press, 2010), 70–100; David J. Silverman, *Thundersticks: Firearms and the Violent Transformation of Native America* (Cambridge, MA: The Belknap Press of Harvard University Press, 2016), 39–43. Indigenous peoples survived this violence and dislocation through resilient kinship ties that enabled them to reconstitute their communities; Heidi Bohaker, "*Nindoodemag:* The Significance of Algonquian Kinship Networks in the Eastern Great Lakes Region, 1600–1701," *WMQ* 63, no. 1 (2006): 23–52; Michael Witgen, *An Infinity of Nations: How the Native New World Shaped Early North America* (Philadelphia: University of Pennsylvania Press, 2012), 46–54.

37. Hening, *Statutes at Large,* 2:153; Eric E. Bowne, *The Westo Indians: Slave Traders of the Early Colonial South* (Tuscaloosa: University of Alabama Press, 2005), 49–53, 72–75; Maureen Meyers, "From Refugees to Slave Traders: The Transformation of the Westo Indians," in *Mapping the Mississippian Shatter Zone: The Colonial Indian Slave Trade and Regional Instability in the American South,* ed. Robbie Eth-

ridge and Sheri M. Shuck-Hall (Lincoln: University of Nebraska Press, 2009), 81–103; *NYHM (Delaware Dutch)*, 197, 200, 203; Charles T. Gehring, trans., *Correspondence, 1654–1658*, New Netherlands Documents Series, vol. 12 (Syracuse, NY: Syracuse University Press, 2003), 205; *DRCHSNY*, 13:183; Robert S. Grumet, *The Munsee Indians: A History* (Norman: University of Oklahoma Press, 2009), 72–81; Tom Arne Midtrød, *The Memory of All Ancient Customs: Native American Diplomacy in the Colonial Hudson Valley* (Ithaca, NY: Cornell University Press, 2012), 106–113 ("great power," at 111).

38. William P. Cumming, ed., *The Discoveries of John Lederer* (Charlottesville: University of Virginia Press, 1958), 19, 30, 41; H. Trawick Ward, "Mortuary Patterns at the Fredricks, Wall, and Mitchum Sites," in *The Siouan Project: Seasons I and II*, ed. Roy S. Dickens Jr., H. Trawick Ward, and R. P. Stephen Davis Jr. (Chapel Hill: University of North Carolina, 1987), 89–90; James H. Merrell, *The Indians' New World: Catawbas and Their Neighbors from European Contact through the Era of Removal* (Chapel Hill: University of North Carolina Press, 1989), 8–48. Lederer's other two expeditions relied on Algonquian guides from Virginia's tributary nations, all of whom belied their ignorance of geographies beyond the tidewater by getting lost in the mountains, and who lacked the social connections needed to secure safe passage; April Lee Hatfield, *Atlantic Virginia: Intercolonial Relations in the Seventeenth Century* (Philadelphia: University of Pennsylvania Press, 2004), 20–37.

39. *The Pynchon Papers*, ed. Carl Bridenbaugh (2 vols.; Boston: Colonial Society of Massachusetts, 1982), 1:93–95; Neal Salisbury, "Toward the Covenant Chain: Iroquois and Southern New England Algonquians, 1637–1684," in *Beyond the Covenant Chain: The Iroquois and Their Neighbors in Indian North America, 1600–1800*, ed. Daniel K. Richter and James H. Merrell (1987; rev. ed., University Park: Pennsylvania State University Press, 2003), 67–69.

40. Claude Bernou, ca. 1676–1682, Lac Teiocha-Rontiong, dit communement Lac Erie, Louis C. Karpinski Map Collection, Newberry Library; Marian E. White, "Iroquois Culture History in the Niagara Frontier Area of New York State," *Anthropological Papers*, Museum of Anthropology, University of Michigan, no. 16 (1961), 47; René de Bréhant de Galinée, "The Journey of Dollier and Galinée," in *Early Narratives of the Northwest, 1634–1699*, ed. Louise Phelps Kellog (New York: Charles Scribner's Sons, 1917), 176, 187; Stanley Baker, "Early Seventeenth Century Trade Beads from the Upper Ohio Valley," *Ohio Archaeologist* 36, no. 4 (1986): 21–24; *Archives of Maryland*, 8:517–519; Lakomäki, *Gathering Together*, 13–41; Stephen Warren, *The Worlds the Shawnees Made: Migration and Violence in Early America* (Chapel Hill: University of North Carolina Press, 2014), 48–51, 64–67.

41. Smith, "Map of Virginia," in *Complete Works*, 1:149; *Jesuit Relations*, 33:129; Celeste Marie Gagnon and Sara K. Becker, "Native Lives in Colonial Times: Insights from the Skeletal Remains of Susquehannocks, A.D. 1575–1675," *Historical Archaeology* 54, no. 1 (2020): 262–285; Daniel K. Richter, *The Ordeal of the Longhouse: The Peoples of the Iroquois League in the Era of European Colonization* (Chapel Hill: University of North Carolina Press, 1992), 59; Christian F. Feest, "Virginia Algonquians," in *Handbook of North American Indians*, vol. 15, *Northeast*, ed. Bruce G. Trigger (Washington, DC: Smithsonian Institution, 1978), 257–258; Kent, *Susquehanna's Indians*, 204, 217, 229–230, 235, 243–244, 340. On Indigenous polities as conceptual cores and neighboring territories (including colonies) as peripheries, see Pekka Hämäläinen and Samuel Truett, "On Borderlands," *JAH* 98, no. 2 (2011): 338–361; Michael Witgen, "Rethinking Colonial

History as Continental History," *WMQ* 69, no. 2 (2012): 527–530. Demographics have been extrapolated from estimates of "warriors," or men of fighting age, which Europeans interested in gathering military intelligence frequently recorded to the exclusion of women, children, and elders. I have followed the standard practice for historians of Iroquoian peoples of multiplying these warrior counts by four to yield conservative population estimates; Richter, "War and Culture," 542n57.

42. Hening, *Statutes*, 1:234, 2:43; Jon Kukla, ed., "Some Acts Not in Hening's *Statutes: The Acts of Assembly, October 1660,*" *VMHB* 83, no. 1 (1975): 87; J. M. Sosin, *English America and the Restoration Monarchy of Charles II: Transatlantic Politics, Commerce, and Kinship* (Lincoln: University of Nebraska Press, 1980), 24–38; Amussen, "Punishment, Discipline, and Power," 10–12.

43. *DRCHSNY*, 3:209–210; Ira Berlin, *Many Thousands Gone: The First Two Centuries of Slavery in North America* (Cambridge, MA: The Belknap Press of Harvard University Press, 1998), 369; John J. McCusker and Russell R. Menard, *The Economy of British America, 1607–1789* (Chapel Hill: University of North Carolina Press, 1985), 136; Lord Culpeper's Instructions of 6 December 1679, with marginal comments against each article, 12 December 1681, TNA CO 1/47/106, fol. 269v; Feest, "Virginia Algonquians," 257–258; Christian F. Feest, "Nanticoke and Neighboring Tribes," in *Handbook of North American Indians*, 15:242; *RVCL*, 3:243; T. H. Breen and Stephen Innes, *"Myne owne ground": Race and Freedom on Virginia's Eastern Shore, 1640–1676* (New York: Oxford University Press, 1980); Holly Brewer, "Slavery, Sovereignty, and 'Inheritable Blood': Reconsidering John Locke and the Origins of American Slavery," *AHR* 122, no. 4 (2017): 1038–1078; Brown, *Good Wives*, 107–136; John C. Coombs, "The Phases of Conversion: A New Chronology for the Rise of Slavery in Early Virginia," *WMQ* 68, no. 3 (2011): 332–360; Morgan, *American Slavery*, 154–157; Anthony S. Parent Jr., *Foul Means: The Formation of a Slave Society in Virginia, 1660–1740* (Chapel Hill: University of North Carolina Press, 2003), 55–60; William A. Pettigrew, *Freedom's Debt: The Royal African Company and the Politics of the Atlantic Slave Trade, 1672–1752* (Chapel Hill: University of North Carolina Press, 2013), 22–30; William Thorndale, "The Virginia Census of 1619," *Magazine of Virginia Genealogy* 33, no. 3 (1995): 155–170; Abigail L. Swingen, *Competing Visions of Empire: Labor, Slavery, and the Origins of the British Atlantic Empire* (New Haven, CT: Yale University Press, 2015); Lorena S. Walsh, *Motives of Honor, Pleasure, and Profit: Plantation Management in the Colonial Chesapeake, 1607–1763* (Chapel Hill: University of North Carolina Press, 2010).

44. *NYHM (General Entries)*, 1:1; Daniel K. Richter, *Before the Revolution: America's Ancient Pasts* (Cambridge, MA: The Belknap Press of Harvard University Press, 2011), 236–264; L. H. Roper, *Conceiving Carolina: Proprietors, Planters, and Plots, 1662–1729* (New York: Palgrave Macmillan, 2004), 21–40; Robert C. Ritchie, *The Duke's Province: A Study of New York Politics and Society, 1664–1691* (Chapel Hill: University of North Carolina Press, 1977), 9–24.

45. Hobbes, *Leviathan*, chap. 21, para. 21; *DRCHSNY*, 2:375. For contemporary debates about the relationship between protection and obedience, see Marco Barducci, *Hugo Grotius and the Century of Revolution, 1613–1718: Transnational Reception in English Political Thought* (Oxford: Oxford University Press, 2017), 25–45. On Hobbes's transmission to the colonies, see Alexander B. Haskell, *For God, King, and People: Forging Commonwealth Bonds in Renaissance Virginia* (Chapel Hill: University of North Carolina Press, 2017), 272–352.

46. *NYHM (General Entries)*, 1:5–6; *DRCHSNY*, 3:53; Charles Z. Lincoln, William H. Johnson, and A. Judd Northrup, eds., *The Colonial Laws of New York from the*

Year 1664 to the Revolution (5 vols.; Albany, 1894), 1:40; Jenny Hale Pulsipher, *Subjects unto the Same King: Indians, English, and the Contest for Authority in Colonial New England* (Philadelphia: University of Pennsylvania Press, 2005), 37–69.

47. *DRCHSNY*, 3:69; *NYHM (General Entries)*, 1:48–49; Lincoln, Johnson, and Northrup, *Colonial Laws of New York*, 1:40–42; Allen W. Trelease, *Indian Affairs in Colonial New York: The Seventeenth Century* (Ithaca, NY: Cornell University Press, 1960), 175–203.

48. *CRNC*, 1st ser., 1:203; *NYHM (Delaware English)*, 2–3; *DRCHSNJ*, 1:30–31; Carla Gardina Pestana, *Protestant Empire: Religion and the Making of the British Atlantic World* (Philadelphia: University of Pennsylvania Press, 2009), 100–127; Patricia U. Bonomi, *Under the Cope of Heaven: Religion, Society, and Politics in Colonial America* (1986; rev. ed., New York: Oxford University Press, 2003), 30–33; Evan Haefeli, *New Netherland and the Dutch Origins of American Religious Liberty* (Philadelphia: Pennsylvania University Press, 2012).

49. *Jesuit Relations*, 33:129, 47:71, 111, 48:77–79, 50:205, 54:111, 56:57; *Archives of Maryland*, 1:407, 472; *NYHM (Delaware Dutch)*, 243, 314, 320, 323, 334; John Berry and Francis Moryson, "A True Narrative of the Rise, Progresse, and Cessation of the Late Rebellion in Virginia," TNA CO 5/1371, p. 372; Josiah Coale to George Fox, 2 January 1661, A. R. Barclay Mss. 53, Friends House Library, London (I am grateful to Geoffrey Plank for pointing me toward this source).

50. Richter, "War and Culture," 543–544; *Jesuit Relations*, 56:55–57; Ana Maria Boza Arlotti, "Evolution of the Social Organization of the Susquehannock Society during the Contact Period in South Central Pennsylvania" (PhD diss., University of Pittsburgh, 1997), 168; Dorothy A. Humpf and James W. Hatch, "Susquehannock Demography: A New Perspective on the Contact Period in Pennsylvania," in *Proceedings of the 1992 People to People Conference*, 68–70; Alsop, *Character of the Province*, 61; *Archives of Maryland*, 1:471, 3:549; Governor and Council (Proceedings), 1656–1669, Liber H.H., p. 264, MSA; Gunlög Fur, *A Nation of Women: Gender and Colonial Encounters Among the Delaware Indians* (Philadelphia: University of Pennsylvania Press, 2009), 37–38.

51. Alsop, *Character of the Province*, 62; *Jesuit Relations*, 52:155, 53:255, 56:35–37.

52. *DRCHSNY*, 12:317; John Thornton, A *Map of some of the south and east bounds of Pennsylvania in America* (London, 1681), HSP; *Archives of Maryland*, 1:407, 3:421, 453, 486, 499; *Original Land Titles in Delaware, Commonly Known as the Duke of York Record* (Wilmington, DE: Sunday Star Print, 1903), 162; *NYHM (Delaware English)*, 106; Fur, *Colonialism in the Margins*, 239. On boundary-crossing cosmopolitans in the Delaware Valley, see Christian J. Koot, *A Biography of a Map in Motion: Augustine Herrman's Chesapeake* (New York: New York University Press, 2018).

53. *Jesuit Relations*, 45:207, 51:123, 52:161, 179, 55:35, 63:153; Nicholas Perrot, "Memoir on the Manners, Customs, and Religion of the Savages of North America," in *The Indian Tribes of the Upper Mississippi Valley and Region of the Great Lakes*, ed. and trans. Emma Helen Blair (2 vols.; Lincoln: University of Nebraska Press, 1996), 1:226; *DRCHSNY*, 9:194. For clashing interpretations of the impact of adopted foreigners on Haudenosaunee politics and society, see Richter, *Ordeal of the Longhouse*, 65–74, 105–132; Parmenter, *Edge of the Woods*, 100–105, 124–125, 140–147.

54. *Jesuit Relations*, 35:219, 42:57, 44:21, 54:81; Richter, *Ordeal of the Longhouse*, 69–74; Kathryn Magee Labelle, *Dispersed but Not Destroyed: A History of the Seventeenth-Century Wendat People* (Vancouver: UBC Press, 2013), 120–140;

Kurt A. Jordan, "Incorporation and Colonization: Postcolumbian Iroquois Satellite Communities and Processes of Indigenous Autonomy," *American Anthropologist* 115, no. 1 (2013): 29–43; Bruce G. Trigger, *The Children of Aataentsic: A History of the Huron People to 1660* (Montreal: McGill-Queen's University Press, 1976), 827–829; Charles F. Wray and Harry L. Schoff, "A Preliminary Report on the Seneca Sequence in Western New York, 1550–1687," *Pennsylvania Archaeologist* 23, no. 2 (1953): 58; William Engelbrecht, "Iroquoian Ethnicity and Archaeological Taxa," in *Taming the Taxonomy: Toward a New Understanding of Great Lakes Archaeology,* ed. Roland F. Williamson and Christopher M. Watts (Toronto: Eastend, 1999), 54–56. The prevalence of Susquehannock pottery among the Senecas is partially explained by Haudenosaunee adoption of European-manufactured kettles. However, as archaeologist Lisa Lauria points out, while Susquehannocks used brass and copper for everyday cooking they continued to craft ceramics reflecting a process of social integration among women; Lauria, "Public Kettles, Private Pots," 91–115.

55. McCusker and Menard, *Economy of British America,* 136, 172, 203; *DRCHSNY,* 3:62; *Archives of Maryland,* 1:420–422; Donna Merwick, *Possessing Albany, 1630–1710: The Dutch and English Experiences* (Cambridge: Cambridge University Press, 1990), 171–172; Evan Haefeli, "The Revolt of the Long Swede: Transatlantic Hopes and Fears on the Delaware, 1669," *PMHB* 130, no. 2 (2006): 137–180; Ritchie, *Duke's Province,* 85–93; Brown, *Good Wives,* 149–154; John Donoghue, "'Out of the Land of Bondage': The English Revolution and the Atlantic Origins of Abolition," *AHR* 115, no. 4 (2010): 943–974; "The Servants' Plot of 1663," in "Virginia Colonial Records (Continued)," *VMHB* 15, no. 1 (1907): 39.

56. Hening, *Statutes,* 2:138–143, 194; *Archives of Maryland,* 2:25–27, 200; Bernard Bailyn, "Politics and Social Structure in Virginia," in *Seventeenth-Century America: Essays in Colonial History,* ed. James Morton Smith (Chapel Hill: University of North Carolina Press, 1959), 90–115; Warren M. Billings, "The Growth of Political Institutions in Virginia, 1634 to 1676," *WMQ* 31, no. 2 (1974): 225–242; Morgan, *American Slavery,* 180–249; Lois Green Carr, "Sources of Political Stability and Upheaval in Seventeenth-Century Maryland," *MHM* 79, no. 1 (1984): 44–70; Ritchie, *Duke's Province,* 68–75; John M. Murrin, "English Rights as Ethnic Aggression: The English Conquest, the Charter of Liberties of 1683, and Leisler's Rebellion in New York," in *Authority and Resistance in Early New York,* ed. William Pencak and Conrad Edick Wright (New York: New-York Historical Society, 1988), 56–94. Few historians have examined Indian affairs as a critical weak point of English colonial regimes, but for an exception see Ethan A. Schmidt, *The Divided Dominion: Social Conflict and Indian Hatred in Early Virginia* (Boulder: University Press of Colorado, 2015).

57. Trelease, *Indian Affairs,* 179–180; Helen C. Rountree, *Pocahontas's People: The Powhatan Indians of Virginia through Four Centuries* (Norman: University of Oklahoma Press, 1990), 128–143; John Berry and Francis Moryson, "Names and Characters of and Presents to the Indians &c.," TNA CO 5/1371, p. 266; Cockacoeske to Francis Moryson, 29 June 1678, TNA CO 1/42/101, fol. 276r; Martha W. McCartney, "Cockacoeske, Queen of Pamunkey: Diplomat and Suzeraine," in *Powhatan's Mantle: Indians in the Colonial Southeast,* ed. Gregory A. Waselkov, Peter H. Wood, and Tom Hatley (1989; rev. ed., Lincoln: University of Nebraska Press, 2006), 243–266.

58. Patrick Wolfe, "Settler Colonialism and the Elimination of the Native," *Journal of Genocide Research* 8, no. 4 (2006): 387–409; Rice, *Nature and History,* 121–142;

Archives of Maryland, 3:489; Tayac, "To Speak with One Voice," 112–122; *NYHM (General Entries),* 1:457.

59. Hening, *Statutes,* 2:141, 185; Kristalyn Marie Shefveland, *Anglo-Native Virginia: Trade, Conversion, and Indian Slavery in the Old Dominion, 1646–1722* (Athens: University of Georgia Press, 2016), 21–48; Paul Kelton, *Epidemics and Enslavement: Biological Catastrophe in the Native Southeast, 1492–1715* (Lincoln: University of Nebraska Press, 2007), 108–120; C. S. Everett, "'They shalbe slaves for their lives': Indian Slavery in Colonial Virginia," in *Indian Slavery in Colonial America,* ed. Alan Gallay (Lincoln: University of Nebraska Press, 2009), 67–108; H. Trawick Ward and R. P. Stephen Davis Jr., "Tribes and Traders on the North Carolina Piedmont, A.D. 1000–1710," in *Societies in Eclipse,* 125–141. A similar mix of Indian slave trading and political factionalism plagued Carolina; see Alan Gallay, *The Indian Slave Trade: The Rise of the English Empire in the American South, 1670–1717* (New Haven, CT: Yale University Press, 2002), 40–69.

60. *Archives of Maryland,* 1:400, 416, 539, 2:47–48, 3:403; Francis Jennings, "Indians and Frontiers in Seventeenth-Century Maryland," in *Early Maryland in a Wider World,* ed. David B. Quinn (Detroit, MI: Wayne State University Press, 1982), 221; Rice, *Nature and History,* 143–146.

61. *Archives of Maryland,* 2:25, 3:413, 426; Hening, *Statutes,* 2:141.

62. [Sherwood], "Virginias Deploured Condition," 164; *Archives of Maryland,* 1:264; Morgan, *American Slavery,* 215–234; Brown, *Good Wives,* 137–139.

63. Hening, *Statutes,* 2:138; "Excerpts from the Charles City County Records (1655–1666) (Continued)," *VMHB* 43, no. 4 (1935): 347–348.

2. Rumors of Wars

1. *Archives of Maryland,* 2:428–430, 462; *Jesuit Relations,* 59:251; Nicholas Perrot, "Memoir on the Manners, Customs, and Religion of the Savages of North America," in *The Indian Tribes of the Upper Mississippi Valley and Region of the Great Lakes,* ed. and trans. Emma Helen Blair (2 vols.; Lincoln: University of Nebraska Press, 1996), 1:226; T[homas] M[athew], "The Beginning, Progress, and Conclusion of Bacon's Rebellion, 1675–1676 (1705)," in Andrews, *Narratives,* 18. For clashing interpretations of the Susquehannocks' southern migration, see Francis Jennings, "Glory, Death, and Transfiguration: the Susquehannock Indians in the Seventeenth Century," *PAPS* 112, no. 1 (1968): 33–34; Elisabeth Tooker, "The Demise of the Susquehannocks: A 17th Century Mystery," *Pennsylvania Archaeologist* 54, nos. 3–4 (1984): 1–10. Indirect evidence, including a surge of Susquehannock captives in Iroquoia after 1674, strongly suggests that they suffered a military defeat beyond the range of colonial observations; *Andros Papers,* 1:131–132; *Jesuit Relations,* 58:225–227, 237, 59:245.

2. *Archives of Maryland,* 2:428–430, 462, 3:420–421; James D. Rice, *Nature and History in the Potomac Country: From Hunter-Gatherers to the Age of Jefferson* (Baltimore: Johns Hopkins University Press, 2009), 47–50.

3. *Archives of Maryland,* 2:429, 5:65; M[athew], "Bacon's Rebellion," 18.

4. On rumor as conversation, see Luise White, *Speaking with Vampires: Rumor and History in Colonial Africa* (Berkeley: University of California Press, 2000), 81–85. The best comprehensive study of rumor in early America is Gregory Evans Dowd, *Groundless: Rumors, Legends, and Hoaxes on the Early American Frontier* (Baltimore: Johns Hopkins University Press, 2015). In addition to the scholarship subsequently cited in this chapter, important works on the history and sociology of rumor

include Arlette Farge and Jacques Revel, *The Vanishing Children of Paris: Rumor and Politics before the French Revolution,* trans. Claudia Miéville (Cambridge, MA: Harvard University Press, 1991); Gary Alan Fine, Véronique Campion-Vincent, and Chip Heath, eds., *Rumor Mills: The Social Impact of Rumor and Legend* (New Brunswick, NJ: Aldine Transaction, 2005); Gary Alan Fine and Patricia A. Turner, *Whispers on the Color Line: Rumor and Race in America* (Berkeley: University of California Press, 2001); Anjan Ghosh, "The Role of Rumour in History Writing," *History Compass* 6, no. 5 (2008): 1235–1243; Georges Lefebvre, *The Great Fear of 1789: Rural Panic in Revolutionary France,* trans. Joan White (New York: Pantheon, 1973); Hans-Joachim Neubauer, *The Rumour: A Cultural History,* trans. Christian Braun (London: Free Association, 1999); Tamotsu Shibutani, *Improvised News: A Sociological Study of Rumor* (Indianapolis, IN: Bobbs-Merrill, 1966); Anand A. Yang, "A Conversation of Rumors: The Language of Popular *Mentalités* in Late Nineteenth-Century Colonial India," *Journal of Social History* 20, no. 3 (1987): 485–505.

5. On rumor in times of war, see Marc Bloch, "Reflections of a Historian on the False News of the War," trans. James P. Holoka, *Michigan War Studies Review* (2013): 1–11. On rumor in connection to group violence, see Jonathon Glassman, *War of Words, War of Stones: Racial Thought and Violence in Colonial Zanzibar* (Bloomington: Indiana University Press, 2011); Donald L. Horowitz, *The Deadly Ethnic Riot* (Berkeley: University of California Press, 2001), 74–88; Ed White, *The Backcountry and the City: Colonization and Conflict in Early America* (Minneapolis: University of Minnesota Press, 2005), 28–72. On "frontier" and "front" in early America, see Patrick Spero, *Frontier Country: The Politics of War in Early Pennsylvania* (Philadelphia: University of Pennsylvania Press, 2016).

6. [M]athew, "Bacon's Rebellion," 17 (emphasis in original); *PSWB,* 485; John Berry and Francis Moryson, "A Narrative of the Rise, Progresse and Cessation of the Late Rebellion in Virginia," *Wiseman's Book,* 142–143; Thomas Campanius Holm, *Description of the Province of New Sweden. Now called, by the English, Pennsylvania, in America,* trans. Peter S. du Ponceau (Philadelphia, 1834), 158; Rice, *Nature and History,* 137–138.

7. [Sherwood], "Virginias Deploured Condition," 165; M[athew], "Bacon's Rebellion," 17; John Berry and Francis Moryson, "A True Narrative of the Rise, Progresse, and Cessation of the Late Rebellion in Virginia," TNA CO 5/1371, p. 372; *PSWB,* 485.

8. *PSWB,* 486–487, 492.

9. David Coast, *News and Rumour in Jacobean England: Information, Court Politics and Diplomacy, 1618–25* (Manchester: Manchester University Press, 2014); David Cressy, *Dangerous Talk: Scandalous, Seditious, and Treasonable Speech in Pre-Modern England* (Oxford: Oxford University Press, 2010); Adam Fox, *Oral and Literate Culture in England, 1500–1700* (Oxford: Oxford University Press, 2000), 1–50, 335–405; Jane Kamensky, *Governing the Tongue: The Politics of Speech in Early New England* (New York: Oxford University Press, 1997); Robert St. George, "'Heated' Speech and Literacy in Seventeenth-Century New England," in *Seventeenth-Century New England,* ed. David D. Hall and David Grayson Allen (Boston: Colonial Society of Massachusetts, 1984), 275–322; Hening, *Statutes,* 1:361; *Archives of Maryland,* 1:343; Charles Z. Lincoln, William H. Johnson, and A. Judd Northrup, eds., *The Colonial Laws of New York from the Year 1664 to the Revolution* (5 vols.; Albany, 1894), 1:45; J. Hammond Trumbull and Charles J. Hoadly, eds., *The Public Records of the Colony of Connecticut* (15 vols.; Hartford, 1850–1890), 1:538; Nathaniel B. Shurtleff, ed., *Records of the Governor and*

Company of the Massachusetts Bay in New England (5 vols.; Boston, 1853–1854), 2:104.

10. "Excerpts from the Charles City County Records (1655–1666) (Continued)," *VMHB* 43, no. 4 (1935): 347–348; Samuel Johnson, *A Dictionary of the English Language . . .*, vol. 1 (London, 1755), s.v. "Jealousy," def. 6; Alexander Mazzaferro, "'Such a Murmur': Innovation, Rebellion, and Sovereignty in William Strachey's 'True Reportory,'" *Early American Literature* 53, no. 1 (2018): 3–32. On the connection between rumors about Native Americans and popular insurrection, see James D. Rice, *Tales from a Revolution: Bacon's Rebellion and the Transformation of Early America* (New York: Oxford University Press, 2012); Antoinette Sutto, *Loyal Protestants and Dangerous Papists: Maryland and the Politics of Religion in the English Atlantic, 1630–1690* (Charlottesville: University of Virginia Press, 2015), 129–158.

11. *PSWB*, 486.

12. *Archives of Maryland*, 15:47–49, 57.

13. *Archives of Maryland*, 2:481–483; William N. Fenton, "Northern Iroquoian Culture Patterns," in *Handbook of North American Indians*, vol. 15, *Northeast*, ed. Bruce G. Trigger (Washington, DC: Smithsonian Institution, 1978), 319.

14. *Archives of Maryland*, 2:481–483, 501; "Col. John Washington: Further Details of His Life from the Records of Westmoreland Co., Virginia," *WMQ* 2, no. 1 (1893): 39–43. Depositions from Maryland colonists placed blame squarely on Washington, claiming that he ordered the executions, while Virginian depositions implied that Truman had given the order. The royal investigators' final report artfully elided the agency behind the murders with phrases such as the "greate men . . . were at last murdered"; Berry and Moryson, "Narrative of the . . . Late Rebellion," *Wiseman's Book*, 143. Such deliberate obfuscation underlines a point that history teachers strenuously try to impress on their students: the surreptitious violence of the passive voice.

15. Alice L. L. Ferguson, "The Susquehannock Fort on Piscataway Creek," *MHM* 36, no. 1 (1941): 1–9; Berry and Moryson, "Narrative of the . . . Late Rebellion," *Wiseman's Book*, 143; [John Cotton], "The History of Bacon's and Ingram's Rebellion, 1676," in Andrews, *Narratives*, 47–48; Anne Cotton, "An Account of Our Late Troubles in Virginia," in *Tracts and Other Papers Relating Principally to the Origin, Settlement, and Progress of the Colonies in North America: From the Discovery of the Country to the Year 1776*, comp. Peter Force (4 vols.; Washington, DC, 1836–1846), vol. 1, doc. 9, p. 3; [M]athew, "Bacon's Rebellion," 19; *Archives of Maryland*, 2:482, 15:50. The number of militia claiming recompense for lost mounts during the siege testifies to the Susquehannocks' successful horse-hunting; *Archives of Maryland*, 66:268–269; Lancaster County Orders, 1666–1680, pp. 383–384, LVA.

16. Philip Lanyon to [Secretary Joseph] Williamson, 14 April 1676, TNA SP 29/380, fol. 242r; [Cotton], "Bacon's and Ingram's Rebellion," 48; *Archives of Maryland*, 2:501.

17. "Causes of Discontent in Virginia, 1676," *VMHB* 3, no. 1 (1895): 35; Anthony F. C. Wallace, "Dreams and the Wishes of the Soul: A Type of Psychoanalytic Theory among the Seventeenth Century Iroquois," *American Anthropologist* 60, no. 2 (1958): 234–248; Bruce G. Trigger, *The Children of Aataentsic: A History of the Huron People to 1660* (Montreal: McGill-Queen's University Press, 1976), 81–84; *Archives of Maryland*, 23:188; *Jesuit Relations*, 57:171; Thomas Chalkley, *A Journal; or, Historical Account of the Life, Travels and Christian Experiences, of*

that Antient, Faithful Servant of Jesus Christ, Thomas Chalkley (London, 1751), 50–51. The precise timing of Midwinter Ceremonies depended on the nation celebrating it, but they typically began five to nine days after the January new moon and lasted between five and eight days; Elisabeth Tooker, *The Iroquois Ceremonial of Midwinter* (Syracuse, NY: Syracuse University Press, 1970), 84–103. No European ethnographer ever recorded the Susquehannocks' version of the Midwinter Ceremony, but for an imaginative reconstruction, see Barry C. Kent, *Jacob My Friend: His 17th Century Account of the Susquehannock Indians* (Philadelphia: Xlibris, 2004), 334. According to calculations by astrophysicist Fred Espenak, the new moon of January 1676 was on January 15, or January 5 in the Old Style calendar in common use by the English; "Phases of the Moon, 1601–1700," last updated 21 December 2014, http://astropixels.com/ephemeris/phasescat/phases1601 .html. Thus, the Susquehannocks launched their raids somewhere between three and ten days after the conclusion of the Midwinter Ceremony.

18. *PSWB*, 498, 507; Letter from Rappahannock in Virginia, 23 May 1676, Coventry Papers, vol. 77, fol. 86r; [Cotton], "Bacon's and Ingram's Rebellion," 50; [Sherwood], "Virginias Deploured Condition," 176; Enclosure in Giles Bland to Thomas Povey, 8 July 1676, TNA CO 1/37/27 I, fol. 86r. On mutilation as symbolic communication, see Juliana Barr, *Peace Came in the Form of a Woman: Indians and Spaniards in the Texas Borderlands* (Chapel Hill: University of North Carolina Press, 2007), 159–196; Jill Lepore, *The Name of War: King Philip's War and the Origins of American Identity* (New York: Alfred A. Knopf, 1998), 71–124; Peter Silver, *Our Savage Neighbors: How Indian War Transformed Early America* (New York: W. W. Norton, 2008), 39–71.

19. "Causes of Discontent," 35; "The Virginians' plea for opposing the Indians without the Governor's order," June (?) 1676, TNA CO 1/37/14, fol. 29r; M[athew], "Bacon's Rebellion," 20. Giles Bland, who like Bacon was a recent immigrant and wrote to an English audience, also invoked comparisons to the 1622 massacre; Giles Bland to Charles Berne, 20 April 1676, in John Daly Burk, *The History of Virginia from Its First Settlement to the Present Day* (4 vols.; Petersburg, VA, 1804–1816), 2:247. It may be telling that the precedent of past Indian wars was most salient for those who had the least experience with Virginia and its Indigenous peoples.

20. Elizabeth Bacon, "A copy of Mrs. Bacon's letter, the wife of Nathaniel Bacon, in Virginia, June the 29th, 76, sent to her Sister," in "Bacon's Rebellion," *WMQ* 9, no. 1 (1900): 4–5; Account of Mr. Nathaniel Bacon Jr.'s Estate, 11 May 1677, TNA CO 5/1371, p. 450–453, 456; Michael Leroy Oberg, *Dominion and Civility: English Imperialism and Native America, 1585–1685* (Ithaca, NY: Cornell University Press, 1999), 174–176. On women during Bacon's Rebellion, see Kathleen M. Brown, *Good Wives, Nasty Wenches, and Anxious Patriarchs: Gender, Race, and Power in Colonial Virginia* (Chapel Hill: University of North Carolina Press, 1996), 162–167; Susan Westbury, "Women in Bacon's Rebellion," in *Southern Women: Histories and Identities*, ed. Virginia Bernhard et al. (Columbia: University of Missouri Press, 1992), 30–46.

21. *Archives of Maryland*, 5:135; "Charles City County Grievances 1676," *VMHB* 3, no. 2 (1895): 137. On war and manhood, see Ann M. Little, *Abraham in Arms: War and Gender in Colonial New England* (Philadelphia: University of Pennsylvania Press, 2007), 12–55. These grievances written by the inhabitants of Charles City County are one of many sets of grievances—one from each county—that were solicited by royal investigators in 1677. Collectively, they are an extraordinarily rich source on colonists' views of the Susquehannock-Virginia War and Bacon's Rebel-

lion. However, because these documents were written in the aftermath of a failed rebellion, they were composed with an eye toward justifying the writers' actions after the fact and must be used with care. I have limited my use of grievances to cases where their accounts or their rhetoric can be corroborated by sources written in 1676. On domestic distress, for example, see also "Virginians' plea," TNA CO 1/37/14.

22. "Charles City County Grievances," 137–138. On Indigenous violence and patriarchal failure, see Krista Camenzind, "Violence, Race, and the Paxton Boys," in *Friends and Enemies in Penn's Woods: Indians, Colonists, and the Racial Construction of Pennsylvania*, ed. William A. Pencak and Daniel K. Richter (University Park: Pennsylvania State University Press, 2004), 201–220; Honor Sachs, *Home Rule: Households, Manhood, and National Expansion on the Eighteenth-Century Kentucky Frontier* (New Haven, CT: Yale University Press, 2015).

23. "Virginians' plea," TNA CO 1/37/14, fol. 29r; Mary Byrd, "Mrs. Bird's Relation," in "Bacon's Rebellion," *WMQ* 9, no. 1 (1900): 10; Memorandum by William Moore, 16 February 1676, Coventry Papers, vol. 77, fol. 56r; Berry and Moryson, "Narrative of the . . . Late Rebellion," *Wiseman's Book*, 144; Berry and Moryson, "A Review Breviary, and Conclusion drawn from the foregoing Narrative," *Wiseman's Book*, 178; "Causes of Discontent," 39–42. On the discourse of "frontier people," see Spero, *Frontier Country*.

24. *PSWB*, 504; [Cotton], "Bacon's and Ingram's Rebellion," 49.

25. Hening, *Statutes*, 2:326–328, 330, 332.

26. "Virginians' plea," TNA CO 1/37/14, fol. 29r; "Causes of Discontent," 39; [Cotton], "Bacon's and Ingram's Rebellion," 52; [M]athew, "Bacon's Rebellion," 20.

27. On literacies among American Indians, see Lisa Brooks, *The Common Pot: The Recovery of Native Space in the Northeast* (Minneapolis: University of Minnesota Press, 2008); Stephanie Fitzgerald and Hilary E. Wyss, "Land and Literacy: The Textualities of Native Studies," *Early American Literature* 45, no. 2 (2010): 241–250; Alyssa Mt. Pleasant, Caroline Wigginton, and Kelly Wisecup, "Materials and Methods in Native American and Indigenous Studies: Completing the Turn," *WMQ* 75, no. 2 (2018): 207–236; Andrew Newman, *On Records: Delaware Indians, Colonists, and the Media of History and Memory* (Lincoln: University of Nebraska Press, 2012). On Indigenous communication networks, see Alejandra Dubcovsky, *Informed Power: Communication in the Early American South* (Cambridge, MA: Harvard University Press, 2016); Katherine Grandjean, *American Passage: The Communications Frontier in Early New England* (Cambridge, MA: Harvard University Press, 2015), 76–109; Helen C. Rountree, "The Powhatans and Other Woodland Indians as Travelers," in *Powhatan Foreign Relations, 1500–1722*, ed. Helen C. Rountree (Charlottesville: University Press of Virginia, 1993), 21–52. On rumor and other unreliable communications, see Lauric Henneton, "Rumors, Uncertainty and Decision-Making in the Greater Long Island Sound (1652–1654)," in *Fear and the Shaping of Early American Societies*, ed. Lauric Henneton and L. H. Roper (Leiden: Brill, 2016), 115–136; Tom Arne Midtrød, "Strange and Disturbing News: Rumor and Diplomacy in the Colonial Hudson Valley," *Ethnohistory* 58, no. 1 (2011): 91–112; Joshua Piker, "Lying Together: The Imperial Implications of Cross-Cultural Untruths," *AHR* 116, no. 4 (2011): 964–986.

28. Lisa Brooks, *Our Beloved Kin: A New History of King Philip's War* (New Haven, CT: Yale University Press, 2018); James D. Drake: *King Philip's War: Civil War in New England, 1675–1676* (Amherst: University of Massachusetts Press, 1999);

Douglas Edward Leach, *Flintlock and Tomahawk: New England in King Philip's War* (New York: Macmillan, 1958); Daniel R. Mandell, *King Philip's War: Colonial Expansion, Native Resistance, and the End of Indian Sovereignty* (Baltimore: Johns Hopkins University Press, 2010); Jenny Hale Pulsipher, *Subjects unto the Same King: Indians, English, and the Contest for Authority in Colonial New England* (Philadelphia: University of Pennsylvania Press, 2005), 101–134.

29. *PSWB*, 504–505, 509; *DRCHSNY*, 12:543; Richard Watts to Joseph Williamson, 28 August 1676, TNA SP 29/385, fol. 18r; Wilcomb E. Washburn, "Governor Berkeley and King Philip's War," *New England Quarterly* 30, no. 3 (1957): 363–377.

30. *PSWB*, 504; [Cotton], "Bacon's and Ingram's Rebellion," 49. For casualty reports— most of them suspiciously vague numbers rounded off to the nearest hundred—see *PSWB*, 507; Mary Byrd, "Mrs. Bird's Relation," 10; Berry and Moryson, "Narrative of the . . . Late Rebellion," *Wiseman's Book*, 144; *Archives of Maryland*, 5:135.

31. "Causes of Discontent," 36–37; "Instructions from the inhabitants of Lancaster County to their Burgesses Colonel William Ball and Major Edward Dale, to be by them presented to the Assembly for redress," March 1677, TNA CO 1/39/77, fol. 217r; Letter from Rappahannock, Coventry Papers, vol. 77, fol. 86r; [Cotton], "Bacon's and Ingram's Rebellion," 49.

32. [Sherwood], "Virginias Deploured Condition," 165–166; Hening, *Statutes*, 2:332; *DRCHSNY*, 3:196; *JHBV*, 2:64.

33. *PSWB*, 504, 509; April Lee Hatfield, *Atlantic Virginia: Intercolonial Relations in the Seventeenth Century* (Philadelphia: University of Pennsylvania Press, 2004), 8–38; Helen Hornbeck Tanner, "The Land and Water Communication Systems of the Southeastern Indians," in *Powhatan's Mantle: Indians in the Colonial Southeast*, ed. Gregory A. Waselkov, Peter H. Wood, and Tom Hatley (1989; rev. ed., Lincoln: University of Nebraska Press, 2006), 27–42. On colonial dependence on Indigenous communication networks, see Dubcovsky, *Informed Power*; Grandjean, *American Passage*, 45–75. On the intentional use of rumors by Natives, see Dowd, *Groundless*, 81–101; Julie A. Fisher and David J. Silverman, *Ninigret, Sachem of the Niantics and Narragansetts: Diplomacy, War, and the Balance of Power in Seventeenth-Century New England and Indian Country* (Ithaca, NY: Cornell University Press, 2014), 54–55, 108–112; Grandjean, *American Passage*, 76–109; Midtrød, "Strange and Disturbing News," 91–112.

34. "The humble Appeale of the Voluntiers to all well minded, and Charitable People," TNA CO 5/1371, p. 253.

35. *PSWB*, 504.

36. *PSWB*, 492, 504; Bland to Berne, in Burk, *History of Virginia*, 2:247.

37. Gordon W. Allport and Leo Postman, *The Psychology of Rumor* (New York: H. Holt, 1947), 159; Steven Hahn, *A Nation under Our Feet: Black Political Struggles in the Rural South from Slavery to the Great Migration* (Cambridge, MA: The Belknap Press of Harvard University Press, 2004), 57–60; Glassman, *War of Words*, 75–146; Ranajit Guha, *Elementary Aspects of Peasant Insurgency in Colonial India* (Oxford: Oxford University Press, 1983), 251–277; Jean-Noël Kapferer, *Rumors: Uses, Interpretations, and Images*, trans. Bruce Fink (New Brunswick, NJ: Transaction, 1990), 14–15; James C. Scott, *Domination and the Arts of Resistance: Hidden Transcripts* (New Haven, CT: Yale University Press, 1990), 144–148.

38. Brown, *Good Wives*, 94–100, 140–149, 162–163; Sarah Hand Meacham, *Every Home a Distillery: Alcohol, Gender, and Technology in the Colonial Chesapeake* (Baltimore: Johns Hopkins University Press, 2009), 64–81; Terri L. Snyder, *Brab-*

bling Women: Disorderly Speech and the Law in Early Virginia (Ithaca, NY: Cornell University Press, 2003); Westbury, "Women in Bacon's Rebellion," 30–39.

39. *PSWB*, 536–537; Berry and Moryson, "Narrative of the . . . Late Rebellion," *Wiseman's Book*, 144–145. The 50 lb. poll tax paid for agents in England to represent the colony against a proprietary claim to the Northern Neck held by the Culpeper family, which mostly threatened the economic interests of wealthy planters; Hening, *Statutes*, 2:311–313; Edmund S. Morgan, *American Slavery, American Freedom: The Ordeal of Colonial Virginia* (1975; repr. ed., New York: W. W. Norton, 2003), 244–247. The amount of the general public levy changed from year to year but was generally far below the amount of the tax to pay for the Susquehannock-Virginia War. Even during the expensive Anglo-Dutch Wars, for example, the tax was 53 lbs. in 1665, 26 lbs. in 1672, 15 lbs. in 1673, and 12 lbs. in 1674; *JHBV*, 2:30, 58, 61, 63. In postrebellion grievances submitted by county representatives, complaints about the war tax and its misuse were almost universal, even in areas that remained loyal to the government; TNA CO 1/39/58, 60, 62, 64, 68, 69, 77, 80, 82, 86, 92, 94–96.

40. "humble Appeale of the Voluntiers," TNA CO 5/1371, pp. 248–51. Military historians agree that the fortifications did not deter Indigenous incursions, but disagree about the effectiveness of ranger patrols; John Grenier, *The First Way of War: American War Making on the Frontier, 1607–1814* (Cambridge: Cambridge University Press, 2005), 34–36; William L. Shea, *The Virginia Militia in the Seventeenth Century* (Baton Rouge: Louisiana State University Press, 1983), 101–102.

41. *PSWB*, 508; "Charles City County Grievances," 137, 159; Wilcomb E. Washburn, *The Governor and the Rebel: A History of Bacon's Rebellion in Virginia* (Chapel Hill: University of North Carolina Press, 1957), 35; Angelo T. Angelis, "'By Consent of the People': Riot and Regulation in Seventeenth-Century Virginia," in *Colonial Chesapeake: New Perspectives,* ed. Debra Meyers and Melanie Perreault (Lanham, MD: Lexington, 2006), 126–127; Stephen A. Higginson, "A Short History of the Right to Petition Government for the Redress of Grievances," *Yale Law Journal* 96, no. 1 (1986): 142–166; Derek Hirst, "Making Contact: Petitions and the English Republic," *Journal of British Studies* 45, no. 1 (2006): 26–50; Brian Weiser, "Access and Petitioning during the Reign of Charles II," in *The Stuart Courts,* ed. Eveline Cruickshanks (Stroud: Sutton, 2000), 203–213.

42. Hening, *Statutes*, 2:336–338; *PSWB*, 537; Berry and Moryson, "Narrative of the . . . Late Rebellion," *Wiseman's Book*, 145; Pierre Marambaud, "William Byrd I: A Young Virginia Planter in the 1670s," *VMHB* 81, no. 2 (1973): 131–150; Kristalyn M. Shefveland, "Cockacoeske and Sarah Harris Stegge Grendon: Bacon's Rebellion and the Roles of Women," in *Virginia Women: Their Lives and Times,* vol. 1, ed. Cynthia A. Kierner and Sandra Gioia Treadway (Athens: University of Georgia Press, 2015), 33–54.

43. Berry and Moryson, "Narrative of the . . . Late Rebellion," *Wiseman's Book*, 145; [Sherwood], "Virginias Deploured Condition," 165; Westbury, "Women in Bacon's Rebellion, 41–43.

44. *PSWB*, 491–493; [Cotton], "Bacon's and Ingram's Rebellion," 52–53; M[athew], "Bacon's Rebellion," 20; Berry and Moryson, "Narrative of the . . . Late Rebellion," *Wiseman's Book*, 146; Bacon, "Mrs. Bacon's Letter," 4. Contemporary portrayals of Bacon's character focus on his ambition, arrogance, and lust for power. The royal commissioners, for example, described him as having "an ominous pensive melancolly aspect, of a Pestilent and prevalent Logicall discourse tendinge to Atheisme in most Companyes," with "a most Imperious and dangerous hidden pride of heart."

All of these descriptions came from his enemies after his death, however, and his ownership of a "Large byble" suggests that not all their aspersions were accurate; Berry and Moryson, "Narrative of the . . . Late Rebellion," *Wiseman's Book*, 146; Account of Bacon's Estate, TNA CO 5/1371, p. 450. On the other hand, his youth in England suggest that he was something of a dilettante, rake, and con artist; Rice, *Tales from a Revolution*, 26–28.

45. *PSWB*, 497–498. On petitions as preemptive loyalty, see David M. Luebke, "How to Become a Loyalist: Petitions, Self-Fashioning, and the Repression of Unrest (East Frisia, 1725–1727)," *Central European History* 38, no. 3 (2005): 353–383.

46. Philip Ludwell, "Philip Ludwell's Account," in "Bacon's Rebellion," *VMHB* 1, no. 2 (1893): 180; [Sherwood], "Virginias Deploured Condition," 166–167; "Letter from Virginia to the Counc[ilo]rs for Trade and Plantations," 31 May 1676, Coventry Papers, vol. 77, fol. 95r; "The Names and Short Characters of those that have bin Executed for Rebellion," *Wiseman's Book*, 113.

47. *PSWB*, 516, 529–531.

48. "Letter from Virginia," Coventry Papers, vol. 77, fols. 95v–96r; Ludwell, "Philip Ludwell's Account," 180.

49. [Anonymous], "Nathaniel Bacon's Victory over the Indians," in *The Old Dominion in the Seventeenth Century: A Documentary History of Virginia, 1606–1700,* ed. Warren M. Billings (1975; rev ed., Chapel Hill: University of North Carolina Press, 2007), 330–333; Nathaniel Bacon, "Mr. Bacon's Acct of Their Troubles in Virginia by ye Indians, June ye 18th, 1676," in "Bacon's Rebellion," *WMQ* 9, no. 1 (1900): 6–10; Wilcomb E. Washburn, ed., "Sir William Berkeley's 'A History of Our Miseries,'" *WMQ* 14, no. 3 (1957): 403–413; [Sherwood], "Virginias Deploured Condition," 167–168; Ludwell, "Philip Ludwell's Account," 180–182; "Letter from Virginia," Coventry Papers, vol. 77, fols. 95v–96r; Abraham Wood to Sir William Berkeley, 24 May 1676, *PSWB*, 522–523; *Rashomon,* directed by Akira Kurosawa (1950).

50. With the exception of Bacon's account and the Indigenous account reported by Wood, each of the accounts cited in the previous paragraph supports this general summary. On Monacans and their relationship with the Occaneechis, see Jeffrey L. Hantman, *Monacan Millennium: A Collaborative Archaeology and History of a Virginia Indian People* (Charlottesville: University of Virginia Press, 2018), 129–156.

51. M[athew], "Bacon's Rebellion," 21; "Nathaniel Bacon's Victory," 330–333; Ludwell, "Philip Ludwell's Account," 180–81; "Letter from Virginia," Coventry Papers, vol. 77, fol. 95v.

52. Ludwell, "Philip Ludwell's Account," 181; "Letter from Virginia," Coventry Papers, vol. 77, fol. 95v; [Sherwood], "Virginias Deploured Condition," 168; "Nathaniel Bacon's Victory," 332–333; M[athew], "Bacon's Rebellion," 21; *PSWB*, 523, 569–570.

53. *PSWB*, 492, 495. For arguments that Bacon was motivated by access to the Native slave trade, see C. S. Everett, "'They shalbe slaves for their lives': Indian Slavery in Colonial Virginia," in *Indian Slavery in Colonial America,* ed. Alan Gallay (Lincoln: University of Nebraska Press, 2009), 84–90; Hatfield, *Atlantic Virginia,* 33–35; Maureen Meyers, "From Refugees to Slave Traders: The Transformation of the Westo Indians," in *Mapping the Mississippian Shatter Zone: The Colonial Indian Slave Trade and Regional Instability in the American South,* ed. Robbie Ethridge and Sheri M. Shuck-Hall (Lincoln: University of Nebraska Press, 2009), 98; Kristalyn Marie Shefveland, *Anglo-Native Virginia: Trade, Conversion, and Indian Slavery*

in the Old Dominion, 1646–1722 (Athens: University of Georgia Press, 2016), 49–50. For depictions of the Occaneechis as shattered or dispersed, see Robbie Ethridge, *From Chicaza to Chickasaw: The European Invasion and the Transformation of the Mississippian World, 1540–1715* (Chapel Hill: University of North Carolina Press, 2010), 155–156; Everett, "They shalbe slaves," 83, 88; Morgan, *American Slavery*, 259–260; Ethan A. Schmidt, *The Divided Dominion: Social Conflict and Indian Hatred in Early Virginia* (Boulder: University Press of Colorado, 2015), 165–166.

54. "Letter from Virginia," Coventry Papers, vol. 77, fol. 95v; Ludwell, "Philip Ludwell's Account," 181; "Nathaniel Bacon's Victory," 331–332. As with the Occaneechis, scholars cited in the previous note have tended to ignore the surviving Susquehannock group and imply that the southern migrants were destroyed.

3. The Susquehannock Scattering

1. Nathaniel Bacon, "Mr. Bacon's Acct of Their Troubles in Virginia by ye Indians, June ye 18th, 1676," *WMQ* 9, no. 1 (1900): 7–8; *PSWB*, 509, 527, 536.

2. Penelope B. Drooker, "The Ohio Valley, 1550–1750: Patterns of Sociopolitical Coalescence and Dispersal," in *The Transformation of the Southeastern Indians, 1540–1760,* ed. Robbie Ethridge and Charles Hudson (Jackson: University Press of Mississippi, 2002), 120–121; Robert Wall and Heather Lapham, "Material Culture of the Contact Period in the Upper Potomac Valley: Chronological and Cultural Implications," *Archaeology of Eastern North America* 31 (2003): 169–171; William N. Fenton, "Northern Iroquoian Culture Patterns," in *Handbook of North American Indians,* vol. 15, *Northeast,* ed. Bruce G. Trigger (Washington, DC: Smithsonian Institution, 1978), 300–301; James D. Rice, *Nature and History in the Potomac Country: From Hunter-Gatherers to the Age of Jefferson* (Baltimore: Johns Hopkins University Press, 2009), 35–37; April M. Beisaw, "Environmental History of the Susquehanna Valley around the Time of European Contact," *Pennsylvania History* 79, no. 4 (2012): 373.

3. I have chosen to use the word *scattering* rather than *diaspora* to describe the Susquehannock experience in the 1670s. Several scholars have made compelling cases that Indigenous diasporas—networks of dispersed populations—were central to some nations' social and political formations; Sami Lakomäki, *Gathering Together: The Shawnee People through Diaspora and Nationhood, 1600–1870* (New Haven, CT: Yale University Press, 2014); Gregory D. Smithers, *The Cherokee Diaspora: An Indigenous History of Migration, Resettlement, and Identity* (New Haven, CT: Yale University Press, 2015); Gregory D. Smithers and Brooke N. Newman, eds., *Native Diasporas: Indigenous Identities and Settler Colonialism in the Americas* (Lincoln: University of Nebraska Press, 2014); Laura Keenan Spero, "'Stout, Bold, Cunning and the Greatest Travellers in America': The Colonial Shawnee Diaspora" (PhD diss., University of Pennsylvania, 2010); Stephen Warren, *The Worlds the Shawnees Made: Migration and Violence in Early America* (Chapel Hill: University of North Carolina Press, 2014). However, I do not believe this model of diasporic communities accurately describes Susquehannock social and political structures, which were far-reaching but centered in Gandastogue. As subsequent chapters demonstrate, their dispersal was immediately followed by efforts to reconstitute into fewer communities, or even a single community, rather than remain distributed. Therefore I believe *scattering* best captures the transitory nature of this phase in their history.

4. On households as the building blocks of larger political structures, or the "elementary units of political order," see James C. Scott, *The Art of Not Being Governed: An Anarchist History of Upland Southeast Asia* (New Haven, CT: Yale University Press, 2009), 36–39 (quotation, 36); Julie Hardwick, Sarah M. S. Pearsall, and Karin Wulf, "Introduction: Centering Families in Atlantic Histories," *WMQ* 70, no. 2 (2013): 205–224; Matthew Kruer, "Bloody Minds and Peoples Undone: Emotion, Family, and Political Order in the Virginia-Susquehannock War," *WMQ* 74, no. 3 (2017): 401–436.

5. [John Cotton], "The History of Bacon's and Ingram's Rebellion, 1676," in Andrews, *Narratives*, 48.

6. On the politics of oratory and social fission as the result of a failure to achieve consensus among the Haudenosaunee, see Daniel K. Richter, *The Ordeal of the Longhouse: The Peoples of the Iroquois League in the Era of European Colonization* (Chapel Hill: University of North Carolina Press, 1992), 45–48.

7. William P. Cumming, ed., *The Discoveries of John Lederer* (Charlottesville: University of Virginia Press, 1958), 24–25; "Letter from Virginia to the Counc[ilo]rs for Trade and Plantations," 31 May 1676, Coventry Papers, vol. 77, fols. 95v–96r; H. Trawick Ward, "Mortuary Patterns at the Fredricks, Wall, and Mitchum Sites," in *The Siouan Project, Seasons I and II*, ed. Roy S. Dickens Jr., H. Trawick Ward, and R. P. Stephen Davis Jr. (Chapel Hill: University of North Carolina, 1987), 98–100.

8. [Sherwood], "Virginias Deploured Condition," 167; Philip Ludwell, "Philip Ludwell's Account," in "Bacon's Rebellion," *VMHB* 1, no. 2 (1893): 180. Throughout this chapter I have made corrections to transcription errors in Ludwell's account based on the original manuscript in TNA CO 1/37/16.

9. "Letter from Virginia," Coventry Papers, vol. 77, fol. 95v; Douglas W. Boyce, "Iroquoian Tribes of the Virginia-North Carolina Coastal Plain," in *Handbook of North American Indians*, 15:286; *Discoveries of John Lederer*, 33; Lewis R. Binford, "An Ethnohistory of the Nottoway, Meherrin and Weanock Indians of Southeastern Virginia," *Ethnohistory* 14, nos. 3–4 (1967): 152–156; Robbie Ethridge, *From Chicaza to Chickasaw: The European Invasion and the Transformation of the Mississippian World, 1540–1715* (Chapel Hill: University of North Carolina Press, 2010), 95, 102–103; April Lee Hatfield, *Atlantic Virginia: Intercolonial Relations in the Seventeenth Century* (Philadelphia: University of Pennsylvania Press, 2004), 34–35; Thomas C. Parramore, "The Tuscarora Ascendency," *NCHR* 59, no. 4 (1982): 315–316; Lars C. Adams, "'Sundry Murders and Depredations': A Closer Look at the Chowan River War, 1676–1677," *NCHR* 90, no. 2 (2013): 157–160; *CRNC*, 1st ser., 2:643. North Carolina colonists in 1726 identified the nationality of the attackers that forced the flight from Cowinchahawkon as "Sennecco Indians," a southern term for the four western Haudenosaunee nations. However, Haudenosaunee raids in this region were unknown prior to the late 1670s, and their recollections were undoubtedly distorted by decades of mourning war raids between Haudenosaunee and southeastern Native nations. The petitioners' comment that the migrants were "disturbed by the sapponie Indians" suggests the attackers were Occaneechis and their Siouan allies; *CRNC*, 1st ser., 2:643; James H. Merrell, "'Their Very Bones Shall Fight': The Catawba-Iroquois Wars," in *Beyond the Covenant Chain: The Iroquois and Their Neighbors in Indian North America, 1600–1800*, ed. Daniel K. Richter and James H. Merrell (1987; rev. ed., University Park: Pennsylvania State University Press, 2003), 116–117.

10. *CRNC*, 1st ser., 2:643. In 1726 the Meherrin nation petitioned the North Carolina government to protect their land from encroaching colonists. Settlers complained

that "those Indians who are not original Inhabitants of any Lands within this Government . . . were formerly called Susquahannahs" and therefore had no rightful claim to territory; *CRNC,* 1st ser., 2:643. As Shannon Lee Dawdy has pointed out, this claim was an attempt to smear Meherrin landowners, violate their sovereignty, and dispossess them by law; Shannon Lee Dawdy, "The Meherrin's Secret History of the Dividing Line," *NCHR* 72, no. 4 (1995): 387–415 (esp. 409n88). Elsewhere Dawdy suggests the claim was a garbled description of an actual mixing of populations, with Susquehannocks slowly incorporated into the Meherrin nation over time; Dawdy, "The Secret History of the Meherrin" (MA thesis, College of William and Mary, 1994), 100–101. An influx of Susquehannocks probably accounts for the stable Meherrin population between 1669 and 1709 amid disease, dislocation, and escalating slave raids that caused the population of neighboring Nottoways to plummet by two-thirds; Boyce, "Iroquoian Tribes," 286–287.

11. *CRNC,* 1st ser., 1:658; Adams, "Sundry Murders," 152–156, 161–164; Dawdy, "Meherrin's Secret History," 394. Ethnic mixing during the turbulent seventeenth century remains a contentious issue among Meherrins to this day, in large part because it has so often been used by colonizers as an excuse to strip the Meherrin nation of its sovereignty on the grounds that its Indigenous identity is insufficiently authentic; Adams, "Sundry Murders," 172. On Indigenous identities and colonialism, see Eva Marie Garroutte, *Real Indians: Identity and the Survival of Native America* (Berkeley: University of California Press, 2003).

12. Edmund Andros to Edmund Cantwell, 22 February 1676, Francis J. Dreer Autograph Collection, series 2, box 51, folder 2, HSP; *NYHM (Delaware English),* 104; *Andros Papers,* 1:377–378; *PWP,* 3:453; Warrant for William Markham and Jacob Pellison, 9 May 1689, RG-17/D-81-98, p. 195, PSA. On "familiar" to describe a spectrum of real and fictive kinship relations, including descent, marriage, and adoption, see Sarah M. S. Pearsall, *Atlantic Families: Lives and Letters in the Later Eighteenth Century* (New York: Oxford University Press, 2008), 56–79; Bianca Premo, "Familiar: Thinking beyond Lineage and across Race in Spanish Atlantic Family History," *WMQ* 70, no. 2 (2013): 295–316.

13. *MECPNY,* 2:499, 501–502; Robert S. Grumet, *The Munsee Indians: A History* (Norman: University of Oklahoma Press, 2009), 135–136.

14. Jean R. Soderlund, *Lenape Country: Delaware Valley Society before William Penn* (Philadelphia: University of Pennsylvania Press, 2015), 132–138; *NYHM (Delaware English),* 71–72; *NYHM (General Entries),* 2:93; *DRCHSNY,* 12:543; Andros to Cantwell, 22 February 1676, Dreer Collection, series 2, box 51, folder 2, HSP.

15. *Andros Papers,* 1:105, 131–132, 178, 195–196, 203, 352–353; *NYHM (General Entries),* 2:16, 35, 69, 84. This alliance chain, as I am suggestively calling it, was the beginning of the Anglo-Iroquois alliance that came to be called the Covenant Chain; Daniel K. Richter, "Rediscovered Links in the Covenant Chain: Previously Unpublished Transcripts of New York Indian Treaty Minutes, 1677–1691," *Proceedings of the American Antiquarian Society* 92, no. 1 (1982): 48–72. Historians have stressed the piecemeal and ad hoc nature of these alliances in 1675, which only later became formalized; Richard L. Haan, "Covenant and Consensus: Iroquois and English, 1676–1760," in *Beyond the Covenant Chain,* 43–46; Francis Jennings, *The Invasion of America: Indians, Colonialism, and the Cant of Conquest* (Chapel Hill: University of North Carolina Press, 1975), 313–326. Andros's experience with Kalinago (Caribs) in the Caribbean may have taught him the importance of such alliances, and there is no question that he pursued them with speed and determination

in North America; Stephen Saunders Webb, *1676: The End of American Independence* (New York: Alfred A. Knopf, 1984), 318–321.

16. Chief Jacob Thomas, with Terry Boyle, *Teachings from the Longhouse* (Toronto: Stoddart, 1994), 17; Francis Jennings, *The Ambiguous Iroquois Empire: The Covenant Chain Confederation of Indian Tribes with English Colonies from Its Beginnings to the Lancaster Treaty of 1744* (New York: W. W. Norton, 1984), 145–151.

17. Andros to Cantwell, 22 February 1676, Dreer Collection, Series 2, Box 51, folder 2, HSP; *NYHM (Delaware English)*, 104; *Andros Papers*, 1:377; Mark L. Thompson, *The Contest for the Delaware Valley: Allegiance, Identity, and Empire in the Seventeenth Century* (Baton Rouge: Louisiana State University Press, 2013), 181–195.

18. *Andros Papers*, 1:377–378. On Indigenous treaty protocols, see Daniel K. Richter, *Facing East from Indian Country: A Native History of Early America* (Cambridge, MA: Harvard University Press, 2003), 129–149. On matchcoats, see Marshall Joseph Becker, "Matchcoats: Cultural Conservatism and Change in One Aspect of Native American Clothing," *Ethnohistory* 54, no. 4 (2005): 727–787; Laura E. Johnson, "'Goods to clothe themselves': Native Consumers and Native Images on the Pennsylvania Trading Frontier, 1712–1760," *Winterthur Portfolio* 43, no. 1 (2009): 115–140; Gail DeBuse Potter, "The Matchcoat," in *Rethinking the Fur Trade: Cultures of Exchange in an Atlantic World*, ed. Susan Sleeper-Smith (Lincoln: University of Nebraska Press, 2009), 411–413.

19. *Andros Papers*, 1:378–379.

20. *Andros Papers*, 1:132, 178; Grumet, *Munsee Indians*, 135–137.

21. *NYHM (General Entries)*, 2:84.

22. *NYHM (General Entries)*, 2:84.

23. *Andros Papers*, 1:178; *Archives of Maryland*, 15:120–121. Francis Jennings, who gives credit to Andros for brokering the Haudenosaunee-Susquehannock peace, underestimates the importance of Indigenous initiatives; Francis Jennings, "Glory, Death, and Transfiguration: the Susquehannock Indians in the Seventeenth Century," *PAPS* 112, no. 1 (1968): 36–39.

24. *Andros Papers*, 1:379.

25. *Andros Papers*, 1:379.

26. *Andros Papers*, 1:379. Most historians depict the Susquehannock–New York council as a victory for Andros, citing Francis Jennings as the preeminent expert on Susquehannock history. Unfortunately, Jennings himself was contradictory on this point, variously arguing that "his invitation won small acceptance" but more recently that "his offer of protection had been gratefully received." Jennings, "Glory, Death, and Transfiguration," 39; Jennings, *Ambiguous Iroquois Empire*, 151. Subsequent historians often attribute success to Andros by making the error of reading Susquehannock political decisions in 1677 back into this earlier meeting, but for a notable exception see Grumet, *Munsee Indians*, 139.

27. *Archives of Maryland*, 15:122, 126; Barry C. Kent, *Susquehanna's Indians* (1984; Harrisburg: Pennsylvania Historical and Museum Commission, 2001), 48–49.

28. *Archives of Maryland*, 2:488–449, 15:57–58, 17:20. Despite the similarity in name, the Maryland Pamunkys were distinct from the Virginia Pamunkeys. Pamunkys were historically affiliated with the Piscataway paramount chiefdom while the Pamunkeys were the core of the Powhatan paramount chiefdom; Rice, *Nature and History*, 53.

29. George E. Gifford Jr. and Marion Tinling, eds., "A Relation of a Voyage to the Head of the Bay," *The Historian* 20, no. 3 (1958): 350; Russell R. Menard, "Population, Economy, and Society in Seventeenth-Century Maryland," *MHM* 79, no. 1 (1984):

72; *Archives of Maryland,* 1:250, 533 (emphasis added), 3:283–284, 5:10; Darold D. Wax, "Black Immigrants: The Slave Trade in Colonial Maryland," *MHM* 73, no. 1 (1978): 30–45. On African slavery in early Maryland, see Demetri D. Debe and Russell R. Menard, "The Transition to African Slavery in Maryland: A Note on the Barbados Connection," *Slavery and Abolition* 32, no. 1 (2011): 129–141; Gloria Lund Main, *Tobacco Colony: Life in Early Maryland, 1650–1720* (Princeton, NJ: Princeton University Press, 1982), 97–139; Russell R. Menard, "The Maryland Slave Population, 1658 to 1730: A Demographic Profile of Blacks in Four Counties," *WMQ* 32, no. 1 (1975), 29–54. Although there has been a surge of excellent studies of Indigenous slavery in the last two decades, Maryland has not received any dedicated treatment.

30. *Archives of Maryland,* 15:58, 90.
31. *Archives of Maryland,* 2:478, 512, 540.
32. *Archives of Maryland,* 15:65; James D. Rice, *Tales from a Revolution: Bacon's Rebellion and the Transformation of Early America* (New York: Oxford University Press, 2012), 55–56; Antoinette Sutto, *Loyal Protestants and Dangerous Papists: Maryland and the Politics of Religion in the English Atlantic, 1630–1690* (Charlottesville: University of Virginia Press, 2015), 81–103.
33. *Archives of Maryland,* 2:475–476, 485–486, 494, 501.
34. *Archives of Maryland,* 2:486, 500–501, 504.
35. *Archives of Maryland,* 2:479.
36. *Archives of Maryland,* 2:488–489, 493, 501–502, 15:78.
37. *Archives of Maryland,* 2:480, 15:90–91; Rice, *Tales from a Revolution,* 56–57.
38. *Archives of Maryland,* 2:505–506, 15:90–92.
39. *Archives of Maryland,* 15:91–92.
40. *Archives of Maryland,* 2:557–560.
41. *Archives of Maryland,* 5:247, 15:120; Hening, *Statutes,* 2:153.
42. Helen C. Rountree, *Pocahontas's People: The Powhatan Indians of Virginia Through Four Centuries* (Norman: University of Oklahoma Press, 1990), 128–143. On Indian hating as the cause of Anglo-Indian violence during this period, see Ethan A. Schmidt, *The Divided Dominion: Social Conflict and Indian Hatred in Early Virginia* (Boulder: University Press of Colorado, 2015); Wilcomb E. Washburn, *The Governor and the Rebel: A History of Bacon's Rebellion in Virginia* (Chapel Hill: University of North Carolina Press, 1957), 37–39; Webb, *1676,* 14, 411. On Indian hating in general, see Richard Drinnon, *Facing West: The Metaphysics of Indian-Hating and Empire-Building* (Minneapolis: University of Minnesota Press, 1980).
43. "Rappahannock in Virginia," 23 May 1676, Coventry Papers, vol. 77, fol. 86r; William Travers to Giles Cale, 13 May 1676, TNA CO 1/36/65, fol. 138r; Northumberland County Order Book, 1666–1678, pp. 241–242, LVA; Hening, *Statutes,* 2:327–328; "Causes of Discontent in Virginia, 1676," *VMHB* 3, no. 1 (1895): 36. Given the timing it is possible that Smith's militia was also responsible for the decision of Matchotics to take refuge among Mattawomans in Maryland; *Archives of Maryland,* 15:90.
44. Francis Moryson to [Henry Coventry?], 9 September 1676, Coventry Papers, vol. 77, fol. 205r; "The humble Appeale of the Volunters to all well minded, and Charitable People," TNA CO 5/1371, p. 252; [Sherwood], "Virginias Deploured Condition," 166, 168.
45. [Sherwood], "Virginias Deploured Condition," 168; Ludwell, "Philip Ludwell's Account," 180. Despite colonists' tendency to see swamps as desolate wastes—an assumption that modern readers often share—the Great Dragon Swamp and other

marshes were resource-rich extensions of Algonquian homelands; Lisa Brooks, "'Every Swamp is a Castle': Navigating Native Spaces in the Connecticut River Valley, Winter 1675–1677 and 2005–2015," *Northeastern Naturalist* 24 (2017): 45–80; Helen C. Rountree, "Look Again, More Closely: 18th Century Indian Settlements in Swamps," *Journal of Middle Atlantic Archaeology* 20 (2004): 7–12.

46. "Rappahannock in Virginia," Coventry Papers, vol. 77, fol. 86r.
47. Ludwell, "Philip Ludwell's Account," 180; *PSWB*, 521–522.
48. *PSWB*, 523, 525–528.
49. *PSWB*, 520; "Memor[ia]lls relateing to Present state of Virg[ini]a," Sir William Berkeley Letters and Documents, 1674–1677, Tracy W. McGregor Collection, Small Library; Ludwell, "Philip Ludwell's Account," 182; [Sherwood], "Virginias Deploured Condition," 169; Sir Henry Chicheley to Col. Nathaniel Bacon, 2 June 1676, Coventry Papers, vol. 77, fol. 102r.
50. "The Virginians' plea for opposing the Indians without the Governor's order," June (?) 1676, TNA CO 1/37/14, fol. 29v; *PSWB*, 537, 630. Nearly one-third of the assembly's statutes were related to the Susquehannock-Virginia War, the rebellion arising from that war, and crimes related to Anglo-Indian violence; Hening, *Statutes*, 2:341–365.
51. *JHBV*, 2:65; John Berry and Francis Moryson, "A Narrative of the Rise, Progresse and Cessation of the Late Rebellion in Virginia," *Wiseman's Book*, 151. The records for the June assembly do not give a full accounting of the sitting burgesses, but government loyalists claimed it was dominated by Nathaniel Bacon and his supporters. Berkeley later complained, "but eight of the Burgesses" were "not of his faction and at his direction," and Isaac Allerton Jr. testified that "a considerable partie of the Burgesses, were of his side"; *PSWB*, 570; Isaac Allerton to Thomas Ludwell, 4 August 1676, Coventry Papers, vol. 77, fols. 160r–160v. Although such vague aspersions from partisan sources are not very helpful, one of the recorded burgesses was Thomas Blayton, described as "Bacon's great engin," and another was James Minge, one of "Bacon's Great friends in formeing the lawes" in his position as clerk of the assembly; "Defense of Col. Edward Hill," *VMHB* 3, no. 3 (1896): 249.
52. [Cotton], "Bacon's and Ingram's Rebellion," 55; Berry and Moryson, "Narrative of the . . . Late Rebellion," *Wiseman's Book*, 151; Ludwell, "Philip Ludwell's Account," 183–184; [Sherwood], "Virginias Deploured Condition," 170–171; *PSWB*, 570–571; Rice, *Tales from a Revolution*, 59–72.
53. John Berry and Francis Moryson, "Names and Characters of . . . the Indians," TNA CO 5/1371, p. 266; T[homas] M[athew], "The Beginning, Progress, and Conclusion of Bacon's Rebellion, 1675–1676 (1705)," in Andrews, *Narratives*, 24–27; Martha W. McCartney, "Cockacoeske, Queen of Pamunkey: Diplomat and Suzeraine," in *Powhatan's Mantle: Indians in the Colonial Southeast*, ed. Gregory A. Waselkov, Peter H. Wood, and Tom Hatley (1989; rev. ed., Lincoln: University of Nebraska Press, 2006), 245–247; Rice, *Tales from a Revolution*, 65–68; Schmidt, *Divided Dominion*, 157–158. A 1669 census counted fifty adult males, suggesting that the twelve Pamunkey scouts represented about one-quarter of the nation's total fighting strength; Hening, *Statutes*, 2:274–275.
54. Ludwell, "Philip Ludwell's Account," 183–184; Naomi Tadmor, *Family and Friends in Eighteenth-Century England: Household, Kinship, and Patronage* (Cambridge: Cambridge University Press, 2001), 18–43; Carole Shammas, *A History of Household Government in America* (Charlottesville: University of Virginia Press, 2002), 35–39. The assembly's reforms lacked a strong popular mandate and were primarily the work of a few opposition leaders who hijacked the proceedings, including

Richard Lawrence, William Drummond, Giles Bland, and Joseph Ingram; *PSWB*, 538; M[athew], "Bacon's Rebellion, 24–25; Washburn, *Governor and the Rebel*, 49–67.

55. Ludwell, "Philip Ludwell's Account," 185.
56. Hening, *Statutes*, 2:341–344, 346–347, 349–352; Gregory Ablavsky, "Making Indians 'White': The Judicial Abolition of Native Slavery in Revolutionary Virginia and Its Racial Legacy," *University of Pennsylvania Law Review* 159, no. 5 (2011): 1467–1472. Historians have interpreted the provision legalizing Indian slavery as a pivotal event in the development of an Indian slave trade; C. S. Everett, "'They shalbe slaves for their lives': Indian Slavery in Colonial Virginia," in *Indian Slavery in Colonial America*, ed. Alan Gallay (Lincoln: University of Nebraska Press, 2009), 86–88; Owen Stanwood, "Captives and Slaves: Indian Labor, Cultural Conversion, and the Plantation Revolution in Virginia," *VMHB* 114, no. 4 (2006): 446–447. However, the June assembly's outlawing of Indian trade complicates this story, because it would have destroyed the existing practice of trading guns to allied Natives in exchange for captives of other nations. Indeed, Bacon's expressed intent was not to expand the Indigenous slave trade but to destroy trade altogether, creating clear lines between English colonists and Native enemies. He argued that in his attempts to enter the trade, he had learned first-hand that "trading with the Indians has proved soe fatall to these parts of the world, that I feare wee shall bee all lost." Bacon, "Mr. Bacon's Acct," 6. Of course, the legislative ban left open the possibility of a Native slave trade conducted by English slavers, but such a trade would have been far more limited in its geographical reach and geopolitical impact than a slave trade that depended on Indigenous partners.
57. Hening, *Statutes*, 2:342–343, 348; Northumberland County Order Book, 1666–1678, p. 275, LVA.
58. Hening, *Statutes*, 2:352–353.
59. Ludwell, "Philip Ludwell's Account," 185; "Gloster County Grievances and Answers," *Wiseman's Book*, 247.

4. The Contagion of Conspiracy

1. Philip Ludwell, "Philip Ludwell's Account," in "Bacon's Rebellion," *VMHB* 1, no. 2 (1893): 179; *PSWB*, 498; Gov. Sir Jonathan Atkins to Sec. Sir Joseph Williamson, 14 November 1675, TNA CO 1/35/41, fol. 252r. On rebellion as contagion, see Ashli White, *Encountering Revolution: Haiti and the Making of the Early Republic* (Baltimore: Johns Hopkins University Press, 2010), 124–165.
2. Thomas Hobbes, *Leviathan or The Matter, Forme and Power of a Common-Wealth Ecclesiasticall and Civill* (1651), chap. 29, paras. 2, 20. On disease and the body politic, see Kathleen M. Brown, *Foul Bodies: Cleanliness in Early America* (New Haven, CT: Yale University Press, 2009), 121–131, 159–211; Simon Finger, *The Contagious City: The Politics of Public Health in Early Philadelphia* (Ithaca, NY: Cornell University Press, 2012); Cristobal Silva, *Miraculous Plagues: An Epidemiology of Early New England Narrative* (New York: Oxford University Press, 2011), 62–100; Kelly Wisecup, *Medical Encounters: Knowledge and Identity in Early American Literatures* (Amherst: University of Massachusetts Press, 2013).
3. The foundational work on conspiracy theory in American history is Richard Hofstadter, "The Paranoid Style in American Politics," in *The Paranoid Style in American Politics and Other Essays* (New York: Alfred A. Knopf, 1965), 3–40. For classic studies of the subject, see Bernard Bailyn, *The Ideological Origins of the American*

Revolution (1967; rev. ed., Cambridge, MA: Belknap Press of Harvard University Press, 1992); David Brion Davis, *The Slave Power Conspiracy and the Paranoid Style* (Baton Rouge: Louisiana State University Press, 1969); Gordon S. Wood, "Conspiracy and the Paranoid Style: Causality and Deceit in the Eighteenth Century," *WMQ* 39, no. 3 (1982): 402–441. James Rice argues that conspiracy theory played an important role in Bacon's Rebellion, stating that "such theories . . . can, by some mysterious, almost magical process, create a new reality." James D. Rice, *Tales from a Revolution: Bacon's Rebellion and the Transformation of Early America* (New York: Oxford University Press, 2012), 224. This chapter builds on that insight by delving more rigorously into the processes by which conspiracy theories shape political movements.

4. Barry Coward and Julian Swann, "Introduction," in *Conspiracies and Conspiracy Theory in Early Modern Europe: From the Waldensians to the French Revolution,* ed. Barry Coward and Julian Swann (Aldershot: Ashgate, 2004), 3–5; Wood, "Conspiracy and the Paranoid Style," 406–411; *MCGCCV,* 210; Robert Beverley, *The History and Present State of Virginia,* ed. Susan Scott Parrish (Chapel Hill: University of North Carolina Press, 2013), 53; "The Servants' Plot of 1663," in "Virginia Colonial Records (Continued)," *VMHB* 15, no. 1 (1907): 38–43; Carla Gardina Pestana, *The English Atlantic in an Age of Revolution, 1640–1661* (Cambridge, MA: Harvard University Press, 2004), 183–212; Edmund S. Morgan, *American Slavery, American Freedom: The Ordeal of Colonial Virginia* (1975; repr. ed., New York: W. W. Norton, 2003), 235–249.

5. *PSWB,* 531, 540; [John Cotton], "The History of Bacon's and Ingram's Rebellion, 1676," in *Narratives of the Insurrections,* 56; [Sherwood], "Virginias Deploured Condition," 173.

6. John Berry and Francis Moryson, "A Review Breviary, and Conclusion drawn from the foregoing Narrative," *Wiseman's Book,* 181; *PSWB,* 540–541; Isaac Allerton to Thomas Ludwell, 4 August 1676, Coventry Papers, vol. 77, fol. 160v; [Cotton], "Bacon's and Ingram's Rebellion," 56; M[athew], "The Beginning, Progress, and Conclusion of Bacon's Rebellion, 1675–1676 (1705)," in *Narratives of the Insurrections,* 34.

7. Berry and Moryson, "Review Breviary, and Conclusion," *Wiseman's Book,* 180; [Cotton], "Bacon's and Ingram's Rebellion," 56–57.

8. Peter Lake, "'The Monarchical Republic of Elizabeth I' Revisited (by its Victims) as a Conspiracy," in *Conspiracies and Conspiracy Theory,* 87–112; Mark Knights, "Faults on Both Sides: The Conspiracies of Party Politics under the Later Stuarts," in *Conspiracy and Conspiracy Theory,* 153–172; John Berry and Francis Moryson, "A Narrative of the Rise, Progresse and Cessation of the Late Rebellion in Virginia," *Wiseman's Book,* 153.

9. Berry and Moryson, "Narrative of the . . . Late Rebellion," *Wiseman's Book,* 153–154; M[athew], "Bacon's Rebellion," 34.

10. Mark Fenster, *Conspiracy Theories: Secrecy and Power in American Culture* (1999; rev. ed., Minneapolis: University of Minnesota Press, 2008), 118–154; Jeffrey Ostler, "The Rhetoric of Conspiracy and the Formation of Kansas Populism," *Agricultural History* 69, no. 1 (1995): 1–27; Justin Pope, "Inventing an Indian Slave Conspiracy on Nantucket, 1738," *EAS* 15, no. 3 (2017): 505–538; Jason T. Sharples, *The World that Fear Made: Slave Revolts and Conspiracy Scares in Early America* (Philadelphia: University of Pennsylvania Press, 2020); Ed White, "The Value of Conspiracy Theory," *American Literary History* 14, no. 1 (2002): 1–31.

11. "The Declaration of the People," in "Proclamations of Nathaniel Bacon," *VMHB* 1, no. 1 (1893): 59–61; Rice, *Tales from a Revolution,* 79–80. On the "common-

alty" as an emergent idea during Bacon's Rebellion, see Peter Thompson, "The Thief, the Householder, and the Commons: Languages of Class in Seventeenth-Century Virginia," *WMQ* 63, no. 2 (2006): 253–280.

12. "Nathaniel Bacon Esq'r, his manifesto concerning the present troubles in Virginia," in "Proclamations of Nathaniel Bacon," *VMHB* 1, no. 1 (1893): 57–58 (hereafter "Bacon's Manifesto"); [Cotton], "Bacon's and Ingram's Rebellion," 58–59. I have corrected errors in the transcribed manifesto based on a manuscript copy of the lost original; TNA CO 1/37/51. Another contemporary copy can be found in Coventry Papers, vol. 77, fol. 167.

13. "Bacon's Manifesto," 57; Lauren Benton, *A Search for Sovereignty: Law and Geography in European Empires, 1400–1900* (Cambridge: Cambridge University Press, 2010), 64–65, 91–100; Ronald Dale Karr, "'Why Should You Be So Furious?': The Violence of the Pequot War," *JAH* 85, no. 3 (1998): 876–909; Dylan Ruediger, "'Neither Utterly to Reject Them, Nor Yet to Drawe Them to Come in': Tributary Subordination and Settler Colonialism in Virginia," *EAS* 18, no. 1 (2020): 1–31; Jenny Hale Pulsipher *Subjects unto the Same King: Indians, English, and the Contest for Authority in Colonial New England* (Philadelphia: University of Pennsylvania Press, 2005), 135–159.

14. *Archives of Maryland,* 15:98, 121, 126. For other emotional bowel movements, see "The Virginians' plea for opposing the Indians without the Governor's order," June (?) 1676, TNA CO 1/37/14, fol. 29r; *DRCHSNY,* 3:274.

15. *Archives of Maryland,* 15:99–102.

16. *Archives of Maryland,* 15:122–123. Francis Jennings portrays Susquehannocks as pawns in Maryland's intercolonial intrigues to secure possession of the Delaware Valley, but fails to account for the Susquehannocks' initiative and misconstrues Maryland's precarious situation by neglecting the expanding rebellion in Virginia; Francis Jennings, "Glory, Death, and Transfiguration: the Susquehannock Indians in the Seventeenth Century," *PAPS* 112, no. 1 (1968): 32–39.

17. *Archives of Maryland,* 15:126.

18. *Archives of Maryland,* 2:424, 5:153, 15:128, 131, 137–138.

19. *Archives of Maryland,* 5:136–137, 15:128–129, 131.

20. *Archives of Maryland,* 5:153, 15:128.

21. Fenster, *Conspiracy Theories,* 100–107; Hofstadter, "Paranoid Style," 35–37; "An Act for preventing Dangers which may happen from Popish Recusants," in *Statutes of the Realm,* vol. 5, 1628–80, ed. John Raithby et al. (Great Britain Record Commission, 1819), 782; John Miller, *Popery and Politics in England, 1660–1688* (Cambridge: Cambridge University Press, 1973), 108–153; Owen Stanwood, *The Empire Reformed: English America in the Age of the Glorious Revolution* (Philadelphia: University of Pennsylvania Press, 2011), 1–21, 54–63; Antoinette Sutto, *Loyal Protestants and Dangerous Papists: Maryland and the Politics of Religion in the English Atlantic, 1630–1690* (Charlottesville: University of Virginia Press, 2015).

22. *Archives of Maryland,* 5:134–135, 140, 145–146. The transcript of the Complaint printed in the *Archives of Maryland* contains many errors, so I have made changes throughout this chapter and Chapter 5 based on the original manuscript; TNA CO 1/36/78. The National Archives of the UK conjecturally dates the document May 1676, but it references the September Clifts uprising and was probably written sometime in late 1676.

23. *Archives of Maryland,* 5:134, 141, 147, 152.

24. Melinda S. Zook, *Radical Whigs and Conspiratorial Politics in Late Stuart England* (University Park: Pennsylvania State University Press, 1999); *Jesuit Relations,* 59:73–75; Daniel K. Richter, *The Ordeal of the Longhouse: The Peoples of the*

Iroquois League in the Era of European Colonization (Chapel Hill: University of North Carolina Press, 1992), 105–132; *Andros Papers*, 1:431–433; extract of a letter from Sieur de la Salle, written from Techirogen to the governor, 10 August 1673, in *Découvertes et établissements des Français dans l'ouest et dans le sud de l'Amérique septentrionale (1614–1754),* ed. Pierre Margry (6 vols.; Paris, 1876–1886), 1:241; *NYHM (General Entries),* 2:132; *DRCHSNY,* 12:557.

25. *Archives of Maryland,* 5:145. Wilcomb Washburn dismisses the Complaint, arguing it "is so full of absurd and false accusations as to be of little use as a source of reliable information," and Francis Jennings similarly states, "its only value is as evidence of popular misinformation." Wilcomb E. Washburn, *The Governor and the Rebel: A History of Bacon's Rebellion in Virginia* (Chapel Hill: University of North Carolina Press, 1957), 184n33; Francis Jennings, *The Ambiguous Iroquois Empire: The Covenant Chain Confederation of Indian Tribes with English Colonies from Its Beginnings to the Lancaster Treaty of 1744* (New York: W. W. Norton, 1984), 140n86. Stephen Saunders Webb, on the other hand, uses the Complaint as the sole piece of evidence to prove that a republican uprising originating in Virginia had spread to become a Chesapeake Confederation with mass support in Maryland; Stephen Saunders Webb, *1676: The End of American Independence* (New York: Alfred A. Knopf, 1984), 70–75. James Rice's analysis of the Complaint as conspiratorial narrative is the most judicious and useful approach; James D. Rice, *Nature and History in the Potomac Country: From Hunter-Gatherers to the Age of Jefferson* (Baltimore: Johns Hopkins University Press, 2009), 151.

26. Hofstadter, "Paranoid Style," 30–31.

27. Lancaster County Order Books, 1666–1680, p. 359, LVA; Berry and Moryson, "Narrative of the . . . Late Rebellion," *Wiseman's Book,* 156; "Declaration signed by Thomas Swann and 69 others," 3 August 1676, TNA CO 1/37/42, fols. 130r–130v.

28. "Declaration," TNA 1/37/42, fol. 131r; [Cotton], "Bacon's and Ingram's Rebellion," 62; "Personall grievances of divers Inhabitants," *Wiseman's Book,* 285; *PSWB,* 571; Herbert R. Paschal, ed. "George Bancroft's 'Lost Notes' on the General Court Records of Seventeenth-Century Virginia," *VMHB* 91, no. 3 (1983): 355, 358–359.

29. Nathaniel Bacon, "Mr. Bacon's Acct of Their Troubles in Virginia by ye Indians, June ye 18th, 1676," *WMQ* 9, no. 1 (1900): 9; "Bacon's Manifesto," 57; Kristalyn Marie Shefveland, *Anglo-Native Virginia: Trade, Conversion, and Indian Slavery in the Old Dominion, 1646–1722* (Athens: University of Georgia Press, 2016), 54; "Proclamation by Nathaniel Bacon, addressed to Colonel John Washington and the rest of the Commissioners for Westmorland county," 4 August 1676, TNA CO 1/37/43, fol. 133r; *PSWB,* 542; Webb, *1676,* 50–53, 68–69; Paschal, "George Bancroft's 'Lost Notes,'" 357–358. Bacon's opposition to Drummond's republicanism was evident in letters to his father, writing "noe hopes of Redresse is to be had by any other meanes then an Appeale to his Sacred Majestie." TNA CO 5/1371, p. 241.

30. Nicholas Spencer to [Henry Coventry], 6 August 1676, Coventry Papers, vol. 77, fol. 170r; [Sherwood], "Virginias Deploured Condition," 175; Ludwell, "Philip Ludwell's Account," 186. On officially promulgated conspiracy theories, see Kathryn S. Olmsted, *Real Enemies: Conspiracy Theories and American Democracy, World War I to 9/11* (New York: Oxford University Press, 2009).

31. [Cotton], "Bacon's and Ingram's Rebellion," 66.

32. Berkeley's commission to Thomas Larramore, August 30 1676, Huntington Mss., HM 21810, Huntington; [Sherwood], "Virginias Deploured Condition," 174–175;

PSWB, 542; Berry and Moryson, "Narrative of the . . . Late Rebellion," *Wiseman's Book, 158.*

33. David Brion Davis, "Some Themes of Counter-Subversion: An Analysis of Anti-Masonic, Anti-Catholic, and Anti-Mormon Literature," *Mississippi Valley Historical Review* 47, no. 2 (1960): 205–224; Robert Alan Goldberg, *Enemies Within: The Culture of Conspiracy in Modern America* (New Haven, CT: Yale University Press, 2001), 150–188; Hofstadter, "Paranoid Style," 31–33; Donald L. Horowitz, *The Deadly Ethnic Riot* (Berkeley: University of California Press, 2001), 74–88, 194–223.

34. Richard S. Dunn, *Sugar and Slaves: The Rise of the Planter Class in the English West Indies, 1624–1713* (1972; repr. ed., Chapel Hill: University of North Carolina Press, 2000), 256–262, 312; Jonathan Atkins to Sir Joseph Williamson, 3 October 1675, TNA CO 1/35/29, fol. 231r; [Anonymous], *A Continuation of the State of New-England . . . Together with an Account of the Intended Rebellion of the Negroes in the Barbadoes* (London, 1676), 19; [Anonymous], *Great Newes from the Barbadoes, or, A True and Faithful Account of the Grand Conspiracy of the Negroes against the English . . .* (London, 1676); Governor Lord Vaughan to Sir Robert Southwell, 20 February 1676, TNA CO 1/36/26, fol. 51r; Michael Craton, *Testing the Chains: Resistance to Slavery in the British West Indies* (Ithaca, NY: Cornell University Press, 1982), 61–80; Jerome S. Handler, "Slave Revolts and Conspiracies in Seventeenth-Century Barbados," *New West Indian Guide/Nieuwe West-Indische Gids* 56, no. 1/2 (1982): 5–42; Barbara Klamon Kopytoff, "The Early Political Development of Jamaican Maroon Societies," *WMQ* 35, no. 2 (1978): 287–307; [Cotton], "Bacon's and Ingram's Rebellion," 65; Andrew Marvell to Sir Henry Thompson, 14 November 1676, Huntington Mss., HM 21813, Huntington; "letter from Virginia," George Chalmers Collection, vol. 19: Virginia, 1606–1683 [p. 179], NYPL; *JHBV*, 2:74; "Bacon's Manifesto," 57.

35. Berry and Moryson, "Narrative of the . . . Late Rebellion," *Wiseman's Book, 159.* On Indigenous understandings of eliminationist intentions, see Jeffrey Ostler, "'To Extirpate the Indians': An Indigenous Consciousness of Genocide in the Ohio Valley and Lower Great Lakes, 1750s–1810," *WMQ* 72, no. 4 (2015): 587–622.

36. Berry and Moryson, "Narrative of the . . . Late Rebellion," *Wiseman's Book, 158–161*; John Berry and Francis Moryson, "A True Narrative of the Rise, Progresse, and Cessation of the Late Rebellion in Virginia," TNA CO 5/1371, p. 393.

37. Berry and Moryson, "Narrative of the . . . Late Rebellion," *Wiseman's Book, 160–163*; Berkeley's orders to Captain Thomas Larrimore, 9 December 1676, Huntington Mss., HM 21812, Huntington; Berry and Moryson, "True Narrative," TNA CO 5/1371, p. 393; Captain William Cookeson and Captain Edward Ahearne, 7 September 1676, Coventry Papers, vol. 77, fol. 216r; Anne Cotton, "An Account of Our Late Troubles in Virginia," in *Tracts and Other Papers Relating Principally to the Origin, Settlement, and Progress of the Colonies in North America: From the Discovery of the Country to the Year 1776*, comp. Peter Force (4 vols.; Washington, DC, 1836–1846), vol. 1, doc. 9, p. 8; Kathleen M. Brown, *Good Wives, Nasty Wenches, and Anxious Patriarchs: Gender, Race, and Power in Colonial Virginia* (Chapel Hill: University of North Carolina Press, 1996), 165–166.

38. *PSWB*, 572; Berry and Moryson, "Narrative of the . . . Late Rebellion," *Wiseman's Book, 171, 175*; [Cotton], "Bacon's and Ingram's Rebellion," 73; Berry and Moryson, "True Narrative," TNA CO 5/1371, p. 393; Rice, *Tales from a Revolution*, 90–117, 232n4; Washburn, *Governor and the Rebel*, 77–91; Webb, *1676*, 87–124.

39. Thomas Grantham to Henry Coventry, n.d., Coventry Papers, vol. 77, fols. 301r–301v; Petition of Edward Lloyd [Mulatto] of James City County, Planter, to His

Majesty's Commissioners for Virginia, 11 April 1677, TNA CO 1/40/24, fols. 26r, 27r. I have found only one other source that points toward Black histories during the rebellion: the alleged rape of an English girl named Bridgett Ellis by George, a "Negro servant," which went uninvestigated for over a year because county justices were incapacitated by "the unquietness of the times." Westmoreland County Deeds, Wills, Patents, etc., 1675–1677, fols. 307v–309v, LVA. Such fragments provide little additional detail on the relationship between George and Bridgett, or the political allegiances of Lloyd and his unnamed wife. They suggest, perhaps, the process of patriarchal authority breaking down at the level of the household, but this hypothesis would require further research to confirm. Historians have often assumed that the most salient context for Black histories during Bacon's Rebellion was an instinctive fear among planters of a biracial alliance between white servants and black slaves; see for example Theodore W. Allen, *The Invention of the White Race*, 2 vols. (New York: Verso, 1994–1997); T. H. Breen, "A Changing Labor Force and Race Relations in Virginia 1660–1710," *Journal of Social History* 7, no. 1 (1973): 6–9; Anthony S. Parent Jr., *Foul Means: The Formation of a Slave Society in Virginia, 1660–1740* (Chapel Hill: University of North Carolina Press, 2003), 141–147. However, evidence of these fears dates from after Bacon's Rebellion, and even then planter fears of servile labor invariably focus on white servants as the real danger.

40. Depositions of William Armiger and John Deery, 26 July 1677, Westmoreland County Deeds, Wills, Patents, etc., 1665–1677, fols. 324v–325r, LVA; [Cotton], "Bacon's and Ingram's Rebellion," 94–95. J. Kēhaulani Kauanui trenchantly observes that the cause uniting black and white Volunteers was Indigenous genocide; J. Kēhaulani Kauanui, "Tracing Historical Specificity: Race and the Colonial Politics of (In)Capacity," *American Quarterly* 69, no. 2 (2017): 261. On freedom struggles and the fraught structure of Black-Native relationships in a settler colonial society, see Yael Ben-Zvi, *Native Land Talk: Indigenous and Arrivant Rights Theories* (Hanover, NH: Dartmouth College Press, 2018); Alaina E. Roberts, *I've Been Here All the While: Black Freedom on Native Land* (Philadelphia: University of Pennsylvania Press, 2021).

41. *Archives of Maryland*, 5:134, 137, 147.

42. Letter from [?] to [Governor Andros], n.d., All Souls Mss. 257, f. 169r, Codrington Library; Letter to Governors of New England, 3 November 1676, All Souls Mss. 253, fol. 94r, Codrington Library; Kings Letter to Lord Baltimore about Nath[aniel] Bacon, 30 September 1676, TNA CO 5/1355, p. 110; To New Engl[an]d not to assist Bacon, 3 November 1676, TNA CO 5/1355, pp. 115–116; Admiralty Journal, 1 October 1676, TNA ADM 3/276 Part I, p. 119; Orders and Warrants, 30 September 1676, TNA ADM 1/1738, p. 39; Letters and Orders, 2 October 1676, TNA ADM 2/1747, p. 500; *Archives of Maryland*, 15:121; "A List of the Names of those worthy persons whose Services and Sufferings by the Late Rebell Nathaniell Bacon Junior and his Party," *Wiseman's Book*, 279; Thomas Ludwell to [Henry Coventry], 13 October 1676, Coventry Papers, vol. 77, fol. 254r.

43. *Archives of Maryland*, 15:102, 124, 17:216; Ludwell to [Coventry], Coventry Papers, vol. 77, fol. 254r; Raphael Semmes, *Captains and Mariners of Early Maryland* (Baltimore: Johns Hopkins University Press, 1937), 437–441; Rebecca Seib and Helen C. Rountree, *Indians of Southern Maryland* (Baltimore: Maryland Historical Society, 2014), 80–81; Kelly L. Watson, "Mary Kittamaquund Brent, 'The Pocahontas of Maryland': Sex, Marriage, and Diplomacy in the Seventeenth-Century Chesapeake," *EAS* 19, no. 1 (2021): 24–63.

44. Warren M. Billings, "Sir William Berkeley and the Carolina Proprietary," *NCHR* 72, no. 3 (1995): 329–342; Lindley S. Butler, "The Governors of Albemarle County:

1663–1689," *NCHR* 46, no. 3 (1969): 282–285; *PSWB*, 403; *CRNC*, 1st ser., 1:235, 259, 269, 290, 317; Jacquelyn H. Wolf, "The Proud and the Poor: The Social Organization of Leadership in Proprietary North Carolina, 1663–1729" (PhD diss., University of Pennsylvania, 1977), 72–75; Noeleen McIlvenna, *A Very Mutinous People: The Struggle for North Carolina, 1660–1713* (Chapel Hill: University of North Carolina Press, 2009), 49–52.

45. *PSWB*, 567; Rice, *Tales from a Revolution*, 112–113; Lars C. Adams, "'Sundry Murders and Depredations': A Closer Look at the Chowan River War, 1676–1677," *NCHR* 90, no. 2 (2013): 162–164; *CRNC*, 1st ser., 1:292. Goode's recall of this conversation with Nathaniel Bacon is suspect because it provided Berkeley with exactly the ammunition he needed to condemn Bacon in exchange for his own pardon; Rice, *Tales from a Revolution*, 120–121. Nevertheless, the sentiments attributed to Bacon were no doubt prevalent among some Volunteer factions, particularly those aligned with Sarah Drummond and her husband William.

46. *CRNC*, 1st ser., 1:226, 278; Adams, "'Sundry Murders,'" 163–164.

47. *CRNC*, 1st ser., 1:259, 278, 292, 294–295; Adams, "'Sundry Murders,'" 164–165; Butler, "Governors of Albemarle," 291; Wolf, "Proud and the Poor," 67–68.

48. The following discussion does not include Andros's efforts to manage spillover violence from King Philip's War across Long Island Sound and the Hudson River, which was the most direct threat to New York's security and occupied most of his energies between 1676 and 1677. On Andros's role in that crisis, see Francis Jennings, *The Invasion of America: Indians, Colonialism, and the Cant of Conquest* (Chapel Hill: University of North Carolina Press, 1975), 313–326; Michael Leroy Oberg, *Dominion and Civility: English Imperialism and Native America, 1585–1685* (Ithaca, NY: Cornell University Press, 1999), 160–170; Webb, *1676*, 363–374.

49. *Andros Papers*, 1:423, 436; *DRCHSNY*, 3:225; John M. Murrin, "English Rights as Ethnic Aggression: The English Conquest, the Charter of Liberties of 1683, and Leisler's Rebellion in New York," in *Authority and Resistance in Early New York*, ed. William Pencak and Conrad Edick Wright (New York: New-York Historical Society, 1988), 66–67; *MCARS*, 2:177; Donna Merwick, "Becoming English: Anglo-Dutch Conflict in the 1670s in Albany, New York," *NYH* 62, no. 4 (1981): 389–414; Indian deeds and grants to John Fenwick, 1675–1676, MG 3: West Jersey, 1648–1829, docs. 3–8, NJHS; *DRCHSNJ*, 1:187; Brendan McConville, *These Daring Disturbers of the Public Peace: The Struggle for Property and Power in Early New Jersey* (Ithaca, NY: Cornell University Press, 1999), 12–20.

50. *Andros Papers*, 1:424, 436; *MCARS*, 1:177, 181; *DRCHSNJ*, 1:187–92; *DRCHSNY*, 12:559, 568–569; *NYHM (Delaware English)*, 132–136; *RCNCD*, 1:37–39.

51. *Archives of Maryland*, 15:122–123; *NYHM (Delaware English)*, 162; Minute of the New Castle Court, 25 May 1678, Milligan Papers, DHS. Francis Jennings speculates that Cantwell colluded with Marylanders to profit by orchestrating the conquest of Susquehannock territory; Jennings, "Glory, Death, and Transfiguration," 37–38. However, Jacob's efforts in organizing these talks, as well as the Maryland Council's continued attempts to arrange peace talks in November–December 1676, suggest a more amicable plan; *Archives of Maryland*, 7:387.

52. *NYHM (Delaware English)*, 112, 119–121, 123; *DRCHSNY*, 12:553; *NYHM (General Entries)*, 2:130–131; *RCNCD*, 1:3–4; *RCUP*, 39–43; *Pennsylvania Archives*, 2nd ser., 5:719–720.

53. *NYHM (General Entries)*, 2:131–132.

54. Stanwood, *Empire Reformed*, 70–81, 96–106.

55. Edward Earl of Clarendon, *The History of the Rebellion and Civil Wars in England* (8 vols.; new ed., Oxford: Clarendon Press, 1826), 3:83; Thomas H. Robinson,

"Lord Clarendon's Conspiracy Theory," *Albion* 13, no. 2 (1981): 96–116; "An Act of Free and Generall Pardon Indempnity and Oblivion," in *Statutes of the Realm,* 5:226.

56. "Letter to the Grand Assembly," *Wiseman's Book,* 88; Washburn, *Governor and the Rebel,* 92–113.

57. Berry and Moryson, "Narrative of the . . . Late Rebellion," *Wiseman's Book,* 142, 172. The title "True Narrative" appears in the copy of the report held in the National Archives of the UK; TNA CO 5/1371, p. 369. The copy in the Pepys Library has the variant title that lacks the telling claim to truth: "Narrative of the Rise . . . ," Samuel Wiseman's Book of Record, Mss. 2582, Pepys Library, Magdalene College, Cambridge.

58. *PSWB,* 530; Berry and Moryson, "Narrative of the . . . Late Rebellion," *Wiseman's Book,* 146–147, 156, 164.

59. Berry and Moryson, "Narrative of the . . . Late Rebellion," *Wiseman's Book,* 147, 156. On feminizing rebellion, see Brown, *Good Wives,* 170–172.

60. *PSWB,* 569; Philip Ludwell to [Alexander Culpeper?], 12 June 1676, Coventry Papers, vol. 77, fol. 119r.

5. Covenants

1. *Archives of Maryland,* 5:152. Because of the many errors in the transcript of the Complaint printed in the *Archives of Maryland,* I have made changes in this chapter and Chapter 4 based on the original manuscript; TNA CO 1/36/78. James Rice contends that the "second part" referred to a "shift in strategy" among "Bacon's followers" to continue armed struggle against their governments; James D. Rice, *Tales from a Revolution: Bacon's Rebellion and the Transformation of Early America* (New York: Oxford University Press, 2012), 137, 139.

2. *Archives of Maryland,* 5:134, 148.

3. On Baltimore in England, see Antoinette Sutto, *Loyal Protestants and Dangerous Papists: Maryland and the Politics of Religion in the English Atlantic, 1630–1690* (Charlottesville: University of Virginia Press, 2015), 119–125.

4. *NYHM (Delaware English),* 112; *Archives of Maryland,* 5:247, 15:120, 122.

5. *Archives of Maryland,* 5:152, 7:387; *RCNCD,* 1:66; George P. Donehoo, *Indian Villages and Place Names in Pennsylvania* (Baltimore: Gateway, 1928), 185–186. The "bakeside" route probably refers to the Minquas Path between Gandastogue and the mouth of the Schuylkill River; Paul A. W. Wallace, "Historic Indian Paths of Pennsylvania," *PMHB* 76, no. 4 (1952): 433.

6. *RCUP,* 49, 52–53; *Archives of Maryland,* 5:247. I have corrected errors in the printed Upland minutes based on the manuscript original in Logan Family Papers (Collection 379), series 1b, box 48, p. 16, HSP.

7. *Archives of Maryland,* 5:247; *RCUP,* 49.

8. *Archives of Maryland,* 5:247.

9. *Andros Papers,* 2:183; *Archives of Maryland,* 5:153.

10. Hening, *Statutes,* 2:395; "Notes and Other Documents Chronicling the Activities and Concerns of the Commissioners," *Wiseman's Book,* 193; Kathleen M. Brown, *Good Wives, Nasty Wenches, and Anxious Patriarchs: Gender, Race, and Power in Colonial Virginia* (Chapel Hill: University of North Carolina Press, 1996), 167–169; Peter Thompson, "The Thief, the Householder, and the Commons: Languages of Class in Seventeenth-Century Virginia," *WMQ* 63, no. 2 (2006): 253–280; John Berry and Francis Moryson, "A true and faithfull account in what condition wee

found your Majesties Colllony of Virginia," *Wiseman's Book,* 173; "To the Governor from Sir John Berry and Col. Moryson," *Wiseman's Book,* 73; "Memorandum of the names of the officers and soldiers going on board the men-of-war to Virginia," October 1676, TNA CO 1/38/13–14, fols. 27r–29r; "An Account of the draught of soldiers for the ships for Virginia," October 1676, TNA CO 1/37/65, fol. 227r; Francis Moryson's answers to questions posed by the King and Council, 6 October 1676, Rawlinson A Mss. 185, fol. 256, Bodleian Library; James Scott, Duke of Monmouth, to Thomas Wyndham, 8 February 1675, TNA WO 26/3, p. 106; John Childs, *The Army of Charles II* (London: Routledge, 1976), 158–161; *Archives of Maryland,* 5:154; Edmund S. Morgan, *American Slavery, American Freedom: The Ordeal of Colonial Virginia* (1975; repr. ed., New York: W. W. Norton, 2003), 271–274; Rice, *Tales from a Revolution,* 126–127. In contrast to the vitriol directed at rebellious servants, victorious loyalists inflicted no punishments on enslaved black people and made no comment on their participation in the rebellion.

11. *Archives of Maryland,* 5:153; "Royal Company of Negroes at Jamaica," 12 July 1676, TNA CO 1/37/31, fol. 108v; "Declaration to his Majesties Loving Subjects," *Wiseman's Book,* 68–70; Winfred T. Root, "The Lords of Trade and Plantations, 1675–1696," *AHR* 23, no. 1 (1917): 20–41; Warren M. Billings, *Sir William Berkeley and the Forging of Colonial Virginia* (Baton Rouge: Louisiana State University Press, 2004), 248–266; Brent Tarter, "Bacon's Rebellion, the Grievances of the People, and the Political Culture of Seventeenth-Century Virginia," *VMHB* 119, no. 1 (2011): 2–41; Wilcomb E. Washburn, *The Governor and the Rebel: A History of Bacon's Rebellion in Virginia* (Chapel Hill: University of North Carolina Press, 1957), 92–138; Stephen Saunders Webb, *1676: The End of American Independence* (New York: Alfred A. Knopf, 1984). On the early modern conception of revolution as "properly a rolling back, or whirling round," as in the return of celestial objects to their original place after a given period of time—a particularly apt description of the Civil Wars culminating in the Restoration—see Edward Phillips, *The New World of English Words, or, a General Dictionary* (London, 1658), s.v. "Revolution"; Thomas Hobbes, *Behemoth, or, The Long Parliament,* ed. Ferdinand Tönnies (Chicago: University of Chicago Press, 1990), 204. Edmund Morgan aptly called the county grievances "a bill of particulars of the ways in which the few were fleecing the many," covering issues ranging from tax relief, tobacco subsidies, official corruption, voting rights, and more; Morgan, *American Slavery,* 277. Few historians have explored Native peoples as one of the grievances' central issues but for an exception see Brown, *Good Wives,* 169–170. Remarkably, not one county—even in the heavily loyalist areas that charged Volunteers with an extensive catalog of sins—mentioned the black men who joined the rebellion or expressed concern about their cooperation with English laborers.

12. "Letter from the Commissioners to Mr. Secretary Coventry," *Wiseman's Book,* 101; Charles Cogan to Sir Joseph Williamson, 11 April 1677, TNA SP 29/393, fol. 25r; Hening, *Statutes,* 2:397; *PSWB,* 606; "Commissioners to Mr. Watkins," *Wiseman's Book,* 118; *JHBV,* 2:77, 105.

13. "Grievances of the inhabitants of Henrico County," March 1677, TNA CO 1/39/90, fol. 238r; "The first grievances presented by the inhabitants of Nancymond County to His Majesty's Commissioners for Virginia," March 1677, TNA CO 1/39/96, fol. 246v; *JHBV,* 2:102, 107–108, 110.

14. *JHBV,* 2:107; "Nathaniel Bacon Esq'r, his manifesto concerning the present troubles in Virginia," in "Proclamations of Nathaniel Bacon," *VMHB* 1, no. 1 (1893): 57–58; Hening, *Statutes,* 1:323–325. On Algonquian and Susquehannock practices

of tattooing and body painting, see Helen C. Rountree, *The Powhatan Indians of Virginia: Their Traditional Culture* (Norman: University of Oklahoma Press, 1989), 73–78; C. A. Weslager, "Susquehannock Indian Religion from an Old Document," *Journal of the Washington Academy of Sciences* 36, no. 9 (1946): 303; Margaret Holmes Williamson, *Powhatan Lords of Life and Death: Command and Consent in Seventeenth-Century Virginia* (Lincoln: University of Nebraska Press, 2003), 247–254.

15. "Instructions for Our Trusty and Welbeloved Herbert Jeffreys Esqr., Sir John Berry Knight, and Francis Morison, Esqr.," *Wiseman's Book,* 37; "By His Majesties' Commissioners for the Affaires of Virginia," *Wiseman's Book,* 93; "Notes and Other Documents," *Wiseman's Book,* 192; "Henrico County Grievances and Answers," *Wiseman's Book,* 241–242; Webb, *1676,* 199–220.

16. "Interlocutory Heads of such matters, in Conference with Sir William Berkeley . . . ," *Wiseman's Book,* 58; "A Letter from the Commissioners to His Majesties Principal Secretaries of State," *Wiseman's Book,* 60; "A Letter to the Grand Assembly," *Wiseman's Book,* 89; Dylan Ruediger, "'Neither Utterly to Reject Them, Nor Yet to Drawe Them to Come in': Tributary Subordination and Settler Colonialism in Virginia," *EAS* 18, no. 1 (2020): 27–28. Stephen Saunders Webb argues that the commissioners imposed "garrison government," a military dictatorship directed from Whitehall, which underestimates the commissioners' interest in coopting colonists; Webb, *1676.*

17. "Letter to the Grand Assembly," *Wiseman's Book,* 89–90; "Nancymond County Grievances First Presented Us and Answers," *Wiseman's Book,* 250. The counties that connected war taxes to rebellion included Charles City, Gloucester, Isle of Wight, James City, Lancaster, Lower Norfolk, Nansemond, Rappahannock, Stafford, and Surry; "Charles City County Grievances 1676," *VMHB* 3, no. 2 (1895): 135–136; *JHBV,* 2:101–113; Warren M. Billings, ed., *The Old Dominion in the Seventeenth Century: A Documentary History of Virginia, 1606–1700* (1975; rev. ed., Chapel Hill: University of North Carolina Press, 1997), 346–349; TNA CO 1/39/64, 96.

18. "Letter to the Grand Assembly," *Wiseman's Book,* 89–90.

19. *JHBV,* 2:68, 69, 70, 88–89; Henrico County Records: Deeds and Wills, 1677–1692, p. 33, LVA; Hening, *Statutes,* 2:410–412.

20. Berry and Moryson, "True and faithfull account," *Wiseman's Book,* 175. I have made minor corrections to the transcription based on one of the manuscript copies of the commissioners' report; TNA CO 5/1371, p. 425.

21. Berry and Moryson, "Narrative of the . . . Late Rebellion," *Wiseman's Book,* 148; *New World of English Words,* s.v. "Colours"; Henrico Grievances, TNA CO 1/39/90, fol. 238r; Joyce E. Chaplin, "Race," in *The British Atlantic World, 1500–1800,* ed. David Armitage and Michael J. Braddick (2002; 2nd ed., New York: Palgrave Macmillan, 2009), 173–191. On Native peoples and race, see Kathleen M. Brown, "Native Americans and Early Modern Concepts of Race," in *Empire and Others: British Encounters with Indigenous Peoples, 1600–1850,* ed. Martin Daunton and Rick Halpern (Philadelphia: University of Pennsylvania Press, 1999), 79–100 (esp. 97–98); Joshua Piker, "Indians and Race in Early America," *History Compass* 3 (2005): 1–17. On racial thinking, see Irene Silverblatt, *Modern Inquisitions: Peru and the Colonial Origins of the Civilized World* (Durham, NC: Duke University Press, 2004); Jonathon Glassman, *War of Words, War of Stones: Racial Thought and Violence in Colonial Zanzibar* (Bloomington: Indiana University Press, 2011).

22. *JHBV,* 2:89–90; Brown, *Good Wives,* 170–172; Berry and Moryson, "True Narrative," TNA CO 5/1371, p. 393; "Account of Mr. James Crewes," TNA CO 5/1371, pp. 447–448; Samuel Johnson, *A Dictionary of the English Language* . . . , vol. 1 (London, 1755), s.v. "Entertain," def. 4. On Indigenous petitioning, see Craig Yirush, "'Chief Princes and Owners of All': Native American Appeals to the Crown in the Early-Modern British Atlantic," in *Native Claims: Indigenous Law against Empire, 1500–1920,* ed. Saliha Belmessous (New York: Oxford University Press, 2011), 129–151.

23. Robert Beverley, *The History and Present State of Virginia,* ed. Susan Scott Parrish (Chapel Hill: University of North Carolina Press, 2013), 51–52; Francis Moryson to [Coventry?], 6 September 1676, Coventry Papers, vol. 77, fol. 205v; Cockacoeske to Francis Moryson, 29 June 1678, TNA CO 1/42/101, fol. 276r; Martha W. McCartney, "Cockacoeske, Queen of Pamunkey: Diplomat and Suzeraine," in *Powhatan's Mantle: Indians in the Colonial Southeast* (1989; rev. ed., Lincoln: University of Nebraska Press, 2006), 248–249, 254–257.

24. Nicholas Spencer to Charles Lord Baltimore, 24 May 1677, TNA CO 1/40/89, fol. 188r; Commissioners to Coventry, *Wiseman's Book,* 99, 101; "A Perticular Account how wee your Majesties Commissioners for the affaires of Virginia have observed and complied with the Severall Articles of our Instructions," *Wiseman's Book,* 130; McCartney, "Cockacoeske," 254–255; *PSWB,* 609–61; "Declaration of Col. Jeffreys," in "Virginia in 1677 (Continued)," *VMHB* 22, no. 1 (1914): 44–47; Billings, *Sir William Berkeley,* 266. On Indigenous influence over such negotiations, see Saliha Belmessous, "Introduction: The Problem of Indigenous Claim Making in Colonial History," in *Native Claims,* 3–18.

25. Cockacoeske to Moryson, TNA CO 1/42/101, fol. 276r; "Names and Characters of and Presents to the Indians," TNA CO 5/1371, p. 267–268; Rountree, *Powhatan Indians,* 79–80. Inquiries by the Lords of Trade and Plantations revealed that the Weyanoke "young boy," Queen Catherine's brother, came under the charge of Thomas Lord Culpeper, a future governor of Virginia, and stayed at his estate in Kent. It is likely that he remained enslaved but it is impossible to be certain because he thereafter disappears from the archives; Journal of Trade and Plantations, 6 December 1679, TNA CO 391/2, p. 179.

26. Governor Herbert Jeffreys to Secretary Sir Joseph Williamson, 11 June 1677, TNA CO 1/40/104, fol. 225r; Hening, *Statutes,* 2:49; "A Form of Prayer with Thanksgiving to be used yearly upon the XXIX day of May; Being the day of His Majesties Birth, and happy Return to His Kingdoms," *Book of Common Prayer* (1662), [unpaginated]; "The Commissioners for Virginia to Mr. Watkins," 4 May 1677, TNA CO 1/40/66, fols. 130v–131r.

27. "Treaty of Middle Plantation," *Wiseman's Book,* 135–136; "Order for Printing the Articles of Peace w[i]th the Indian Princes in Virginia" TNA PC 2/66, pp. 138–139; *Articles of Peace Between the Most Serene and Mighty Prince Charles II . . . And Several Indian Kings and Queens . . .* (London, 1677), TNA CO 1/40/96, fol. 204r.

28. "Treaty," *Wiseman's Book,* 135–136, 138.

29. "Treaty," *Wiseman's Book,* 137–138; "A List of the Names of those worthy persons whose Services and Sufferings by the Late Rebell Nathaniell Bacon Junior and his Party," *Wiseman's Book,* 286. On composite sovereignty in European empires, see Lauren Benton, *A Search for Sovereignty: Law and Geography in European Empires, 1400–1900* (Cambridge: Cambridge University Press, 2010).

30. *London Gazette,* 30 July to 2 August 1677, no. 1221, p. 1; Berry and Moryson, "True and faithfull account," *Wiseman's Book,* 176; *Articles of Peace,* TNA CO

1/40/96, fols. 212r–212v; Herbert Jeffreys to Henry Coventry, 30 December 1677, Coventry Papers, vol. 78, fol. 164r; "Articles of Peace between the Most Mighty Prince and our Dread Soveraigne Lord Charles III . . . and the severall Indian Kings and Queens . . . ," Virginia Company of London and the Colony, Miscellaneous Papers, 1606–1692, Thomas Jefferson Papers, series 8, vol. 13, pp. 226–233, LoC. The Treaty of Middle Plantation has usually been interpreted as a waypoint on the Virginia Indians' path to declension—James Rice calls it "a major step in the colony's conquest of the nations within"—but the results over time should be distinguished from the intent of its design, especially given Cockacoeske's influence over its architecture; James D. Rice, "Bacon's Rebellion in Indian Country," *JAH* 101, no. 3 (2014): 743. According to Bradley Dixon, the treaty is better understood as establishing an English equivalent to the Spanish *republica de indios,* a separate system of rule for Indigenous subjects; Bradley Dixon, " 'Darling Indians' and 'Natural Lords': Virginia's Tributary Regime and Florida's Republic of Indians in the Seventeenth Century," in *Justice in a New World: Negotiating Legal Intelligibility in British, Iberian, and Indigenous America,* ed. Brian P. Owensby and Richard J. Ross (New York: New York University Press, 2018), 183–212.

31. Thomas Ludwell to Sir Joseph Williamson, 28 June 1677, Lee Family Papers, Mss1 L51, folder 8, VHS; McCartney, "Cockacoeske," 255–256; Buck Woodard and Danielle Moretti-Langholtz, " 'They will not admitt of any werowance from him to governe over them': The Chickahominy in Context: A Reassessment of Political Configurations," *Journal of Middle Atlantic Archaeology* 25 (2009): 85–96.

32. *JHBV,* 2:74–75; *CRNC,* 1st ser., 1:226; "Isle of Wight County: Papers Related to Bacon's Rebellion," *WMQ* 4, no. 2 (1895): 114–115.

33. *CRNC,* 1st ser., 1:246, 272, 292; Secretary of State Records, Council Minutes, Wills and Inventories, 1677–1701, p. 5, NCSA.

34. *CRNC,* 1st ser., 1:229, 232–233, 278, 296; Lars C. Adams, " 'Sundry Murders and Depredations': A Closer Look at the Chowan River War, 1676–1677," *NCHR* 90, no. 2 (2013): 166.

35. *CRNC,* 1st ser., 1:658; Adams, "Sundry Murders," 166–169.

36. *CRNC,* 1st ser., 1:249. The connection between the fiscal strain of Anglo-Indian war and popular rebellion is based on a narrative by Timothy Biggs once held by NYPL, with a copy in NCSA; Timothy Biggs, "A Narrative of the Transactions past In the Conty of Albemarle In Carolina Sence Mr. Tho. Miller his Arrivall there . . . ," [January, 1678], Arents Tobacco Collection, NYPL. The narrative now seems to be missing or lost from both archives. Fortunately, Mattie Erma Parker published a detailed description of Biggs's narrative, and this paragraph draws on her work; Mattie Erma E. Parker, "Legal Aspects of 'Culpeper's Rebellion,' " *NCHR* 45, no. 2 (1968): 122–123.

37. *CRNC,* 1st ser., 1:281, 297–299; Noeleen McIlvenna, *A Very Mutinous People: The Struggle for North Carolina, 1660–1713* (Chapel Hill: University of North Carolina Press, 2009), 54–64; Parker, "Legal Aspects," 123–124.

38. *CRNC,* 1st ser., 1:658; "Articles of Peace," Jefferson Papers, series 8, vol. 13, pp. 226–233, LoC; Adams, "Sundry Murders," 169–171; Shannon Lee Dawdy, "The Meherrin's Secret History of the Dividing Line," *NCHR* 72, no. 4 (1995): 394–396. On the Chowanokes' struggles to shape the system of their subjection, see Bradley J. Dixon, " 'His one Netev ples': The Chowans and the Politics of Native Petitions in the Colonial South," *WMQ* 76, no. 1 (2019): 41–74.

39. Daniel K. Richter, *The Ordeal of the Longhouse: The Peoples of the Iroquois League in the Era of European Colonization* (Chapel Hill: University of North Carolina Press, 1992), 133–149; Holly A. Rine, "Mohawk Reinvention of the Fort Orange

and Albany Courthouses, 1652–77," *Journal of Early American History* 2, no. 1 (2012): 3–31.

40. Jon Parmenter, *The Edge of the Woods: Iroquoia, 1534–1701* (East Lansing: Michigan State University Press, 2010), 150–156, 291; *NYHM (General Entries)*, 2:132; *Archives of Maryland*, 5:153, 244–245.

41. *Archives of Maryland*, 5:244–247, 250–251; *Andros Papers*, 2:53–54; *DRCHSNY*, 12:572, 13:503; Francis Jennings, "Indians and Frontiers in Seventeenth-Century Maryland," in *Early Maryland in a Wider World*, ed. David B. Quinn (Detroit, MI: Wayne State University Press, 1982), 234–235; Neal Salisbury, "Toward the Covenant Chain: Iroquois and Southern New England Algonquians, 1637–1684," in *Beyond the Covenant Chain: The Iroquois and Their Neighbors in Indian North America, 1600–1800*, ed. Daniel K. Richter and James H. Merrell (1987; University Park: Pennsylvania State University Press, 2003), 61–73.

42. *Archives of Maryland*, 5:247–248, 7:388.

43. *DRCHSNY*, 13:507–508; *Archives of Maryland*, 5:251–252; Lord Baltimore to William Blathwayt, 11 March 1682, TNA CO 1/48/43, fol. 169r; Francis Jennings, "Glory, Death, and Transfiguration: the Susquehannock Indians in the Seventeenth Century," *PAPS* 112, no. 1 (1968): 41–42.

44. "Propositions made to the Maques and Sinnequo Indians by Henry Coursey Esqr," 20 July 1677, TNA CO 1/40/56 V, fol. 81r; *Archives of Maryland*, 2:246, 248. On Indigenous treaty protocols, see Daniel K. Richter, *Facing East from Indian Country: A Native History of Early America* (Cambridge, MA: Harvard University Press, 2003), 129–149. On Haudenosaunee diplomacy, see Mary A. Druke, "Linking Arms: The Structure of Iroquois Intertribal Diplomacy," in *Beyond the Covenant Chain*, 29–40. Coursey's proposals and the responses of the Five Nations are easily accessible in *LIR*, 42–48. However, the Livingston transcripts of the 1677 Albany conference omit portions of the conference and contain punctuation and orthography that sometimes obscures the text's meaning. For clarity, in the remainder of this chapter I quote the manuscript copies in The National Archives of the United Kingdom.

45. Daniel K. Richter, "Garakonte [Daniel Garakontié]," in *Oxford Dictionary of National Biography*, ed. H. C. G. Matthew and Brian Harrison (60 vols.; Oxford: Oxford University Press, 2004), 21:392–393; "The Onnondages Answer," 21 July 1677, TNA CO 1/40/56 V, fol. 81v; Charles T. Gehring, ed. and trans., *Fort Orange Court Minutes, 1652–1660*, New Netherland Documents Series vol. 16, part 2 (Syracuse, NY: Syracuse University Press, 1990), 453; *Archives of Maryland*, 7:475; Francis Jennings, *The Ambiguous Iroquois Empire: The Covenant Chain Confederation of Indian Tribes with English Colonies from Its Beginnings to the Lancaster Treaty of 1744* (New York: W. W. Norton, 1984), 53–55; Richard L. Haan, "Covenant and Consensus: Iroquois and English, 1676–1760," in *Beyond the Covenant Chain*, 41–46.

46. "The Onneydes Answer," 21 July 1677, TNA CO 1/40/56 V, fol. 82r; *LIR*, 51; Matthew L. Rhoades, *Long Knives and the Longhouse: Anglo-Iroquois Politics and the Expansion of Colonial Virginia* (Lanham, MD: Fairleigh Dickinson University Press, 2011), 32–33.

47. "The Maques Answer," 6 August 1677, TNA CO 1/40/56 V, fols. 82v–83r.

48. "The Sinnondowannes and Cajouges Answer," 22 August 1677, TNA CO 1/40/56 V, fols. 83r–83v.

49. *Archives of Maryland*, 5:247–248, 269; *Andros Papers*, 2:184; Jennings, *Ambiguous Iroquois Empire*, 159–162. The gendered language of Delawares as women changed over time; by the 1740s it had become more insult than honor. On the

meaning and transformation of this metaphor, see Gunlög Fur, *A Nation of Women: Gender and Colonial Encounters among the Delaware Indians* (Philadelphia: University of Pennsylvania Press, 2009), 160–198 ("made women," 163).

50. *Archives of Maryland*, 5:251, 7:475; Coursey's Propositions, TNA CO 1/40/56 V, fol. 81r; Jennings, *Ambiguous Iroquois Empire*, 162–164; Richard Hill, "Oral Memory of the Haudenosaunee: Views of the Two Row Wampum," *Northeast Indian Quarterly* 7, no. 1 (1990): 21–30; Jon Parmenter, "The Meaning of *Kaswentha* and the Two Row Wampum Best in Haudenosaunee (Iroquois) History: Can Indigenous Oral Tradition be Reconciled with the Documentary Record?" *Journal of Early American History* 3 (2013): 82–109.

6. Capturing Iroquoia

1. *Jesuit Relations*, 60:173; Henry R. Schoolcraft, *Notes on the Iroquois: or, Contributions to the Statistics, Aboriginal History, Antiquities, and General Ethnology of Western New-York* (New York, 1846), 29; *Archives of Maryland*, 15:239. Based on the work of Francis Jennings, the last historian to conduct an in-depth study of the Susquehannocks, scholars have generally taken contemporary sources at face value when they state that Susquehannocks "instigated" Haudenosaunee violence; Francis Jennings, *The Ambiguous Iroquois Empire: The Covenant Chain Confederation of Indian Tribes with English Colonies from Its Beginnings to the Lancaster Treaty of 1744* (New York: W. W. Norton, 1984), 168. However, scholarship on Haudenosaunee mourning war suggests that Susquehannocks should have become subordinated peoples rather than leaders with the influence to instigate much of anything; Daniel K. Richter, *The Ordeal of the Longhouse: The Peoples of the Iroquois League in the Era of European Colonization* (Chapel Hill: University of North Carolina Press, 1992), 31–38, 65–74; William A. Starna and Ralph Watkins, "Northern Iroquoian Slavery," *Ethnohistory* 38, no. 1 (1991): 34–57.

2. Richard W. Hill Sr., "Making a Final Resting Place Final: A History of the Repatriation Experience of the Haudenosaunee," in *Cross-Cultural Collaboration: Native Peoples and Archaeology in the Northeastern United States*, ed. Jordan E. Kerber (Lincoln: University of Nebraska Press, 2006), 10–11; Richter, *Ordeal of the Longhouse*, 50–74; James W. Bradley, "Change and Survival among the Onondaga Iroquois since 1500," in *Societies in Eclipse: Archaeology of the Eastern Woodlands Indians, A.D. 1400–1700*, ed. David S. Brose, C. Wesley Cowan, and Robert C. Mainfort Jr. (Washington, DC: Smithsonian Institution Press, 2001), 27–36; William Engelbrecht, "Iroquoian Ethnicity and Archaeological Taxa," in *Taming the Taxonomy: Toward a New Understanding of Great Lakes Archaeology*, ed. Roland F. Williamson and Christopher M. Watts (Toronto: Eastend, 1999), 51–59; Kurt A. Jordan, "Incorporation and Colonization: Postcolumbian Iroquois Satellite Communities and Processes of Indigenous Autonomy," *American Anthropologist* 115, no. 1 (2013): 29–43. On captives' connections to natal identities and influence on captor societies, see Catherine M. Cameron, *Captives: How Stolen People Changed the World* (Lincoln: University of Nebraska Press, 2016).

3. On the outsized influence of small but highly networked Indigenous groups, see Elizabeth Ellis, "Petite Nation with Powerful Networks: The Tunicas in the Eighteenth Century," *Louisiana History* 58, no. 2 (2017): 133–178.

4. *Archives of Maryland*, 15:175–176; *DRCHSNY*, 3:271.

5. *JHBV*, 2:115; "The Aggrievances of the Queen of Pamunkey and her son Captain John West," 5 June 1678, TNA CO 1/42/88, fols. 177r–177v; Sarah M. S. Pearsall,

Polygamy: An Early American History (New Haven, CT: Yale University Press, 2019), 108–110; David J. Silverman, *This Land Is Their Land: The Wampanoag Indians, Plymouth Colony, and the Troubled History of Thanksgiving* (New York: Bloomsbury, 2019), 205–252; Thomas Ludwell to Sir Joseph Williamson, 28 June 1678, Lee Family Papers, Mss L51, folder 8, VHS; Cockacoeske to Francis Moryson, 29 June 1678, TNA CO 1/42/101, fol. 276r; Thomas Ludwell to Henry Coventry, 30 January 1678, Coventry Papers, vol. 78, fol. 202v. Cockacoeske's challengers may have been partially motivated by a crisis of masculinity in the generation that grew up after 1646; Ethan A. Schmidt, "Cockacoeske, Weroansqua of the Pamunkeys, and Indian Resistance in Seventeenth-Century Virginia," *American Indian Quarterly* 36, no. 3 (2012): 288–317.

6. Ludwell to Williamson, Mss L51, folder 8, VHS; John Pocock to Joseph Williamson, 16 April 1678, TNA SP 29/403, fol. 70r; Thomas Ludwell to Henry Coventry, 15 March 1678, Coventry Papers, vol. 78, fol. 208r.

7. *Archives of Maryland,* 15:145–146, 162, 172–175, 190–191; Ludwell to Coventry, Coventry Papers, vol. 78, fol. 208r.

8. Ludwell to Coventry, Coventry Papers, vol. 78, fol. 208r; Herbert Jeffreys to Henry Coventry, 2 April 1678, Coventry Papers, vol. 78, fol. 216r; Jeffreys to Coventry, 7 August 1678, Coventry Papers, vol. 78, fol. 283r; Jeffreys to Coventry, 10 July 1678, Coventry Papers, vol. 78, fols. 273r–273v; *Archives of Maryland,* 15:175, 183; Ludwell to Coventry, 3 August 1678, Coventry Papers, vol. 78, fol. 281r. On the Manahoacs, see Raymond J. Demallie, "Tutelo and Neighboring Groups," in *Handbook of North American Indians,* vol. 14, *Southeast,* ed. Raymond D. Fogelson (Washington, DC: Smithsonian Institution, 2004), 286–300.

9. Ludwell to Coventry, Coventry Papers, vol. 78, fol. 208r; "Cornelius Dabney, Interpreter to the Queen of Pamunkey, to Colonel Francis Moryson," 29 June 1678, TNA CO 1/42/102, fol. 277r; Jeffreys to Coventry, Coventry Papers, vol. 78, fol. 273v; Ludwell to Coventry, Coventry Papers, vol. 78, fol. 281r; *Archives of Maryland,* 15:178–179, 184, 186.

10. Herbert Jeffreys to Henry Coventry, n.d., Coventry Papers, vol. 78, fol. 293r; Philip Ludwell to Henry Coventry, 16 June 1679, Coventry Papers, vol. 78, fol. 386r; Joseph Ewan and Nesta Ewan, eds., *John Banister and His Natural History of Virginia, 1678–1692* (Urbana: University of Illinois Press, 1970), 38–39; *MCGCCV,* 519; *DRCHSNY,* 3:277; *LIR,* 57.

11. Ludwell to Coventry, Coventry Papers, vol. 78, fol. 281r; Jeffreys to Coventry, Coventry Papers, vol. 78, fol. 283r; Mattie Erma Edwards Parker, ed., *North Carolina Higher-Court Records, 1670–1696* (Raleigh, NC: State Department of Archives and History, 1968), 417; *CRNC,* 1st ser., 1:228, 233, 286–287; Thomas C. Parramore, "The Tuscarora Ascendency," *NCHR* 59, no. 4 (1982): 312–316.

12. *Archives of Maryland,* 15:403; Jeffreys to Coventry, Coventry Papers, vol. 78, fol. 293v; Jeffreys to Coventry, Coventry Papers, vol. 78, fol. 283v; Ludwell to Coventry, Coventry Papers, vol. 78, fols. 386r–386v.

13. *Archives of Maryland,* 15:180–181, 197–198, 218; Jeffreys to Coventry, Coventry Papers, vol. 78, fol. 293v; *DRCHSNY,* 3:277–288; *MCGCCV,* 519.

14. Ewan and Ewan, *John Banister,* 39; *Archives of Maryland,* 7:23–24; Henry Coventry to Herbert Jeffreys, 5 December 1678, Add. Mss. 25120, p. 136, British Library.

15. Henry Coventry to Sir Henry Chicheley, 1 April 1679, Add. Mss. 25120, p. 140, British Library; Sir Henry Chicheley to Henry Coventry, 20 May 1679, TNA CO 5/1355, p. 361 (emphasis added).

16. Marshall Joseph Becker, "Wampum Held by the Oneida Indian Nation, Inc. of New York: Research Relating to Wampum Cuffs and Belts," *The Bulletin: Journal of the New York State Archaeological Association* 123 (2007): 1–18; *Archives of Maryland*, 15:239; Jon Parmenter, *The Edge of the Woods: Iroquoia, 1534–1701* (East Lansing: Michigan State University Press, 2010), xlviii–xlix.

17. Nancy Shoemaker, *A Strange Likeness: Becoming Red and White in Eighteenth-Century North America* (New York: Oxford University Press, 2004), 90–95; Christina Snyder, *Slavery in Indian Country: The Changing Face of Captivity in Early America* (Cambridge, MA: Harvard University Press, 2010), 114–122; Ludwell to Coventry, Coventry Papers, vol. 78, fol. 281v; *Archives of Maryland*, 15:239. On "amphibious" identities and their power as camouflage, see James C. Scott, *The Art of Not Being Governed: An Anarchist History of Upland Southeast Asia* (New Haven, CT: Yale University Press, 2009), 24, 238–282.

18. Jay F. Custer, "An Unusual Land Claim from Lancaster County," *Pennsylvania Archaeologist* 65, no. 2 (1985): 41–47; David J. Minderhout and Andrea T. Frantz, *Invisible Indians: Native Americans in Pennsylvania* (Amherst, NY: Cambria, 2008), 55.

19. *Archives of Maryland*, 15:239–240; Shoemaker, *Strange Likeness*, 91–92.

20. *Archives of Maryland*, 15:217–222, 240, 242.

21. Hening, *Statutes*, 2:433; Ewan and Ewan, *John Banister*, 39–40; Philip Ludwell to Henry Coventry, 19 June 1679, Coventry Papers, vol. 78, fol. 406v; Ludwell to Coventry, Coventry Papers, vol. 78, fol. 386r; *Archives of Maryland*, 15:251; *NYHM (Delaware English)*, 314; Journal of Trade and Plantations, 20 May 1679, TNA CO 391/3, p. 5.

22. Scott Sowerby, "Opposition to Anti-Popery in Restoration England," *Journal of British Studies* 51, no. 1 (2012): 26–49; TNA CO 391/3, p. 5; *Domestick Intelligence, or, News from Both City and Country*, issue 7, 28 July 1679. On coffeehouses and British public culture, see Brian Cowan, *The Social Life of Coffee: The Emergence of the British Coffeehouse* (New Haven, CT: Yale University Press, 2005); Steve Pincus, "'Coffee Politicians Does Create': Coffeehouses and Restoration Political Culture," *Journal of Modern History* 67, no. 4 (1995): 807–834.

23. Instructions to Colonel Jeffreys, n.d., All Souls Mss. 254, fol. 345, Codrington Library; Herbert Jeffreys to Henry Coventry, 11 February 1678, Coventry Papers, vol. 78, fol. 206v; Jeffreys to Coventry, 2 April 1678, Coventry Papers, vol. 78, fol. 218r; Francis Moryson to Sir William Jones, *Wiseman's Book*, 126–127; Wayne E. Lee, "The Military Revolution of Native North America: Firearms, Forts, and Polities," in *Empires and Indigenes: Intercultural Alliance, Imperial Expansion, and Warfare in the Early Modern World*, ed. Wayne E. Lee (New York: New York University Press, 2011), 49–79; J. Frederick Fausz, "Merging and Emerging Worlds: Anglo-Indian Interest Groups and the Development of the Seventeenth-Century Chesapeake," in *Colonial Chesapeake Society*, ed. Lois Green Carr, Philip D. Morgan, and Jean B. Russo (Chapel Hill: University of North Carolina Press, 1988), 54–55; Hening, *Statutes*, 2:433–437.

24. Hening, *Statutes*, 2:489; *Archives of Maryland*, 15:251.

25. *DRCHSNY*, 3:277; Ludwell to Coventry, Coventry Papers, vol. 78, fol. 386r; *Archives of Maryland*, 5:270; *Andros Papers*, 3:137–138; *DRCHSNY*, 13:536–537; *JHBV*, 2:151.

26. *LIR*, 50, 53.

27. *LIR*, 51–52, 55–56, 60.

28. *LIR*, 53, 56; *Archives of Maryland*, 15:241. On Euro-American captives assimilating into Indigenous societies, see James Axtell, "The White Indians of Colonial America," *WMQ* 32, no. 1 (1975): 55–88; John Demos, *The Unredeemed Captive: A Family Story from Early America* (New York: Alfred A. Knopf, 1994); Ann M. Little, *The Many Captivities of Esther Wheelwright* (New Haven, CT: Yale University Press, 2016); Ian K. Steele, *Setting All the Captives Free: Capture, Adjustment, and Recollection in Allegheny Country* (Montreal: McGill-Queen's University Press, 2013).

29. *Jesuit Relations*, 44:21; Richter, *Ordeal of the Longhouse*, 32–33, 69–74; Kathryn Magee Labelle, *Dispersed but Not Destroyed: A History of the Seventeenth-Century Wendat People* (Vancouver: UBC Press, 2013), 120–140; Bruce G. Trigger, *The Children of Aataentsic: A History of the Huron People to 1660* (Montreal: McGill-Queen's University Press, 1976), 827–829.

30. Charles City County Order Book, 1677–1679, p. 338, LVA; Hening, *Statutes*, 2:283, 490–491; Gregory Ablavsky, "Making Indians 'White': The Judicial Abolition of Native Slavery in Revolutionary Virginia and Its Racial Legacy," *University of Pennsylvania Law Review* 159, no. 5 (2011): 1457–1476; Kathleen M. Brown, *Good Wives, Nasty Wenches, and Anxious Patriarchs: Gender, Race, and Power in Colonial Virginia* (Chapel Hill: University of North Carolina Press, 1996), 107–136; Michael Guasco, "To 'Doe Some Good Upon Their Countrymen': The Paradox of Indian Slavery in Early Anglo-America," *Journal of Social History* 41, no. 2 (2007): 389–411; Jennifer L. Morgan, *Laboring Women: Reproduction and Gender in New World Slavery* (Philadelphia: University of Pennsylvania Press, 2004); Hayley Negrin, "Possessing Native Women and Children: Slavery, Gender and English Colonialism in the Early American South, 1670–1717" (PhD diss., New York University, 2018); Kristalyn Marie Shefveland, "The Many Faces of Native Bonded Labor in Colonial Virginia," *Native South* 7 (2014): 68–91; Owen Stanwood, "Captives and Slaves: Indian Labor, Cultural Conversion, and the Plantation Revolution in Virginia," *VMHB* 114, no. 4 (2006): 434–463. On the alienation of enslaved people and their defiant assertions of social and political vitality, see Vincent Brown, "Social Death and Political Life in the Study of Slavery," *AHR* 114, no. 5 (2009): 1231–1249.

31. Abstract of a letter from Sir Edmund Andros to [William Blathwayt?], 26 February 1680, TNA CO 1/44/31, fol. 80r.

32. *Archives of Maryland*, 5:247, 15:283, 17:5.

33. *Archives of Maryland*, 15:239–240, 17:14.

34. Chief Jacob Thomas, with Terry Boyle, *Teachings from the Longhouse* (Toronto: Stoddart, 1994), 17; Richter, *Ordeal of the Longhouse*, 66–72; Gabrielle Astra Tayac, "'To Speak with One Voice': Supra-Tribal American Indian Collective Identity Incorporation among the Piscataway, 1500–1998" (PhD diss., Harvard University, 1999), 100–102, 132–133; Margaret Holmes Williamson, *Powhatan Lords of Life and Death: Command and Consent in Seventeenth-Century Virginia* (Lincoln: University of Nebraska Press, 2003), 161–163. On slow violence, see Rob Nixon, *Slow Violence and the Environmentalism of the Poor* (Cambridge, MA: Harvard University Press, 2011).

35. *Archives of Maryland*, 15:280–285.

36. *Archives of Maryland*, 15:281, 284–285, 301–303.

37. Nicholas Spencer to Henry Coventry, 9 July 1680, TNA CO 1/45/43, fol. 189v; Bartlett Burleigh James and J. Franklin Jameson, eds., *Journal of Jasper Danckaerts*,

1679–1680, trans. Henry C. Murphy (New York: Charles Scribner's Sons, 1913), 181; "Extracts from letters to Lord Culpeper from Virginia," 18 June 1681 and 25 July 1681, TNA CO 1/47/36, fols. 80r–80v; William Fitzghugh to Captain Partis, 11 June 1680, *William Fitzhugh and His Chesapeake World, 1676–1701: The Fitzhugh Letters and Other Documents*, ed. Richard Beale Davis (Chapel Hill: University of North Carolina Press, 1963), 80.

38. Nicholas Spencer to Henry Coventry, 15 January 1680, Coventry Papers, vol. 78, fol. 438r.

39. *JHBV*, 2:146–147; Nicholas Spencer to Lords of Trade and Plantations, 18 March 1680, TNA CO 1/44/42, fol. 131r.

40. Hening, *Statutes*, 2:480; Cadwallader Jones to Lord Baltimore, 6 February 1682, TNA CO 1/48/22, fol. 115r; "Mr. Byrd's proposals for regulating the Indian trade," [February?] 1683, TNA CO 1/51/56, fol. 149r; Fairfax Harrison, "Western Exploration in Virginia between Lederer and Spotswood," *VMHB* 30, no. 4 (1922): 323–340; Pierre Marambaud, "Colonel William Byrd I: A Fortune Founded on Smoke," *VMHB* 82, no. 4 (1974): 442–443; C. S. Everett, "'They shalbe slaves for their lives': Indian Slavery in Colonial Virginia," in *Indian Slavery in Colonial America*, ed. Alan Gallay (Lincoln: University of Nebraska Press, 2009), 67–108; Kristalyn Marie Shefveland, *Anglo-Native Virginia: Trade, Conversion, and Indian Slavery in the Old Dominion, 1646–1722* (Athens: University of Georgia Press, 2016), 44–60. For a vivid narrative of how dangerous these trading expeditions could be, see Richard Traunter, *The Travels of Richard Traunter on the Main Continent of America from Appomattox River in Virginia to Charles Town in South Carolina* (1699), Mss 5:9 T6945:1, VHS.

41. Alan Gallay, *The Indian Slave Trade: The Rise of the English Empire in the American South, 1670–1717* (New Haven, CT: Yale University Press, 2002), 53–79; Paul Kelton, *Epidemics and Enslavement: Biological Catastrophe in the Native Southeast, 1492–1715* (Lincoln: University of Nebraska Press, 2007), 120–143; Carolina B. Whitley, comp., *North Carolina Headrights: A List of Names, 1663–1744* (Raleigh: North Carolina Department of Cultural Resources, 2001), 7, 83, 94–96, 98, 100, 112, 125, 137–139, 190; *DRCHSNY*, 13:551; *Andros Papers*, 3:173–174; Marion Tinling, ed., *The Correspondence of the Three William Byrds of Westover, Virginia, 1684–1776* (2 vols.; Charlottesville: University Press of Virginia, 1977), 1:163; *DRCHSNY*, 13:537–538.

42. *Archives of Maryland*, 15:284, 286, 293–294, 299–300.

43. Lord Culpeper to Lords of Trade and Plantations, 12 December 1681, TNA CO 1/47/105, fol. 259r; "Most humble proposalls on behalfe of the Indian Kings and Queenes," TNA CO 5/1371, pp. 265–271; Jewel House Warrant Books, 1677–1709, TNA LC 5/108, fol. 28v; Wardrobe Accounts, 1675–1679, TNA LC 9/275, fols. 264r–267r; Spencer to Coventry, TNA CO 1/45/43, fol. 189v; *EJCCV*, 1:4; *JHBV*, 2:146.

44. *Archives of Maryland*, 15:284, 305.

45. Spencer to Coventry, Coventry Papers, vol. 78, fol. 438v; Hening, *Statutes*, 2:463, 469–471, 484; *EJCCV*, 1:13–14.

46. *Archives of Maryland*, 15:294, 302–305, 313.

47. *Archives of Maryland*, 7:388, 15:175, 295, 305, 310–312; William B. Marye, "The Old Indian Road," *MHM* 15, no. 2 (1920): 111–115.

48. *Archives of Maryland*, 7:384, 391.

49. *Archives of Maryland*, 3:277, 7:391–392, 15:239, 383; *DRCHSNY*, 3:328; Paul A. W. Wallace, "Historic Indian Paths of Pennsylvania," *PMHB* 76, no. 4

(1952): 436–437; William B. Marye, "Indian Paths of the Delmarva Peninsula," *Bulletin of the Archaeological Society of Delaware* 2, no. 3 (1937): 5–22.

50. *Archives of Maryland,* 17:85–86; *DRCHSNY,* 13:555.

7. Susquehannock Resurgence and Colonial Crisis

1. *Archives of Maryland,* 7:111.
2. Philip Ludwell to Henry Coventry, 19 July 1679, Coventry Papers, vol. 78, fol. 406v. On the seasonal cycle of Native warfare, see James D. Rice, *Nature and History in the Potomac Country: From Hunter-Gatherers to the Age of Jefferson* (Baltimore: Johns Hopkins University Press, 2009), 40–42.
3. James Bray's address to the General Court, 26 September 1677, Coventry Papers, vol. 78, fol. 89r; "Petition of Sarah Drummond to Jeffreys," TNA CO 5/1371, pp. 527–528; "Acc[oun]tt of A Discourse That Coll Phillip Ludwell Offered in his owne house," Coventry Papers, vol. 78, fol. 135r; "Testimony of Griffith Jones regarding Philip Ludwell," 20 December 1677, Coventry Papers, vol. 78, fol. 173r; Herbert Jeffreys, "A Narrative of some Affaires in Virginia since his Majestyes Comiss[ione]rs Departed The Collony," Coventry Papers, vol. 78, fols. 168r–168v; Thomas Ludwell to Henry Coventry, 30 January 1678, Coventry Papers, vol. 78, fol. 202r; Surry County Order Book, 1671–1691, p. 133, LVA (and for similar cases see pp. 154–155); Frances Berkeley to Sir William Berkeley, 9 August 1677, Mss. 10301, Small Library; Kathleen M. Brown, *Good Wives, Nasty Wenches, and Anxious Patriarchs: Gender, Race, and Power in Colonial Virginia* (Chapel Hill: University of North Carolina Press, 1996), 168–169; Mary Beth Norton, *Separated by Their Sex: Women in Public and Private in the Colonial Atlantic World* (Ithaca, NY: Cornell University Press, 2011), 9–36; Terri L. Snyder, *Brabbling Women: Disorderly Speech and the Law in Early Virginia* (Ithaca, NY: Cornell University Press, 2003), 22–32; Susan Westbury, "Theatre and Power in Bacon's Rebellion: Virginia, 1676–77," *Seventeenth Century* 19, no. 1 (2004): 69–86.
4. Journal of Trade and Plantations, 20 May 1679, TNA CO 391/3, p. 6; Philip Ludwell to Henry Coventry, 19 July 1679, Coventry Papers, vol. 78, fol. 406v; "Notes and Other Documents Chronicling the Activities and Concerns of the Commissioners," *Wiseman's Book,* 198; Herbert Jeffreys to Henry Coventry, 2 April 1678, Coventry Papers, vol. 78, fol. 218r; Thomas Ludwell to Sir Joseph Williamson, 28 June 1678, Lee Family Papers, Mss. L51, folder 8, VHS.
5. Thomas Eastchurch to Herbert Jeffreys, 25 December 1677, Coventry Papers, vol. 78, fol. 152r; "Letter from the Rebells in Carolina," 27 December 1677, Coventry Papers, vol. 78, fol. 154r; John Berry and Francis Moryson, "A true and faithfull account in what condition wee found your Majesties Collony of Virginia," *Wiseman's Book,* 177; Frances Berkeley to William Berkeley, Small Library; Thomas Ludwell to Henry Coventry, 29 December 1677, Coventry Papers, vol. 78, fols. 155r–155v.
6. Herbert Jeffreys to Henry Coventry, 11 February 1678, Coventry Papers, vol. 78, fol. 206v; Lord Culpeper to Lords of Trade and Plantations, 12 December 1681, TNA CO 1/47/105, fol. 261r; Council Minutes, Wills and Inventories, 1677–1701, p. 153, Secretary of State Records, SS 874.2, NCSA; Petition of Captain Henry Wilkinson to King Charles II, 17 May 1680, Blathwayt Papers, vol. 18, folder 9, Rockefeller Library; Lords Proprietors to the Governor and Council of Albamarle, 5 February 1679, TNA CO 5/286, p. 140; *CRNC,* 1st ser., 1:247–248, 261, 288, 298, 346–347, 350–352, 368–370; Mattie Erma Edwards Parker, ed., *North Carolina*

Higher-Court Records, 1670–1696 (Raleigh, NC: State Department of Archives and History, 1968), 333; Mattie Erma E. Parker, "Legal Aspects of 'Culpeper's Rebellion,'" *NCHR* 45, no. 2 (1968): 125–127.

7. J. R. Jones, *The First Whigs: The Politics of the Exclusion Crisis, 1678–1683* (London: Oxford University Press, 1961); J. P. Kenyon, *The Popish Plot* (London: Heinemann, 1972); Melinda S. Zook, *Radical Whigs and Conspiratorial Politics in Late Stuart England* (University Park: Pennsylvania State University Press, 1999); *Journals of the House of Lords* (42 vols.; London: Her Majesty's Stationary Office, 1767–1830), 13:367–368; James D. Rice, *Tales from a Revolution: Bacon's Rebellion and the Transformation of Early America* (New York: Oxford University Press, 2012), 150–151.

8. *Archives of Maryland,* 15:245–246; *DRCHSNY,* 3:272; Bartlett Burleigh James and J. Franklin Jameson, eds., *Journal of Jasper Danckaerts, 1679–1680,* trans. Henry C. Murphy (New York: Charles Scribner's Sons, 1913), 137; Thomas Ludwell to Secretary Sir Joseph Williamson, 17 April 1678, TNA CO 1/42/55, fol. 111v; Antoinette Sutto, *Loyal Protestants and Dangerous Papists: Maryland and the Politics of Religion in the English Atlantic, 1630–1690* (Charlottesville: University of Virginia Press, 2015), 148–151.

9. Sir Henry Chicheley to Henry Coventry, 20 May 1679, CO 5/1355, p. 361; "Letter from [?] to [Thomas Lord Culpeper]," n.d., All Souls Mss. 257, fol. 167r, Codrington Library; Ludwell to Coventry, Coventry Papers, vol. 78, fols. 406v–407r; *EJCCV,* 1:10–12; *JHBV,* 2:118; Ludwell to Coventry, Coventry Papers, vol. 78, fol. 202v. The king's tight-fisted fiscal policy was understandable: on top of the £11,000 price tag for the 1677 expedition, the Office of Ordinance estimated that military expenditures for Virginia cost the royal treasury more than £3,000 annually. This was more than any other colony except Jamaica, outstripping expenses for the vastly more lucrative sugar islands in the Caribbean. The cost was sufficiently high that King Charles II mentioned it in his 1678 address to Parliament, alongside the escalating naval war against Algiers, to justify his request for funding; "A memorial of all the estimates delivered from the Office of Ordnance for his Majesty's service upon this present expedition to Virginia," 8 November 1676, TNA CO 1/38/34, fol. 76r; "Order for Allowances to the Officers of the Plantations," 27 June 1679, TNA CO 324/4, pp. 64–65; *His Majesties Gracious Speech to Both Houses of Parliament, on Munday the 28th of January, 1677/8* (London, 1678), 6.

10. *Archives of Maryland,* 7:363, 475–476.

11. *Archives of Maryland,* 7:384, 15:329–330, 375, 17:5; Rice, *Nature and History,* 154.

12. *Archives of Maryland,* 15:329–330, 336.

13. *Archives of Maryland,* 15:353, 358–359, 373–374, 17:14.

14. *Archives of Maryland,* 15:374, 376; Alex J. Flick et al., "'. . . a place now known unto them': The Search for Zekiah Fort" (unpublished report, St. Mary's City: St. Mary's College of Maryland, 2012), 33–34.

15. "Extracts from letters to Lord Culpeper," 18 June 1681 and 25 July 1681, TNA CO 1/47/36, fol. 80r; Nicholas Spencer to Sir Leoline Jenkins, 13 May 1681, TNA CO 1/46/137, fol. 324r; *Archives of Maryland,* 15:336, 360.

16. *Archives of Maryland,* 15:374–376, 385, 418, 17:6–7; *Oxford English Dictionary,* 2nd ed. (20 vols.; Oxford: Oxford University Press, 1989), s.v. "Jackanapes," def. 2c. How Passanucohanse got his nickname, and whether this bears on his role in propagating an elaborate conspiracy theory, is anybody's guess.

17. Lord Baltimore to William Blathwayt, 11 March 1682, TNA CO 1/48/43, fol. 169r; "Extract of a letter from Virginia," 22 July 1681, TNA CO 1/47/35, fol.

79r; "Extracts from letters to Lord Culpeper," TNA CO 1/47/36, fols. 8or–8ov; *MCGCCV,* 521; *Archives of Maryland,* 15:360.

18. *Archives of Maryland,* 15:355–356, 360–373, 393–395, 415–416, 17:11–12; "Extract of a letter from Virginia," TNA CO 1/47/35, fol. 79r; "Extracts from letters to Lord Culpeper," TNA CO 1/47/36, fol. 8or.

19. "Extract of a letter from Virginia," TNA CO 1/47/35, fol. 79r; *Archives of Maryland,* 15:376, 386, 388, 399, 420.

20. *Archives of Maryland,* 5:313–314, 15:388–391, 420; "Extracts from letters to Lord Culpeper," TNA CO 1/47/36, fol. 8or; Philip Calvert to Henry Meese, 20 December 1681, TNA CO 1/47/120, fol. 321r; David W. Jordan, "John Coode, Perennial Rebel," *MHM* 70, no. 1 (1975): 1–28.

21. *Archives of Maryland,* 15:379, 388–392; Philip Ludwell to [?], 30 July 1681, TNA 1/47/43, fol. 92r.

22. *Archives of Maryland,* 15:387, 406, 409, 420.

23. *Archives of Maryland,* 15:387, 393, 420. On horse racing and sociability, see T. H. Breen, "Horses and Gentlemen: The Cultural Significance of Gambling among the Gentry of Virginia," *WMQ* 34, no. 2 (1977): 239–257. Communication and media scholars describe the ironic propagation of suppressed information as "the Streisand effect," usually attributing its power to the echo chambers of the Internet. Although journalists have used it to describe phenomena ranging from celebrity lawsuits to populist revolutions around the world, it has received remarkably little study; but see Sue Curry Jansen and Brian Martin, "The Streisand Effect and Censorship Backfire," *International Journal of Communication* 9 (2015): 656–671; Rolien Hoyng and Murat Es, "Conspiratorial Webs: Media Ecology and Parallel Realities in Turkey," *International Journal of Communication* 11 (2017): 4219–4238.

24. *Archives of Maryland,* 5:312, 15:391, 402–404.

25. "Extract of a letter from Virginia," TNA CO 1/47/35, fol. 79r; *Archives of Maryland,* 5:281, 15:407–408; Ludwell to [?], TNA CO 1/47/43, fol. 92r.

26. *Archives of Maryland,* 15:408–409, 17:5–6, 199; *LIR,* 65–66. Piscataways estimated the attacking force numbered six hundred, while Haudenosaunee stated it was three hundred; *Archives of Maryland,* 15:408, 17:3.

27. *Archives of Maryland,* 15:374, 17:3–4.

28. *Archives of Maryland,* 17:4–5.

29. *Archives of Maryland,* 17:4–7, 11–12.

30. *Archives of Maryland,* 17:14–15, 20.

31. *Archives of Maryland,* 5:328, 331–332, 334, 17:78; *EJCCV,* 1:14.

32. Holly Brewer, "Slavery, Sovereignty, and 'Inheritable Blood': Reconsidering John Locke and the Origins of American Slavery," *AHR* 122, no. 4 (2017): 1038–1078; Brown, *Good Wives,*179–185; John C. Coombs, "The Phases of Conversion: A New Chronology for the Rise of Slavery in Early Virginia," *WMQ* 68, no. 3 (2011): 350–353; David W. Galenson, "White Servitude and the Growth of Black Slavery in Colonial America," *Journal of Economic History* 41, no. 1 (1981): 39–47; Edmund S. Morgan, *American Slavery, American Freedom: The Ordeal of Colonial Virginia* (1975; repr. ed., New York: W. W. Norton, 2003), 295–315; William A. Pettigrew, *Freedom's Debt: The Royal African Company and the Politics of the Atlantic Slave Trade, 1672–1752* (Chapel Hill: University of North Carolina Press, 2013), 22–30; Allan Kulikoff, *Tobacco and Slaves: The Development of Southern Cultures in the Chesapeake, 1680–1800* (Chapel Hill: University of North Carolina Press, 1986), 37–44; Gloria L. Main, *Tobacco Colony: Life in Early Maryland, 1650–1720* (Princeton, NJ: Princeton University Press, 1982); John J. McCusker and Russell R. Menard, *The Economy of British America, 1607–1789* (Chapel Hill:

University of North Carolina Press, 1985), 136; Russell Menard, "From Servants to Slaves: The Transformation of the Chesapeake Labor System," *Southern Studies* 16, no. 4 (1977): 355–390; Anthony S. Parent Jr., *Foul Means: The Formation of a Slave Society in Virginia, 1660–1740* (Chapel Hill: University of North Carolina Press, 2003), 55–79; Lorena S. Walsh, *Motives of Honor, Pleasure, and Profit: Plantation Management in the Colonial Chesapeake, 1607–1763* (Chapel Hill: University of North Carolina Press, 2010), 200–205.

33. Hening, *Statutes*, 2:491; Coombs, "Phases of Conversion," 353–358; Hayley Negrin, "Possessing Native Women and Children: Slavery, Gender and English Colonialism in the Early American South, 1670–1717" (PhD diss., New York University, 2018), 115–148 (esp. 134); Kristalyn Marie Shefveland, "The Many Faces of Native Bonded Labor in Colonial Virginia," *Native South* 7 (2014): 68–91; Owen Stanwood, "Captives and Slaves: Indian Labor, Cultural Conversion, and the Plantation Revolution in Virginia," *VMHB* 114, no. 4 (2006): 434–463.

34. Hening, *Statutes*, 2:481–482 (emphasis added), 491–492, 3:449; Gregory Ablavsky, "Making Indians 'White': The Judicial Abolition of Native Slavery in Revolutionary Virginia and Its Racial Legacy," *University of Pennsylvania Law Review* 159, no. 5 (2011): 1471–1472; Brown, *Good Wives,* 179–180, 185–186; Kathleen M. Brown, "Native Americans and the Early Modern Concept of Race," in *Empire and Others: British Encounters with Indigenous Peoples, 1600–1850,* ed. Martin Daunton and Rick Halpern (Philadelphia: University of Pennsylvania Press, 1999), 79–100; Rebecca Anne Goetz, *The Baptism of Early Virginia: How Christianity Created Race* (Baltimore: Johns Hopkins University Press, 2012); Kristofer Ray, "Constructing a Discourse of Indigenous Slavery, Freedom and Sovereignty in Anglo-Virginia, 1600–1750," *Native South* 10 (2017): 19–39. On "Moors," see Sylviane A. Diouf, *Servants of Allah: African Muslims Enslaved in the Americas* (New York: New York University Press, 1998); Michael A. Gomez, *Exchanging Our Country Marks: The Transformation of African Identities in the Colonial and Antebellum South* (Chapel Hill: University of North Carolina Press, 1998), 59–87.

35. The body of scholarship on racial slavery is enormous, but for helpful reviews of debates about its origins see Alden T. Vaughan, "The Origins Debate: Slavery and Racism in Seventeenth-Century Virginia," in *Roots of American Racism: Essays on the Colonial Experience* (New York: Oxford University Press, 1995), 136–174; John C. Coombs, "Beyond the 'Origins Debate': Rethinking the Rise of Virginia Slavery," in *Early Modern Virginia: Reconsidering the Old Dominion,* ed. Douglas Bradburn and John C. Coombs (Charlottesville: University of Virginia Press, 2011), 239–278. For major works on the evolution of African slavery in North America, see Theodore W. Allen, *The Invention of the White Race,* 2 vols. (New York: Verso, 1994–1997); Ira Berlin, *Many Thousands Gone: The First Two Centuries of Slavery in North America* (Cambridge, MA: The Belknap Press of Harvard University Press, 1998); Brown, *Good Wives;* David Brion Davis, "Constructing Race: A Reflection," *WMQ* 54, no. 1 (1997): 7–18; David Eltis, *The Rise of African Slavery in the Americas* (Cambridge: Cambridge University Press, 2000); Barbara Jeanne Fields, "Slavery, Race and Ideology in the United States of America," *New Left Review* 181 (1990): 95–118; Winthrop D. Jordan, *White over Black: American Attitudes toward the Negro, 1550–1812* (Chapel Hill: University of North Carolina Press, 1968); Morgan, *American Slavery;* Jennifer L. Morgan, *Laboring Women: Reproduction and Gender in New World Slavery* (Philadelphia: University of Pennsylvania Press, 2004); Parent, *Foul Means;* Peter H. Wood, *Black Majority: Negroes in Colonial South Carolina from 1670 through the Stono Rebellion* (New York: Alfred A.

Knopf, 1974). Relatively few scholars have examined the ways that African and Indigenous slaveries were intertwined, but that is beginning to change; Rebecca Anne Goetz, "Rethinking the 'Unthinking Decision': Old Questions and New Problems in the History of Slavery and Race in the Colonial South," *JSH* 75, no. 3 (2009): 599–612; Heather Miyano Kopelson, *Faithful Bodies: Performing Religion and Race in the Puritan Atlantic* (New York: New York University Press, 2014); Margaret Ellen Newell, *Brethren by Nature: New England Indians, Colonists, and the Origins of American Slavery* (Ithaca, NY: Cornell University Press, 2015); Joshua Piker, "Indians and Race in Early America," *History Compass* 3 (2005): 1–17; Brett Rushforth, *The Bonds of Alliance: Indigenous and Atlantic Slaveries in New France* (Chapel Hill: University of North Carolina Press, 2012); Jennifer M. Spear, "Race Matters in the Colonial South," *JSH* 73, no. 3 (2007): 579–588; Daniel H. Usner Jr., *Indians, Settlers, and Slaves in a Frontier Exchange Economy: The Lower Mississippi Valley before 1783* (Chapel Hill: University of North Carolina Press, 1992); Wendy Warren, *New England Bound: Slavery and Colonization in Early America* (New York: Liveright, 2016). A distinct body of scholarship focusing on the development of "white" and "Indian" identities in the context of eighteenth-century frontier warfare emphasizes English fears of Indigenous violence as a major driver of racial formation, but this literature has seldom been in conversation with scholarship on racial slavery; Jane T. Merritt, *At the Crossroads: Indians and Empires on a Mid-Atlantic Frontier, 1700–1763* (Chapel Hill: North Carolina University Press, 2003); William A. Pencak and Daniel K. Richter, eds., *Friends and Enemies in Penn's Woods: Indians, Colonists, and the Racial Construction of Pennsylvania* (University Park: Pennsylvania State University Press, 2004); Daniel K. Richter, *Facing East from Indian Country: A Native History of Early America* (Cambridge, MA: Harvard University Press, 2003), 189–236; Nancy Shoemaker, "How Indians Got to Be Red," *AHR* 102, no. 3 (1997): 625–644; Peter Silver, *Our Savage Neighbors: How Indian War Transformed Early America* (New York: W. W. Norton, 2008).

36. Hening, *Statutes*, 2:433, 438–439, 481–482; Nicholas Spencer to Henry Coventry, 15 January 1680, Coventry Papers, vol. 78, fol. 438r; *Archives of Maryland*, 15:281.

37. Spencer to Coventry, Coventry Papers, vol. 78, fol. 438r; *JHBV*, 2:162; *Archives of Maryland*, 15:400; Hilary McD. Beckles, "Kalinago (Carib) Resistance to European Colonisation of the Caribbean," *Caribbean Quarterly* 38, no. 2/3 (1992): 1–14, 123–124; Michael Craton, "From Caribs to Black Caribs: The Amerindian Roots of Servile Resistance in the Caribbean," in *In Resistance: Studies in African, Caribbean, and Afro-American History*, ed. Gary Y. Okihiro (Amherst: University of Massachusetts Press, 1986), 96–116.

38. *JHBV*, 2:159; "Extract of a letter from Virginia," TNA CO 1/47/35, fol. 79r; *Archives of Maryland*, 17:98.

39. "Extract of a letter from Virginia," TNA CO 1/47/35, fol. 79r.

40. *Archives of Maryland*, 17:70, 72; Baltimore to Blathwayt, TNA CO 1/48/43, fol. 169r.

41. Parent, *Foul Means*, 81–83; "Council and Burgesses of Virginia to the King," 26 July 1681, TNA CO 1/47/37, fol. 83r; "Letter from the King to the Lieut[enant] Gov[erno]r of Virginia," 21 January 1682, TNA CO 5/1356, pp. 11–12; *JHBV*, 2:162, 168–169; King Charles II to Lt. Governor and Council of Virginia, 30 November 1681, All Souls Mss. 225, pp. 76–78, Codrington Library; "Proclamation to prorogue the assembly," 18 April 1682, TNA CO 5/1405, p. 98.

42. Nathaniel Bacon Sr. to [William Blathwayt], 10 July 1683, Blathwayt Papers, Beinecke Library; [Sir] Hen[ry] Chicheley, "An Account of an insurrection in Gloucester

County, Virginia," 8 May 1682, Blathwayt Papers, BL 86, Huntington; Nicholas Spencer to Sir Leoline Jenkins, 8 May 1682, TNA CO 1/48/69, fol. 230v; *EJCCV*, 1:18–23; Nicholas Spencer to Sir Leoline Jenkins, 7 June 1682, TNA CO 1/48/95, fol. 313r; Nicholas Spencer to Sir Leoline Jenkins, 28 May 1682, TNA CO 1/48/81, fol. 261r; *Archives of Maryland*, 5:357; "The Plant-Cutter Riots," in *The Old Dominion in the Seventeenth Century: A Documentary History of Virginia, 1606–1700*, ed. Warren M. Billings (1975; rev. ed., Chapel Hill: University of North Carolina Press, 2007), 349–355; Snyder, *Brabbling Women*, 39–44.

43. *EJCCV*, 1:33–34; Spencer to Jenkins, TNA 1/48/95, fol. 313r.

44. Lord Culpeper to Lords of Trade and Plantations, 12 December 1681, TNA CO 1/47/105, fol. 261r; *DRCHSNY*, 3:263, 271; *Archives of Maryland*, 5:148; Owen Stanwood, *The Empire Reformed: English America in the Age of the Glorious Revolution* (Philadelphia: University of Pennsylvania Press, 2011), 25–30; Journal of Trade and Plantations, 20 December 1681, TNA CO 391/3, p. 329. The Lords of Trade's hesitation to infringe on charter liberties contradicts Stephen Saunders Webb's portrayal of a Stuart military takeover after 1676; Stephen Saunders Webb, *1676: The End of American Independence* (New York: Alfred A. Knopf, 1984).

45. *Archives of Maryland*, 17:102, 207–208; Thomas Ludwell to Henry Coventry, 29 December 1677, Coventry Papers, vol. 77, fol. 155r; Herbert Jeffreys to Henry Coventry, 30 December 1677, Coventry Papers, vol. 78, fol. 164v; "Lord Culpeper's projects for the relief and improvement of Virginia," 18 October 1681, TNA CO 1/47/76, fol. 180v; *DRCHSNY*, 3:271. April Lee Hatfield depicts intercolonial cooperation increasing smoothly throughout the 1670s and 1680s; April Lee Hatfield, *Atlantic Virginia: Intercolonial Relations in the Seventeenth Century* (Philadelphia: University of Pennsylvania Press, 2004), 191–218.

46. "To the Inhab[i]tants and planters of the province of pensilvania," Cadwalader Papers, series 3, box 53, folder 3, HSP; *DRCHSNY*, 12:666–667; *NYHM (Delaware English)*, 349; Charles Calvert to Cecilius, Lord Baltimore, 2 June 1673, *The Calvert Papers* (2 vols.; Baltimore: Maryland Historical Society, 1889), 1:288–290; Leon deValinger Jr., "The Burning of the Whorekill, 1673," *PMHB* 74, no. 4 (1950): 473–487.

47. "Deed—John Fenwick [et al] to William Penn (1682)," Chew Family Papers, series 4K, box 191, folder 7, and "Release of Land Rights—John Fenwick to William Penn (1682)," box 196, folder 13, HSP; Counterpart of deed from John Fenwick to William Penn for his interest in West Jersey, 23 March 1682, MG 3: West Jersey Manuscript Collection, 1648–1829, doc. 12, NJHS; *DRCHSNJ*, 1:507–508; "To the Inhab[i]tants," Cadwalader Papers, series 3, box 53, folder 3, HSP; *PWP*, 2:112; Charles Calvert, Lord Baltimore, to William Penn, 24 June 1683, folder 27, p. A, Pratt Library; *Archives of Maryland*, 5:350, 375; Depositions of John Nummers, James Graham, and Samual Land, Cadwalader Papers, series 3, box 56, folder 27, HSP; William Welch to William Penn, 5 April 1684, Ferdinand J. Dreer Autograph Collection, series 1, box 25, folder 53, HSP; Patrick Spero, *Frontier Country: The Politics of War in Early Pennsylvania* (Philadelphia: University of Pennsylvania Press, 2016), 14–33.

48. Daniel K. Richter, "Land and Words: William Penn's Letter to the Kings of the Indians," in *Trade, Land, Power: The Struggle for Eastern North America* (Philadelphia: University of Pennsylvania Press, 2013), 145–146; *PWP*, 2:129; *Archives of Maryland*, 5:380; William Penn to Charles, Lord Baltimore, 6 June 1683, *Calvert Papers*, 1:328–329; "Reports of Conferences Between Lord Baltimore and William

Penn, and Their Agents," in *Narratives of Early Maryland, 1633–1684,* ed. Clayton Colman Hall (New York: Charles Scribner's Sons, 1910), 440.

49. *Archives of Maryland,* 17:202–203, 215, 369; *DRCHSNY,* 13:563–564; *Jesuit Relations,* 62:67; *Archives of Maryland,* 17:100.

50. "Extract of a letter from Virginia," TNA CO 1/47/35, fol. 79r; *Archives of Maryland,* 17:100.

51. *Archives of Maryland,* 17:214; *DRCHSNY,* 3:322–323; Jon Parmenter, *The Edge of the Woods: Iroquoia, 1534–1701* (East Lansing: Michigan State University Press, 2010), 163–175. Printed transcriptions of this conference contain errors that cause unnecessary confusion, so I have made corrections based on the originals in TNA CO 1/49/18, fols. 84–94.

52. *Archives of Maryland,* 17:215; *DRCHSNY,* 3:324–325.

53. *DRCHSNY,* 3:325–327; Richard L. Haan, "Covenant and Consensus: Iroquois and English, 1676–1760," in *Beyond the Covenant Chain: The Iroquois and Their Neighbors in Indian North America, 1600–1800,* ed. Daniel K. Richter and James H. Merrell (1987; rev. ed., University Park: Pennsylvania State University Press, 2003), 46–52.

54. *DRCHSNY,* 3:326, 328. Coursey and Lloyd did not name their source, but it must have been someone in Albany. Just two days before asking their question they had proposed Jacob as the fulcrum of a Maryland-Seneca alliance, and surely would not have done so if they suspected that Jacob was responsible for organizing Haudenosaunee attacks.

55. *DRCHSNY,* 3:327; *Archives of Maryland,* 17:113–114.

56. *Archives of Maryland,* 15:239–240.

57. *Archives of Maryland,* 17:364–365, 367.

58. *Archives of Maryland,* 17:366–367.

59. Nathaniel Bacon Sr. to William Blathwayt, 23 July 1683, Blathwayt Papers, vol. 13, folder 1, Rockefeller Library; John Berry and Francis Moryson, "A True Narrative of the Rise, Progresse, and Cessation of the Late Rebellion in Virginia," TNA CO 5/1371, p. 372; *Archives of Maryland,* 17:5.

60. "Kekelappan to William Penn for that half of all my lands betwixt the Susquehanna and Delaware which lieth on the Susquehanna side," 10 September 1683, Basic Documents of Pennsylvania Including Proprietary Charters and Deeds, Indian Deeds, and State Constitutions, 1681–1873, RG-26/AOSC/2, item 27, PSA; "Machaloha to William Penn for lands on the Delaware River, Chesapeak Bay, and up to the Falls of the Susquehanna," 18 October 1683, RG-26/AOSC/2, item 28, PSA; Commission to James Graham and William Haige for treating with the Indians, 2 August 1683, Chew Papers, series 2G, box 23, folder 8, HSP; *PWP,* 2:128; Francis Jennings, "The Indian Trade of the Susquehanna Valley," *PAPS* 110, no. 6 (1966): 406–424; Gary B. Nash, "The Quest for the Susquehanna Valley: New York, Pennsylvania, and the Seventeenth-Century Fur Trade," *NYH* 48, no. 1 (1967): 3–27.

61. *LIR,* 69–70; *DRCHSNY,* 3:417–418; "Propositions made by the Cajouges and Onnondages Sachims to the Commissaryes of Albany," 26 September 1683, Ferdinand J. Dreer Autograph Collection, series 1, box 18, folder 29, HSP; Peter R. Christoph, ed., *The Dongan Papers, 1683–1688* (2 vols.; Syracuse, NY: Syracuse University Press, 1993), 2:36. On the Haudenosaunee's fictitious conquest, see Francis Jennings, "Glory, Death, and Transfiguration: the Susquehannock Indians in the Seventeenth Century," *PAPS* 112, no. 1 (1968): 49.

Epilogue

1. *Archives of Maryland,* 7:386–392, 399.
2. Raphael Semmes, *Crime and Punishment in Early Maryland* (Baltimore: Johns Hopkins University Press, 1938), 33–37; Alison Thorne, "Women's Petitionary Letters and Early Seventeenth-Century Treason Trials," *Women's Writing* 13, no. 1 (2006): 23–43; *Archives of Maryland,* 7:495, 558, 571, 13:21.
3. Francis Jennings, "Jacob Young: Indian Trader and Interpreter," in *Struggle and Survival in Colonial America,* ed. David G. Sweet and Gary B. Nash (Berkeley: University of California Press, 1981), 354–359; *Archives of Maryland,* 7:485, 507, 518, 591, 598; Lois Green Carr, Russell R. Menard, and Lorena S. Walsh, *Robert Cole's World: Agriculture and Society in Early Maryland* (Chapel Hill: University of North Carolina Press, 1991), 77–118.
4. On the embrace of politically convenient falsehoods, see Joshua Piker, "Lying Together: The Imperial Implications of Cross-Cultural Untruths," *AHR* 116, no. 4 (2011): 964–986.
5. Warren M. Billings, ed., *The Papers of Francis Howard, Baron Howard of Effingham, 1643–1695* (Richmond: Virginia State Library and Archives, 1989), 149, 213; *LIR,* 74, 86; Nathaniel Bacon Sr. to [William Blathwayt], 20 June 1685, Blathwayt Papers, Beinecke Library; *EJCCV,* 1:70–71; *Archives of Maryland,* 5:426; Francis Jennings, *The Ambiguous Iroquois Empire: The Covenant Chain Confederation of Indian Tribes with English Colonies from Its Beginnings to the Lancaster Treaty of 1744* (New York: W. W. Norton, 1984), 172–219; Michael Leroy Oberg, *Dominion and Civility: English Imperialism and Native America, 1585–1685* (Ithaca, NY: Cornell University Press, 1999), 217–228.
6. Richard L. Haan, "Covenant and Consensus: Iroquois and English, 1676–1760," in *Beyond the Covenant Chain: The Iroquois and Their Neighbors in Indian North America, 1600–1800,* ed. Daniel K. Richter and James H. Merrell (1987; rev. ed., University Park: Pennsylvania State University Press, 2003), 52–57; Timothy J. Shannon, *Iroquois Diplomacy on the Early American Frontier* (New York: Viking, 2008); Robert A. Williams Jr., *Linking Arms Together: American Indian Treaty Visions of Law and Peace, 1600–1800* (New York: Oxford University Press, 1997).
7. James H. Merrell, "'Their Very Bones Shall Fight': The Catawba-Iroquois Wars," in *Beyond the Covenant Chain,* 115–134; James D. Rice, "Bacon's Rebellion in Indian Country," *JAH* 101, no. 3 (2014): 726–750.
8. Robbie Ethridge, *From Chicaza to Chickasaw: The European Invasion and the Transformation of the Mississippian World, 1540–1715* (Chapel Hill: University of North Carolina Press, 2010), 149–254; Robbie Ethridge and Sheri M. Shuck-Hall, eds., *Mapping the Mississippian Shatter Zone: The Colonial Indian Slave Trade and Regional Instability in the American South* (Lincoln: University of Nebraska Press, 2009); Alan Gallay, *The Indian Slave Trade: The Rise of the English Empire in the American South, 1670–1717* (New Haven, CT: Yale University Press, 2002), 53–98; Paul Kelton, *Epidemics and Enslavement: Biological Catastrophe in the Native Southeast, 1492–1715* (Lincoln: University of Nebraska Press, 2007), 120–143; David J. Silverman, *Thundersticks: Firearms and the Violent Transformation of Native America* (Cambridge, MA: The Belknap Press of Harvard University Press, 2016), 56–91; Christina Snyder, *Slavery in Indian Country: The Changing Face of Captivity in Early America* (Cambridge, MA: Harvard University Press, 2010).
9. Ira Berlin, *Many Thousands Gone: The First Two Centuries of Slavery in North America* (Cambridge, MA: The Belknap Press of Harvard University Press, 1998),

109–141; Sharon Block, *Colonial Complexions: Race and Bodies in Eighteenth-Century America* (Philadelphia: University of Pennsylvania Press, 2018); Kathleen M. Brown, *Good Wives, Nasty Wenches, and Anxious Patriarchs: Gender, Race, and Power in Colonial Virginia* (Chapel Hill: University of North Carolina Press, 1996), 194–211; Kathleen M. Brown, *Foul Bodies: Cleanliness in Early America* (New Haven, CT: Yale University Press, 2009); Barbara Jeanne Fields, "Slavery, Race and Ideology in the United States of America," *New Left Review* 181 (1990): 95–118; Kirsten Fischer, *Suspect Relations: Sex, Race, and Resistance in Colonial North Carolina* (Ithaca, NY: Cornell University Press, 2002), 159–190; Rebecca Anne Goetz, *The Baptism of Early Virginia: How Christianity Created Race* (Baltimore: Johns Hopkins University Press, 2012); Edmund S. Morgan, *American Slavery, American Freedom: The Ordeal of Colonial Virginia* (1975; repr. ed., New York: W. W. Norton, 2003), 316–337; Jennifer L. Morgan, *Laboring Women: Reproduction and Gender in New World Slavery* (Philadelphia: University of Pennsylvania Press, 2004); Philip D. Morgan, *Slave Counterpoint: Black Culture in the Eighteenth-Century Chesapeake and Lowcountry* (Chapel Hill: University of North Carolina Press, 1998), 257–317; Mark M. Smith, *How Race Is Made: Slavery, Segregation, and the Senses* (Chapel Hill: University of North Carolina Press, 2006), 1–28.

10. On Indian-fearing and racialization in the eighteenth century, see Krista Camenzind, "Violence, Race, and the Paxton Boys," in *Friends and Enemies in Penn's Woods: Indians, Colonists, and the Racial Construction of Pennsylvania*, ed. William A. Pencak and Daniel K. Richter (University Park: Pennsylvania State University Press, 2004), 201–220; Jane T. Merritt, *At the Crossroads: Indians and Empires on a Mid-Atlantic Frontier, 1700–1763* (Chapel Hill: North Carolina University Press, 2003); Peter Silver, *Our Savage Neighbors: How Indian War Transformed Early America* (New York: W. W. Norton, 2008).

11. James D. Rice, *Tales from a Revolution: Bacon's Rebellion and the Transformation of Early America* (New York: Oxford University Press, 2012), 183–201.

12. "The Treaty of Middle Plantation," *Wiseman's Book,* 135, 138; Bradley J. Dixon, "'His one Netev ples': The Chowans and the Politics of Native Petitions in the Colonial South," *WMQ* 76, no. 1 (2019): 41–74; Michelle LeMaster, "In the 'Scolding Houses': Indians and the Law in Eastern North Carolina, 1684–1760," *NCHR* 83, no. 2 (2006): 193–232; Helen C. Rountree, *Pocahontas's People: The Powhatan Indians of Virginia Through Four Centuries* (Norman: University of Oklahoma Press, 1990), 144–277; "Pamunkey Tribe's Federal Recognition Finalized," *Native American Rights Fund (NARF) Legal Review* 41, no. 1 (2016): 9.

13. *Archives of Maryland,* 7:399.

14. "Treaty of Middle Plantation," *Wiseman's Book,* 135.

15. George Alsop, *A Character of the Province of Mary-Land* (London, 1666), 61; Lord Culpeper to [Sir Leoline Jenkins?], 20 March 1683, TNA CO 1/51/68, fol. 171v.

16. Barry C. Kent, *Susquehanna's Indians* (1984; Harrisburg: Pennsylvania Historical and Museum Commission, 2001), 56–57; *LIR,* 116; *Archives of Maryland,* 8:181, 207.

17. *PWP,* 2:546; Warrant for William Markham and Jacob Pellison, 9 May 1689, RG-17/D-81-98, p. 195, PSA; *Archives of Maryland,* 8:378, 13:234–235, 283, 310.

18. *Archives of Maryland,* 8:517–518 (emphasis added); Stephen Warren, *The Worlds the Shawnees Made: Migration and Violence in Early America* (Chapel Hill: University of North Carolina Press, 2014), 157–179.

19. *Archives of Maryland,* 8:343; Samuel Hazard, ed., *Minutes of the Provincial Council of Pennsylvania* (10 vols.; Harrisburg, 1838–1852), 1:448; Kent, *Susquehanna's*

Indians, 72–78, 105–106; James D. Rice, *Nature and History in the Potomac Country: From Hunter-Gatherers to the Age of Jefferson* (Baltimore: Johns Hopkins University Press, 2009), 161–173.

20. Francis Jennings, "The Indian Trade of the Susquehanna Valley," *PAPS* 110, no. 6 (1966): 406–424; Peter C. Mancall, *Valley of Opportunity: Economic Culture along the Upper Susquehanna, 1700–1800* (Ithaca, NY: Cornell University Press, 1991), 48–50; James H. Merrell, "The Other 'Susquahannah Traders': Women and Exchange on the Pennsylvania Frontier," in *Cultures and Identities in Colonial British America,* ed. Robert Olwell and Alan Tully (Baltimore: Johns Hopkins University Press, 2006), 197–219; Gary B. Nash, "The Quest for the Susquehanna Valley: New York, Pennsylvania, and the Seventeenth-Century Fur Trade," *NYH* 48, no. 1 (1967): 3–27; *PWP,* 3:453; *Archives of Maryland,* 19:519–20; Hazard, *Minutes of the Provincial Council,* 2:15.

21. *Archives of Maryland,* 8:517–518, 19:519. On Conestogas and European clothing, see Laura E. Johnson, "'Goods to clothe themselves': Native Consumers and Native Images on the Pennsylvania Trading Frontier, 1712–1760," *Winterthur Portfolio* 43, no. 1 (2009): 115–140.

22. On the importance of recognizing Indigenous futurity, see Alejandra Dubcovsky, "Defying Indian Slavery: Apalachee Voices and Spanish Sources in the Eighteenth-Century Southeast," *WMQ* 75, no. 2 (2018): 295–322; Joshua L. Reid, *The Sea Is My Country: The Maritime World of the Makahs* (New Haven, CT: Yale University Press, 2015), 276–281; Eve Tuck and K. Wayne Yang, "Decolonization Is Not a Metaphor," *Decolonization: Indigeneity, Education and Society* 1, no. 1 (2012): 1–40.

· ACKNOWLEDGMENTS ·

This book is about a tumultuous ten-year span of American history, but from start to finish it took twelve years to write. That is, to put it mildly, a long time. A lot of that time has been lonely hours in archive dust and digital ghostlight. But in the end what I remember most are the hours I spent with all the people to whom this project has connected me over the years, a rich and expansive web of humans scattered all over the place. Those people taught me and connected me to others who could teach me more. They corrected my mistakes and held me accountable. They inspired me to do better. They told me stories and made me laugh and, amid all this seemingly solitary labor, brought the joys of community into my life and work. I am pleased to have the chance now to thank them for everything that they have given to me, and all the ways they helped this book come into being.

The most important people for any historian are the librarians and archivists that make our work possible. I owe a deep debt to the knowledge, dedication, and professionalism of the staffs at the archives where I conducted research for this book, including the American Philosophical Society; Weston Library (Special Collections) of the Bodleian Libraries; British Library; John Carter Brown Library at Brown University; Earl Gregg Swem Library at the College of William and Mary; John D. Rockefeller Jr. Library at Colonial Williamsburg; Delaware Historical Society; Friends House Library, London; Historical Society of Pennsylvania; Huntington Library; Library Company of Philadelphia; Library of Congress; Library of Virginia; Maryland Historical Society; Maryland State Archives; The National Archives of the United Kingdom; New Jersey Historical Society; North Carolina State Archives; Oklahoma Historical Society; Pennsylvania State Archives; Pepys Library of Magdalene College at the University of Cambridge; Codrington Library of All Souls College at the University of Oxford; Albert and Shirley Small Special Collections Library at the University of Virginia; Virginia Historical Society; and Beinecke Library at Yale University. I'm also grateful to the staffs of many university libraries, especially those in the Interlibrary Loan departments, upon whom I have inflicted untold multitudes of requests and who have never failed to come through: British

Museum Library; Houghton Library and Tozzer Library at Harvard University; Joseph Regenstein Library at the University of Chicago; Senate House Library and the Wohl Library at the Institute of Historical Research, University of London; Bizzell Memorial Library at the University of Oklahoma; Merton College Library and Vere Harmsworth Library at the University of Oxford; and Van Pelt Library at the University of Pennsylvania.

I have had the privilege of receiving financial assistance from many institutions whose generosity made the research for this book possible. The University of Pennsylvania, Huntington Library, Colonial Williamsburg Foundation, Virginia Historical Society, American Philosophical Society, American Historical Association, Maass Manuscript Society, and Jamestowne Society supported early research that helped turn an idea into a viable project. A scholarship from the University of Oxford enabled me to spend a year researching in Britain, and a writing fellowship from the Andrew W. Mellon Foundation and American Council of Learned Societies offered the magnificent pleasure of drafting most of these chapters in the British Library. Additional research was made possible by a faculty fellowship from the Vice President for Research of the University of Oklahoma, the National Endowment from the Humanities, and the Library Company of Philadelphia. The Mahindra Humanities Center at Harvard offered valuable time to reflect and a brilliant community of scholars to think with as I revised the manuscript. A Dobbert Research Grant from the History Department at the University of Chicago kindly paid for the images in this book. Institutions, of course, are nothing without the labor and dedication of the people that make them run. It is seldom acknowledged and often thankless work, and so to them I offer my most sincere gratitude.

A vast distributed network of scholars and intellectuals offered constructive criticism of work-in-progress and contributed ideas that made their way into this book. As a graduate student in Philadelphia I was fortunate to spend four years at the McNeil Center for Early American Studies, an extraordinary gathering of talent, energy, and collegial spirit thanks in large part to the culture nurtured by its director, Daniel Richter. The McNeil was the first place I had the opportunity to test out my ideas, and it will always feel like home no matter where I go. Steven Gunn offered the singular experience of discussing Indigenous history with the Early Modern Britain Seminar at Oxford. I am grateful to Pekka Hämäläinen and Peter Thompson for inviting me to the American History Seminar at the Rothermere American Institute to hone my arguments about emotional cultures. *Time of Anarchy* got its real road testing at the Colloquium of the Omohundro Institute of Early American History and Culture (thanks to Karin Wulf and Joshua Piker), the Washington Area Early American History Seminar (Holly Brewer and Richard Bell), Mahindra Humanities Seminar (Joyce Chaplin and Matthew Liebmann), and the Boston Area Early American History Seminar (Linford Fisher). Members of the US History Workshop at the University of Chicago were extraordinarily helpful in refining my arguments about captivity, especially Kathleen Belew, Destin Jenkins, and Amy Lippert. The Chicagoland Native American and Indigenous Studies Working Group has been a brilliant and welcoming community for exploring NAIS methods, and its members inspired me to travel in new directions as this work evolved. My special thanks to Melissa Adams-Campbell, Rose Miron, Teresa

Montoya, Hayley Negrin, Sarah Pierce Taylor, Anna Elena Torres, Isaiah Wilner, Kelly Wisecup, and SJ Zhang. I have also benefited from the audiences at conferences of the American Historical Association, American Society for Ethnohistory, Omohundro Institute, Organization of American Historians, Society of Early Americanists, Southern Historical Association, and Western Historical Association. Finally, I owe a debt to my students, both undergraduate and graduate, from whom I learn as much as I teach. Taken together, hundreds of people have generously engaged with the work in this book. It was shaped by their incisive questions, challenging provocations, and creative suggestions.

Several people in this distributed community have been especially important to the shaping of this book, ranging from one-time interlocutors who probably don't remember me to dear friends who I delight in seeing during the seasonal round of scholarly migration. All of them are valued colleagues: Gregory Ablavsky, Chief Lynette Allston, Allard Allston, Cheikh Babou, Juliana Barr, Susan Brandt, Kathleen Brosnan, Valeria Castelli, Jon Connolly, Lori Daggar, Jennifer Davis, Jeremy Dell, Philip Deloria, Matthew Dennis, Jane Dinwoodie, Gregory Dowd, Alejandra Dubcovsky, Elizabeth Dyer, Elizabeth Ellis, Isaac Emrick, Robbie Ethridge, Paul Gilje, Cassandra Good, Onur Günay, Steven Hahn, James Hart, Lauric Henneton, Eric Hinderaker, Anne Hyde, Mandy Izadi, Sumayya Kassamali, Catherine Kelly, Paul Kelton, Judith Lewis, Jonathan Lyon, Jack Maddex, George Milne, Kathryn Olivarius, Jeffrey Ostler, Rachel Parikh, Christopher Parsons, Geoff Planck, Justin Pope, Eve Troutt Powell, William Ramsay, Bryan Rindfleisch, Jessica Roney, Kristalyn Shefveland, Rachel Shelden, Anooradha Iyer Siddiqi, Susan Sleeper-Smith, Laura Keenan Spero, Robert St. George, Taylor Stoermer, Fredrika Teute, Charles Watson, Moira Gillis Watson, Michael Witgen, Buck Woodard, and David Wrobel. Love and solidarity to my comrades in the Praxis Collective, Craig Franson, Danielle Holtz, and Justin Simard. Most important of all are my mentors, Daniel Richter and Kathleen Brown. They put me through as rigorous and demanding a program of study as any student ought to have, but even more important are their generosity, advice, support, unfailing good humor, and bottomless warmth. They are inspiring scholars and wonderful friends. I owe them everything.

The scholars who read this entire manuscript deserve a special thanks. James Rice, who has been a model of collegiality since we met, read the *William and Mary Quarterly* article that forms the spine of this book, as well as the book itself. Several University of Chicago faculty, along with outside readers Sarah Pearsall and Ned Blackhawk, participated in an all-day manuscript workshop: Mark Bradley, Emilio Kourí, Jonathan Levy, Steven Pincus, Eric Slauter, and James Sparrow. Additional readers included Julie Fisher, Katherine Grandjean, and David Silverman. Their careful readings and thoughtful suggestions have improved every aspect of this book.

Another special thanks goes to William Keegan, who designed the maps for this book. I deeply appreciate his collaborative spirit, willingness to experiment, and shared conviction that maps are not just illustrated references, but vehicles for making arguments that text cannot make on its own. I offer Bill my immense respect and gratitude.

As much as I have to thank my friends and colleagues, I owe infinitely more to my family, both born and made. My parents, Rick and Eileen Kruer, have offered unwavering love and support from the beginning. I would never have made it this far without them. My brother Patrick and grandmother Antoinette Bell complete this beloved circle. Allen Whitt is no less my brother by the standards of familiarity, and it has been an enormous pleasure watching his daughters Saffana and Noomi grow up. The Hickersons and a small army of Bissells have been a source of laughter and adventure over the years. Most of all, I am thankful for Katie Hickerson, for her strength, power, wisdom, brilliance, and grace.

I sat down to write these acknowledgments in March 2020, in the early days of the coronavirus pandemic. I finished them in May, when it started sinking in that what seemed to be a short-term emergency was actually going to be a long-term crisis that transformed our lives and our world. Composing these acknowledgments has been a poignant and illuminating experience at a time when none of us can safely leave our homes and all of us are struggling for a sense of connection. It has reminded me of the vast web of humanity to which I am bound, the community of people who have sustained and nourished me, giving of themselves to teach me how to become a better human. I have felt that web's painful fragility as well as its ferocious strength. I am overcome with gratitude, and I will try to give back that gift.

328   *Index*

Susquehannocks (*continued*)
230–231; enslaved by English, 93, 216; influence on Haudenosaunee, 43, 174–175, 183–184, 200, 221, 245, 300n1; and Jacob My Friend, 1–3, 206–207, 237–239; language of, 2, 53, 93, 197–198; leadership of, 15–16, 40–42, 56–57, 81–82, 88; migration to Potomac, 51–52; military strength of, 10, 28, 31–32, 40; names of, xii; origins of, 15–18; militia's accidental attack on, 53; Peri-, 15; political organization of, 6–7, 15–16, 244; and power, 10–12, 42, 48, 111, 175, 182–183, 190, 200–202, 243–244; Proto-, 15, 34; reconstitution of, 146–148, 171–172, 244–248; retaliation for militia attack, 55; scattering of, 4, 78–85, 92–93, 100–101, 112, 149, 281n3; sources about, 7–8; sovereignty of, 31, 225, 245; space of, 18, 30–31, 33–36, 43, 78–79, 232; spiritual practices of, 8, 59, 259n12; subsistence of, 78–79; territory of, 30–31, 224–225, 245; trade networks of, 17, 33–34, 140, 236; transportation to Iroquoia, 42–43, 90, 148–149, 174–175, 182; travel routes of, 198–199, 215, 231; women and gender among, 8, 188–189, 272n54. *See also* Gandastogue
Susquehannocks, relations with: Albemarle, 84, 136–138, 163–166; Algonquians in Maryland, 27–28, 46, 51, 93–96, 98, 100, 121, 178–180, 183–184, 191–192, 197, 207–209, 214–216, 221, 225, 231–232, 245–246; Algonquians in New England, 34; Algonquians in Virginia, 66–67, 103, 178–180, 184, 221; Chowanokes, 82–83, 137, 165–166; Haudenosaunee, 15, 17–18, 31–32, 34–35, 40–43, 46, 50–51, 78, 89–90, 147–149, 174–175, 190, 245–246, 273n1; Eries, 31, 33; Lenapes, 25, 84–88, 167–168; Maryland, 26–31, 42, 46, 50–51, 55–57, 93–97, 121, 171, 197–201, 207–211, 215–217, 245; Meherrins, 82–83, 137, 165–166, 283n10; Munsees, 30, 33, 84, 89, 215; New Netherland, 25, 30–31, 33; New Sweden, 25, 31; New York, 83–92, 139–141, 147–148, 236, 239; Neutrals, 31; Pennsylvania, 232–236, 239, 245–247; Petuns, 31; Shawnees, 34, 245; Siouans, 33–34, 73–76, 81–82, 184, 192–193, 246; Virginia, 13–14, 24–26,

31, 53–57, 59–66, 73, 100–101, 184–185, 221; Wendats, 25–26, 31–33
Susquehannock-Virginia War, 70, 78, 101, 113, 116, 137, 143, 154
Svanahändär, 31
Swerisse, 170, 186; granddaughter of, 186, 188–189

Tackaniennondi, 229
taxes, 69–70, 203, 218, 224, 279n39; as catalyst for rebellion, 154–155, 165, 221–222, 296n17; and customs duties, 37, 128, 164, 203, 221; and fiscal strain of Anglo-Indian war, 46, 69–70, 122, 153–154, 165, 186, 221–222, 279n39
Tekanistapendacquo, 198, 229–230
Time of Anarchy: beginning of, 52–59; definition and meaning of, 6–7; ending of, 230–236; geographical scope of, 36; legacies of, 239–243; pattern of violence during, 243–244
tobacco, 23, 37, 69, 196, 221–222. *See also* plantations
Tonnahoorn, 30
trade: and alliance, 17, 26, 30–31, 42, 140, 232–236; competition over, 27–28, 46–47, 76, 194–195; and corruption, 71, 118; prohibition on, 109; regulation of, 39, 70–71, 194; and smuggling, 45–46, 119, 138. *See also* fur trade; markets; slave trade, African; slave trade, Indigenous
treaty: of Albany (1677), 166–173, 176, 186, 201, 229; of Albany (1679), 186–190; of Albany (1682), 228–230, 238; of Albany (1685), 239; Algonquian-Maryland, 44, 47, 98, 220; Algonquian-Virginia, 24, 67, 104, 152; Gandastogue-Maryland, 29–30, 56, 198–199; Haudenosaunee-New York, 38–39; of Middle Plantation, 157–163, 166–168, 176, 195, 223, 242–243; as protection compact, 24, 51, 104, 208; of Shackamaxon, 147–149, 166, 172, 200; Tuscarora-Albemarle, 179
tributaries. *See* subjecthood
Truman, Thomas, 55–57, 93, 96–98, 211–212, 275n14
Tsenacomoco, 22. *See also* Powhatan
Tuscaroras, 73, 179, 185, 194, 246
Tyrling, John, 213–214

Unnacokassimon, 177
Ununtsquero, 166